Battle for Bed-Stuy

Battle for Bed-Stuy

The Long War on Poverty in New York City

Michael Woodsworth

▌▌▌
▌▌▌
Harvard University Press

Cambridge, Massachusetts
London, England
2016

First printing

Library of Congress Cataloging-in-Publication Data
Names: Woodsworth, Michael, 1978- author.
Title: Battle for Bed-Stuy : the long war on poverty in New York City / Michael Woodsworth.
Description: Cambridge, Massachusetts : Harvard University Press, 2016. |
Includes bibliographical references and index.
Identifiers: LCCN 2015036137 | ISBN 9780674545069 (alk. paper)
Subjects: LCSH: Urban policy—New York (State)—New York. |
Poverty—Political aspects—New York (State)—New York—History—20th century. |
African Americans—New York (State)—New York—Politics and government—20th century. |
African American women—Political activity—New York (State)—New York. |
Bedford-Stuyvesant (New York, N.Y.)—Economic conditions—20th century. |
Bedford-Stuyvesant (New York, N.Y.)—History—20th century.
Classification: LCC HC108.N7 .W66 2016 | DDC 362.5/561097471—dc23
LC record available at http://lccn.loc.gov/2015036137

Contents

Abbreviations

AATA	African-American Teachers Association
APOB	Antipoverty Operations Board
BCSP	Brooklyn Council for Social Planning
CAA	Community Action Agency
CBCC	Central Brooklyn Coordinating Council
CDC	Community Development Corporation
CHIP	Community Home Improvement Program
CORE	Congress of Racial Equality
D&S	Bedford-Stuyvesant Development and Services Corporation
HARYOU	Harlem Youth Opportunities Unlimited
JOIN	Job Orientation in Neighborhoods
LENA	Lower Eastside Neighborhood Association
LISC	Local Initiatives Support Corporation
MFY	Mobilization for Youth
OEO	Office of Economic Opportunity
PCJD	President's Committee on Juvenile Delinquency
R&R	Bedford-Stuyvesant Renewal and Rehabilitation Corporation
SIP	Special Impact Program
UDC	Unity Democratic Club
WTC	Women's Talent Corps
YIA	Bedford-Stuyvesant Youth in Action

Introduction

The Senator and the Secretary

> Of prime necessity in any meaningful program for the elimi-
> nation of poverty and the culture it sustains is the need for a
> total and coordinated commitment to its eradication. Central
> to this program is the elimination of slum conditions, the cre-
> ation of job opportunities and other economic and social im-
> provements which will undoubtedly result in decent, sanitary
> and safe housing.
>
> —CENTRAL BROOKLYN COORDINATING COUNCIL, 1964

Elsie Richardson stood shivering on a windy street corner in Brooklyn's Bedford-Stuyvesant district, one of the poorest places in New York City. A gray midwinter sky hung low above her head; beneath her feet, a thin layer of wet snow concealed crumbling sidewalks. Richardson was a mother of three who spent her days working as a school secretary and packed her nights and weekends with community organizing and committee meetings. The next few hours would define her career as an activist—but the main thing on her mind was the cold.[1]

It was February 4, 1966. That afternoon, Richardson would provide a tour of Bedford-Stuyvesant for an important visitor: Robert F. Kennedy, the junior senator from New York. Richardson's group, the Central Brooklyn Coordinating Council (CBCC), brought together more than one hundred civic clubs, churches, block associations, and civil-rights groups. For years, members had worked to raise awareness among politicians about the plight of their community. Bedford-Stuyvesant was a sprawling and inexactly defined area housing between 250,000 and 500,000 people—less of a neighborhood than a "city within a city" the size of Cincinnati.[2] In the mid-1960s, around 80 percent of the community's residents were black; 10

1

Elsie Richardson of the Central Brooklyn Coordinating Council and Shirley Chisholm, then a New York State assemblywoman, conferring in 1966. *Photo courtesy Bedford-Stuyvesant Restoration Corporation*

to 15 percent claimed Puerto Rican descent. Prior to the summer of 1964, when anger at police brutality had boiled over into a riot, few outside Brooklyn had heard of the place. Since then, Bedford-Stuyvesant had gained national notoriety. Bigwigs had dropped in and pledged to help; none had delivered. Even President Lyndon B. Johnson's 1964 declaration of "unconditional war" against poverty had so far amounted to little beyond a flurry of studies and grant applications—though it had raised great hopes at the grass roots.

Richardson hoped this time would be different. Maybe Kennedy would be genuinely moved by the poverty and anger he encountered in Brooklyn. Maybe he would sit up and listen when she told him what she always told white visitors: that Bedford-Stuyvesant was a *community*, not a "ghetto." Maybe he would offer more than promises. She wasn't holding her breath.

Forty-four years earlier, Richardson had been born to working-class immigrants from the tiny Caribbean island of Nevis. As a young child, she lived on Manhattan's West Side, in a neighborhood later razed to make room for Lincoln Center. When Elsie was ten and her family was living in East Harlem, her father lost his job working in a tie factory; days later, the family saw everything they owned disappear in a tenement fire that killed five people. It was 1932—the depths of the Great Depression. They'd seen the fire coming, suspecting the landlord might burn the building down to collect an insurance payout. Elsie's father had even placed a ladder by the back window of their third-floor apartment, just in case. The ladder saved Elsie and her three siblings. But they reached safety too late for their father to scramble up and salvage his last paycheck, which sat neatly folded in the pocket of his work pants, waiting to be cashed. Elsie desperately held onto his legs, afraid he would try to clamber back into the blaze. Then the air filled with the screams of children—Elsie's neighbors—burning to death. For the rest of her days, that indelible memory would inspire Richardson's activism.[3]

Her parents revered Marcus Garvey, the Jamaican-born prophet of black empowerment, whose organization, the United Negro Improvement Association, had galvanized Harlemites in the 1920s. Paraphrasing Garvey, they instilled in Elsie a simple philosophy: "You're as good as anyone else." Elsie took up civil-rights causes as a teenager, when wartime Harlem crackled with political ferment. The 1941 bus boycott (led by an up-and-coming Adam Clayton Powell Jr., later a congressman) made an indelible impact on the nineteen-year-old, who graduated as the only black student in her class at Manhattan's Washington Irving High School. After the war, Elsie married and moved to the Crown Heights neighborhood of Brooklyn, bordering on Bedford-Stuyvesant; the Richardsons landed in the Albany Houses, an integrated public-housing project. There she began building her reputation as an activist, organizing tenants and doing youth-outreach work at the nearby Stuyvesant Community Center. By the mid-1950s, the Richardsons had saved enough to buy the townhouse of their dreams, a stone's throw from the projects. Now a mother of three and a full-time school secretary, Elsie became a force in block associations, PTAs, and her church. Somehow, she found time to take college classes at night.[4]

Meanwhile, Brooklyn was undergoing a dramatic transformation. Thousands of blacks arrived each year—from the South, from the West Indies, from Harlem—and thousands of whites decamped. The newcomers often encountered grim housing options; in a redlined neighborhood, prospective homeowners navigated a predatory mortgage market, while tenants typically paid exorbitant rents. As credit dried up, city services declined. Further, until the 1960s, black Brooklynites were mostly shut out of the Democratic Party clubhouses that dominated the borough's politics. To fill the gap, they built a dense network of civic clubs, block associations, social-outreach initiatives, and other benefit societies. Many were led by the sons and daughters of West Indian immigrants, who tended to occupy higher income brackets than their neighbors with roots in the American South.[5]

In 1958, the Central Brooklyn Coordinating Council emerged as an umbrella organization for these various groups and began serving as the de facto political broker between Brooklyn's black citizens and the municipal government. Its original mandate was to oversee an outreach program for youth gangs, a major concern of New York's reformers in the postwar years. But Richardson and CBCC soon began lobbying Mayor Robert F. Wagner Jr. for more comprehensive efforts to control juvenile delinquency, rehabilitate housing, and create jobs. Partnering with political reformers and civil-rights advocates, CBCC dramatized the woefully inadequate housing, schools, and city services in Bed-Stuy. In 1964, President Johnson and Mayor Wagner jointly launched the War on Poverty and pledged to "empower" the residents of poor neighborhoods. CBCC, primed for action, teamed up with Brooklyn's leading churchmen and launched an ambitious new Community Action Agency to coordinate antipoverty programs in Bedford-Stuyvesant. Funds, however, trickled in slowly. The local mood began to sour.[6]

Elsie Richardson had been in the middle of it all. But as 1966 dawned, she, like many others in Brooklyn and around the country, felt a heightened sense of urgency. With jobs disappearing, schools failing, poverty deepening, and crime rates rising, Bed-Stuy's activist leadership group worried that their community might soon spiral out of control. After years of half-measures, Richardson believed a comprehensive solution must be found. Eloquent, forceful, and driven, Richardson would spend fourteen years earning her college degree in night school, all while raising three children, working in public schools, and dedicating her evenings and weekends to endless community meetings. She could be counted on to voice the community's frustrations without mincing words, and she was not about to swoon at the sight of a Kennedy.

Richardson's personality and politics made her an appropriate host for the junior senator from New York. By early 1966, Kennedy, too, was seeking to jumpstart a new antipoverty initiative that would succeed where Johnson's much-hyped programs were failing. Several years earlier, during his tenure as U.S. attorney general, Kennedy had overseen the President's Committee on Juvenile Delinquency, which popularized the model of "community action" that would later underpin the War on Poverty. But the erstwhile poverty warrior had grown disillusioned with the federal antipoverty programs, which he saw as ineffectual, bureaucratic, and underfunded. The riots in the Watts section of Los Angeles in 1965 had convinced him that despite recent civil-rights gains, masses of urban blacks were angry, alienated, and disillusioned. Far more would have to be done—by governments, foundations, the private sector, and society at large—to help them. Like Richardson, Kennedy hoped to design new approaches that would harness the energies unleashed by the War on Poverty while learning from its failures. For that to happen, the poverty program would have to shift gears from promoting "empowerment" to creating jobs, from repairing torn psyches to rebuilding decrepit streets.[7]

And so Elsie Richardson met Bobby Kennedy. Along with Donald Benjamin, a social worker who served as CBCC's staff director, the school secretary led the senator on a ninety-minute tour of Bed-Stuy. Characteristically, Kennedy braved the chill hatless and scarfless. Trailing the senator's vehicle was a ten-car caravan of journalists, handlers, local politicos, and officials from the federal Department of Housing and Urban Development and the Housing and Home Finance Agency. But it was Richardson who sat by Kennedy's side as he asked question after question.

They got out to walk down a grim stretch of Atlantic Avenue, where locals could scarcely believe their eyes at the sight of the slain president's kid brother. Richardson, Kennedy, and their entourages climbed up into a sparsely furnished apartment where an obese, bedridden woman burst into tears as the senator entered her room; on her wall were pictures of Jesus, Martin Luther King Jr., and John F. Kennedy. They rang doorbells along a run-down block of Gates Avenue, where the houses, according to a local saying, weren't even worthy of the rats who infested them. A five-year-old boy emerged from one such dwelling only to slam the front door shut when Kennedy asked where his parents were and why he wasn't in school. Elsewhere, Kennedy noted litter-strewn lots, boarded-up stores, and crumbling tenement buildings. But Richardson also insisted that he see Bedford-Stuyvesant's tidier streets, where a striving middle class, much of it of Caribbean descent, had restored elegant Victorian brownstones, planted trees, and organized block associations. These were the homes, Richardson explained, of the area's leading activists. Far from succumbing to despair, these men and women were hard at work, drawing up the blueprints for

Senator Robert F. Kennedy chatting with five-year-old Ricky Taggart on Gates Avenue during his tour of Bedford-Stuyvesant on February 4, 1966. *Photo by Dick DeMarsico. New York World-Telegram and the Sun Newspaper Photograph Collection, Library of Congress Prints and Photographs Division. LC-USZ62-133361*

the neighborhood's revitalization. With private capital rapidly fleeing the city, they demanded that governments fill the gap.[8]

The final stop of the tour was the Bedford Avenue YMCA. Hundreds had crammed into the auditorium to hear Senator Kennedy speak—and most wanted to give him a piece of their mind. These activists had spent years "building a better Bedford-Stuyvesant," as CBCC's slogan went. They were the foot soldiers of the War on Poverty, and they simmered with anger at the slow pace of change. Richardson, who chaired the meeting, set the tone. "We are tired of what we call 'getting the business,'" she volleyed in her opening remarks. She added that although she trusted Kennedy's good intentions, she had been wary of hosting him when she heard he wanted to tour Bedford-Stuyvesant. "What? Another tour?" she recalled asking herself. "Are we to be punished by being forced again to look at what we look at all the time?"[9]

Kennedy was taken aback. On the defensive, he insinuated that community leadership of antipoverty programs had so far left much to be desired, and he suggested that the city government designate an official who could tie together Bed-Stuy's political factions. In the meantime, he promised that his staff would carry out a thorough study of the area's problems. His audience, representing the best and brightest of black Brooklyn—the very leaders he seemed to be denigrating—took that as a slap in the face.

"We've been studied to death," Richardson shot back before yielding the floor. A parade of local notables rose to echo her refrain. "You know what, I am tired Mr. Kennedy, I am tired," added Ruth Goring, an assistant to the Brooklyn borough president. "We've got to have something concrete now—not tomorrow, not yesterday." Civil Court Judge Thomas R. Jones, who had made his name battling Brooklyn's Democratic machine, leapt to his feet with a pointed challenge. "I'm weary of speeches, weary of promises that aren't kept," he said, his voice rising. "The Negro people are angry, Senator, and judge that I am, I'm angry too."

The encounter embarrassed the senator. "Brooklyn Negroes Harass Kennedy" read the *New York Times* headline the next morning. "I don't have to take that shit," he reportedly told an aide. "I could be smoking a cigar in Palm Beach." Yet the neighborhood's demands fell on receptive ears. Following his tense encounter with Bedford-Stuyvesant's civic leaders, Kennedy asked his staff to begin working with CBCC on strategies for a new front in the War on Poverty. What emerged was the country's first federally funded Community Development Corporation (CDC)—a new model of urban revitalization that, despite seemingly overwhelming obstacles, would offer new hope for cities in the decades to come.[10]

The Forgotten Fight

"The War on Poverty," one of its planners mused in the late 1960s, was "a story in superlatives." Lyndon Johnson's "unconditional" crusade against want came wrapped in military rhetoric designed to inspire a country reeling from the assassination of John F. Kennedy. Along with the Civil Rights Act of 1964, the War on Poverty formed the centerpiece of Johnson's Great Society agenda. The president promised an unprecedented federal effort to dismantle structures of political, social, and economic exclusion, especially as they affected African Americans. Beyond that, the poverty program would redefine federalism itself by funneling cash to grassroots groups around the country, often without using state or local governments as intermediaries. What Johnson called "creative federalism" would encourage big thinking, ambitious goals, and a new brand of place-based politics.[11]

The executive agency created to run the War on Poverty was the Office of Economic Opportunity (OEO), with Kennedy's brother-in-law, Sargent Shriver, at the helm. Between 1964 and 1974, OEO funded dozens of initiatives, including the Community Action Program, which encouraged the poor to pursue their own empowerment; Upward Bound, a program to help low-income students make it through college; Head Start, which provided free preschool education; the Job Corps, which offered vocational training to teenagers; neighborhood-based legal services, health clinics, and consumer-education drives; and the CDCs that sprang up around the country in the years following Robert Kennedy's visit to Bedford-Stuyvesant. Several Great Society programs supplemented the assault on poverty: Medicare and Medicaid, food stamps, federal aid to education, Model Cities, and the Fair Housing Act of 1968. All told, Johnson envisioned the Great Society growing into "a beautiful woman . . . so big and beautiful that the American people couldn't help but fall in love with her, and once they did, they'd want to keep her around forever, making her a permanent part of American life, more permanent even than the New Deal."[12] And so they did. Even the most controversial aspects of the War on Poverty lived on in altered form after Richard Nixon abolished OEO in 1974. Despite the sustained rhetorical attacks of both conservative politicians and left-wing critics, War on Poverty programs proved widely popular and today account for what Annelise Orleck calls "some of the most enduring and unassailable strands of the national social safety net."[13]

For all that, poverty endured in America. Fifty years on, the very notion of a president promising to end poverty feels fantastical. After several decades of rising inequality and as a different war—the War on Drugs—ravages black neighborhoods, Elsie Richardson's hope that the federal government might intervene benevolently in her community seems quaint. But the people of Bed-Stuy had good reason to believe they could use the new antipoverty bureaucracy as a foothold from which to increase their political power and access desperately needed resources. Indeed, they had been doing just that with city government initiatives for years. To activists like Richardson, Great Society programs represented the logical continuation of an ongoing local struggle, which this book dubs the "long" War on Poverty.

In narrating that struggle, *Battle for Bed-Stuy* offers several fresh perspectives on the origins, goals, and legacies of this transformational moment in twentieth-century social policy. Shining a light on a key locale of black politics, it opens up new ways of thinking about the continuity of reform efforts across the civil-rights era, and it illustrates the importance of activist women who, though ignored at the federal level, often took the lead in organizing communities. Seen through this lens, the War on Poverty appears as something more complex than a set of federal programs handed down from above. It was a social movement that spanned several decades, and it both grew out of and fed into other overlapping campaigns: the fight for black political power, the revolt against urban renewal, the drive to purify local politics, and the neighborhood-conservation movement later known as "brownstoning." Like other movements of the time, the antipoverty struggle featured bold experimentation tinged with wide-eyed idealism and a heartfelt communitarian impulse. The activists of Bedford-Stuyvesant were central players in this national drama.[14]

This book illustrates how *creative* "creative federalism" could be. Examining postwar New York City as a key policy laboratory, it uncovers how municipal elites and neighborhood-level actors spawned ideas and institutions that were later appropriated by federal policymakers. In the transition period bridging the New Deal and the Great Society, city agencies and grassroots organizers forged a series of new policymaking coalitions. At first, such partnerships tended to center around a mutual commitment to controlling youth crime; gradually, they began to tackle a broader range of urban issues. As they did so, the top-down forms of governance associated with the post–New Deal state (as embodied in the urban-renewal regime of Robert Moses) began, slowly, to integrate elements of participatory democracy. In the mid-1960s, decentralized planning became an article of faith among the city's policy elites. Meanwhile, federal poverty programs presented activists with a new set of institutions through which to pursue their agenda.

Battle for Bed-Stuy recounts how the middle-class leadership group affiliated with CBCC spent years trying to tap the resources of the expanding liberal state. Their hope: to "save" a neighborhood they treasured from a future they dreaded. Striving to uplift Bedford-Stuyvesant's poorest citizens and to protect their own homes from "slum conditions," Bed-Stuy's home-owning professionals recognized that sweat equity and community organizing could not by themselves stem capital flight. They demanded that governments join the fight. In so doing, these educators, social workers, lawyers, ministers, and secretaries paved the way for the federal War on

Poverty and, once it was launched, adapted it to serve long-cherished goals. Members of this group put forth an ideal of community stability tied to safe streets, home ownership, and citizen participation in planning. While they embraced Johnson's sweeping goal of eradicating poverty, Brooklyn's black poverty warriors also demanded that government programs create jobs, repair crumbling streetscapes, fix failing schools, and counter the effects of redlining. Some of those demands resulted in successful programs; others fell on deaf ears. As a whole, though, the War on Poverty opened up a wider panorama of policy possibilities than is often assumed—as is evident when it is viewed through the eyes of its foot soldiers in Bed-Stuy.[15]

At the same time, as this book shows, the new place-based politics ultimately left many black New Yorkers feeling frustrated and disillusioned. In the 1950s and 1960s, the city and federal governments actively courted local leaders by launching successive programs dedicated to community planning, community control, and community development. Such programs provided activists with bases from which to expand their policy influence, access patronage networks, and extract concessions from the state. In the 1970s, a new generation of black politicians emerged, many of them empowered by their experiences in the poverty programs. That said, alliances with elites also disarmed local people by channeling their ideas and energies into bureaucratized, ritualized channels. By making neighborhoods the main unit of analysis for theorizing social change, community-based reform ended up reinforcing the boundaries of impoverished, segregated urban spaces. Meanwhile, the state was entering a period of retrenchment, as conservatives slashed spending and proclaimed the Great Society dead. As Ronald Reagan famously put it, "We fought a war on poverty, and poverty won."[16]

Not surprisingly, most historical accounts of the War on Poverty have dwelt on its shortcomings. Dismissed by conservatives as an emblem of government overreach, Johnson's crusade has also been skewered on the left as a cheap trick to defuse urban unrest. The Community Action Program, in particular, with its high aspirations and messy implementation, has often served as a parable for the declension of postwar liberalism. Scholars have most often found fault among federal planners and politicians, who, it is variously argued, adopted faulty theoretical premises, consciously avoided wealth redistribution, failed to grapple with racism, set impossibly high expectations, belittled the poor, and alienated key constituents.

Even those accounts most sympathetic to OEO's efforts point out that programs authorized by the Economic Opportunity Act never drew more than $2 billion in federal funds—less than 2 percent of the budget at a time when 20 percent of all Americans lived in poverty. No society has ever succeeded in disproving the biblical dictum that, "The poor you will always have with you." What made Americans think they could break the trend, especially when squandering so much wealth fighting in the far-away jungles of Southeast Asia?[17]

Of late, scholars have taken a fresh look at the War on Poverty. In an age of glaring inequality, liberal economists and policymakers have been more inclined to praise the contributions of the Great Society to the American social safety net.[18] It has long been known that official poverty rates declined precipitously in the decade following Johnson's declaration of war, from 19 percent in 1964 to 11 percent in 1973—a record unsurpassed to this day.[19] That drop has often been attributed to the era's brisk economic growth, but recent research makes clear that governments also played a role. Further, the hardships of low-income Americans today would be significantly worse absent the forms of noncash income the Great Society made available. In 2014, the official poverty rate was 14.8 percent; according to one study, however, the real poverty rate in America—taking into account contributions to family incomes made by social programs and tax subsidies—sat below 5 percent. More broadly, scholars have credited LBJ with establishing poverty as a legitimate target for government programs and mobilizing a policy community around the issue. "The most important lesson from the War on Poverty," declared a 2014 report issued by President Barack Obama's Council of Economic Advisors, "is that government programs and policies *can* lift people from poverty; indeed they *have* for the past 50 years."[20]

Such optimistic assessments provide an important counterpoint to past accounts of failure. But the War on Poverty, as a fragmented policy experiment that reached into hundreds of neighborhoods around the country, evades master narratives. Many of those neighborhoods have continued to suffer from disinvestment, job loss, and, increasingly, mass incarceration.[21] Ideas and institutions once employed to justify and structure federal aid to urban communities gradually came to underpin what sociologist Herbert Gans has called "the war against the poor." Given the discrepancy between Johnson's stated goals and the weapons used to achieve them, maybe fighting poverty was never really the point of the War on Poverty.

Critics in the 1960s and 1970s interpreted it as a "riot insurance program" intended to buy off angry urbanites with patronage and summer jobs. Another line of analysis reinterprets the War on Poverty as a transitional moment in federal urban policy, one that paved the way for more repressive interventions in minority communities. Others have argued that the White House cynically used the poverty programs, together with the Voting Rights Act, to cement black allegiances to the Democratic Party.[22]

Each interpretation has merit, but a bottom-up perspective shows that the political goals of Johnson and the Democrats were not hegemonic. In the past decade, a wave of case studies has shown how federally funded Community Action Agencies reshaped power dynamics in neighborhoods around the country even when they left economic inequality intact. Recent work suggests that the War on Poverty breathed new life into the participatory structures of American democracy, notably by empowering black women at the neighborhood level and providing local leaders with the tools to pursue community control and build new bases of black political power. Furthermore, the community-based organizations spawned by the War on Poverty—thousands of which endure to this day—continue to provide key services in the realms of housing, health, early-childhood education, legal services, tenant advocacy, and cultural preservation. That legacy offers further proof that the War on Poverty, as a social movement and as a set of policy innovations, was adapted by many different actors to suit divergent political goals.[23]

The View from Brooklyn

Nowhere were the War on Poverty's complex local realities—the limitations and possibilities, the deep roots and lasting legacies—more vividly on display than in Bedford-Stuyvesant. Long overlooked by historians, Central Brooklyn and the activists it nurtured have sparked renewed interest in recent years. Bed-Stuy fascinates, in part, because it was simultaneously emblematic and exceptional. It epitomized the processes by which urban black communities in the mid-twentieth century grew in population, were ravaged by capital flight, and organized to take political action. In the 1960s and 1970s, it was often described as the "largest ghetto" in America.[24] But Bed-Stuy was exceptionally diverse, crisscrossed with unique ethnic, class, and gender divisions. The area housed a mix of desperately poor people and upwardly mobile ones, and those socioeconomic

12

contrasts often overlapped with the cultural cleavages between people whose roots were in the American South and those who hailed from the Caribbean. Far from being a monolithic zone of suffering and blight, as implied by the "ghetto" designation, Bed-Stuy was a diverse collection of micro-neighborhoods where a multinational population had laid down roots. These dynamics would affect the structure of the poverty programs launched there.

Bedford-Stuyvesant is also notable as an urban space where borders were defined by racism. The term "Bedford-Stuyvesant" came into common usage in the 1930s, just as large numbers of African Americans were moving into the neighborhoods of Bedford and Stuyvesant Heights. Thereafter, the boundaries of Bed-Stuy were progressively enlarged to match the spreading radius of black settlement. This reached a point of absurdity by the late 1960s, when an area encompassing half a million people was still being spoken of as a single "neighborhood." When War on Poverty programs targeted "Bedford-Stuyvesant," and when local groups defined "Bedford-Stuyvesant" as synonymous with "community," they were tacitly acknowledging that racism set the parameters for their efforts. The vision of "comprehensive" urban renaissance that emerged from Bedford-Stuyvesant was thus bounded simultaneously (and sometimes contradictorily) by class, space, and race.

Within these limits, postwar Bed-Stuy served as a testing ground for a series of pioneering ideas about urban reform and community action. In the late 1940s and early 1950s, policymakers and local organizers alike supported experiments designed to curtail juvenile delinquency and disarm teen gangs. The first of these unfolded thanks to the initiative of the Brooklyn Council for Social Planning, which employed novel social-work techniques that were later adopted by a new government agency, the New York City Youth Board. The Youth Board's gang-outreach programs assumed that citizens of the neighborhoods where needs were greatest should participate in planning and running the programs that affected them. In the late 1950s, under Wagner, the city broadened the scope of its thinking about youth gangs. Henceforth the government would seek not only to control delinquency but also to prevent it by addressing "root causes": discrimination, family breakdown, decaying housing, and poverty.

Activists in Brooklyn's rapidly expanding black neighborhoods picked up on this vision of community action and ran with it. In 1958, a coalition of block associations, civic groups, churches, and social workers formed

CBCC, with an assist from the Youth Board. As a city-funded agency, CBCC acted as a broker between streets and elites while fostering community participation in the government's gang-outreach programs. But the locals had their eyes on a bigger prize. Most CBCC devotees were active in the civil-rights movement, and many also spent their time organizing block associations. Though keen to see youth gangs disarmed, such activists also used CBCC to push the Wagner administration to take action on other fronts: schools, housing, jobs, and more. At the same time, the federal government was endorsing the Youth Board's mode of community action through the President's Committee on Juvenile Delinquency, overseen by Robert F. Kennedy.

The early 1960s were a time of extraordinary fluidity in New York politics. Insurgent reformers challenged political machines, grassroots activists confronted institutionalized racism, and a revolt against urban renewal bubbled up in neighborhoods around the city. From Wagner's perspective, it seemed like sound politics and good policy to partner with the Kennedys to empower community-based organizations; the most important antidelinquency efforts in the country were based in Manhattan and cosponsored by Wagner. In Brooklyn, CBCC activists worked to gain federal and municipal support for a similar program. Their efforts paid off with the creation of a new agency, Bedford-Stuyvesant Youth in Action (YIA), in early 1964.

Launched only days after Johnson and Wagner each declared war against poverty, Youth in Action was Brooklyn's first official Community Action Agency. Bed-Stuy's middle-class activists, who directed its work, hoped to turn YIA into a vehicle for pursuing not only youth programs but also a broader campaign of community revitalization. As it turned out, the agency mirrored the flaws that plagued CAAs around the country: unreliable funding streams, chaotic managerial structures, and rampant infighting. Increasingly, YIA struggled to manage social-service provision while also serving as a conduit for participatory democracy. Despite it all, YIA initiated popular programs and showed that it was possible for neighborhood-based organizations to adapt the War on Poverty to their own purposes. Its attention to the needs of low-income women in Bed-Stuy—especially in the realms of education and career advancement—marked it as a particularly valuable resource during the mid-1960s.

There was another side to the poverty war, too: a drive to repair the physical resources of the "ghetto." The frustrations of community action—and the invalidation of old models of urban renewal—spurred federal policy-makers and local activists to develop new models of neighborhood redevelopment. In the mid-1960s, Elsie Richardson and CBCC reached out to advocacy planners from the nearby Pratt Institute for Design for help in addressing challenges that previous antipoverty initiatives had failed to address: disinvestment, job loss, and crumbling brownstones. Eventually, they attracted Kennedy, and a fresh vision of community renewal emerged. That vision led to the creation, in 1967, of the Bedford-Stuyvesant Restoration Corporation, which captured the energy the War on Poverty had unleashed and turned it into a program of physical revitalization. Restoration reaffirmed the spirit of community action while seeking to sidestep its pitfalls. But serious policy differences soon arose. Would Restoration think big or would it think small? Would it answer to elites or to the grass roots? The debates brought into focus preexisting class and gender divisions, and they precipitated a reconfiguration of power in Bed-Stuy.

In many ways, Restoration's accomplishments reflected the goals community activists had been putting forth since the 1950s. The corporation's vision of neighborhood revival was premised on holding the middle class. By creating a mortgage pool, extending credit to small businessmen, and fostering home ownership, Restoration attempted to make Bed-Stuy more attractive, more livable. Under the directorship of Franklin Thomas, Restoration aimed to reunite the community by taking up bricks-and-mortar programs; the most popular initiative hired young men to help repair brownstones and tidy up historic blocks. In the late 1960s, another campaign—for a community-controlled college in Central Brooklyn—gained traction and temporarily united the various factions in the community. But the extent of their clout remained in question. Though Restoration provided a model for hundreds of Community Development Corporations nationwide, there was only so much community groups could do to fight the headwinds of deindustrialization, disinvestment, and austerity.

1

A Suitcase Full of Knives

We know from our experience in New York City that a combination of under-privilege, discrimination and frustration provides an ideal soil for juvenile delinquency—and for adult delinquency, too—in all the worst manifestations, including narcotics addiction and crimes of extreme violence.

—ROBERT F. WAGNER JR., 1962

In the summer of 1945, as war in the Pacific hurtled toward its dénouement, American teenagers were waging a violent struggle on the home front. The years since Pearl Harbor had seen a spike in youth crime, and strife among teenage gangs intensified alongside the conflict overseas. Nowhere was the trend more alarming than in the nation's largest city. That summer, New York teenagers grabbed headlines by robbing, vandalizing, rampaging, and, most sensationally, staging massive "rumbles." Outbreaks of hand-to-hand combat featured young men wielding baseball bats, switchblades, chains, car antennas, and the handles of trashcans, improvised as brass knuckles. Fifteen-year-olds stabbed each other with icepicks, penknives, and bayonets, while serious gangsters packed "zip" guns— homemade firearms cobbled together by using curtain rods, coffee percolators, blocks of wood, rubber bands, and toy-gun parts.[1]

Though riveted to the carnage in the Pacific, growing numbers of parents, social workers, and government officials also fretted about the violence in their own backyard. Across the country, juvenile courts were handling a rapidly increasing caseload; J. Edgar Hoover of the FBI warned that juvenile delinquency was "approaching a national scandal." The teen murder rate had doubled since 1940, and alarming reports circulated that returning veterans, often still in their teens, were rejoining gangs and adding an element of paramilitary leadership to the raw enthusiasm of younger boys.[2]

16

Teenagers brought into police custody in Brownsville after what the *Brooklyn Eagle* described as "a street free-for-all" between the Saints and the Socialistic Gents, 1949. Brooklyn Eagle, *1949. Brooklyn Public Library, Brooklyn Collection*

Many young brawlers were just getting their kicks. But, increasingly, the worst violence followed ethnic fault lines. In Upper Manhattan, along the rapidly shifting frontiers dividing majority-white from majority-black areas, angry teenagers organized into warring factions with names like "Irish Dukes" and "Negro Sabers." Across the river in the Bronx, posses representing Italians, Irish, Puerto Ricans, and African Americans vied for control of disputed public spaces. Among the stoops and steeples of Brooklyn, it was common for rival gangs to join forces in the name of ethnic solidarity. In a city where memories of the 1943 Harlem riot were fresh, many feared that violence was turning the melting pot into a cauldron of hatred. Such fears were especially pronounced in Bedford-Stuyvesant, an area where the white population was rapidly being replaced by black migrants from Harlem, the West Indies, and the American South.[3]

Parents feared for the welfare of their children. "I am a respectable American Negro citizen, mother of eight children," one Brooklyn woman wrote Mayor Fiorello La Guardia. "In the community where I live . . . conditions are becoming so that our children's lives are in constant jeopardy, day and night. Will you please advise us what we, the decent Negro mothers of Brooklyn, can do to get the protection necessary to shield our children?"[4]

What to do about the wild youth? On August 2, 1945, the same day the Potsdam Conference concluded, a group of reformers gathered in an elegant brownstone on Macon Street to discuss juvenile delinquency in Bedford-Stuyvesant. The area suddenly seemed to be teeming with violent youth gangs. The Greene Avenue Stompers, the Robins, the Bishops, the Socialistic Gents, the Brewery Rats, the Red Skin Rhumbas: together, they added up to what the *Amsterdam News*, New York's preeminent black newspaper, dubbed a "terrifying display of gangsterism." Among the notables gathered in the Macon Street townhouse were community leaders from the NAACP, the YMCA, and several black churches. They were joined by representatives of the city's welfare department and from La Guardia's Committee on Unity, which aimed to foster cooperation among the city's ethnic and racial groups. The assembled group declared itself determined to "weed out the delinquency that has engulfed many otherwise fine and respectable-familied youths." All agreed that doing so would require a combination of grassroots organizing, innovative social work, and government funds.[5]

That vision, and the coalition that articulated it, helped lay the foundations for New York's long War on Poverty. For the next two decades, the city's social scientists, municipal officials, social workers, and community organizers would treat juvenile delinquency as a matter of paramount concern. Because they were so worried about crime, municipal elites developed an ever-growing interest in poor communities. Beginning in the late 1940s, Brooklyn reformers launched a series of experimental programs aimed at disarming, controlling, and reforming the fighting gangs of Kings County. The social-work methods they employed were novel and bold; so were accompanying efforts to galvanize grassroots support by organizing community councils in the affected neighborhoods. The new approach was soon picked up by a fledgling municipal-government agency, the New York City Youth Board, which in the 1950s tried to suppress teen violence in a city suddenly transfixed by the ominous yet strangely romantic specter of the juvenile delinquent. Initially, the archetypical delinquent was white, and early efforts to control youth behavior in postwar Bedford-Stuyvesant targeted youngsters of Italian and Irish extraction. By the mid-1950s, however, ideas about youth crime had become increasingly racialized, and most of the city's antidelinquency efforts were targeting groups of African Americans and Puerto Ricans.

In part, this shift reflected the discourse emanating from those very communities, where "respectable-familied" citizens and "decent Negro mothers" linked the intensifying struggle for racial justice to campaigns for safe streets and improved city services. Meanwhile, Mayor Robert F. Wagner Jr., who served three terms in office between 1954 and 1965, was pushing local communities to take a more active role in planning municipal programs in their neighborhoods. A vocal supporter both of civil rights and of citizen participation in government, Wagner oversaw the emergence of community-based youth programs that aimed not only to disarm the gangs but also to address the "root causes" of their behavior. Under Wagner, expanded Youth Board programs in the late 1950s and early 1960s would tap local expertise to address the spectrum of social ills that, the theory went, caused young people to misbehave: deteriorated housing, shoddy schools, joblessness, racism, and, above all, poverty.

Who's Afraid of the Brewery Boys?

What did it mean to be a juvenile delinquent in postwar New York? Definitions varied wildly. Strictly speaking, a juvenile delinquent was someone under the age of twenty-one who had been arrested for a crime. "Delinquency," opined a 1947 study titled *Jailbait: The Story of Juvenile Delinquency*, "is only a nicer word for crime, for transgression against society." However, the federal Children's Bureau estimated that only one in eleven young criminals was actually arrested. New York City tabulated delinquency figures by adding arrest figures to the number of referrals handled by the NYPD's youth division. Such referrals could be for any number of behaviors, criminal or not, adjudged to be "antisocial." In the 1950s, the city classified cases in children's court into "delinquency types." In addition to serious crimes such as robbery, car theft, and sexual assault, the list included relatively benign forms of youthful rebellion: running away, truancy, and "carelessness and mischief." One category of delinquent listed by the city Youth Board was simply tagged "ungovernable." A lot could get you labeled a delinquent.[6]

And what of gangs? Their rumbles grabbed headlines, fed hysteria, and lived on in the stories the gangs themselves mythologized. But pitched battles were rare, especially after 1950. Nor were all gang members criminals.

19

Some held down jobs; others took their schoolwork seriously. More commonly, gang members could be found playing cards, hanging around candy stores, drinking wine, and crashing dances.[7] Sonny Carson, who would gain fame in the 1960s as a prominent black nationalist and protest leader, in the late 1940s ranked among the leaders of the Bishops, a notorious Bedford-Stuyvesant gang made up of black teenagers. In his telling, gang life was all about routine—to wit, his daily activities while he was nominally attending George Westinghouse High School in downtown Brooklyn:

> Purchasing a coconut-custard pie, then walking all the way uptown, shaking people down who looked like they had money (in The Black Community that means making them give you a nickel or a dime), buying wine, looking for the pushers to purchase some marijuana. Going to someone's pad, getting high, winding up in bed with one of the girls. Invading the present enemy, The Beavers, or maybe The Robins or The Socialistic Gents. Dodging the police all the time.[8]

Viewed through Carson's eyes, such daily activities liberated teenagers for whom adult life ultimately promised little. The Brooklyn delinquent, not unlike James Dean's character in *Rebel without a Cause*, appeared as an authentic, masculine figure parading across landscapes shot through with apathy and despair. "It was a beautiful life, man," Carson concluded. Not surprisingly, elders disagreed. Why, reformers wondered, were teenagers spending so much time invading enemies and dodging police? Why did the Bishops, the Robins, and the Socialistic Gents take such mirthful pleasure in killing each other? Far from beautiful, such behavior seemed to betray a rising tide of nihilism that threatened to engulf entire communities.[9]

On a mid-November day in 1946, another Bed-Stuy gang, the Brewery Boys, decided to drop in on a community center in nearby South Williamsburg. It was not a friendly visit. The Brewery Boys—also known as the Brewery Rats—made their home base in a burned-out old brewery nestled among the three-story tenements of Pulaski Street, in northern Bedford-Stuyvesant. Most of them belonged to the area's shrinking Italian American community. The Brewery Boys had made a name for themselves by fighting African American gangs like Sonny Carson's Bishops, whose turf lay farther south, in the majority-black section of Bed-Stuy. Of late, though, they had turned their attention to a group of Jewish boys who hung out at the South Williamsburg community center. On this particular day, the Brewery Rats demanded entrance to the center on the grounds that it should serve all local youth, not just Jews. After the center's directors—themselves Jewish—locked the doors, the Brewery Rats forced their way in and trashed the place. No one was hurt, but the incident shocked local Jews. With the center shuttered, concerned parents formed a vigilante committee and swore to protect their families by any means necessary. Clearly, though, long-term solutions were needed. What could be done? For answers, local Jewish leaders sought advice from the Brooklyn Council for Social Planning (BCSP). Without knowing it, the Brewery Rats had ushered in a new era of social reform.[10]

The Brooklyn Council for Social Planning had been founded in 1933 as one of four outer-borough affiliates of the New York City Welfare Council, an umbrella group that brought together social-welfare experts from the voluntary sector and the city government. BCSP received the bulk of its monies from the Greater New York Fund, a precursor to the United Way, and its support network included more than one hundred settlement houses, charities, and religious groups. It was an explicitly multiracial, multifaith, progressive endeavor. Jews, Italians, and Irish Catholics made up the bulk of BCSP's directors; in the 1940s, they were joined by a small number of African Americans, including the head of the New York Urban League, Robert T. Elzy, and Maude B. Richardson, a well-known community activist from Bedford-Stuyvesant. People involved with BCSP hoped to make Brooklyn safer, more livable, and more equal.[11]

Throughout the 1930s and 1940s, BCSP worked to improve health services, housing, and youth programs in Brooklyn, particularly for blacks and Puerto Ricans. When, in 1943, a Kings County grand jury investigating crime in Bedford-Stuyvesant recommended robust police work to counter "a most unusual and extremely deplorable state of lawlessness" in the area—language many black Brooklynites interpreted as a thinly veiled racial slur—BCSP responded by calling instead for better housing, schools, and hospitals. In 1946, BCSP released a report on growing criminality and racial tensions among Brooklyn youth, which helped initiate a citywide effort to reform policies toward youth crime. Among other things, BCSP called for a new, government-run youth bureau to coordinate community services and design comprehensive youth-outreach programs. Following this recommendation, Mayor William O'Dwyer in 1948 set up the New

York City Youth Board to coordinate the multitudinous agencies providing services for troubled teenagers. In the meantime, BCSP began plotting how it would deal with the Brewery Rats.[12]

For inspiration, the Brooklynites looked to Chicago, where community organizers, social workers, and academics had been experimenting with new methods of categorizing, measuring, and treating juvenile delinquency. In the 1930s, Clifford R. Shaw, a sociologist from the University of Chicago, put forth the thesis that youth crime resulted not from individual pathologies but from "social disorganization"—the breakdown of social structures within rapidly changing urban communities. To test his theory, and to try out solutions, he founded the Chicago Area Project in 1934. The effort, which operated in six high-delinquency areas, downplayed professional casework and instead emphasized grassroots leadership in antidelinquency initiatives. Under Shaw's guidance, neighborhood workers provided "curbstone counseling," venturing out to meet gangs in their day-to-day hangouts, getting to know them, and gradually helping them channel their energies into socially acceptable activities. Shaw also encouraged local adults, including former criminals, to act as mediators between delinquent youths and the police. A onetime student of Shaw's, Saul Alinsky, added a twist on the Chicago Area Project when he founded the Back of the Yards Neighborhood Council in a working-class area of Chicago's South Side. Under Alinsky, community organizing became less focused on reestablishing social control within individual neighborhoods than on confronting outside power structures and demanding better services.[13]

The Chicago experiments directly inspired the effort undertaken by BCSP in 1946, dubbed the Tompkins Park Youth Leadership Project. (A similar program was launched in Harlem in 1947 under the aegis of the Welfare Council of Manhattan.) The park in question was the only significant green space in central Bedford-Stuyvesant, and the Brewery Rats were among several gangs who staked claims to the turf. But Tompkins Park was not only a battleground for bat-wielding teens; it also loomed as a symbolic battleground for the reformers struggling to reassert a sense of order, community cohesion, and sovereignty over public space. A slew of agencies signed up to help plan and fund the project: the Brooklyn Jewish Community Council, the Urban League, the Catholic Youth Organization, the Italian Board of Guardians, the Brooklyn Division of the Protestant Council, the Board of Education, and the 79th Police Precinct.[14]

To lead the Tompkins Park project, BCSP turned to Leo Laughlin, a streetwise social worker in his late twenties. Laughlin came on as a "detached worker," meaning he would operate outside the traditional structures of settlement houses and social-work agencies. His charge: to seek out gang members in their indigenous setting and divert their aggressive urges into more fruitful pursuits. In June 1947, Laughlin began insinuating himself into the Brewery Rats' world. He hung out in candy stores, betting shops, and empty lots. He threw coins into jukeboxes, flipped cards, and spent long hours chatting on stoops. He helped to organize dances and managed a sandlot baseball team. He picked up the gang's slang and befriended its leaders. To convince the boys he wasn't a cop, he scampered away like one of them when officers raided their hideouts.[15]

Laughlin soon learned that the Brewery Rats were only the most notorious faction in a shifting network of a hundred or so young men and boys who gravitated to the derelict brewery on Pulaski Street. Their home turf was a forbidding strip of decrepit houses, empty lots, abandoned storefronts, and bookie shops. It seemed an ideal spot to "fight it out." The brewery itself served as a fortress during battles; inside, a "maze of rooms and cellars overrun by rats," in the words of the *Brooklyn Eagle*, provided hiding places and storage space for stolen loot. Pulaski Street factions tended to scrap against one another, but they would sometimes band together—and rebrand themselves the Pulaski Street Boys—for rumbles against outside gangs. Among the Brewery Boys, Italians predominated, although a select few Puerto Ricans and even two Jews moved in Pulaski Street circles.[16]

As Laughlin gained the trust of the Brewery Boys, he began asking questions about what drove their behavior. Many boys saw themselves as defenders of their neighborhood and of their "kind." They posed as protectors of a white, Catholic, working-class milieu besieged by hostile forces, including the expanding Hassidic enclave to the north and the bustling black community to the south and east. "Some boys seem to feel need of gangs to act as vigilantes to protect white people when Negro groups have uprisings," Laughlin reported to BCSP in 1947. He also found that most whites in the area were primed to flee once they sensed an easing of the postwar housing shortage: "A common attitude among many of the older residents was that they were living in this neighborhood only until they could find housing elsewhere and that once the housing situation improved the entire section would be occupied by Negroes."[17]

Racial strife aside, the Pulaski Street gangs also reflected postwar malaise and economic stress. Some of the older members had held jobs during the war but had since been laid off; in response, Laughlin helped them find work again, and he observed that their violent activity soon waned. Others among the "boys" were in fact men who had joined gangs some years earlier, left to serve in overseas combat, and then rejoined upon returning to a tight job market. Traumatized, shiftless, and uneasy about the future, they found stability, structure, and leadership opportunities among the Pulaski Street Boys. Indeed, as Laughlin learned, postwar youth gangs were strictly hierarchical affairs. New recruits dreamed of climbing the ranks and gaining titles like "war counselor" or "combat director." The more experienced members drafted younger boys, including their brothers, and—perhaps inspired by the legendary farm system of baseball's Brooklyn Dodgers—organized them into feeder groups dubbed "Midgets" or "Juniors." Some gangs even sponsored ladies' auxiliaries: the Tigers of Gowanus had their Regits—"tiger" spelled backward—and the Robins of Bed-Stuy had their Robinettes. ("The distaff gangs indulge in varying degrees of unladylike behavior, from tomboy roughness to knife-toting and sex delinquency," the *Times* observed.) The Brewery Boys were led by a nucleus of ten young men aged between seventeen and twenty-one, including some veterans; below them was a faction of twelve- to sixteen-year-olds, known as the Pulaski Street Boys Jr.[18]

The proliferation of such organizations, combined with the knowledge of weaponry that returning GIs lent the groups, made some Brooklynites fear an outbreak of open urban warfare. Laughlin was less worried. He reported back to the BCSP board that most boys engaged in combat not for the love of violence but because rumbles built group solidarity and helped insecure teens gain a sense of self-worth. The Brewery Boys, like the youth gangs that were proliferating across the city, fought for turf and pride and bragging rights—but there were rarely profits at stake. Laughlin maintained that "constructive activities can be substituted for destructive ones" as long as such activities offered prestige and opened doors. Jobs were part of the solution. Laughlin also aimed to institutionalize the Brewery Boys by strengthening the gang's internal structure. Having aligned himself with the older members, Laughlin convinced the boys to move out of the brewery and into a row of abandoned storefronts on Pulaski Street, which they spent much of 1948 renovating, painting, and cleaning. By year's end, they had opened an official clubhouse they called Club Caliph. Laughlin

encouraged the boys to collect dues and run the club according to democratic procedures; so they did, electing officers and writing a constitution.
They held weekly meetings, where they discussed club rules, policies, and
finances. (They decided early on to buy a ping-pong table.) Given a stake
in their neighborhood, they quit vandalism and resisted rumbles. Instead,
they organized baseball tournaments, dances, and fundraisers. The boys
even painted a shuffleboard court on the Pulaski Street pavement, where
fists and knives had once determined winners and losers. In 1950, the
Brooklyn Eagle reported that Pulaski Street had become "a quiet spot in
a normal neighborhood. . . . The tension and fear provoked by the gang
has disappeared." According to Laughlin, the project had been so successful that a modicum of racial tolerance prevailed. "Negro children play
in the empty lot next to the old clubhouse," he wrote. "A few years ago
a Negro youth would not have been able to walk down Pulaski Street
unmolested."[19]

And so the Brewery Rats became good citizens. In the meantime, their
elders had come together in a parallel organizing effort. Through the
Tompkins Park initiative, BCSP attempted to foster "indigenous leadership" not only among the gangs but also within the wider community. In
order to "increase neighborhood planning and responsibility," BCSP
founded a new body called the Tompkins Park Neighborhood Council,
with Municipal Court Justice Milton Wecht presiding. The thirty-five
members included priests, policemen, shopkeepers, teachers, and parents.
At first, their mandate was to supervise Laughlin's street work and raise
funds for the Brewery Rats' clubhouse. After two years, Laughlin bowed
out, his mission accomplished, and the neighborhood council began
working directly with representatives of the Brewery Boys. The council also
drummed up community support for a campaign to clean up streets, whose
deterioration they blamed in part for teen violence. Meanwhile, they convinced the city to demolish the abandoned brewery building and fence in
empty lots nearby.[20]

By 1950, BCSP was trumpeting its work among the Brewery Boys as an
unqualified success—one that offered lessons for the future. First conceived as an "action-demonstration" program, the Tompkins Park project
had pursued a limited set of goals by using experimental social-work techniques alongside relatively novel forms of community organizing. Now the
gang had gone straight, the citizens group had banded together to take action, and a fresh community spirit was burgeoning. All told, the results

supported BCSP's premise that a previously undefined neighborhood with no set borders or unifying characteristics could redefine itself as a "community," and that through such a process a new form of place-based political organizing could proceed.

The demonstration did not go unnoticed. As the Tompkins Park project unfolded, BCSP began setting up a network of "Youth Councils" elsewhere in Bedford-Stuyvesant, as well as in "each neighborhood where intensive co-ordination and citizen participation are needed." The councils acted as informal town halls where representatives aged fifteen to twenty-one met to discuss their problems and mediate disputes. In some neighborhoods, the kids organized track meets to promote harmony among otherwise hostile ethnic groups. Other councils led cleanup drives, hosted dances, and petitioned the city to build playgrounds on abandoned lots. By 1950, BCSP had replicated the Tompkins Park experiment across the borough by placing at least one social worker in Brownsville, East New York, Brighton Beach, Park Slope, and South Brooklyn.[21]

Meanwhile, the New York chapter of the National Urban League, one of the country's foremost civil-rights organizations, was planning an anti-delinquency project of its own. The Urban League's perspective on youth problems aligned neatly with that of BCSP; the chapter's executive secretary, Robert Elzy, was a Brooklyn social worker who sat on the BCSP board. A 1947 report about delinquency in Brooklyn's rapidly growing black enclaves argued that "young people roam the streets, or gather at soda fountains and beer taverns because they have no other place to go and no constructive outlets for their youthful energies." In response, the Urban League proposed to sponsor sports teams, clubhouses, debating societies—anything that might cultivate a sense of "social responsibility" among troubled teens. Meanwhile, adults in each of the neighborhoods were expected to come together and discuss how teen behavior reflected deeper social problems. "In such fashion," the Urban League proposal stated, "the sponsorship of a youth activities program could become the springboard to neighborhood action for improved housing, increased health facilities, family service, et cetera." In other words, a community's attempts to reform delinquents must inevitably lead to broader reforms—and, it was hoped, to political empowerment. In the short term, little came of the project other than a summer leadership camp. But, like BCSP's work, the Urban League's efforts suggested that Brooklynites were increasingly linking youth behavior, social conditions, grassroots community action, and political power.[22]

To Reach the Unreached

One reason the Urban League project never got off the ground was because government action rendered it moot. In 1948, Mayor William O'Dwyer established the New York City Youth Board, with the mandate of coordinating efforts to protect and control the city's young people. Armed with matching state and city monies, the Youth Board sponsored programs that expanded on the model of youth-outreach work that BCSP and other private welfare agencies had pioneered. Heads of the city's health, welfare, housing, education, and parks departments joined the board, alongside a coterie of magistrates and, later, emissaries from the Brooklyn Catholic Youth Organization, the Federation of Protestant Welfare Agencies, the Jewish Family Service, the Children's Aid Society, Columbia's School of Social Work, and several settlement houses. The Youth Board promoted an aggressive form of social work that targeted children and families who had not requested help and, in some cases, resisted it. The animating goal was to "reach the unreached." In 1949, the city set up referral units in public schools and housing projects. Staffed by social workers, these units existed to track teenagers categorized as "troubled" (as well as their families, when possible) and refer them to private agencies that provided vocational training, after-school supervision, and sports programs.[23]

Despite the success of the Tompkins Park project, violence among teen gangs was escalating around the city—particularly in Brooklyn. According to the Youth Board, "anti-social activity reached an unprecedented peak" in early 1950. Reporting from Bedford-Stuyvesant later that year, the *Times* announced that "warfare among teen-age street gangs has risen to fever pitch." New outfits proliferated while existing ones grew in strength, thanks to their farm systems. Brooklyn gangs were reputed to engage in "the most highly organized street and park warfare in the city." Rivals waged pitched battles in Prospect Park, where a gently sloping meadow near the park's western edge was christened Massacre Hill. On Easter Sunday 1950, the NYPD youth squad only barely managed to preempt an epic rumble in which multiple Brooklyn gangs were to have fought a Manhattan confederacy on the boardwalk of Coney Island.[24]

Faced with such challenges and armed with meager funds ($2.3 million in fiscal 1950), the Youth Board attempted to "reach the unreached" by targeting programs to closely circumscribed areas. In doing so, the agency looked to the work of Leo Laughlin and BCSP among the Brewery Rats.

The Youth Board's chairman, Nathaniel Kaplan, served as a judge in Brooklyn's Domestic Relations Court and had watched closely as the Tompkins Park project unfolded. Impressed, Kaplan released funds in July 1950 to make Brooklyn "a laboratory for a coordinated, reasonable approach" to juvenile delinquency, as the *Brooklyn Eagle* put it. As they designed the new approach, Youth Board officials and the Kings County assistant district attorney worked closely with BCSP's chairman, Henry Carpenter, and its executive secretary, Louise Simsar. Albert Edwards of the interracial Stuyvesant Community Center, where a young Elsie Richardson would soon begin volunteering her time, also provided his input.[25]

Dubbed the Brooklyn Detached Worker Program, the new antigang effort stationed social workers in four of the borough's most turbulent areas—Bedford-Stuyvesant, Williamsburg, Brownsville, and South Brooklyn—and tasked them with infiltrating and reforming fighting gangs. "The New York City Youth Board will invade Bedford-Stuyvesant in the near future with a small army of workers to break up the juvenile gang menace" the *Amsterdam News* reported when the detached-worker program launched on December 15, 1950. That "small army" in Bed-Stuy was small indeed: it initially numbered only three, though it would soon include a dozen men. Like Laughlin, the new batch of detached workers would be given considerable leeway to tailor programs to neighborhoods. Many followed Laughlin's lead by establishing structured spaces—sports teams, clubhouses, dances—where they could introduce gang members to "mainstream" social norms.[26]

One of the first to hit the ground in Bed-Stuy was Kenneth Marshall. A twenty-five-year-old social worker, Marshall epitomized the kind of "indigenous leader" that Clifford Shaw had sought to recruit and train in his Chicago Area Project. Although he would go on to a successful academic career, Marshall, who was black, had belonged to a youth gang himself less than a decade earlier. Having grown up on the streets of Bed-Stuy, he knew his way around: he knew where to find gang members, he knew what parties to crash, he knew how to handle a zip gun, and he knew who spoke what slang. After the Youth Board assigned him to work with one of Brooklyn's fiercest fighting gangs, the Greene Avenue Stompers, Marshall made himself popular by organizing dances in rented halls on neutral territory—which precluded the beefs that typically resulted from gangs crashing parties on foreign turf. Meanwhile, he used his government contacts to find jobs for motivated Stompers, which earned him a nickname: "The Job

The Youth Board's Kenneth Marshall appears before a Senate Judiciary subcommittee on November 20, 1953. Marshall holds a "zip" gun of the kind used by teen gangs on the streets of Brooklyn. *Associated Press*

Man." Three years on, Marshall found himself testifying before a titillated U.S. Senate Judiciary Committee, telling tales of gang hangouts infiltrated and rumbles averted. According to the *Times*, he "amazed the Senators with a generous sample of the jargon employed by the bands of warring youths." His portrait of the mean streets of Brooklyn, told with wide-eyed intensity and while waving a zip gun, was the first many legislators had heard of the pioneering work going on in New York City.[27]

Marshall's efforts with the Greene Avenue Stompers proved the first step in a long career as a social-policy leader. He later attended Columbia's School of Social Work and wrote his dissertation under Richard Cloward, one of the country's most influential scholars of poverty and juvenile delinquency. In the early 1960s, Marshall collaborated with Cloward to draw up plans for a community-action experiment on Manhattan's Lower East Side called Mobilization for Youth, which in the 1960s served as a blueprint for the War on Poverty. Fresh off that experience, Marshall helped psychologist Kenneth Clark found another key War on Poverty program, Harlem Youth Opportunities Unlimited, of which he eventually became executive director. Marshall's trajectory from Brooklyn gang member to Youth Board worker to War on Poverty official typifies a key thread in the Great Society's policy genealogy. "The Job Man" was just one among a generation of social workers and community activists who in the 1950s gained policy experience through the city's juvenile-delinquency programs and a decade later graduated into leadership positions within the antipoverty bureaucracy.[28]

The detached-worker program that gave Marshall his start in 1950 was part of a citywide initiative known as the Council of Social and Athletic Clubs. Beyond Brooklyn, the Youth Board adopted "target areas" in Manhattan (East and Central Harlem, the West Side of Central Park, Washington Heights) and the Bronx (Morrisania, Mott Haven), as well as South Jamaica, Queens. The selected locales accounted for about a third of the city's youth population but almost two-thirds of delinquency cases. Each area housed large numbers of recently arrived migrants from the South and from Puerto Rico, and already strained social services had diminished. Packed schools in Harlem, Bed-Stuy, and the Bronx were forced to run double shifts, leaving students with half a day to kill. Meanwhile, interethnic conflicts flared up, often provoked by teen gangs.[29]

At the outset, Youth Board workers didn't try to break up the gangs, fearing that would demonstrate bad faith. Like Laughlin and BCSP, the Youth Board recognized how important it was for teenagers to gain a sense of belonging and social solidarity. As a 1957 report explained, there was nothing inherently wrong with joining a youth gang. "The gang means a great deal," the report observed. The goal for detached workers would be to divert boys' energies away from "anti-social" activities like rumbles, vandalism, sexual violence, and drugs—but to do so "within the gang framework." Young gang members, the Youth Board posited, sought status and recognition. In some ways, their membership in a tightly structured organization indicated a laudable desire to take a measure of responsibility for their own lives and for the communities around them. Government's role, then, was to "help them achieve in more socially acceptable ways the recognition and status they need and crave. . . . Their horizons must be broadened, individual personal and social adjustments must be improved and there must be increased democratic participation within the gang itself."

Some Youth Board workers reorganized gangs into straitlaced "street clubs" dedicated to sports, dances, and theater. Others took boys to amusement parks or bucolic locations. But those who managed to find jobs for the boys were always the most popular.[30]

This approach contrasted with the antigang strategies adopted by other major American cities during the 1950s. Whereas Chicago and Los Angeles pioneered policing tactics aimed at suppressing gang violence but employed little in the way of social work, New York stood out for its efforts to mitigate the repressive aspects of policing with neighborhood-specific planning and group work. Detached workers were expected to keep an ear to the ground for rumors of rumbles; in cases of imminent violence, they were instructed to call the cops if mediation failed. Some Youth Board workers resented this guideline because it undermined their status among the gangs, and some also mistrusted the NYPD. But the city's creative mix of social work and inconspicuous policing seemed to be working—at least for the time being.[31]

In 1953, the Youth Board reported that there had been a 9.5 percent drop in delinquency rates citywide over the previous five years and a 12.5 percent drop in arrests and referrals in the Youth Board's target areas. Even so, delinquency rates in Manhattan and Brooklyn remained much higher than in other big American cities, and the drop in youth crime proved fleeting. In February 1955, the Youth Board's executive secretary, Ralph Whelan, announced that the number of sixteen- to twenty-one-year-olds either arrested or named in complaints had shot up an eye-popping 52.7 percent in a year. In response, Whelan called for government and communities to cooperate in the fight against youth crime. Otherwise, he warned, more and more young people would become "enemies of society."[32]

Such alarmist rhetoric abounded in the mid-1950s, when juvenile delinquency was turning into a national obsession. Delinquency, Elizabeth A. Wells has written, loomed during those years as "an overwhelming and terrifying unknown, on par only with communism as a threat to the very fabric of American society." The press, smelling good copy, abounded in tales of young toughs marauding through the streets of the country's aging cities. More than that, teen gangs were springing up in affluent suburbs, raising the possibility that violent kids might just as well be motivated by boredom and alienation as they were by poverty or racism. J. Edgar Hoover announced that he had "sickening information about

American adolescents." Congressional subcommittees heard endless hours of testimony about youth crime, hoping "to find out what turns a child into a mugger, a 'goof pill' addict, a car thief, even a killer," as the Associated Press put it.[33]

The hysteria reached fever pitch in 1955. That year, a Senate subcommittee on delinquency demanded that publishers of comic books stop portraying "depraved acts" that might inspire teen violence. In Albany, a group of state assemblymen from Brooklyn pushed through legislation banning zip guns. Also in 1955, the New York City Council voted to ban realistic-looking toy handguns, while a Brooklyn grand jury recommended that all teens be required to carry identification cards. Finally, it was in 1955 that *Blackboard Jungle*, a tale of New York City juvenile delinquents, hit theaters; meanwhile, Steven Sondheim, Leonard Bernstein, and Arthur Laurents began collaborating on *West Side Story*. Teen gangs, objects both of fear and of romance, had permeated the culture. They would soon become the glue that held together new policy coalitions between community groups and governing elites.[34]

"An Affront to Our Principles"

If one man gave voice to the national obsession with juvenile delinquency, it was New York Mayor Robert F. Wagner Jr., who served from 1954 to 1965. Despite the Youth Board's efforts, Wagner often warned that his city could explode in an orgy of racially motivated youth violence, and he continually lobbied federal officials for antigang funds. "Mayor Wagner would bring down his suitcase full of knives and things," one observer quipped of the mayor's repeated appearances before congressional subcommittees on delinquency. "I think he just left the suitcase here each year and opened it up at the hearings."[35]

For all his alarmism about youth crime, Wagner oversaw a period of progressive innovation in city government. He was the only child of Senator Robert F. Wagner Sr., a liberal titan who sponsored such landmark New Deal laws as the National Labor Relations Act (commonly known as the Wagner Act), the Social Security Act, and the 1937 Housing Act. The younger Wagner inherited his father's faith in the capacity of big government to solve big problems. During his mayoralty, New York City embraced the hallmarks of New Deal liberalism: unions, public works, urban renewal. But Wagner also sought to align himself with a new mode of liberal politics, especially after 1960. A supporter of civil rights and of citizen participation in government, he oversaw new partnerships linking city agencies to neighborhood groups. Though New York's robust version of the New Deal had won the approval of the city's African Americans, the Democratic Party had nonetheless failed to incorporate the views, concerns, and aspirations of black voters into a durable governing apparatus. Under Wagner, the post–New Deal state would pioneer new forms of racial liberalism.[36]

Wagner, whose mother died when he was nine, grew up surrounded by icons of the New York Democracy: Tammany boss "Silent" Charles Francis Murphy, Governor Al Smith, and Mayor Jimmy Walker. Only weeks after graduating from Yale Law School in 1937, he ran for the State Assembly as the Democratic candidate from the Yorkville district on Manhattan's Upper East Side. He gave up his seat to join the Army Air Corps during World War II; upon his return, Wagner took successive jobs as a city tax commissioner, housing commissioner, and chairman of the City Planning Commission. In 1949, he became Manhattan borough president, backed by Tammany Hall. At the time, borough presidents retained significant appointive powers and held a voting seat on the city's powerful Board of Estimate, which was tasked with setting budgetary priorities. From this perch, Wagner spoke out against poverty, prejudice, and slums. He campaigned for mayor in 1953 with the support of the Democratic bosses of Manhattan and the Bronx, Carmine DeSapio and Ed Flynn, who had recruited him to take on anti-Tammany incumbent Vincent Impellitteri. Thus, Wagner arrived in Gracie Mansion as both a Tammany man and a true-blue progressive. He proudly presented himself as his father's son, a man devoted to "fighting for schools, for hospitals, for a fair shake for labor." Yet if Wagner Sr. was known for his legislative triumphs, he passed along a creed of forbearance. "When in doubt, don't," went the senator's advice—and his son would remain true to the motto. Later, as New York lurched from one crisis to another and as its finances plunged toward the abyss, Wagner would come in for intense criticism because of his belief that "delay could allay."[37]

The city Wagner took over in 1954 was at the height of its success. New York stood proudly as the world's preeminent manufacturing center, as well as the global capital of finance and diplomacy, not to mention publishing, advertising, and, increasingly, the arts. The projects of master builder Robert Moses loomed as symbols of triumphant modernism: majestic expressways thrusting through yesterday's slums, gleaming public spaces replacing gang-ridden alleys, imposing housing projects where rat-infested rookeries once slouched. Supporting such growth was a powerful alliance of developers, institutions such as hospitals and universities, liberal planners, and the federal, state, and city governments. Blessed with seemingly bottomless pockets, City Hall increased its budget in 1955 to almost $1.72 billion—more than the amounts spent by all but two states. In the decade to come, New Yorkers would consolidate an already imposing welfare state, in many ways anticipating the Great Society programs launched under Lyndon Johnson. Under Wagner, New York established the City University system, expanded welfare benefits, and built unparalleled networks of schools, playgrounds, and public housing projects. The city also became the first place in the country to allow collective bargaining for its municipal employees. (The measure was dubbed the "Little Wagner Act.") For Wagner, as for his father, the attainment of democratic freedoms was premised on decisive action by a benevolent state. As he put it in 1954, "America grew to be the mightiest nation in all the world because its people have learned to expect their government to be an ever increasing source of public service."[38]

At the same time, Wagner encouraged individual citizens and grassroots groups to participate in governing processes. Even before his election as mayor, Wagner had, according to the *Times*, "built up tremendous goodwill in all five boroughs by adroit and untiring application of three time-tested rules—write a letter, show your face, take an interest." As borough president, he forged close alliances with parent–teacher associations and good-government groups. Wagner was a savvy campaigner and a keen student of political behavior. Despite his pedigree, he cultivated an earthy charm; even as he surrounded himself with real-estate men who gloried in Manhattan's orgiastic building boom of the 1950s and early 1960s, Wagner fashioned himself a friend of the common man. (Writer Gay Talese reported that Wagner once shook 515 hands in an hour during a rally at Madison Square Garden, after which "his hand hung there like a dead fish.") He excelled at speeches delivered from the back of a sound truck; through decades of practice, he became a master at spontaneously tailoring his words to the ethnic or class makeup of the neighborhood he was driving through.[39]

Wagner recognized that migration in and out of New York in the postwar decades was changing how votes were won. The city's Democratic Party was fracturing, and he was mindful of binding citizens' loyalties to his person rather than to his party. In 1951, as borough president, Wagner sponsored a pioneering exercise in political decentralization when he divided Manhattan into twelve community-planning districts and urged the formation of a neighborhood council in each one. These semiofficial bodies were meant to encourage citizen participation in government policy, and Wagner asked them for feedback about housing, social services, schools, parks, and libraries. Beyond policy, the planning councils made political sense for Wagner. Though he owed his ascendance to the Democratic machines, he was eager to burnish his credentials as a reformer. Community-planning bodies linked the young politician directly to his diverse constituents at a time when regular Democratic Party structures had yet to open up to the city's minority groups. Wagner hired a black woman, Thelma Berlack Boozer, to set up and oversee the twelve planning councils, of which he praised Harlem's as "the most effective and the most active." Taken more broadly, Wagner's experiments in community planning represented a forward-looking response to what political scientist Seth Forman has described as the "postwar fear that, to an ever increasing extent, people's lives were controlled by large, faceless bureaucracies."[40]

And yet each day powerful bureaucracies were transforming the way many New Yorkers lived. More than any other city, New York embraced the federal urban-renewal program authorized by the Housing Act of 1949. Urban renewal was couched as a way of clearing low-income neighborhoods—which were routinely written off as "blighted"—and relocating poor families into modern housing. The program reflected old progressive ideas about maintaining urban order, as well as a modernist faith in new, efficient forms of dwellings. But in the hands of Moses, one man's utopia was the nightmare of thousands. Using the Title I program, which provided federal funds for slum clearance, New York's building czar routinely destroyed vibrant working-class communities and sent poor New Yorkers scrambling to rebuild their lives. People across the city saw their homes bulldozed and mourned the destruction of social networks that had sustained them only yesterday.[41]

New Yorkers were hardly alone in experiencing such wrenching change; slum clearance left deep wounds nationwide. In cities across the country, majority-black neighborhoods were disproportionately targeted, and urban renewal came to be known as "Negro removal." To compound the problem, most cities never erected anything approaching an adequate supply of new housing to accommodate the people displaced. New York, ever the exception, erected a network of low- and middle-income housing projects on a scale unmatched anywhere in North America for both quantity and quality. Yet even that failed to alleviate the city's tight postwar housing market. (The citywide vacancy rate in 1955 was the lowest in the United States, and one study found the rate in tenements to be just 0.1 percent.) This was especially true for African Americans, who faced extensive housing discrimination. Many had no choice but to move into cramped, shabby rooming houses in areas like Bedford-Stuyvesant.[42]

Though Wagner arrived in office vowing to curtail the enormous powers Moses had amassed under Impellitteri, he initially made few moves to sideline the master builder. Instead, he presided over an urban-renewal regime that traumatized, uprooted, and ghettoized poor New Yorkers, many of them black or Puerto Rican. And yet Wagner also funded extensive social-welfare programs; few elected officials in the country spoke as ardently on behalf of civil rights. In that juxtaposition, Wagner encapsulates the contradictory nature of postwar urban liberalism. Even as African Americans faced an urban landscape growing steadily more unequal, thanks in part to the discriminatory housing policies of the post–New Deal state, they also flocked to a Democratic Party whose northern wing had erected the foundations of a welfare state that was extremely popular among black voters.[43]

"We in New York have moved further and faster toward the goal of equal rights and equal opportunities than in any other period of our city's history," Wagner proudly wrote to civil-rights leader A. Philip Randolph in 1961. A supporter of the black freedom struggle since the 1930s, Wagner took office promising to fight inequality by building more public housing, opening new schools while desegregating existing ones, and promoting job opportunities for blacks and Puerto Ricans. "The depressed and segregated areas of our city are an affront to our principles of equality in a democracy," the new mayor declared in March 1954. Two months later, Wagner celebrated the Supreme Court's *Brown v. Board of Education* decision as a "magnificent opinion which will strengthen the wellsprings of democracy."[44]

In subsequent years, Wagner worked with the City Council to put New York at the forefront of the national struggle to upend legalized racism. In 1955, the city issued Local Law 55, which set up the Commission on Intergroup Relations (later renamed the Commission on Human Rights) to investigate and uproot "prejudice, intolerance, bigotry, and discrimination" in the city. Three years later, New York became the first city to ban housing discrimination in the private market. Meanwhile, Wagner promoted African Americans and Puerto Ricans in city government and unabashedly presented himself as a leader in the struggle for racial justice.[45] An emblematic incident occurred in 1956, when Hulan E. Jack, Wagner's successor as Manhattan borough president and one of the top black elected officials in the country, suddenly faced accusations of harboring Communist sympathies after traveling to Louisiana to promote desegregation. Told that the House Committee on Un-American Activities had uncovered evidence of Jack's associations with "subversive groups," Wagner brushed the charges aside and defended Jack as "the highest grade of American that I know of." In 1958, Wagner began to promote a brand of urban renewal that stressed community participation in planning. And he offered early support for the kinds of community-based antipoverty groups that would flourish during the War on Poverty, especially in majority-black neighborhoods. "Wagner was good," Elsie Richardson later recalled, "he really tried to help us."[46]

Root Causes

Increasingly, Wagner and the policymakers surrounding him linked their fight against youth crime to the national struggle against discrimination and poverty. By the late 1950s, the social workers, social scientists, and policymakers within the Youth Board's orbit were embracing an environmentalist interpretation of juvenile delinquency. The issue of youth crime—its causes, its effects, and its remedies—was becoming a prism through which reformers of all stripes began to consider the most significant challenges facing the modern city.

Soon after his accession to the mayoralty in 1954, Wagner put Deputy Mayor Henry Epstein to work crafting a new approach to reducing delinquency in the city. The following year, Wagner asked sociologist Robert M. MacIver to put together a research group named the Mayor's Juvenile Delinquency Evaluation Project. In 1958, Wagner declared delinquency to be "the Number One project for the city."[47] By the early 1960s, Wagner was trumpeting the fact that the city spent upward of a billion dollars annually on youth. (The vast majority of that money went to the general education budget.) The number of detached workers in the Youth Board stable swelled from 40 in 1955 to 150 a decade later. The number of guidance counselors in public schools increased from 100 to

600 in the eight years after 1955. City spending on treatment for young drug addicts increased fourfold. New York also built hundreds of playgrounds, community centers, and recreation rooms in housing projects to alleviate what Wagner called "the conditions under which delinquent tendencies develop."[48]

That said, the city wasn't only serving up carrots. There were sticks aplenty: stepped-up police patrols, expanded prisons, and the institutionalization of delinquents. During the election year of 1957, Wagner ratcheted up his law-and-order rhetoric to new heights, calling for "vigorous police action" to deal with "hard-core problem children." That September, Wagner announced that the city would be escalating its assault on the "menace of irresponsible adolescent delinquency." Among the get-tough measures he floated was an archipelago of camps modeled on the old Civilian Conservation Corps, where troublemakers would be sent to undergo work training and disciplinary training. (The idea quietly disappeared soon afterward.) "Mayor Mobilizes Full City Attack on Teen Violence," read the *Times* headline.[49]

Wagner linked youth behavior to broader cultural shifts. "There has been a serious breakdown in the moral fiber of our society and this has been a major contributory factor to many of the ills that now beset us," he said in 1959. This moral breakdown was particularly salient among what he and other reformers in the late 1950s sometimes termed "multi-problem families." In such households, the theory went, teenagers would be more inclined to join gangs because of the "breakdown of family life and the resultant weakening of the authority of the home." But lax parental discipline could only explain so much. "Much of the criticism attributing to parents responsibility for juvenile delinquency is essentially uncharitable," Epstein wrote in "Perspectives on Delinquency Protection," a landmark report released on May 12, 1955. Epstein and others held that gang members were just like other adolescents, except that they lacked access to "constructive channels" through which to find a sense of belonging and play out their urges and fantasies.[50]

According to a 1957 booklet about gangs published by the Youth Board, the origins of delinquents' behavior lay in their physical and socioeconomic surroundings. "For the most part, their homes may be found in rundown areas of the city," the report observed. "Apartments here are overcrowded; every room is a bedroom. Privacy is all but impossible. Family sociability is difficult at best." Beyond that, such neighborhoods had overcrowded schools, poor community resources, and overtaxed health and welfare services. "Moreover," the Youth Board opined, "these areas are composed of many minority groups—so that the destructive influence of discrimination is at work early in the lives of the area's young inhabitants." Deeply enmeshed in a web of social problems, such youngsters seemed almost predestined to fail. Clearly, not all children in poor areas of the city journeyed into gangland; nor was it obvious that criminal behavior was a natural response to discrimination. Yet the Youth Board was prepared to assume, for policy purposes, that most delinquents were either poor or members of minority groups—and, most often, both. These assumptions racialized the issue of delinquency.[51]

Though white youth gangs endured throughout the 1950s, antidelinquency efforts in Wagner-era New York increasingly targeted black and Hispanic teenagers—who, policymakers assumed, were more likely to commit crimes because of the circumstances in which they had been raised. "We know from our experience in New York City," Wagner said in 1962, "that a combination of under-privilege, discrimination and frustration provides an ideal soil for juvenile delinquency—and for adult delinquency, too. . . . It is also true that when we are talking about the root causes of delinquency, we must include unemployment; we must include lack of educational opportunity; we must include the decreasing demand for unskilled labor; we must include the lure of easy money through crime."[52]

How to act on this interpretation? These "root causes" were deeply embedded in the American political economy. Such things as segregation, alienation, and shifting patterns of industrial development could scarcely be addressed at the national level, let alone in a single city. But that didn't stop New York's reformers from thinking big. Activists and academics in the late 1950s theorized an antidelinquency policy that simultaneously aimed to control young people's behavior and alter the socioeconomic circumstances in which they lived. If black and Hispanic teenagers were especially likely to engage in criminal activities, as the Youth Board assumed, then preventing such activities implied taking on a whole range of issues that specifically affected racial minorities. This entailed, on the one hand, neighborhood-based interventions tailored to "at-risk" youth—remedial reading instruction, new playgrounds in housing projects, vocational training, and the like—and, on the other, macro-scale programs aimed at improving housing, creating jobs, fostering healthier living conditions, and combating discrimination. In this comprehensive vision lay a template for the War on Poverty.

As for the detached-worker program that remained the centerpiece of the Youth Board's efforts, evidence began to emerge in the late 1950s that it had scored some notable successes in inducing gang members to go straight. The Wagner administration claimed that there had been only one serious rumble between March 1956 and September 1959 among the gangs serviced by the Council of Social and Athletic Clubs. The summer of 1958 was notable for having witnessed no gang killings. By 1959, the Youth Board claimed to be working with 80 of the city's 110 known youth gangs, although it was difficult to tell for sure just how many were active at any given moment. But the street-club program was not a cure-all. "The street club worker cannot change the living conditions of teenage gang members," a 1957 Youth Board report argued. "He cannot give a member a better home life. He cannot hope to eliminate discrimination in a neighborhood nor can he modify other social and economic pressures which act on these young people and their families." The question facing Wagner-era reformers, then, was what *could* address such "social and economic pressures."[53]

One answer was to foster policy innovation from the bottom up. In the late 1950s, the Youth Board stepped up its efforts to promote grassroots participation in combating juvenile delinquency and addressing root causes. As Epstein put it in his 1955 report, "civic groups have an invaluable part to play in overall welfare planning and in encouraging constructive social action on the part of youth." This squared with Wagner's previously stated belief that "community leaders share with municipal officials the responsibility for formulating a program for improving conditions in their own neighborhood."[54]

In August 1957, Wagner announced that he was asking Ralph Whelan, the Youth Board's executive director, to accelerate the fight against youth crime "with particular emphasis on local community action programs." Citywide, this meant building alliances between city agencies and neighborhood groups and softening some of the suspicion with which black and Latino citizens tended to view government agencies. In each target area, the Youth Board would sponsor town-hall meetings where local leaders could talk to city officials and lay the groundwork for permanent community councils. Several neighborhoods, most notably the Lower East Side, had preexisting community groups devoted to working with teen gangs; in such cases, the city stepped in with funds, manpower, and political support. In other places, the Youth Board spawned new institutions that would keep one foot in the world of community organizing while dipping a toe in the waters of government bureaucracy. That was the case in Bedford-Stuyvesant, where the Youth Board brought together a network of civic groups, civil-rights organizations, churches, and block associations in 1958. The new group would take on a dual role, helping to implement youth programs in Bed-Stuy while also advising the city on how to address the "root causes" of delinquency.[55]

In and of itself, the goal of community participation in planning was hardly new. Like the Brooklyn Detached Worker Program launched in 1950, this latest phase in the Youth Board's work closely mimicked approaches pioneered by the Brooklyn Council for Social Planning. Not coincidentally, BCSP itself ceased to exist in 1957, when it lost the support of its parent organization, the Greater New York Fund. (The same fate befell BCSP's sister councils in each of the other boroughs.)[56] To some extent, the council was a victim of its own success in dramatizing urban problems and demonstrating new approaches to solving them. The city government's expansion of social-welfare programs, along with the Youth Board's sponsorship of community action and antigang programs, represented a transitional moment in which the post–New Deal state was forging new relationships not only with grassroots groups but also with the voluntary sector. Whereas the major delinquency efforts of the 1940s had been launched by nonprofit groups such as the BCSP and then migrated into government policy, the War on Poverty in the 1960s would supersede the voluntary sector by setting up a network of government-sponsored community groups and social-service agencies.[57]

Indeed, what was novel about the Youth Board's work in the late 1950s was that it put the *government*—as opposed to settlement houses, religious charities, and other nonprofit groups—in the position of mobilizing neighborhood activists and tapping into grassroots energies. Youth Board programs represented the city government's embrace of a set of theoretical assumptions and social-work techniques that had sprouted from the voluntary sector's gang-outreach programs. Aware of its role as a policy innovator, the Youth Board sponsored "demonstration programs" that adopted neighborhood activism as an important component of social policy.

New York City was not alone in testing such approaches: the Ford Foundation in the late 1950s was funding a national network of community-action experiments known as the Gray Areas program, which aimed to tackle delinquency and other urban problems. But what happened in New York was especially significant because of the city's size, its mayor's prominence, national interest in Gotham's gangs, and the influential neighborhood-based coalitions that arose around the goal of changing youth behavior. The city's youth programs would soon wield outsize policy influence in the emerging national assault on the "root causes" of juvenile delinquency.

The Youth Board's work also marked a new beginning in the relationship of the municipal state to African Americans. Though New Deal programs had been popular among New York's black residents, the post–New Deal state remained an inadequate vehicle for advancing the cause of racial equality. For one thing, macro-scale processes like redlining, urban renewal, and subsidized white flight—all of them shaped by New Deal legislation—were contributing to the ghettoization of New York's growing black population. Meanwhile, the city's Democratic clubhouses remained poorly equipped, and often unwilling, to act as intermediaries between minority communities and the government. Under Wagner, the state became more permeable, providing the city's African Americans with platforms from which to voice their concerns and articulate a set of complex community aspirations that transcended formal recognition of their "civil rights." The Youth Board community councils, like the community planning boards and, later, War on Poverty agencies, offered access points to the state, and they furthered the Wagner administration's quest to secure political partners at the grassroots. At first, the devolution of power to local decision-making bodies was mostly symbolic. But symbolism mattered. The new, neighborhood-based bureaucracy opened up fresh possibilities in minority neighborhoods. In the 1960s, New York's community-action groups would incubate more radical visions. On the other hand, the incorporation of the black leadership class into government agencies threatened to exert a moderating influence on the discourse emanating from places like Bedford-Stuyvesant.

2

Mobilizing the Forces

Bedford-Stuyvesant is a community of great personal resources
on the one hand and of marked social disorganization on the
other. It is a community which has all the factors to deal with
the tremendous human and physical problems it faces provided
it can reach some consensus about them and move in concerted fashion to resolve them.

—REV. J. ARCHIE HARGRAVES, 1956

As 1958 dawned, the Youth Board was plotting an "all-out fight against
Bedford-Stuyvesant juvenile delinquency." It had been twelve years
since the Brooklyn Council for Social Planning had launched its gang
project in Bedford-Stuyvesant; seven years had passed since the Youth
Board's Nathaniel Kaplan had announced that a "small army" of social
workers would "invade" the area. The Youth Board had mostly managed
to stop groups like the Bishops and the Greene Avenue Stompers from
staging the kinds of rumbles that had bloodied parks, playgrounds, streets,
and subways a decade earlier. That counted as a success. But gangs of
armed (and often drug-addled) teenagers still haunted the city. Muggings,
stabbings, and rapes abounded. Battles for turf and revenge could erupt
at any moment.[1]

A wave of teen violence during the winter of 1957–1958 spurred the Youth
Board to step up its efforts in Brooklyn. The city's newest drive against delinquency would thrust neighborhood activists onto center stage. "We
feel that many community groups have ideas of their own on methods of
combating delinquency, and that these groups are able to initiate their
programs," declared Charles A. Ward, the Youth Board's point man in
Bedford-Stuyvesant. "The Youth Board is not going to impose any ideas
on the cooperating groups." But how would those "cooperating groups"

A 1961 ad for brewed-in-Brooklyn Rheingold beer, saluting the community service of Charles A. Ward Jr. An employee of the New York City Youth Board, Ward helped organize the Central Brooklyn Coordinating Council in 1958.
Foote, Cone & Belding, 1961, for Liebmann Breweries, Inc., Brooklyn, New York.
Photograph by Patston-Hesse

be selected? Now that the city was turning to communities for input, who should speak for those communities? The answers were far from simple.[2]

Bedford-Stuyvesant in the 1950s was a sprawling tapestry of micro-neighborhoods in which a diverse and rapidly changing population lived, worked, and defined common goals. Complex ethnic and class cleavages made Bed-Stuy a difficult political terrain for city policymakers to navigate. Even the neighborhood's borders were contested—and the very notion of a community named "Bedford-Stuyvesant" was itself a recent invention. To outsiders, Bedford-Stuyvesant was synonymous with crime, poverty, and social dissolution. But that imagery obscured what lay beneath: a vibrant, organized, energetic community. An emerging destination for black culture, the area bubbled with block associations, voluntary agencies, and political clubs. For the preachers and professionals who led most of those organizations, the late 1950s were a moment of crisis but also a time of hope. Intense organizing on a variety of fronts, combined with the progressive policies of the Wagner administration, was ushering in a new era in the relationship of the state to black Brooklynites.

That's where Ward came in. Because the Kings County Democratic bosses had largely excluded African Americans from positions of influence, there were few patronage ties linking City Hall to black Brooklynites. Ward, a social worker with experience both in government and as an activist, was perfectly positioned to translate into policy the yearnings of Bedford-Stuyvesant's vocal yet politically marginalized citizens. In 1958, he set about organizing a new, community-based delinquency initiative dubbed the Central Brooklyn Coordinating Council for Youth (CBCC). The project attracted political reformers, church ministers, and club-women; civil-rights leaders, homeowner advocates, and fraternity brothers also came onboard. Together, they would advise the Youth Board on methods for reforming and retraining local youth. But distrust of the city government lingered. Not content to play an advisory role, CBCC activists would soon put forward a vision of community renewal that went far beyond the immediate challenge of suppressing youth gangs. That vision was nourished by a rich tradition of local activism—and by the long legacy of racial exclusion in Brooklyn.

Inventing a Community

Writer Alfred Kazin once remarked that each Brooklynite's knowledge of his home borough tended to encompass only that part of it separating his own home from the East River. Many neighborhoods were more foreign to one another than each was to Manhattan—which Brooklyn residents usually called "The City." Whereas Manhattan had some 600 streets, most of them neatly aligned to the island's iconic grid, Brooklyn had 1,800. A 1955 handbook for newcomers to the borough advised buying a detailed street map before doing anything else: "Plot your course before you start out. Everyone gets lost at least once in Brooklyn."[3]

Neighborhoods in postwar Brooklyn knew no formal definitions. Borders were unofficial, fluid, and contested. Like villagers of bygone days, Kings County residents tended to identify their surroundings according to what historian Suleiman Osman calls "a palimpsest of memories, symbols, and imagined places." When people talked about community, they meant different things. Some referred to ethnic enclaves, others to gang turfs, and still others to church parishes, political districts, block associations, or even nearby union halls, parks, and playgrounds. That was changing, though. At a time when Americans in all walks of life were redefining the meanings of "community," Brooklynites sought to reinvent urban space in ways that would signify belonging and authenticity. Increasingly, they drew boundaries that reflected changing populations and new political coalitions. Beginning in the early 1960s, local maps would become dotted with newly christened neighborhoods: Cobble Hill, Boerum Hill, Carroll Gardens, Lefferts Gardens, Prospect Heights, and more. Self-conscious invocations of a distant, more bucolic past, the names also evoked shifting power dynamics and real-estate trends. Some neighborhood names consecrated efforts to keep out newcomers; others sought to attract them. In the case of Bedford-Stuyvesant, the space that would later become known as "America's largest ghetto" was defined almost entirely by racism.[4]

Once, there had been two towns: Bedford Corners and Stuyvesant Heights. Each dated back to colonial times, and they retained distinct identities well into the twentieth century. The term "Bedford-Stuyvesant" had occasionally featured in nineteenth-century real-estate classifieds touting fancy new homes in the area. But the double-barreled neighborhood name only entered common usage during the Great Depression, when the black population of Central Brooklyn began to expand rapidly. By the late 1930s, city newspapers had taken to calling the area "Little Harlem," in reference to what the *Brooklyn Eagle* described as "Brooklyn's largest colored colony." In the 1950s, some African Americans embraced the term "Stuyford," and neighborhood socialites occasionally called themselves Stuyfordites. But it was "Bedford-Stuyvesant" that stuck. The neighborhood would gain national notoriety during the riots of 1964, and by 1966 "Bedford-Stuyvesant" had become a byword for "ghetto problems." Local residents proudly appropriated the new name and its diminutive; by the 1960s, "Bed-Stuy" had caught on.[5]

By most calculations, some 250,000 people lived in Bedford-Stuyvesant in the 1950s. The neighborhood was not always depicted on maps, but its generally accepted borders were Broadway and Saratoga Avenue to the East, Flushing Avenue or Myrtle Avenue to the north, Classon Avenue to the west, and Fulton Avenue or Atlantic Avenue to the south. Yet as the *Brooklyn Eagle* explained in 1954, those boundaries "mysteriously enlarge each year as the press of increasing population forces more and more Negroes to find homes in nearby 'fringe' areas." By the mid-1960s, expansive renderings of the area called Bedford-Stuyvesant put the local population at 450,000 people—200,000 more than a decade earlier. The reason for this blurriness was that Bedford-Stuyvesant's borders had become racial rather than geographic. "The definition most commonly used, both by the daily press and by some residents and leaders of the community, is that Bedford-Stuyvesant is 'wherever Negroes happen to live,'" one study declared. Elsie Richardson joked in 1966 that when someone asked her to define the borders of Bedford-Stuyvesant, she answered, "What date do you want?" As the Great Migration proceeded, enclaves that had once been, or would later be, seen as separate neighborhoods—Crown Heights, Weeksville, Clinton Hill, parts of Brownsville and Fort Greene—got absorbed into the rapidly expanding "ghetto." One local resident quipped in 1967, "I think pretty soon Harlem and Bedford-Stuyvesant is going to meet some place."[6]

The implication was that African Americans were intruders, whose very presence in the borough required a redefinition of boundaries. In fact, African Americans had inhabited Brooklyn from the dawn of European settlement. Most early black Brooklynites were exploited as slave labor on Dutch farms, and by the time of the Revolutionary War, Kings County had become one of the slaveholding capitals of the North. In 1790, 60 percent of the county's white families held fellow humans in bondage; only 3 percent of Kings County's blacks were free. Yet Brooklyn would soon

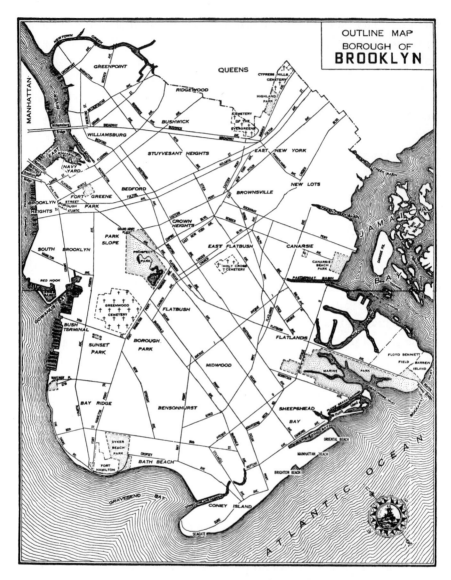

A map of Brooklyn, circa 1950. Several neighborhoods that would be familiar to future generations had yet to be named, including Cobble Hill, Carroll Gardens, Lefferts Gardens, Prospect Heights, Boerum Hill, and Ditmas Park. Nor had the term "Bedford-Stuyvesant" come into widespread use. *Papers of the Brooklyn Council for Social Planning, Brooklyn Public Library*

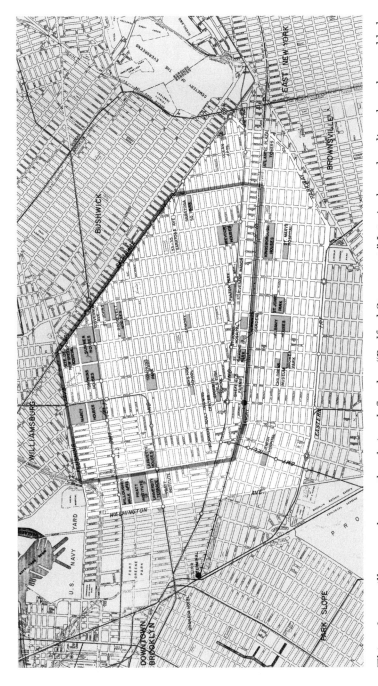

This 1967 map illustrates the area then being defined as "Bedford-Stuyvesant." Interior boundary lines have been added to show where Bed-Stuy's borders tend to be drawn today. The western rectangle of the shaded area is Clinton Hill; the parallelogram to the south is Crown Heights; and the southeastern slice is often considered part of Ocean Hill-Brownsville. *Brooklyn Public Library, Brooklyn Collection (Maps Collection)*

become a bastion of free black culture. In the years following the 1827 abolition of slavery in New York State, many African Americans moved to a semirural area of Brooklyn named Weeksville, wedged between the towns of Bedford and Flatbush. By mid-century, Weeksville's plucky residents had launched one of the country's first black newspapers, *The Freedman's Torchlight*, and funded a variety of community institutions, including Colored School No. 2, the Howard Colored Orphanage Asylum, the Zion Home for Aged Relief, and the Berean Baptist Church. A second free-black settlement, Carrsville, sprouted up nearby. At the time of the Civil War, Kings County had a larger percentage of blacks than any other place in New York State—which was itself home to more blacks than any other Northern state. During the draft riots of 1863, the embattled Weeksville community sheltered people fleeing the violence gripping Manhattan; after arsonists torched the Colored Orphan Asylum on Fifth Avenue, many of the traumatized survivors were spirited to Brooklyn.[7]

Weeksville's independent identity was soon swept away amid mass European immigration to Brooklyn. During the nineteenth century, the "City of Churches" underwent a dramatic transformation from a muddy village of 2,378 people into an industrial powerhouse of 1.2 million. Before being absorbed into New York City in 1898, Brooklyn ranked as the fourth most populous city in America. Development was intense along the East River and the Gowanus Canal; nearby areas of Sunset Park, lower Park Slope, Williamsburg, and Red Hook hummed with manufacturing and warehousing. Once-bucolic landscapes became crisscrossed with bustling streets, as the families of longshoremen and factory workers crammed into tenements and rows of hastily erected, plain-faced row houses. Meanwhile, Brooklyn was also developing into an attractive residential enclave for Manhattan's affluent classes. During the first third of the nineteenth century, elegant Brooklyn Heights emerged as America's first commuter suburb, thanks in large part to Robert Fulton's steam ferry. A half-century later, opulent mansions began to rise along the "Gold Coast" that bordered magnificent Prospect Park, designed by Frederick Law Olmsted and Calvert Vaux. The opening of the Brooklyn Bridge in 1883 encouraged Manhattan's moneyed classes to flock across the river. Merchants and other members of the expanding middle class built stately brownstone and limestone houses in Fort Greene, South Brooklyn, and Crown Heights; wealthy bankers and industrialists dominated the northwestern periphery of Prospect Park and toney Brooklyn Heights.[8]

Brooklyn was not a stylish place for whites alone. A small but prominent black bourgeoisie lived in Stuyvesant Heights and Clinton Hill, enclaves known for the splendor of their Victorian building stock. "It will be news to many white persons to learn that many negro men own and occupy brownstone dwellings in fashionable neighborhoods, employ white servants, and ride in their own carriages behind horses driven by liveried coachmen," the *Times* wrote in 1895. "As soon as negro men amass a comfortable fortune they move . . . across the East River." Stuyvesant Heights would remain a stronghold for black strivers in decades to come, and the blocks around historic Weeksville continued to house a small black middle class. At the turn of the century, though, those areas were mostly inhabited by Irish and German merchants, shopkeepers, and professionals. Meanwhile, in neighboring Bedford, developers touted "genteel suburban residences" and rubbed their hands as the new elevated railway along Fulton Street attracted a fresh group of affluent residents. But Central Brooklyn's gentility was short-lived. Most of the elite departed for suburban landscapes during the early decades of the twentieth century, and the streets of Bedford, Stuyvesant Heights, and Crown Heights became home mostly to working-class Jews and Italians. Brooklyn's black population, as a percentage of the whole, had declined significantly since the Civil War, thanks to mass European migration. By 1920, Brooklyn's 32,000 African Americans accounted for a small—and often embattled—fraction of the borough's two million people.[9]

The Great Migration changed that. The black population of Brooklyn more than doubled in the 1920s, heralding the start of a long period of growth. With its bounty of industrial jobs, Kings County was an especially attractive destination for people from the Carolinas and Virginia, for whom the train journey to a new life was short and sweet. But the Southerners soon found themselves facing stubborn discrimination in New York schools, workplaces, and housing markets. They were also greeted by suspicion and condescension from many of their more refined black neighbors. A 1940 study of Brooklyn's freshly arrived black residents found that "social and educational facilities have not kept pace with the needs[,] and there has been exploitation, expressions of hostility, and indifference not only by white citizens but on the part of the older Negro population." Social worker and activist Anna Arnold Hedgeman, who worked at the Brooklyn branch of the YWCA during the 1930s, later recalled how the black elite women who dominated social institutions like the YWCA, though "kindly in intent," were more inclined to identify with white women of their own social class than with poor blacks. "These white and Negro women of 'Old Brooklyn,'" Hedgeman wrote, "had worked together for nearly twenty-five years, and shared a common gentility and determination to maintain the status quo."[10]

Old Brooklyn was disappearing rapidly. Increasingly, Bedford-Stuyvesant's tree-lined streets, elegant brownstones, and air of gentility attracted African Americans of all classes. The completion of the A Train in 1936 made Brooklyn all the more accessible for Harlemites seeking to escape Manhattan's crowded tenements and filthy, dangerous streets. The Depression years also coincided with a generational shift, as many of Bed-Stuy's original homeowners grew too aged (or, in some cases, too poor) to hold onto their properties. Absentee landlordism became commonplace. Often, landlords subdivided brownstones that had once housed single families, renting them out to as many families as there were floors or turning them into rooming houses for the poor, the elderly, or the transient. This process would accelerate in the postwar years as more and more white homeowners headed for the suburbs.[11]

Whites who stayed in Bedford-Stuyvesant often reacted with alarm at the sudden influx of African Americans, and some joined forces to isolate and intimidate the newcomers. The Midtown Civic League, for example, organized resistance and occasional vigilante violence against African Americans in the 1930s. "There appears to be a concerted effort to keep living conditions as undesirable as possible, particularly in the Bedford-Stuyvesant area, where there is the greatest concentration [of black residents], in order to discourage further increases," opined the Brooklyn Council for Social Planning in a 1944 report.[12]

On the other hand, the growing ghetto was good business for slumlords and speculators. Penned in by the urban geography of racism, African Americans tended to pay above-market rents for substandard housing; landlords squeezed every possible penny of profit out of tenants whom they knew to be vulnerable. Many of Brooklyn's new black residents found themselves living in crowded, decrepit, rat-infested dwellings. No wonder, then, that they flocked to the network of low- and middle-income housing projects the New York City Housing Authority erected during the 1940s and 1950s. Kingsborough Houses in Crown Heights, built in 1941, added some 1,100 units to the housing supply, and 4,000 more apartments were built in Central Brooklyn between 1949 and 1957, when the Albany,

Brevoort, and Marcy Houses were erected. The black population of Brooklyn almost doubled in the 1940s, to 213,032, of whom some 122,240 lived in the area known as Bedford-Stuyvesant. By 1950, African Americans made up just shy of a tenth of New York City's citizens, and close to 750,000 black people lived in New York, more than in any other American city. Moreover, whereas black life in New York had once been virtually synonymous with Harlem, by 1950 about half the city's African Americans lived outside of Manhattan.[13]

World War II gave Brooklyn's expanding black working class a rare chance to get ahead. War production created enormous job growth in the borough. The Navy Yard at Wallabout Bay, where George Washington's men had once died by the thousands aboard British prison ships, became the busiest shipbuilding site in the world. At the height of the wartime mobilization, more than 70,000 workers drew their paychecks at the 290-acre facility, which bordered on the neighborhoods of Fort Greene, Williamsburg, Bed-Stuy, and Clinton Hill. The Navy Yard hummed twenty-four hours a day, seven days a week; alone, it produced more battleships than Japan during the war. Black New Yorkers, who had suffered catastrophic unemployment rates during the Depression, jumped at the jobs, and they were joined by tens of thousands of hopeful migrants from the South. The city as a whole buzzed with industrial activity. In 1944, the number of New Yorkers working in factories peaked at 1.86 million—and of those jobs, only 700,000 were directly tied to the war effort.[14]

Brooklyn owed much of its economic vitality to small firms. In 1947, there were 7,298 manufacturers in Brooklyn, 93 percent of which employed fewer than one hundred laborers. Clothing, musical instruments, furniture, paints, potato chips, chewing gum, paper—the list of goods produced by the small firms of Kings County could fill several pages. Several major companies also called Brooklyn home. The borough boasted the world's largest coffee-roasting facility. The Consolidated Edison plant claimed to be the world's biggest generator of steam electricity. Two local firms produced almost all of the type used by the American publishing industry. The Schaefer brewery was among the largest beer purveyors in the country. The North Brooklyn waterfront had once refined 70 percent of the sugar consumed in the United States, and the American Sugar Company still produced enough each day to supply New York's entire population. If counted as a city unto itself, Brooklyn in the late 1940s would have ranked first in foreign trade among North American ports. Some seventy-five steamship companies plied their trade from the docks of Red Hook and Bush Terminal in Sunset Park.[15]

But winds of change were blowing in. As the war industries packed up shop and the Navy Yard phased out the bulk of its operations, the trickle of blue-collar jobs out of the city—which had begun two decades earlier—would turn into a flood. The return to peacetime was particularly difficult for black workers. A study of twenty-five New York area war plants found that between mid-August and mid-September of 1945, some 45 percent of black employees lost their jobs.[16] A bounty of jobs remained, and wages were good thanks to the city's thriving labor movement; still, black Brooklynites often found themselves written out of the city's social-democratic contract. Many companies refused to hire African Americans, and powerful trade unions—notably in the job-rich construction industry—often excluded black workers altogether. Even in those industries that consented to hire African Americans, they were usually forced to take menial and unskilled positions, which paid less. Unemployment rates among black Brooklynites tended to be almost double those that prevailed among whites. For all that, the job market in Brooklyn seemed far more promising than in the rural South. And blacks were not the only group drawn to Brooklyn's industrial waterfront. Migrants from Puerto Rico flocked to neighborhoods such as Williamsburg, Greenpoint, Bushwick, and Sunset Park, where factory jobs abounded and where churches, stores, and sidewalks increasingly took on a Hispanic flavor. The northern sections of Bedford-Stuyvesant, which bordered Williamsburg and Bushwick, also attracted significant numbers of Puerto Ricans.[17]

Brooklyn's white residents, meanwhile, were beginning a migration of their own. Within the approximate borders of Bedford-Stuyvesant, the 1940 census counted 73.3 percent of residents as white; by 1950, that figure had dropped to 47.5 percent.[18] The City Planning Commission reported in 1951 that for the first time since the Revolutionary era, the number of New Yorkers leaving the city exceeded those entering; the trend was most visible in Brooklyn, where net outward migration reached 200,000 in the 1940s. (Owing to the high birth rates of the period, Brooklyn's population still grew slightly in the 1940s, reaching an all-time high of 2.74 million in 1950.) Many whites moved to the suburbs in pursuit of a middle-class American dream suddenly made possible by cheap housing, modern highways, and government-guaranteed mortgages. Some were following jobs gone south or west. Still others fled to areas of the city—Canarsie, Bay

Ridge, Queens—where African Americans had yet to settle; from there, they demanded that African Americans be excluded from union jobs, good schools, and all but the most shoddy housing. Author Pete Hamill of Park Slope later recalled the mixed motives that drove white Brooklynites to the suburbs: "It was race plus despair plus insecurity about money plus desires for the betterment of one's children plus—the most important plus—the loss of a feeling of community." Between 1940 and 1990, Brooklyn would experience a net gain of 1.3 million people of color and a net loss of 1.5 million whites.[19]

Underlying it all was redlining: the practice by which banking and mortgage institutions, with guidance from the federal government, conspired to withhold credit from neighborhoods considered to be risky. Redlining originated in attempts by the Homeowners Loan Corporation and Federal Housing Administration, creations of Franklin D. Roosevelt's New Deal, to revive a collapsed housing market in the late 1930s. As they assessed the viability of urban areas, federal officials cast a wary eye on a variety of ethnic groups—African Americans set off the loudest alarms—and discouraged lenders from investing in places of interracial mingling. As Craig Wilder has shown, many of Brooklyn's older neighborhoods were graded poorly, literally cordoned off on maps in red ink. Bedford-Stuyvesant in its entirety received a D rating from the HOLC, and subsequent assessments by private lenders reinforced the notion that Central Brooklyn, with its expanding black population, should be quarantined. As a result, few prospective homebuyers in the area, black or white, could access federally guaranteed mortgages; existing homeowners, foreseeing plummeting property values, sold out while they could. In effect, redlining made racial purity a goal of federal housing policy and, as Ta-Nahesi Coates has written, "destroyed the possibility of investment wherever black people lived." That sent whites fleeing the urban core for homogeneous suburbs and encouraged residents of those suburbs to keep out African Americans, whose very presence risked damaging the investments all around them. Increasingly, blacks found themselves confined to places like Bed-Stuy.[20]

By 1950, the bulk of Bed-Stuy residents lived at the economic margins. The area's median family income of $2,675 was barely three-quarters of the citywide figure, and only slightly higher than subsistence levels. (The official poverty line, when it was first calculated in the 1960s, was set at $3,000, which was $2,400 in 1950 dollars.) Less than 6 percent of Bed-Stuy families pulled in more than $6,000 a year, as compared with 15.5 percent

55

of Brooklynites as a whole. The share of Bed-Stuy residents in professional or managerial jobs was less than half that of Brooklyn overall. "[It] is general knowledge," a 1953 study declared, "that Bedford-Stuyvesant is an underprivileged area with a large Negro population which is on the increase; that housing is substandard, inadequate, overcrowded, and old; and that incomes are in general low." Far from a "sweet land of liberty," this was a place where frustrations were mounting.[21]

"Buying House"

As a "neighborhood" that was in fact the size of a city, midcentury Bedford-Stuyvesant stood out from surrounding areas because of its poverty. But Central Brooklyn also housed a well-established middle class and was fast becoming a trendy cultural hub for the city's flourishing black elite. This group would drive much of the reform activity in Bedford-Stuyvesant during the 1950s and early 1960s, infusing their politics with a complex and often contradictory blend of racial solidarity and class privilege.

"Society here is based on tradition, old families, and a quiet elegance," a local columnist opined in 1959. "Club life is intense with many organizations and clubs with full programs." Doctors, lawyers, realtors—their names crammed the society columns of the *Amsterdam News*, which reported in detail on their good looks, snappy clothes, and glamorous gatherings. They attended the lavish balls of the Comus Club, which claimed to be "the oldest social club in Negro America" and was also billed as "Brooklyn's snootiest." Others kept up with old friends in the prestigious Alpha Phi Alpha fraternity. Many collected club memberships as if they were lapel pins, splitting time and donations among Greek societies, professional guilds, social-uplift organizations like the YWCA and the Salvation Army, and civil-rights groups like the NAACP and Urban League. At night, they could let loose at supper clubs and jazz joints like the Arlington Inn on Fulton Avenue, the Verona Café on Verona Place, or the Continental on Nostrand Avenue, which featured a parade of bebop giants, including Dizzy Gillespie, Miles Davis, Max Roach, and local legend Randy Weston. (Thelonious Monk was a regular at Tony's, an unassuming bar on Dean Street.) And all took pride in the fact that the most electrifying Brooklynite of them all, the Dodgers' Jackie Robinson, made his home on McDonough Street in Stuyvesant Heights after breaking baseball's color barrier in 1947.[22]

But it was the churches of Central Brooklyn—dozens upon dozens of them—that served as the central cultural institutions in the area. Brooklyn in the 1950s was home to "the greatest concentration of remarkably gifted black preachers America's ever seen," according to Gardner C. Taylor, longtime minister of Concord Baptist Church in Bed-Stuy and a totemic figure in the black freedom struggle. This group included Sandy Ray of Cornerstone Baptist Church, Archie Hargraves of Nazarene Congregational Church, Claude Franklin of Mount Lebanon Church, and Milton Galamison of Siloam Presbyterian Church. All gained national reputations for their ministry and activism, and their churches filled with energetic congregants. On Sunday mornings, the streets of Bedford-Stuyvesant would lie quiet, then come alive when services concluded, as throngs poured out of churches in colorful hats and sharp suits.[23]

In Brooklyn, as in many other Northern cities, long-established black residents sometimes struggled to cope with the rapid in-migration of relatively impecunious Southerners after World War II. Studies of twentieth-century black elites, sometimes described as the "talented tenth" (W. E. B. Du Bois's term) or as the "black bourgeoisie" (E. Franklin Frazier's), have documented their ambivalent attitudes toward the black working class. Paternalism and noblesse oblige, backed by calls for racial uplift, coexisted with thinly veiled disdain for rural folkways. According to historian Robin D. G. Kelley, "African Americans born and raised in the North, particularly those who owned property and maintained a steady income, looked down on these newcomers and blamed them for neighborhood deterioration." This dynamic was certainly at work in Bedford-Stuyvesant. Yet the greenhorns in the postwar years included not only poor "rural folk" but also urbane professionals who had attended the best black colleges, gone to graduate school, and settled among Bed-Stuy's home-owning and increasingly politicized elite. This group included many social workers and, most prominently, several of the crusading churchmen who helped put Brooklyn on the front lines of the national civil-rights struggle. Taylor, for instance, was from Louisiana; Ray was born in Texas; Hargraves hailed from North Carolina; and William A. Jones and Walter Offutt Jr., both of whom preached at Bethany Baptist Church in the 1960s, grew up in Kentucky.[24]

Adding to Bedford-Stuyvesant's distinctive class landscape was a growing group of first- and second-generation West Indian immigrants. Some had immigrated directly to Brooklyn; others had passed through Harlem before taking the A Train to Kings County, hoping to shelter their children from the crime and grime of Manhattan. Though the West Indians of Bed-Stuy experienced high poverty rates, they tended to be better educated and better off than were recent migrants from the American South. Some West Indians first entered the United States on student visas and took up specialized professions after graduating; many others were skilled laborers or shopkeepers. In the 1940s and 1950s, growing numbers eagerly poured their savings and sweat equity into the area's spacious yet run-down brownstones. What was known as "buying house," according to novelist Paule Marshall, who grew up in Brooklyn, was "an obsessive pursuit" among West Indian families. To make their mortgage payments, many took two or three jobs. Often, West Indian women toiled as domestic day laborers; in the mornings, they would gather on street corners in affluent neighborhoods and wait for white housewives to pick them up and offer them a few hours' work. The working conditions were often humiliating, but the jobs were, in Marshall's words, "simply a means to an end: the end being the down payment on a brownstone house, a college education for their children, and the much coveted middle-class status these achievements represented." The second-generation strivers growing up in West Indian households included many who would rise to prominence in 1960s Bedford-Stuyvesant: community organizer Elsie Richardson; Congresswoman Shirley Chisholm; Judge Thomas R. Jones; Assemblyman William Thompson Sr.; Franklin Thomas, president of the Bed-Stuy Restoration Corporation; and Earl Graves, publisher of *Black Enterprise* magazine. A 1973 study remarked that, "Taken collectively, the Bed-Stuy West Indians would be among the most ambitious and hard-working people one would find anywhere."[25]

Chisholm, an early-childhood educator who in 1968 would become the first black woman elected to Congress, described Barbadian immigrants, including her parents, as "bright, thrifty, ambitious people." Because of their work ethic and obsession with their children's education, the Barbadians, Chisholm recalled, were known as the "Black Jews"—a stereotype they proudly adopted. Though West Indians were often at the forefront of efforts to build black political power in the postwar years, it was not uncommon for them to look down on working-class African American culture. According to Chisholm, migrants from the South were perceived as "passive and accommodating in the face of discrimination"—in stark contrast with West Indian men like her father, a well-read laborer who participated actively in union politics and embraced the ideas of Jamaican-born nationalist Marcus Garvey.[26]

Immigrants from the West Indies, whatever their claims to ethnic or class distinctiveness, soon found that in color-coded America they were lumped in with African Americans. Many New Yorkers with roots in the English-speaking Caribbean, according to journalist and Aruba native F. Donnie Forde, "had distinguished themselves in their native lands as members of the privileged class and were more than a bit surprised and disappointed to discover that all their special privileges were abrogated by the policies and practices of segregation once they set foot in the United States." This common experience with American racism, and the common feeling of living in an embattled community, fostered solidarity and sympathy among Brooklynites of African descent. Still, to speak of a singular "black community" in midcentury Brooklyn ignores not only class and gender stratifications but also the divisions between people with roots in the Caribbean and others with roots in the American South. Chisholm herself—who would do more than anyone to smooth over those cleavages—recalled in her memoir that "there was no such thing as a black community" in Brooklyn while she was growing up.[27]

Such divisions often spilled over into the political arena, threatening the kinds of racial unity advocated by black nationalists, including Garvey. Within the electoral realm, black people with roots in the South continued to view the Democratic Party with a measure of mistrust. Even after FDR won the lion's share of black voters nationwide during his second presidential campaign in 1936, many African Americans continued to hold the Democratic Party at arm's length, and vice versa. Not surprisingly, the first nonwhites to carve out niches within the Democratic county organizations in New York City were immigrants from the Caribbean, most notably Nevis-born Bertram Baker, elected to the State Assembly from Brooklyn in 1948, and Hulan Jack, a Saint Lucia native who in 1953 succeeded Robert Wagner Jr. as Manhattan borough president. Beginning with FDR's election, West Indians found ways to capture most of the patronage the Democratic Party was dishing out to black New Yorkers. But there was much less being dished out in Brooklyn than in Manhattan. In Harlem, J. Raymond Jones (who was born in the Virgin Islands) successfully built a power base within the Democratic Party organization; in 1964, he became the first black leader of Tammany Hall. Meanwhile, black Brooklyn's leading political strategist, Wesley Holder (born in Guyana), was forced to run insurgent campaigns against the local Democratic Party clubhouses. It was not until the 1960s that Caribbean Americans really broke through in Brooklyn, gaining election to numerous local and statewide offices.[28]

In the meantime, the West Indians of Brooklyn created a network of self-help groups, fraternal organizations, and mutual-aid societies to cope with life in an increasingly segregated city. The most important of these was the Paragon Progressive Credit Union. Scraped together in 1939, it started with a war chest of two dollars and twenty-five cents. Its early members, almost all of them men born in the Caribbean, were influenced by Garvey's Universal Negro Improvement Association, whose model of racial uplift through business enterprise and ethnic pride continued to resonate long after Garvey himself had passed from the scene. In the 1950s, Paragon's leaders included Holder and Charles Kellar, a civil-rights lawyer for the NAACP. By 1958, Paragon had 7,000 members and total savings of $2 million, and the *New York Age* reported that it was the largest black-run credit union in the country. Despite its deep roots in the West Indian community, the group chose not to target its efforts exclusively toward Caribbean Americans. Adopting the motto "Not for profit, but for service," Paragon donated to the NAACP, the YMCA, and the Negro College Fund, and it offered scholarships to the future doctors, lawyers, teachers, and social workers of Bedford-Stuyvesant. As such, it played a key role in building the middle class that would later provide much of the impetus for urban-redevelopment and antipoverty programs in Central Brooklyn.[29]

Paragon also funded many early efforts at historic preservation, underwriting a group of upwardly mobile "brownstoners" who bought nineteenth-century townhouses and set about renovating them. This was crucial to Bedford-Stuyvesant's development at a time when redlining was bleeding the neighborhood dry. Still, Paragon's funds could only help so many buyers. Unable to access federally guaranteed mortgages, potential homeowners in black Brooklyn "had to buy in a market that had been set aside for certain predatory elements, and pay fantastic moneys for mortgages," according to Thomas R. Jones, a son of Barbadian immigrants who came of age in Bedford-Stuyvesant during the 1930s and 1940s. Homebuyers often paid steep prices to brokers who had only recently scooped up the very same properties for pennies on the dollar, in some cases after using blockbusting techniques to scare white residents into selling cheap. In addition, most black Brooklynites borrowed at usurious terms from storefront lenders, loan sharks, and other middlemen.[30]

Nor was paying off the mortgage the only challenge facing the proud new owner of a Brooklyn home. Half-century-old houses often required extensive renovations and restoration. As many owners soon discovered, the ubiquitous brownstone façades that added so much to Bed-Stuy's charm were also uniquely vulnerable to erosion. (The type of New Jersey sandstone that was widely used by nineteenth-century developers had been selected precisely because its softness allowed for easy cutting and ornamentation.) Restoration projects were doubly challenging for black homeowners, who might find themselves unable to refinance their mortgages or take out home-improvement loans except at exceedingly high interest rates. Even a building in tip-top shape was never safe from plummeting in value. Bed-Stuy's homeowners felt acutely the precariousness of their wealth and status.

Despite those obstacles, swathes of Bed-Stuy, especially Stuyvesant Heights, became what Paule Marshall described as "a relatively stable, well-kept community of proud black homeowners who treated the brownstones they had purchased with the same loving care as the whites whom they had replaced." For the most part, owner-occupied dwellings in Bed-Stuy were sturdy, elegant, attached townhouses, made of limestone or brownstone. Three or four stories high, they lined many of the district's leafy east–west streets. Some blocks featured dozens of plain-faced houses standing shoulder to shoulder, unified in their quiet dignity. Other streets came alive with gorgeous, often ornate, architectural detail—Grecian columns, stone faces, Romanesque archways, stained-glass bay windows, intricate brickwork in the Queen Anne revival style. For decades, those homes "represented the fulfillment of many aspirations among the upwardly mobile families in the Central Harlem ghetto," as a 1965 study put it.[31]

According to various estimates, most dating from the 1960s, between 15 percent and 20 percent of Bed-Stuy homes were owner-occupied. Because many of those homeowners rented out one or more units within their own brownstones, an estimated 25 to 30 percent of local families lived in an owner-occupied building. Another 10 percent of buildings were owned by people who lived nearby. In Stuyvesant Heights, there were many blocks where a majority of residents owned their homes. Not all brownstones were elegant, of course, nor were they all owner-occupied. Many housed either too many people (in the case of those converted into single-room-occupancy dwellings) or too few (in the case of those simply abandoned and left to rot). The north–south avenues, meanwhile, tended to feature four-, five-, or even six-story tenements, many of which were owned by absentee landlords who let them fall into decay. Still, the high home ownership rates in Bedford-Stuyvesant marked a stark contrast with Harlem, and indeed with most other areas that earned the "ghetto" label in the wake of the Great Migration.[32]

The robust presence of homeowners gave a special quality to Bed-Stuy's community organizing. "Many streets are organized into block associations which combine to form powerful area-wide and community-wide organizations," one study observed. "The high proportion of ownership has helped produce a deep commitment to, and involvement with, the community's future." Life in row houses encouraged residents to come together in efforts to preserve and beautify their blocks. The more modest brownstones often stretched in an uninterrupted chain from one end of the block to the other, with little in the way of architectural ornamentation to distinguish one from the next. Physically, aesthetically, and spiritually connected, they demanded a communal effort from owners keen on maintaining property values. Lacking lawns, driveways, or spacious backyards, the houses propelled their inhabitants out onto stoops and sidewalks; with parks scarce, the street was a place to be honored, nurtured, and celebrated. As teen gangs proliferated, some block-level organizers tried to reclaim the streets by joining community-based efforts to fight crime. Such activities were not limited to homeowners. Tenants often participated in the activities of block associations, and former tenant organizers (including Elsie Richardson) sometimes graduated into organizing block groups once they had bought their own homes. Still, the backbone of the block associations were the men and women who had poured their savings and sweat into buying a house and, in many cases, fixing up and preserving the Victorian relics they had grown to love.[33]

Some of the earliest homeowner coalitions in Bed-Stuy, such as the Midtown Civic League, had been white supremacist groups formed to keep blacks out. During the late 1930s and early 1940s, black homeowners started coming together in block associations, often in concert with white neighbors.[34] Their early aims were prosaic: to ensure timely garbage pickup, restore eroding brownstone façades, clean up empty lots, and provide what Jane Jacobs later called "eyes on the street." Some planted maples and sycamores; some trimmed hedges and tended to flowering window boxes. The model caught on fast. "When tired, a walk through an association block provides a refreshing atmosphere," the *Amsterdam News* reported in 1948. "Here and there are found new trees planted along the streets that were bought through the block association. Yards are kept; homes look inviting with trim, neat windows. Radios are always tuned low; all is serene. Dogs travel on leash, and are curbed. Refuse and garbage cans are covered and placed on the sidewalks only a short time before the disposal truck makes its collection."[35]

Before long, block associations began to come together in larger groups, the most active of which was the Bedford-Stuyvesant Neighborhood Council, founded in 1939. This was among the first institutions to identify with the emerging "Bedford-Stuyvesant" label. At a time when the racist Midtown Civic League was at the height of its influence, the Neighborhood Council explicitly embraced its community's dynamism and diversity. By the mid-1950s, it represented more than one hundred block associations and had begun organizing to expand access to public transit and protest the withdrawal of city services from majority-black areas. The Neighborhood Council mobilized annual beautification drives during which residents painted their homes, cleaned up front yards, and cleared trash from vacant lots. They also organized to oppose the opening of several local bars, which, the Neighborhood Council claimed, "could be breeding places for juvenile delinquency." Signs posted around Bedford-Stuyvesant read, "This Is Your Block. Please Help Keep It Clean," "Take Pride in the Appearance of Your Home and Neighborhood," or "Shhh! Watch Your Language, Your Mother May Be Passing." During the holiday season, the Neighborhood Council sponsored an annual Christmas decoration contest; stretches of MacDonough Street, Decatur Street, and Putnam Avenue would twinkle with incandescent bulbs, each block vying for bragging rights.[36]

To an extent, block associations represented an attempt to preserve comfortable living standards and property values in Bed-Stuy; as such, they reflected the efforts of anxious professionals to shield themselves from the poverty and disorder that surrounded them. According to Steven Gregory, an anthropologist who has studied the predominantly black neighborhood of East Elmhurst (which sits seven miles north of Bedford-Stuyvesant, in Queens), block associations in the 1950s "gave institutional form to class divisions within the community, creating an effective organizing base for the growing middle class, one that linked their activism directly to their

A view of Jefferson Avenue in Bedford-Stuyvesant in 1954. The sign above, erected by a block association, reads "This is your block. Keep it clean, safe, beautiful." Such signs are still visible on some blocks of Bed-Stuy six decades later. *Brooklyn Public Library, Brooklyn Collection*

interests as property owners." Indeed, home ownership was quite rare among urban African Americans, and it conferred status upon a select group. As historian N. D. B. Connolly has argued, "it was property owners who mostly set the agendas for formal civil rights protest." Homeowner activism could also lend a conservative flavor to protest. Brownstone activists in the late 1950s and early 1960s perceived poor neighbors not only as allies in the struggle for racial justice, but also as incubators of the "slum conditions" in their midst.[37]

Yet homeowner activism in Bedford-Stuyvesant was more than a narrow expression of class privilege. Block associations supported assertive campaigns for improved city services—more frequent garbage collection, for instance, or increased access to health care—that promised to benefit the entire population. And block-based activism often provided a space in which local organizers could build support for broader causes: political reform, school desegregation, and civil rights. During the 1960s, Bed-Stuy's network of block associations would exert a strong influence on the government programs that unfolded in the neighborhood. Many of Bed-Stuy's political leaders remained well known locally for their dedication to block-level organizing. Through them, streets linked up with elites. When the city and federal governments began seeking out community institutions that might help plan and run new programs, they turned first to churches and then to block associations. Thus, Bed-Stuy's homeowning professionals, along with churchmen, became the first local residents to partner with politicians and bureaucrats when it came time to craft policy. This process would imbue War on Poverty initiatives with political capital and policy expertise. It also meant that the local poverty programs would internalize some decidedly middle-class assumptions about the causes and remedies of poverty.

In Search of Empowerment

Despite ethnic and class cleavages, Bed-Stuy residents in the 1950s increasingly found common ground in protest and politics. Black New Yorkers could draw on a rich local tradition of grassroots action. Although the civil-rights movement is often described as having "moved north" in the mid-1960s, as the triumphant tones of the March on Washington turned to cries of "Black Power," the struggle had been deeply rooted in the North all along. It was in the North, and especially in New York City, that activists could organize, raise funds, make interracial connections, and test the waters of electoral politics without fearing for their lives. Successive campaigns for equal access to schools, jobs, and housing had unfolded throughout the years of Depression and war, before momentarily bowing to the pressures of McCarthyism. If anything, the movement moved *south* after 1954.[38]

New York State's first antidiscrimination law was passed in 1895, a few short months before the *Plessy v. Ferguson* decision validated "separate but equal" facilities. Known as the Malby Bill, the statute declared that "all persons within the jurisdiction of the State shall be entitled to the full and equal accommodations, advantages, facilities, and privileges of trains, restaurants, hotels, eating-houses, bath-houses, barber-shops, theatres, music halls, public conveyances on land and water, and all other places of public accommodation or amusement." Yet the law was routinely flouted in the decades that followed. Segregation hardened. New Yorkers reacted with action on a variety of fronts, from the editorial offices of *The Crisis* to the pageants organized by Garvey's Universal Negro Improvement Association. The "don't buy where you can't work" protests of the 1930s and the "Double-V" campaign of World War II—along with countless boycotts, sit-ins, and picket lines that foreshadowed events of the 1960s—cemented New York's status as a critical battleground in the black freedom struggle.[39]

Beginning in the 1930s, Brooklyn activists embarked on a vigorous campaign to test New York's anti-discrimination statutes. They filed suit against Jim Crow restaurants that refused to seat them and protested segregated swimming pools. The National Negro Congress in 1941 accused the owners of Coney Island's Luna Park of "Hitler-like action" for barring a group of black schoolboys. PTA groups mobilized to protest overcrowded schools, indifferent teachers, and, most troubling, "zoning with a strong suspicion of Jim Crow intent, whereby children who were Negro had to walk or ride long distances to schools almost wholly Negro, while white children from equal distance came to a more modern desirable school nearby." A group called the Brooklyn Inter-Racial Assembly, led by Ada B. Jackson and Maude B. Richardson, was particularly active in trying to expand the New Deal state to include African Americans; the group lobbied for desegregated health facilities, daycares catering to working mothers, after-school programs, enforcement of tenants' rights, consumer protection, and an end to racist mortgage-lending policies. In December 1943, the Inter-Racial Assembly took advantage of Eleanor Roosevelt's visit to

Bed-Stuy to unveil a ten-point program that endorsed the key demands of A. Philip Randolph's March on Washington movement: equal employment opportunities and an end to segregation in the armed forces.[40]

New York's black activists struggled to keep their fight alive amid the fervent anticommunism of the immediate postwar years. But they did mobilize around specific local issues, including police brutality. In the late 1940s and early 1950s, police officers shot several unarmed black New Yorkers and meted out what a city councilman from Harlem, Earl Brown, estimated as "hundreds" of beatings. At a 1949 rally, Brooklyn civil-rights attorney Charles Kellar cited four recent beatings of local black men, each of whom had been hospitalized after his encounter with New York's finest. One of the men eventually died, and another was permanently incapacitated. Said future judge Lewis S. Flagg Jr., then the lead lawyer for the Brooklyn branch of the NAACP, "No one, so long as his face is black, is immune to such treatment."[41]

Another pressing issue was public health. In the postwar decades, rates of infant mortality and venereal disease in Bedford-Stuyvesant were more than twice the national average.[42] Bed-Stuy had no public hospital; at the same time, many African American physicians complained that they lacked access to private hospitals in surrounding areas of Brooklyn. In 1949, the mayoral administration of William O'Dwyer suggested that a new public hospital would open in Bed-Stuy within five years. When nothing came of it, local activists turned the hospital into a cause célèbre. A left-wing group calling itself the Bedford-Stuyvesant Health Congress launched the campaign by gathering 15,000 signatures demanding a 750-bed, city-funded "interracial" hospital in the area. Organizers attempted to link their efforts to the national civil-rights struggle. In 1955, after the City Planning Commission delayed the hospital yet again, Reverend Benjamin Lowry wrote, "This decision condemns to death more of our babies and mothers in childbirth, who make up the highest mortality toll of any community in the United States. . . . Thus a straight line is drawn from the dramatic outrage of judicial sanction in Mississippi of the murder of young Emmett Till to the more subtle form of murder by omission of the hospital project emanating from City Hall."[43]

Lowry was not alone in tying local battles to the broader crusade against racial discrimination. As Till's murder and other events in 1955 thrust the black freedom movement onto the national stage, Brooklyn's black activists gained a renewed sense of purpose and mission. Many took inspiration from the strenuous efforts of Southerners to overthrow the Jim Crow system—all the more so because many had grown up in the South themselves. Upon the arrival of Martin Luther King Jr. in Brooklyn on March 24, 1956, fresh from leading the boycott of public buses in Montgomery, Alabama, the *Amsterdam News* urged all New Yorkers "to come out and support morally and financially the greatest Negro movement in our history—the boycott!" Brooklynites embraced similar efforts to pursue civil rights through economic pressure and independence. "Trade with pride" was one slogan heard on the streets of Bedford-Stuyvesant, where a community savings-and-loan association and a black-run insurance agency had recently taken root.[44]

Meanwhile, activists across New York City worked to end informal segregation by sending out "testers" to hundreds of restaurants known to exclude black clientele. Though largely successful, these challenges gained less press coverage than the wave of lunch-counter sit-ins that swept the South after 1960. Ironically, the problem for New York activists was that segregation was illegal, even if it persisted on the ground. They could not hope to deal a fatal blow to the Jim Crow system, since the Jim Crow system did not officially exist. Because discrimination endured in so many restaurants, hotels, and construction sites, despite laws to the contrary, assailing it required hundreds upon hundreds of individual challenges. No wonder that Brooklynites were eager to identify with the more dramatic—and more dangerous—Southern campaigns, to which Bed-Stuy activists often lent a hand in person.[45]

Increasingly, Brooklyn activists in the 1950s turned their attention to the electoral arena, where African Americans found themselves shockingly underrepresented. Prior to 1960, Brooklyn had elected only two black lawmakers at *any* level of government. Brooklyn's Democratic bosses rarely promoted nonwhite candidates, and they tended to get away with it because a large proportion of black Brooklynites weren't registered to vote. Gerrymandered congressional districts further compounded the problem. Thus, unlike Harlem, which regularly returned Adam Clayton Powell to Congress and tapped into city patronage through Democratic boss J. Raymond Jones, Bed-Stuy's black majority was largely voiceless in Washington, DC, and in City Hall. "Bedford-Stuyvesant," commented one city official in the 1960s, "is the province, Harlem is the capital."[46]

The political empowerment of African Americans was an uneven process, and it proceeded slowly in Brooklyn. The Great Depression and the

New Deal had touched off a nationwide exodus of African Americans from the Republican Party, to which they'd pledged their loyalties since the Civil War. That development, combined with the ongoing migration of blacks to Northern cities and the 1944 Supreme Court ruling against all-white primaries, made African Americans an increasingly potent force in national politics. President Harry Truman's decision in 1948 to embrace civil rights for blacks testified to this newfound clout. At the local level, Mayor Wagner's attention to the concerns of African Americans and his efforts to promote them in city government consecrated a new era of black participation in municipal politics. County politics were another story. Well into the 1960s, the Kings County Democratic organization, which ruled Brooklyn, kept the political spoils firmly in white hands. Whether contesting seats in the City Council, the State Legislature, or Congress, machine-backed Democrats held a massive advantage over any and all challengers—and the machine-backed Democrats were almost always white. Party bosses also picked candidates for judgeships and other non-legislative positions; mounting an insurgent campaign, either in the primary or in the general election, was a massive undertaking. Though the Kings County organization had succumbed to processes of "ethnic succession" in the past, with Jews and Italians managing to penetrate what had once been an Irish stronghold, such changes had only come after decades-long challenges by the disempowered groups.[47]

African Americans had to engage in a similar struggle during the postwar years. Their first task was to challenge the informal segregation practiced by the local Democratic clubhouses. Shirley Chisholm, in her 1970 autobiography, recalled the tense scenes three decades earlier at the "club nights" held every Monday and Thursday by the Democratic club of the 17th Assembly District. As local constituents filed in to air grievances and request favors, the district leader, Vincent Carney, "used to sit with his flunkies on a dais at the far end of the room, while the voters came in and took high-backed chairs to wait their turns for an audience." By the 1940s, the 17th Assembly District was inhabited mostly by blacks but represented by whites at all levels of elective office. At the club nights, Chisholm recalled, "the blacks sat at one side, the whites on the other. There was no sign that said 'Colored Side.' It was an unwritten law. In many clubs even in the 1940s blacks were not welcome, unless they were brought in by a white member. In the 17th A. D. club, they came but they stayed in their place."[48]

69

Brooklyn reformers also had to grapple with challenges embedded in the political geography of New York City. Unlike other cities, such as Chicago, where a single Democratic machine ruled city politics, in New York City each of the county Democratic organizations constituted a machine unto itself. That decentralized structure presented both obstacles and opportunities for African American political reformers. On the one hand, it was difficult for insurgents in one borough to build on the gains achieved in other boroughs. That Harlem's J. Raymond Jones had emerged as a formidable broker within the New York County (Manhattan) Democratic Party by the early 1950s brought few immediate benefits to the African Americans of Brooklyn, who were facing a Kings County Democratic machine bent on preempting independent bases of black political power. In addition, as historian Martha Biondi has pointed out, the sheer size and dispersal of the city's black population hampered efforts at coordinating a citywide reform movement. Harlem and Bedford-Stuyvesant were both big enough to be cities in their own right, and it was an hour-long commute from one neighborhood to the other. The areas of Queens where a growing black middle class was settling (East Elmhurst, Corona, and later South Jamaica) were geographically isolated from the city's two main hubs of black culture and politics, and each area gave birth to its own civic and political institutions. But in isolation lay sources of strength. Focusing their reform efforts on individual districts allowed African American insurgents to build strong, if parochial, bases of black political power. Ultimately, they would force the Democratic county organizations to open up new pathways to political power, patronage, and influence.[49]

In 1946, the two women who had founded the Brooklyn Inter-Racial Assembly, Ada B. Jackson and Maude B. Richardson, ran separately for election in Brooklyn's 6th Assembly District, which included a section of Bedford-Stuyvesant. Jackson, a left-leaning activist, earned the nomination of the American Labor Party, which was enjoying a flush of success. Richardson was a Republican, though she, too, often partnered with radicals to advance her goals. Neither woman outpolled the clubhouse Democrat, John Walsh, but together they received more votes and sent a message to the machine. Two years later, the Democrats, fearing for their hold on an increasingly black district (though clearly not worried about alienating the women who had supported Jackson and Richardson), nominated Bertram Baker for the Assembly seat. Baker, a West Indian immigrant, took the primary and became the first black Brooklynite elected to a legislative post.

Eleven years later, in 1957, J. Daniel Diggs became the second when he was elected to the City Council from Bedford-Stuyvesant. Reformers in Central Brooklyn found little to celebrate in these victories. Baker had been handpicked by the Democratic machine, and he proved a loyal soldier for the next two decades, wielding "Tammany-like clout" over a patronage-dispensing "sub-machine." Diggs, meanwhile, had come through the ranks under Brooklyn borough president John Cashmore, the kingpin of the Democratic machine, and was himself handpicked by Baker. Though both men did carve out new spaces for African Americans within the Brooklyn Democratic machine, they did little to democratize the political system. And the fact that they were men gave proof that the women of Bedford-Stuyvesant would need to find other ways of translating their activism into political power.[50]

A more substantive challenge to the Kings County machine began to emerge in 1951, when another immigrant from the Caribbean, Wesley Holder, founded the insurgent Bedford-Stuyvesant Political League. Holder had abandoned his native Guyana in 1920 so he could join the Garvey movement in New York, and by the 1950s he hoped to harness the incipient political power of Brooklyn's growing black population. The Political League declared itself in favor of reform, good government, and voter registration. Holder launched its first campaign in 1953, backing Lewis S. Flagg Jr. in a race for a civil-court judgeship. Flagg, who was black, faced a white opponent from outside the district, whose only credential was the backing of the Democratic regulars. Not only did the Flagg campaign win the majority of black votes; it also earned the support of the largely Jewish American Labor Party and several white-dominated unions, including the United Electrical Workers Union and the United Auto Workers. Flagg became Brooklyn's first nonwhite civil-court judge, and his supporters celebrated a triumph both for racial equality and for reform. The campaign also energized a generation of young activists, most notably two ambitious members of Holder's club, Thomas Jones and Shirley Chisholm. Each in their own way, Jones and Chisholm gave voice to an upbeat, idealistic vision of politics and social reform. During the 1960s, each would score spectacular electoral victories against entrenched interests, and each would help to dictate the course of antipoverty programs in Bedford-Stuyvesant.[51]

All told, the homeowner organizing, civil-rights activism, and insurgent electoral campaigns of the 1950s put a lie to the notion, sometimes peddled by outsiders, that Bedford-Stuyvesant was an apathetic slum that lacked the leadership necessary to organize collective action. What Bed-Stuy did lack was power: access to capital, access to the political system, and access to government resources. In the late 1950s, those deficits began to shrink, albeit in a small way, thanks to the new coalition uniting Central Brooklyn's leadership class. With the Youth Board's Charles Ward playing matchmaker, that coalition would explore ways of translating the community's myriad activist traditions into policy.

A Community in Action

In matters religious and political, J. Archie Hargraves was a radical. A native of North Carolina who was raised by his grandmother, he began his activist career as a teenager, picketing segregated movie theaters in 1930s Greensboro. He worked his way through college—attending North Carolina Agricultural and Technical State University, future birthplace of the 1960s sit-in movement—before serving in World War II and moving north to attend Union Theological Seminary in Harlem. In 1948, he cofounded a network of storefront churches known as the East Harlem Protestant Parish, which delivered what Hargraves called "hard-working practical religion" to impoverished locals. The churches gave out food, dispensed health services, took on abusive landlords, cleaned up garbage-strewn lots, and promoted interfaith and interracial unity. Hargraves then moved to Chicago and founded the interdenominational West Side Christian Parish, which mixed street-level preaching with social services and political activism.

At a time when many urban churches were fleeing to the suburbs, Hargraves believed that inner-city ministers must live among their flock, advocating for the poor, the oppressed, and the outcast. He accused his colleagues of watching from the sidelines amid wrenching social change. "The church is not simply sleeping through a revolution, it is too often *pussyfooting* through it," he wrote in 1963. Nor was he afraid of publicly disagreeing with those churchmen who did embrace social change. At a moment when most black activists—and just about all clergymen—embraced the ideology and tactics of nonviolence, Hargraves articulated a Christian justification of violence. "The Christian stands before God with his Bible in one hand and the reality of the specific social situation in the other, and responds to each situation as it comes," he wrote in a 1959 column defending Robert C. Williams, an NAACP activist from North Carolina who advocated armed self-defense and was roundly denounced within the movement. "Sometimes the situation demands stronger measures of action than non-violence."[52]

In 1956, Hargraves moved to Brooklyn from Chicago and took the pulpit at Nazarene Congregational Church in Stuyvesant Heights. A relatively affluent congregation, Nazarene traced its roots to the 1870s. Hargraves's flock numbered 475 people, who donated an average of $57 each year, reported to be the highest giving rate of any black Congregational Church in America. Under Hargraves's guidance, the church began to experiment with what the pastor dubbed the "halfway house" technique. Instead of trying to lure new members to the church itself—which sat on a leafy block of MacDonough Street—Hargraves leased a storefront property that he converted into a community-outreach center and staffed with enthusiastic congregants. Most of the activities coordinated there focused on youth: summer field trips and museum visits for young children, talent shows featuring gifted teenagers, and a "godparent" program for "problem boys and girls" who needed reading help, mentoring, or temporary shelter. The church later hired full-time outreach workers to help locals with housing and to forge links between blacks and Puerto Ricans.[53]

Another Hargraves initiative, launched in 1956, was dubbed the Bedford-Stuyvesant Area Project—a reference to Clifford Shaw's juvenile-delinquency programs in Chicago, with which Hargraves was intimately acquainted. Like Shaw, Hargraves believed that community action could help access the great reserves of untapped potential that resided in rebellious young men. For help reaching out to teen gang members in Bed-Stuy, he solicited the backing of three dozen block associations, civic clubs, and PTA groups. He also exhorted fellow preachers to join; churches remained the most powerful institutions in black Brooklyn, and Hargraves hoped they might convince gang members to put down their weapons, stay in school, and forswear the street life. By 1959, Hargraves's brand of "precinct evangelism" was being touted in black newspapers across the country as a promising tool for "coping with the problems of teenage gangs."[54]

And what of the city government's efforts to reform the young criminals of Brooklyn? Hargraves saw municipal agencies as fragmented, overburdened, and understaffed; they could not be expected to craft a comprehensive, flexible response to delinquency. "What is needed is an organization of local people which will devote its attention and energies exclusively to the challenge offered by our children and teenagers," he wrote in a 1956 pamphlet. Such a group, he hoped, would strengthen families, churches, and community ties by improving schools, providing vocational guidance, and pooling scarce resources in a poor community.[55]

Yet, for all his attention to youth gangs, Hargraves also worried about how black crime was being dramatized outside Bedford-Stuyvesant. In February 1958, he joined other prominent Stuyfordites in denouncing press accounts of violence among African American youths, which Milton Galamison of the NAACP called "racist propaganda."[56] Increasing numbers of social scientists, social workers, and policymakers were paying attention to youth gangs and their root causes. But Hargraves viewed such "experts" with a skeptical eye because of their continual emphasis on "ghetto conditions" in Central Brooklyn. "Bedford-Stuyvesant," he wrote in 1956, "is not the slum so often depicted by ignorant outsiders and newspaper reporters who rarely stay here long enough to get even a superficial impression." Rather, this was a community with sufficient strength, leadership, and resources to organize collective solutions to collective problems. "A problem like juvenile delinquency we can handle ourselves," he wrote.[57]

In fact, Hargraves's analysis was shared by the men spearheading the Youth Board's efforts in Brooklyn: Walter Pinkston, the planning coordinator of the agency's Brooklyn borough office, and his delegate in Bedford-Stuyvesant, Charles Ward. Both social workers in their thirties, Pinkston and Ward represented a new generation of reformers. Both had held jobs as civil-rights organizers before moving into city government, and both would go on to play key roles in New York's community-action agencies during the 1960s. Far from "outsiders," they considered themselves integral members of the Bedford-Stuyvesant community.[58]

Pinkston, a Florida native, had earned a master's degree in social work at Atlanta University and begun his career in 1949 as an organizer with the Miami branch of the Urban League. From there he'd moved into a job with the New York City Housing Authority. Along with his wife, Anne, who had once been his boss at the Housing Authority and subsequently founded a creative-arts academy in Crown Heights, Pinkston also devoted a good portion of his time and energies throughout the 1950s to the American Council for Human Rights, a civil-rights lobby rooted in black fraternities and sororities. The couple, impeccably educated and ensconced in stable government jobs, for a time numbered among the very few black residents of Manhattan's Stuyvesant Town, a middle-income housing development originally intended to house whites only. By the late 1950s, Pinkston had gained a reputation as a serious, driven man who imbued his work with a strong sense of moral purpose.[59]

Ward, meanwhile, had attended Columbia University's School of Social Work and worked for the New York City Bureau of Child Welfare and the New York State Training School for Boys. In addition, he'd spent time overseeing the Bronx branch of the Urban League. He was stylish, dynamic, and indefatigable—he claimed at one point to be active in a dozen different community organizations. Like Pinkston, he would draw heavily on his experience as an activist as he set about organizing Bedford-Stuyvesant on behalf of the city government.[60]

In 1958, Pinkston and Ward already saw that their work with the Youth Board would extend beyond their official mandate of combating juvenile delinquency. Headquartered in the Youth Board office on Pierpont Street in downtown Brooklyn, they didn't have to travel far to hear what local people were saying. And it was clear that the ambitions of black Brooklyn extended far beyond the fight against youth crime. Though they had come from elsewhere, both Pinkston and Ward were rooted in the civil-rights struggle, street life, and civic clubs of Brooklyn. They identified themselves as members of the community whose singular role was to translate local desires into concrete government action. As Ward described his work in 1961, "We want to stimulate people, stir up interest, develop fruitful programs, initiate social action—in short, mobilize our Bedford-Stuyvesant forces and improve our community."[61]

During the winter of 1957–1958, Ward began meeting with neighborhood activists for brainstorming sessions about Youth Board initiatives in Bedford-Stuyvesant. In January, he put together an informal steering committee to help recruit a broad swathe of community representatives. The citizens of Bedford-Stuyvesant took their organizing seriously, and soon a constellation of grassroots organizations in the area was coming together under the Youth Board's umbrella. In March, seventeen organizations officially banded together to form the Central Brooklyn Coordinating Council for Youth. Block associations were represented, as were churches, fraternities, business groups, community centers, and civil-rights organizations. The group had no executive staff; its purpose was to advise the Youth Board and, in collaboration with Ward and Pinkston, design programs that would then be implemented in community centers and churches across Bedford-Stuyvesant and Crown Heights. By and large, those who sat on CBCC's board were leaders of existing organizations. They represented the well-educated professionals—doctors, real-estate brokers, teachers, lawyers, social workers, ministers—of Central Brooklyn, and almost all of them were black. CBCC did, however, consider itself to be an interracial group, and a small number of whites participated in its affairs.[62]

In bringing the group together, Ward and Pinkston occupied a new po-sition in the emerging social-welfare polity: that of the bureaucrat as com-munity organizer. Soon after the founding of CBCC, the Youth Board assigned Ward to a full-time position as CBCC's executive secretary; Pinkston later became CBCC's executive director, also on the Youth Board payroll. In taking such positions, both men blurred the lines between their jobs within city government and their work as grassroots advocates. It turned out to be perfect training for their future participation in the War on Poverty, when community organizing emerged as a preferred tool of the antipoverty bureaucracy. Like Kenneth Marshall, whose work with the Greene Avenue Stompers provided the launching pad for a long social-policy career, Pinkston and Ward would leverage their experiences fighting crime in the 1950s into leadership positions in the fight against poverty a decade later. Beginning in the mid-1960s, Ward would direct the Harlem Domestic Peace Corps, an offshoot of the federally funded As-sociated Community Teams initiative; Pinkston was hired in 1966 to run Bedford-Stuyvesant Youth in Action, the area's official Community Action Agency. Their career trajectories—from civil-rights activists to gang workers, to community organizers, to poverty warriors—in many ways mirrored the policy genealogy of the War on Poverty itself.[63]

In 1958, Ward and Pinkston could bring to bear their intimate knowl-edge of Bedford-Stuyvesant as they addressed the skepticism of commu-nity leaders such as Archie Hargraves. At a time when Mayor Wagner was mouthing increasingly muscular law-and-order rhetoric, Hargraves re-mained wary of cooperating with the municipal government's campaign for social control. But the pastor of Nazarene Congregational Church agreed in 1958 to take up a leadership position within CBCC. In doing so, he tacitly admitted that Youth Board knowledge, expertise, and especially funds could help jump-start indigenous organizing efforts. Nonetheless, Hargraves's ambivalence about the city's sudden interest in reforming the young people of his community set a pattern for future interactions be-tween Bed-Stuy's middle-class activists and the city and federal governments. Through the late 1950s and into the 1960s, many such activists embraced government programs out of concern about the mounting crime and poverty in their midst. Having signed up to promote the city's antidelinquency agenda, they later helped plan federal War on Poverty programs that yoked the fight against juvenile delinquency to the fight against poverty. Yet they never fully set aside their mistrust of the state.[64]

Expanded Horizons

CBCC was part of a process by which juvenile delinquency came in the late 1950s and early 1960s to serve as a proxy for all manner of debates about social conditions in impoverished communities, not only in Brooklyn but across urban America. As a public-policy issue, youth crime was intimately tied into individual and community self-perceptions. When neighbors discussed the connections between teenagers' behavior and safe streets, they also confronted sensitive questions about how children were being raised, nurtured, disciplined, and damaged. Nothing struck closer to home. (It was for similar reasons that schools served as the staging grounds for the most visceral debates over community control in the late 1960s.) The implications were wide-ranging. In New York, the willingness of policy elites to investigate the "root causes" of youth crime implied a new approach to urban problems and, quite possibly, progressive solutions to poverty, disinvestment, and discrimination. At the same time, government interest in juvenile delinquency helped to institutionalize a portrait of young African Americans as deviants and criminals. In Bedford-Stuyvesant, activists such as Hargraves had worried about youth crime long before the founding of CBCC. But the council's formation in 1958 demonstrated that alarmist discourses surrounding youth crime and urban disorder were being incorporated into state structures. For Bed-Stuy activists, that represented a strategic choice: talking about wayward youth was a good way of getting politicians to pay attention to their underserved streets.[65]

Few knew more about those streets than Maude B. Richardson, CBCC's founding chairwoman. The woman affectionately known to thousands as "Maude B." was ubiquitous in black Brooklyn. She was a former schoolteacher who had also operated a job-placement agency, dabbled in real estate, written a long-running column in the *Amsterdam News*, and once owned a tea shop on Fulton Street. Her activism spanned decades, and dozens of civic groups had proudly listed her as a member: the Urban

League, the NAACP, the Bedford-Stuyvesant Real Estate Board, the New York City Council of Churches, the New York State Commission Against Discrimination, the Brooklyn Bureau of Social Service, the Brooklyn Home for the Aged, and many more. She presided over her local PTA as well as the 77th Police Precinct community council, through which she had tackled the wartime crime wave by mobilizing grassroots enthusiasm for antigang programs in Bedford-Stuyvesant. Though a lifelong Republican, Maude B. was no conservative. In 1945, a high-water mark of black protest across New York City, it was reported that she actively participated in twenty-three different groups—many of them dedicated to assailing the city's Jim Crow edifice. In the late 1940s, as chair of the Brooklyn Provisional Committee on Jobs, she used boycotts and protests to force local businesses to hire black workers. In 1946, she joined Ada Jackson as the first black women to run for the State Assembly in Brooklyn, coming within seventy-seven votes of beating the incumbent Democrat.[66]

Richardson's frenzied activity made her a local icon. In the late 1950s, there was nobody better equipped to link the various organizers of black Brooklyn, be they involved in electoral politics, civil rights, social welfare, or block associations. And it was Richardson who brought them together under the rubric of CBCC. In the years to come, as the group shifted its focus from crime to root causes, it came to represent the kind of eclectic activism Richardson herself had practiced.

Richardson also paved the way for CBCC's emergence as a significant new platform from which activist women could make their voices heard. As historian Julie Gallagher has argued, women like Richardson and Jackson "understood the necessity of engaging the state, and they frequently endeavored to wrest power from it—the power that made life more bearable, that made the streets safer, that kept the roofs over their heads, that kept the food in stores safe for consumption." Maude B. blazed a trail for a younger generation of politically prominent black women in Brooklyn, including Elsie Richardson, Shirley Chisholm, and Lucille Rose. CBCC provided them with a venue in which to "engage the state" by meeting with organizer-bureaucrats like Pinkston and Ward, who in turn translated grassroots demands into grant proposals and funding requests. CBCC also allowed the women of Bed-Stuy, especially those who were plugged into block associations, to pool their energies and address problems—disinvestment, failing schools, crime—that begged a comprehensive approach. Women's intimate connections to local social networks lent strength and legitimacy to the council's organizing efforts. A 1969 Ford Foundation study observed that the women of CBCC "worked in and for the total community at a time when few others saw beyond the confines of their block, their church, or their club." Many of these women later made the transition from grassroots organizing to positions in city government.[67]

But that was in the future. In 1958, CBCC launched a small number of circumscribed, carefully targeted programs. As a first step, CBCC asked the Youth Board to help train a corps of thirty volunteers to do youth-outreach work on the streets of their own neighborhood. The program—the first of its kind in the city—was designed to combine local knowledge, street smarts, and a new understanding of "the problems of teenagers and the complexities of their behavior." Going forward, the community-led CBCC would have at its disposal a crew of local experts to mediate violent flare-ups, as the Youth Board's "detached workers" had been doing since the early 1950s. The Youth Board also funded a demonstration program dubbed Teens in Industry, which Hargraves directed. In June 1958, Hargraves picked twenty-five "brainy teenagers" to take summer jobs in banks, law firms, insurance companies, retail outlets, and factories that had agreed to participate in the program. Hargraves required his charges, most of them sixteen or seventeen, to volunteer at community centers on weekends and pass a leadership-training course that he taught himself. They also spent several hours a week in group-study sessions, after which they ate dinner together. At the end of their training, it was hoped, this motivated group would form the core of a new youth leadership council for Bed-Stuy. It was an idea the Brooklyn Council for Social Planning had floated years earlier and that local War on Poverty agencies would attempt anew in the 1960s.[68]

Teens in Industry attracted high-profile backers, including the Brooklyn Chamber of Commerce, the AFL-CIO, Borough President John Cashmore, Municipal Court Judge Franklin W. Morton, and Assemblyman Baker. A local banker, Richard Brennan of the Brevoort Savings Bank on Fulton Street, donated money, wrote newspaper editorials trumpeting the approach, and hired interns. Richardson and Ward further publicized the project when each won a "Good Neighbor" cash award handed out by Brooklyn-based Rheingold Beer Company (announced with full-page ads in *Ebony* magazine and several black newspapers) and donated the proceeds to Teens in Industry. The number of enrollees in the program rose steadily, peaking at 200 high-school students per year in the early 1960s. For a time, the New York State Employment Service assigned a full-time professional to Bedford-Stuyvesant, with the charge of finding placements for Teens in Industry graduates. But summer internships were just the start. CBCC also laid out a long-term vision of how to motivate talented youngsters who, the theory went, would otherwise fall into despondency and delinquency. In addition to vocational training, the young were encouraged to take up activism. Inspired by the lunch-counter sit-ins of 1960, the Youth Board hired four full-time counselors to "inculcate training in citizenship and interracial and inter-faith ideals" among enrollees aged sixteen to nineteen. Morton, chairman of the Teens in Industry advisory board, explained the new thrust: "Events in the South have highlighted the great contributions young people are making in equality for us all."[69]

Launched against a background of mounting youth unemployment, Teens in Industry proved popular. Though small in scale, it offered a positive response to the hysteria about wayward youth emanating from politicians and the press. "It has been established that this is the time of year when tempers and tensions soar right along with the temperature and humidity," the *Amsterdam News* wrote in August 1960. "The Teens-in-Industry program has made an effort to solve these hot weather outbursts of violence and crime in the Bedford-Stuyvesant community." The Youth Board's executive director, Ralph Whelan, presented CBCC's initiative as a first step in a citywide drive to make summers more "constructive . . . for our half million older teenagers." Teens in Industry continued into 1964, when the War on Poverty unleashed a far more thorough effort to "unlock opportunities" through job training and youth-leadership programs.[70]

Teens in Industry was hardly a panacea for Bed-Stuy's problems, but its creation marked a promising start to CBCC's work. At a time when black New Yorkers outside of Harlem were mostly frozen out of formal political structures, CBCC marked one of the first institutional linkages between black Brooklynites and the municipal government. Through men like Ward and Pinkston, the city was trying its hand at community organizing, fostering new forms of citizen participation in planning. CBCC created a venue wherein grassroots activists and policy innovators like Maude Richardson and Archie Hargraves could join city officials to exchange ideas and set priorities. This was especially significant given Wagner's support of African American aspirations. Going forward, activists would expect the city government to do more, much more, in New York's most underserved black community.

At the same time, CBCC codified a certain way of thinking about the boundaries and meanings of that community. Wagner recognized CBCC as a representative body for the people of Bedford-Stuyvesant, and the new coalition could credibly claim to represent "community sentiment." Embedded in these claims, however, were latent class, ethnic, and gender tensions—tensions that would surface during the 1960s, when the meanings of community and the boundaries of community participation in planning were repeatedly challenged. Through CBCC, a mostly middle-class, middle-aged leadership group took up the cause of reforming the behavior of poor youths. That group now became the public face of an imagined community named "Bedford-Stuyvesant." With that role came the power to define that particular geographical space—and the character of the diverse people inhabiting it.

Bed-Stuy's activist leadership also sought the power to define the issues facing their community. By cooperating with the Youth Board, they codified their common commitment to reforming teen behavior and preserving social order. But Bed-Stuy activists would spend much of the 1960s demanding that the Wagner administration deal with issues *other* than delinquency. CBCC gave them a platform from which to organize grassroots political pressure on city officials—despite the council's continuing dependence on the Youth Board for staff and operating expenses. Increasingly, Maude Richardson and her successors would insist that all branches of the city government partner with CBCC when it came time to direct services to black Brooklyn. The sincerity of Wagner's promises to revitalize Bed-Stuy, local activists maintained, would be verified not through street clubs and detached workers but through schools and housing programs. As Richardson put it in 1959, echoing the city's "root causes" analysis, CBCC "recognizes the intimate relationship between delinquency and poor housing in Bedford-Stuyvesant." In the 1960s, the rotating cast of activists within CBCC would lobby for a wide variety of programs in their increasingly desperate efforts to gain funding and to shore up an area they worried was rapidly spinning out of control.[71]

3

From the Clubhouse to the White House

> This community needs a leadership that will fight for its fair
> share of democracy, a leadership that will see to it that the com-
> munity obtains the jobs, the city services, the schools, and the
> police protection it both needs and deserves. I hope that the
> people in the community and from all over the City of New
> York will join with us in our fight to end the political planta-
> tion system in Bedford-Stuyvesant.
>
> —THOMAS R. JONES, 1962

The early 1960s in New York City were "days full of tension and danger,
but also of infinite promise," in the words of Robert F. Wagner Jr. On
the one hand, this was the moment when deindustrialization picked up
steam and the middle class quickened its flight to the suburbs; when New
York was fracturing into a "dual city" disproportionately inhabited by
the very rich and the very poor; when crime embarked on its inexorable
ascent; and when the city's finances started slouching toward disaster. The
city where the New Deal had reached its apogee seemed suddenly to be
coming apart, battered by what Wagner called "forces beyond the control
of any municipal government and, in many ways, beyond the control of
even national governments." New York in the 1960s would lurch from one
crisis to the next.[1]

And yet, there was promise, too. Migrants flocked to the city from the
American South, Puerto Rico, and, as always, the rest of the world. Newcomers dreamed of tasting success in the "sweet land of liberty," of living
free from poverty and discrimination. Civil-rights activists ambitiously assailed segregation in workplaces and schools, mobilizing some of the
largest protest actions America had yet seen. In neighborhoods around the
five boroughs, citizens stood up to defend their homes against faceless bureaucracies and rapacious developers. On dozens of run-down yet historic

CUT UP!

...cut up by the county's
political machines run by
double-dealing politicians,
who continue to deny us
—DECENT HOUSING
—EQUAL JOB OPPORTUNITIES
—QUALITY EDUCATION FOR
 OUR CHILDREN

YOU CAN CHANGE THIS NOW!

A mid-1960s poster mapping the five congressional districts overlapping the
Bedford-Stuyvesant area. Though African Americans made up more than
80 percent of Bed-Stuy's population at the time, each of the neighborhood's
representatives—Hugh Carey, John Rooney, Eugene Keogh, Emmanuel Celler,
and Edna Kelly—was white. *The original creator of the poster is unknown*

blocks, middle-class homeowners were repairing foundations and building
communities. Everywhere, citizen movements were sprouting up from
cracked sidewalks and laying siege to deeply rooted institutions. Even
Wagner, a son of Tammany Hall, mounted the barricades, took on the
machine, and started speaking the language of young, upbeat reformers.
Voices once muted were finally heard; the insurgents seemed to be winning. For the dispossessed, accessing the halls of government suddenly
seemed possible.

This sense of possibility reflected a broader impulse coursing through
American culture in the early 1960s: participatory democracy. The term
was popularized by Students for a Democratic Society, who in 1962 made
it the animating principle of their Port Huron manifesto. As a *cri de coeur*
born both of alienation and of optimism—as a critique of bureaucratic

power, as a hopeful call for the reinvigoration of community—participatory democracy reflected ambivalence about suburbanization, militarization, automation, and racism. The revolt against urban renewal, the movement to purify politics, the assault on segregation, the sexual revolution: each reflected, in its own way, the spirit of participatory democracy. A thousand flowers bloomed and a thousand edifices crumbled as citizens demanded power over the decisions that affected their daily lives. Insurgents laid siege to school boards and planning boards, patronage machines and political parties, universities and police departments. From the clubhouse to the White House, the forces of order would come under assault, one by one.[2]

This is not to say that elites lost their sway. During the 1960s, the Cold War alliance of soldiers and capitalists that departing president Dwight D. Eisenhower dubbed the "military-industrial complex" became ever more entrenched in the firmament of American prosperity. The titans of finance, alarmed by the upsurge of urban disorders and the expanding liberal state, launched a counterinsurgency aimed at taming government spending and taking control of the urban-redevelopment agenda. Intellectual elites, peering down from their perches in universities, foundations, and government, appropriated the grievances of outsider groups and devised new ways of incorporating grassroots politics into the structures of an expanding welfare state. New York's municipal government was a pioneer in this domain, unveiling neighborhood planning boards and community councils amid the rumble of bulldozers. By 1961, the presidential administration of John F. Kennedy was following suit, applying the new ideal of "community action" in a series of experiments dedicated to reforming juvenile delinquents. These federal efforts to address the "root causes" of youth crime in poor neighborhoods would in turn inspire the Community Action Program at the heart of Lyndon Johnson's war against poverty.

And so the very power structures assaulted as undemocratic proved all too willing to accommodate demands from below—or, more often, to blunt the sharp edge of such demands by paying them lip service. Therein lies one of the central paradoxes of the era. Bold experiments in participatory democracy were designed from above, conceived among presidential task forces and interdepartmental meetings. Citizen movements tamed the state, but the state tamed them back. Radical impulses were softened, citizen participation ritualized. Yet the innovative structures set up by the federal and municipal governments to incorporate grassroots energies were also adaptable, providing political spaces in which local groups could press for further devolutions of power. "Community action" invited excluded groups to take up policymaking roles, gave them access to state resources, and invited them to dream of better tomorrows.[3]

This process played out in 1960s Bedford-Stuyvesant thanks to the evolving relationships of the Central Brooklyn Coordinating Council with Wagner's mayoral administration and, later, with Robert F. Kennedy. By organizing the community, CBCC incarnated the spirit of participatory democracy and choreographed the *pas de deux* between the street and the state. Though founded with a focus on youth, CBCC in the 1960s expanded its sights beyond juvenile delinquency. Inspired by the new zeitgeist, the group organized to end gerrymandering, desegregate public schools, rehabilitate homes, spark job creation, shape urban-renewal plans, and bring a college to Central Brooklyn. At times, the group functioned as a government agency; at other times, it resembled a social movement. On the one hand, CBCC activists hoped to consolidate their foothold within the municipal bureaucracy and pursue moderate avenues of social reform. On the other, CBCC represented, in the words of political reformer Thomas R. Jones, "the response of the people of Bedford-Stuyvesant to the civil rights movement that then was breaking out all over the country." But how would CBCC capture the fiscal and political capital needed to serve the role Jones claimed for it? In the early 1960s, juvenile delinquency remained the issue most likely to arouse the concern of policymakers—especially given the sudden interest emanating from the White House.[4]

Just at the moment that CBCC was emerging as a political force, the Kennedy administration was beginning to fund a similar neighborhood-based group on the Lower East Side of Manhattan. Dubbed Mobilization for Youth, the project had initially emerged in response to the postwar spike in gang activity. In the late 1950s, local activists had partnered with city officials and professors from Columbia University to turn the Lower East Side into a "great natural laboratory" for the study of crime, poverty, unemployment, discrimination, and thwarted aspirations. By 1961, the experiment had gained nationwide attention and was transforming the way federal officials thought about crime and poverty in American cities. The New York approach was going national.

The President's Committee

March 5, 1961, brought an unusual burst of warmth to New York City. It was a Sunday. A winter chill lingered at dawn, but temperatures hit 70 in the late afternoon. In the streets, people peeled off layers of clothing, baring sun-starved skin to the springtime sun. Ice-cream trucks hopefully came out of hibernation, filling the air with summertime jingles. Mothers gathered on stoops after church; packs of boys in t-shirts tore down chalked-stained sidewalks; clusters of men crackled with talk of Maris and Mantle and the season to come.[5]

That day, the new president's younger brother, Robert F. Kennedy, was in town to tape a TV show. He decided to take advantage of the balmy weather and go for a stroll, or rather, a long walk. Less than two months into his tenure as attorney general, Kennedy wanted to meet some of the city's notorious youth gangs in their native setting. Juvenile delinquency was to be a major focus of the administration's law-enforcement strategy—but what did the "best and the brightest" know about the delinquents themselves? Kennedy had his aides call up the city's Youth Board and arrange a tour of Manhattan's meanest streets. They started on East 66th Street and marched forty blocks north, into East Harlem. There, street workers had lined up appointments with a dozen members of the Viceroys, a Puerto Rican gang. Later, fifteen or twenty Redwings—Italian boys—materialized. (That the local youth workers could convene such posses on short notice no doubt impressed the attorney general.) Kennedy whiled away the warm afternoon chatting with the boys. He was shocked by their casual attitude toward drugs, mesmerized by tales of violence. ("We were very green in understanding the problems," a Kennedy aide, David Hackett, later recalled. "The conversations at the beginning were, perhaps, naïve.") But he couldn't extract a satisfying answer to the question that troubled him most: why did the boys fight? "We just like to get into it," was the best they could offer.[6]

Two days later, on March 9, 1961, the Senate Subcommittee on Juvenile Delinquency opened hearings on a proposed $10 million federal program to counter youth crime. The first witness, fittingly, was the mayor of New York. Wagner bore his usual collection of machetes, zip guns, and knives seized from the clutches of gang members. But the silver-haired solons seemed to be paying him more attention than usual. As Thomas J. Dodd of Connecticut, the committee's chairman, pointed out, youth crime had leapt 177 percent nationwide since 1948. In New York City, juvenile arrests for "injury to person" had quadrupled in the 1950s. Even in affluent suburbs, "white collar" delinquency was setting off increasingly strident alarm bells.[7]

"It cannot be overemphasized that delinquency is a national problem," Wagner told the senators, "and no section, no state, and no community is immune." Though keen to praise his city's Youth Board, Wagner admitted that the problems bearing down on New York surpassed his government's ability to respond. Federal action was critical. Among other things, Wagner asked the subcommittee to move against drug trafficking and the interstate weapons commerce, and to fund a Youth Conservation Corps. But jobs programs would be the key. As Ralph Whelan, New York's commissioner of youth services, explained to the subcommittee, experts had concluded that fighting juvenile delinquency would require, first and foremost, a strategy that targeted high unemployment rates in low-income urban neighborhoods.[8]

Though juvenile delinquency had been a hot-button issue in New York City for years, street gangs became a national obsession in 1961. That year, with the Oscar-winning *West Side Story* lighting up screens, the culture registered the implications of an epochal generational shift. The first baby boomers were turning sixteen. Parents saw signs of youth rebellion everywhere. The lunch-counter sit-ins that began in February 1960 had marked not only the dawn of a new decade but also the new assertiveness of youth in setting the country's moral agenda. The sit-ins were nonviolent political protests led by buttoned-up college students—a far cry from the nihilistic violence the attorney general detected in East Harlem. And yet, the sit-ins were unmistakable acts of rebellion carried out by young people. Unlike their 1950s forebears, the rebels of the 1960s had causes. And men like Wagner and Kennedy suspected that the causes of lunch-counter sit-ins were not all that different from those driving youth gangs into the streets of New York.

By the time Kennedy toured East Harlem, the environmentalist interpretation of juvenile delinquency had come to dominate policy discussions. The prevailing wisdom held that teens turned to crime in response to systemic factors: poverty, joblessness, and poor housing. Most of those youngsters labeled as delinquents had grown up in environments that were "stony hard, cruel, and demoralizing," in Wagner's words. Born with limited horizons, their problems were compounded by racism, which liberal policymakers were increasingly recognizing as a key driver of poverty and juvenile delinquency. "We have learned one fact," Wagner mused during his final year in office. "Of all the problem syndromes, racial injustice and discrimination have the sharpest cutting edges, contribute the most to social pathology, and are the most resistant to the approaches or remedies available to a city government."[9]

Wagner and many others reasoned that, because delinquency resulted from racism, and because racism was a national problem, then any serious antidelinquency effort must be national in scope. And in 1961 the federal government was ready to act. On May 11, 1961, President Kennedy established by executive order the President's Committee on Juvenile Delinquency and Youth Crime (PCJD), which brought together the attorney general; Secretary of Health, Education, and Welfare Abraham Ribicoff; Secretary of Labor Arthur Goldberg; and a gang of delinquency wonks from government, private agencies, and academia. The composition of the PCJD reflected the prevailing diagnosis that tackling youth misbehavior was no simple matter of law and order but would also require social services, mental-health treatments, and jobs programs. Congress, meanwhile, appropriated $30 million over three years through the Juvenile Delinquency and Youth Offenses Control Act.[10]

For the most part, the administration's campaign against youth crime would unfold quietly, overshadowed by foreign-policy issues, fiscal policy, and the civil-rights revolution. Yet the PCJD inspired a new style of federal policymaking—decentralized, experimental, hostile to traditional bureaucracies—that would reach full bloom during the War on Poverty. The committee also became a clearinghouse for ideas about how to tackle the "root causes" of delinquency, and it brought together within the federal bureaucracy a network of academics interested in exploring not only crime but also poverty, discrimination, and urban change. Their policy discussions shaped the federal antipoverty approach as it emerged in late 1963. Most significantly, the PCJD gave the federal seal of approval to a nebulous concept known as community action, which after 1964 would become the centerpiece of the War on Poverty.[11]

In many ways, the Kennedy administration's delinquency programs mimicked what New York's Youth Board had been doing since the early 1950s. The PCJD sponsored a series of local experiments, many of which also received grants from city governments. In some places, federal funders joined forces with the Ford Foundation's Gray Areas program, an effort to revive urban neighborhoods that was launched in the late 1950s. (The best-funded of the Ford efforts was in New Haven, Connecticut.) In keeping with the "demonstration" nature of the program, each local project was rooted in social-scientific theory and subject to systematic evaluation. Though confined to relatively small geographic areas, the projects aimed to articulate "comprehensive" solutions to the problems facing the neighborhoods in question. This meant addressing juvenile delinquency as a collective rather than an individual problem and, in so doing, bringing people together to devise solutions to problems *other than* delinquency—namely, poverty, unemployment, and family breakdown.[12]

Robert Kennedy emerged as the key patron of the federal delinquency program. Though he didn't oversee day-to-day planning, the president's brother would get involved "at times of serious decision making." He also visited several of the projects unfolding in impoverished parts of the country. Kennedy's face-to-face encounters with young people in such places would strongly affect his later work as an antipoverty crusader. In that sense, the juvenile delinquency dossier provided something of a bridge between the early Kennedy—tough, anticommunist—and the compassionate Kennedy of later years who became a devoted ally of the poor and oppressed. To the attorney general's mind, the fight against youth crime was no mere matter of law and order; it was a moral crusade.[13]

Kennedy eloquently laid out his interpretation of youth crime's causes and effects in a 1962 speech before the Citizens Advisory Committee of the PCJD. "Delinquency is steadily spreading throughout our society," he said. The national delinquency rate had increased for a dozen years in a row—largely, Kennedy argued, because of structural problems in the economy. As the attorney general explained, the flight of unskilled migrants from the countryside to cities was exacerbating already stiff competition for work. Meanwhile, automation was eliminating the kinds of jobs typically claimed by young urbanites with minimal skills. Since World War II, birth rates had soared, as had youth unemployment and dropout rates. Some 26 million young people were expected to join the workforce during the 1960s, of which 7.5 million would not have graduated high school. A growing "army of out-of-school, unemployed youth," according to Kennedy, was becoming alienated and indulging in instant gratification: violence, casual sex, drugs, drinking. Their behavior, in turn, exerted intense pressure on straitlaced peers to drop out and join the fun. Based on Kennedy's calculations, somewhere between three million and four million teenagers would "become delinquent in this decade."[14]

What was to be done? The environmentalist interpretation of delinquency assumed that the clearest predictor of which boys would become delinquents was the environment in which they grew up. If that was true, then the most viable long-term strategy for fighting delinquency was to transform those environments. According to sociologist Robert MacIver, who headed New York City's Juvenile Delinquency Evaluation Project, programs should "benefit whole neighborhoods, whole communities, not merely the young who otherwise might become delinquent." PCJD projects would eschew reactive steps against criminal behavior—police raids, imprisonment, reformatories—and instead, according to Kennedy, "offer new and expanded opportunities to young people" through job-placement programs, improved social services, more and better schools, and civil-rights legislation. Wagner, too, believed that these experiments in what he called "community-wide social planning" must devote themselves "to creating new jobs and to training our young people in new skills, and to breaking down the barriers of discrimination."[15]

The model for such action was unfolding on Manhattan's Lower East Side, only a short walk from Wagner's City Hall. Mobilization for Youth (MFY) was born of cooperation among community organizations, the Youth Board, federal agencies, the Ford Foundation, and Columbia University professors. But its institutional roots lay in the social-reform traditions of the Progressive Era. Since the 1890s, when Lillian Wald founded the Henry Street Settlement, various settlement houses had provided health services, education, and support for the huddled masses of the Lower East Side. By the postwar years, a rich mix of ethnic groups coexisted uneasily in the area. In 1954, mounting strife between rival teen gangs the Sportsmen (made up of African Americans), the Dragons (Puerto Ricans), and the May Roses (whites) inspired a slew of settlement houses, churches, and civic groups to band together. The new coalition, christened the Lower Eastside Neighborhood Association (LENA), hoped to ease tensions and create a sense of community cohesion. LENA, aided by a crew of Youth Board workers, strove to avert the most explosive gang conflicts while also steering younger children away from gangs. Initially, this approach resembled what the Brooklyn Council for Social Planning had tried to do with the Brewery Boys some years earlier—although LENA did try to intercede on a broader scale than had the effort surrounding Tompkins Park.[16]

But the Lower East Side initiative spun off in a new direction in 1957, when it gained the attention of Lloyd Ohlin and his colleague at Columbia's School of Social Work, Richard Cloward. In conversations with the Henry Street Settlement, Cloward and Ohlin proposed to expand the LENA project into a more ambitious program of social change. The locals concurred, though there were tensions from the start. Cloward argued that social workers should help poor people launch rent strikes, picket City Hall, and fight the welfare bureaucracy. That was a far cry from the moderate reformism espoused by the director of the Henry Street Settlement, Helen Hall. "The idea of rousing up the people themselves to start raising hell about their housing conditions, having sit-ins in welfare waiting rooms, and things like that just blew their minds," Cloward later recalled. "It threatened to disrupt these long established relationships, which the heads of the settlements had with leading political figures in the city."[17]

Behind this activist agenda lay a sophisticated theoretical framework. Most notably, Cloward and Ohlin's ideas owed a debt to sociologist Leonard Cottrell. A contributor to Clifford Shaw's landmark 1929 study of delinquency in Chicago, Cottrell had trained under Robert Park and other Chicago-school proponents of "social ecology." According to the social ecologists, urban communities inhabited by large numbers of newcomers became "disorganized"; the trauma of rapid change resulted in "pathological" mindsets. For Cottrell, the key to remedying such pathologies was to foster "competent communities" in which local citizens, newly confident in their ability to act, actively participated in collective action aimed at solving their own problems and assimilating deviant behaviors. Mobilization for Youth would push this idea of community competence still further. Simply helping the residents of the Lower East Side to organize their own community would be insufficient; they must also be trained to confront outside power structures.[18]

In a 1960 book, *Delinquency and Opportunity,* Cloward and Ohlin argued that low-income youths engaged in self-destructive behavior not because they were pathological deviants but because they lacked opportunities. The Columbia men posited that delinquency stemmed from "anomie," a concept they borrowed from French sociologist Emile Durkheim and that they defined as meaning "lawlessness, or normlessness . . . a state in which social norms no longer control men's actions." Delinquents,

Cloward and Ohlin argued, came to disregard social norms out of frustration at the disparity between their aspirations and the pathways to achievement; their behavior reflected "not a lack of motivation to conform but quite the opposite." If gang members could be introduced to opportunities in mainstream society, they might behave differently and, in so doing, break the self-perpetuating "circle of poverty" that ensnared them. But for new opportunities to emerge, structural barriers must be assaulted. Cloward and Ohlin, echoing Saul Alinsky, advocated not merely community action but, more critically, community *agitation*, preferably in cooperation with sympathetic academics and bureaucratic insiders who knew where the system was most vulnerable.[19]

In February 1959, Wagner announced the official launch of Mobilization for Youth under the auspices of the city's juvenile-delinquency program. The agency's board at the time reflected the close partnerships the Wagner administration was forging with community groups: twenty city officials sat alongside twenty-three representatives of Lower East Side social agencies, as well as eleven members of Columbia's School of Social Work. This was an undertaking on a different scale from what the Youth Board had put together in Central Brooklyn, and MFY became the flagship youth initiative in New York City.[20] Later that year, the National Institute of Mental Health provided grant monies, and in 1961 both the Ford Foundation and the PCJD followed suit. Finally, on May 30, 1962, Wagner and the Kennedys stood shoulder to shoulder in the White House garden to announce the official rebirth of MFY as a joint city and federal project. The Lower East Side agency would draw $12.6 million—the equivalent of $100 million in 2015—over the next three years, with the majority coming from Wagner's coffers. President Kennedy proclaimed MFY "the most advanced program yet devised to combat delinquency on a broad scale." (The next-best-funded PCJD projects were in New Haven and Cleveland, each of which received $1 million from the federal government by the end of 1963.)[21]

The MFY blueprint, according to Robert Kennedy, foresaw "an integrated program of job opportunities, improved education, increased social services, new recreational activities, and improved community organization." Though MFY would ultimately fall short of those lofty goals, the Lower East Side experiment nonetheless became the standard-bearer for the PCJD's brand of community action. Future projects, like MFY, would have to establish a theoretical framework before launching "action programs" aimed at changing local conditions and confronting local power structures. Interestingly, the Cloward-Ohlin theory was never meant to be hegemonic. One planner, Leonard Stern, later recalled that the PCJD "really worked like hell to fight off the accusation that we were trying to develop all of the cities around the Ohlin and Cloward book." Federal funders encouraged local activists to consult scholars, dive into the sociological literature, and come up with their own, locally specific hypotheses about delinquency's causes and solutions.[22]

The problem was that tailoring theory to a particular neighborhood was long, hard work. An exception that proved the rule was Harlem Youth Opportunities Unlimited (HARYOU), launched with federal and city funds in 1962 and led by Kenneth Clark, a professor of psychology at City College. Armed with intimate knowledge of Harlem and deep immersion in the academic literature, Clark was able to set aside the Cloward-Ohlin thesis and devise an original analysis of delinquency, one more attentive to the legacies of racism. But not every neighborhood had a Kenneth Clark waiting in the wings. In the years to come, as community-action agencies sprouted up by the hundreds, most local reformers read from either the Cloward-Ohlin playbook or Clark's, regardless of whether those theories matched local realities.[23]

At the time of President Kennedy's assassination, it was too early to tell whether his youth-crime initiative would bear fruit. The PCJD had funded pilot projects in sixteen different cities; MFY was the only group to have completed its demonstration phase and moved into action. What mattered more, in the near term, was that the Kennedys had spawned a national network of agencies through which funding could be disbursed directly to grassroots groups in low-income, mostly minority neighborhoods. This new brand of place-based policymaking, which provided a blueprint for the War on Poverty's Community Action Program, held great promise but also presented great dangers. On the one hand, community action validated the democratic ideal that solutions to local problems could be found by tapping into local expertise and helping grassroots groups access the political system. This process nurtured feelings of empowerment among disempowered groups, helped to consolidate the Democratic Party base in urban areas, and laid the groundwork for a sustained effort to improve the lives of America's poorest citizens. On the other hand, there was something illogical about asking neighborhood-based initiatives to tackle enormous structural problems. Local activists might spout social-scientific theory and articulate "comprehensive" solutions, but that didn't change the fact that community action, by definition, must address parochial concerns and unfold within narrow geographic constraints. "What we have learned," Ohlin would remark in 1966, "is that institutional change doesn't come easy." Consecrating community organizing as federal policy entailed risks—that the weapons of the weak might prove lacking, that results might fall short of expectations, that communities might descend into turmoil when they encountered inevitable roadblocks. And how would governments respond if they suddenly faced challenges from the very groups they had helped organize and fund? Such dilemmas, left unresolved, would haunt the War on Poverty.[24]

In the near term, however, the PCJD programs, like the Youth Board experiments before them, signaled that the state might prove an ally to community groups in minority neighborhoods. In Bedford-Stuyvesant, MFY and HARYOU offered political lessons that the activists affiliated with CBCC were quick to learn. The Lower East Side experiment made it clear that old-fashioned casework had fallen out of favor and that "comprehensive" approaches to addressing youth crime could draw serious funding from foundations and the federal government. Further, Kenneth Clark's program in Harlem showed that the federal and city governments were eager to absorb the energy of the civil-rights movement by supporting efforts that explicitly targeted the legacies of racism. Finally, the Manhattan projects reaffirmed the assumption, common to many Wagner-era policy innovations, that social planning should target clearly delineated neighborhoods. In the years to come, the unit of analysis for poverty workers would be "communities" rather than individuals. Grassroots groups would have to map new spaces for themselves and define community aspirations in the heartlands of anomie. CBCC would spend the early 1960s doing just that.

Democratic Voices

Yet another outburst of violence shook Brooklyn in the spring and early summer of 1961, when gang skirmishes in Williamsburg, Crown Heights, and Bedford-Stuyvesant left five teens dead. The rumbles of old seemed to have returned, as rival crews from different housing projects faced off in turf wars. The press pounced on the story, and the *Times* even dusted off the old "Little Harlem" designation to go alongside an unflattering description of Bed-Stuy. CBCC, formed three years earlier to tackle gang violence in the area, begged the city to intervene. "An emergency situation exists in Bedford-Stuyvesant, requiring the introduction of emergency corrective measures," said Robert Palmer, a physician who replaced Maude B. Richardson as CBCC's president that year.[25]

Mayor Wagner apparently concurred. On July 19, 1961, he convened a public meeting at Junior High School 258 in Brooklyn to solicit community viewpoints. Some 500 people packed the school's sweltering auditorium and inundated the mayor with complaints big and small, from Jim Crow unions to sour milk in local grocery stores. A week later, Wagner hosted an hour-long meeting at City Hall with fifteen Central Brooklyn leaders, who presented a set of recommendations. The mayor, mindful of cultivating support among black New Yorkers in an election year, showed himself to be receptive. (That same week, the city's most powerful black politician, Congressman Adam Clayton Powell Jr., had come out for Wagner's opponent in the Democratic primary, Arthur Levitt, decrying the mayor's civil-rights record as little more than tokenism.) Wagner followed up by assigning eight additional Youth Board group workers to Bed-Stuy, stepping up the local police presence, pledging funds to keep schools open at night and on weekends, and opening a Central Brooklyn office of the Commission on Intergroup Relations, the agency tasked with investigating charges of racial discrimination. Most novel was the promise of urban-renewal funds to help revitalize Bed-Stuy's declining housing stock. Community leaders responded with cautious enthusiasm, and the *Amsterdam News* lauded the mayor's approach as "the example of how to launch a good community program."[26]

Results lagged behind rhetoric. More than a year later, in September 1962, the Youth Board's Walter Pinkston admitted to a meeting of CBCC delegates that "too few recreational facilities and youth workers" existed in the areas of Crown Heights and Bed-Stuy surrounding the Albany, Brevoort, and Kingsborough housing projects, where gangs were gaining strength. A month earlier, the City Planning Commission had announced that it was postponing all plans for the physical renewal of Bed-Stuy until the following year. CBCC's leaders, with little to show for four years of organizing activity, increasingly faced questions about their ability to speak for an area in the midst of wrenching transformations. Indeed, CBCC claimed to represent the entire community but was run by—and, arguably, in the interests of—a relatively small network of middle-class activists. Equally problematic was the group's dependence on the city government, which proved better at making promises than executing them.[27]

A series of columns written in September 1962 by respected *Amsterdam News* reporter Simon Anekwe exposed the fault lines within the partnership tying Bed-Stuy activists to municipal officials. Anekwe quoted an unnamed source from within the City Planning Commission slamming Bedford-Stuyvesant's leadership class for pursuing individual agendas and pushing self-interested policy proposals. According to the source, city agencies felt uncomfortable launching new programs in Bed-Stuy because the local leaders seemed to lack the capacity and legitimacy to implement them. Unlike in Harlem, where local leadership was said to be "centralized and organized," Bed-Stuy's leadership was allegedly "diffuse and uncoordinated." The Brooklynites retorted that the city government was unresponsive to the community's needs. "It is a public disgrace that the City Planning Commission would cleverly discriminate against Brooklyn's one-half million Negroes," was one assessment in the *Amsterdam News*. The lesson was clear: CBCC would have to begin acting like more of an activist group and less like a government agency if it hoped to acquire greater political clout. Brooklyn's African American activists continued to lack power, and CBCC had proven to be a flawed vehicle for exerting political pressure. "Basically what the [City Planning Commission] is saying is that Bedford-Stuyvesant has not brought enough pressure on them," an unnamed CBCC official told Anekwe. "We are now re-organizing the Coordinating Council, and we will do that."[28]

The opening phase of CBCC's reinvention began on September 26, 1962, when the council hosted its first annual conference on poverty in Bedford-Stuyvesant. In the keynote speech, the head of the Urban League of Greater New York, Edward S. Lewis, urged those assembled to wield more "organized pressure" on elected officials. "Washington is not going to be interested in Bedford-Stuyvesant if you have a divided front. It will want to deal with a group totally representative and responsible," he said, urging CBCC to broaden its reach. It was significant that Lewis should mention Washington as a target for CBCC's activism. The group to that point had mostly trained its sights on City Hall, but the existence of the President's Committee on Juvenile Delinquency now held out the promise of funds from the federal government.[29]

Lewis's audience responded by reinventing CBCC as a social movement. With the national civil-rights movement picking up steam, CBCC activists began increasingly to echo the language and organizing tactics of the freedom struggle. In October 1962, the Central Brooklyn Coordinating

Council for Youth formally dissolved and reconstituted itself as the Central Brooklyn Coordinating Council, Inc. The name change, though slight, signified a major shift in emphasis. To date, CBCC had accepted its narrow mandate of controlling youth behavior. Now, no longer content merely to assist the city government's antidelinquency efforts, the council would address the broader concerns of area residents while wielding the kind of political pressure Lewis and others were calling for. CBCC intended to pursue the kinds of resources lavished on Harlem and the Lower East Side, where, as one Brooklyn volunteer pointed out, "there are professional organizers to do the job of planning and crystallizing community needs."[30]

As a first step, the new, action-oriented group put together a speaker bureau, through which volunteers pounded the pavement in an attempt to put CBCC in touch with PTA groups, professional guilds, tenant associations, and cultural groups. One organizer, Elsie Richardson, would later recollect, "We made an effort to involve everybody in the community. We went into barbershops, beauty parlors, bars. We made sure that everybody had a voice." Such efforts paid off. CBCC's membership began to expand dramatically: by 1966, the council would claim to represent some 140 local groups, dozens of which participated in its planning meetings at the Bedford Avenue YMCA. "The community meetings would run hour upon hour upon hour," one participant later recalled. "There was a lot of emotion, there was a lot of capacity building. These were really democratic meetings."[31]

The reorganized CBCC brought together a broad-based coalition with connections both to Bed-Stuy's middle-class and, to a lesser extent, its low-income majority. For example, a leadership meeting held on November 1, 1962, attracted forty-five people, each with a specific organizational affiliation. Several coalitions of block associations—the Kingsboro Community Council, the Parkway-Stuyvesant Community Council, the Brower Park Civic Association, and the Bedford-Stuyvesant Neighborhood Council—sent representatives. So did the Lafayette Community Center, the Stuyvesant Community Center, the Bedford Mental Hygiene Clinic, the Willa Hardgrow Mental Health Center, and the Boys Welcome Hall, all of which specialized in youth-outreach work. City agencies, including the Youth Board, the Council of Social and Athletic Clubs, the Board of Education, the Brooklyn Public Library, and the Commission on Human Rights, also attended. Also present were members of business groups such as the Bedford-Stuyvesant Real Estate Board, the Carver Federal Savings

& Loan Association, and the Fulton Street Merchants Association; exclusive clubs for gentlemen (the Comus Club, the YMCA Men's Luncheon Club) and ladies (the National Association of College Women and the National Association of Negro Business and Professional Women's Clubs); a plethora of churches, as well as the Brooklyn Catholic Interracial Council and the Interdenominational Ministers Alliance; five Greek societies and two veterans posts; the NAACP, the Urban League, and the Congress of Racial Equality; and political associations, including the Unity Democratic Club (UDC), the Kings County Voter Registration League, and the 16th Assembly District Regular Republican Club. Notably absent from the roster of officially recognized CBCC groups were tenant associations or other groups explicitly representing poor people, though some would join in subsequent years.[32]

CBCC's new president, elected in November 1962, was Cecil Gloster, an obstetrician notable less for his activism than for his involvement in exclusive social milieus like the Comus Club, the Chi Delta Mu fraternity of physicians, and the influential black fraternity Alpha Phi Alpha. His first vice-president was Bernice Johnson, a housewife who had trained as a teacher. The council's first full-time hire was Walter Pinkston, who as the Youth Board's borough coordinator had helped to found the earlier incarnation of CBCC four years earlier. Pinkston had in fact spent the previous months devoting "75% of his time" to CBCC, and he remained on the Youth Board payroll. In his new job, he helped shape the group into a forceful and reliable advocate for stepped-up city programs in Bedford-Stuyvesant. (Four years later, Pinkston would become the executive director of Bedford-Stuyvesant's federally funded antipoverty agency, Youth in Action, which had begun as a branch of CBCC's Youth Services Committee.) CBCC also counted among its organizers a cohort of politically radical women who helped firm up the council's legitimacy among Bed-Stuy's working class. The most prominent were the teacher turned reformer Shirley Chisholm and Elsie Richardson, the energetic school secretary who in 1966 would broker CBCC's collaboration with Robert F. Kennedy.[33]

Chisholm, more than any other Brooklyn activist, would figure out how to convert grassroots organizing into formal political power. Her father was a Garveyite and proud member of the Confectionery and Bakers International Union; her mother, a seamstress, moonlighted as a domestic to add precious dollars to the family purse. Shirley was born in Brooklyn but spent much of her childhood with her grandmother in rural Barbados, where her immigrant parents thought she would be more comfortable than in hard-scrabble Brownsville. Returning to New York, she gained a radical political education from her father and attended Bed-Stuy's prestigious Girls High School (where she earned a medal for excellence in French). As a student at Brooklyn College, she joined the Harriet Tubman Society, a black student group, and fought to get courses in African American history added to the curriculum. She later earned a master's in early-childhood education from Columbia and began a career as a teacher's aide at a Harlem daycare. By 1960, she was working as an educational consultant for the city's Department of Welfare and devoting most of her free time to political activism.[34]

Chisholm would be elected to the State Assembly in 1964 before gaining national fame in 1968 as the first black woman elected to Congress. In 1972, she mounted an inspirational if quixotic run for the presidency, again becoming the first black woman to do so. "Unbought and Unbossed": so went the motto of a woman who weighed less than 100 pounds and threw every ounce of her weight into pushing progressive causes. In Albany and DC, "Fighting Shirley" pursued such measures as funding for low-income college students, subsidized daycare for working mothers, increases to the minimum wage, unemployment insurance for domestic workers, legalized abortions, and the Equal Rights Amendment. As a black woman, she faced what she called "double discrimination" (and it was being a woman, she said, that posed greater challenges). She instinctively sympathized with the underdog and didn't hesitate to criticize Bed-Stuy's elites, whom she derided as "the nose-in-the-air black bourgeoisie." For this, for her flamboyant fashions, for her plainspoken earthiness, and for her fluency in Spanish, she would become wildly popular in Brooklyn, especially among working-class women.[35]

In 1962, though, Chisholm was best known as an early-childhood educator with a seemingly inexhaustible appetite for community activism and political campaigning. For several years, she had pounded the pavement on behalf of Democratic reform candidates, turning heads with her "colorful and dramatic manner of dress." Along with Thomas Jones, Chisholm was the face of the Unity Democratic Club, which was just then mounting an unprecedented challenge to Brooklyn's political powerbrokers. Though she was said to belong to "17 or more" organizations or clubs, it was the UDC that Chisholm officially represented within CBCC. In the fall of 1962, Chisholm was elected as the council's vice-president in charge of program development. It was an important position at a time when CBCC was turning its attention to all "major problems and needs that affect the welfare of the people of this area." That a woman of Chisholm's political sensibilities occupied the position demonstrated that CBCC's new activism would take on a crusading tone to match the spirit of the times.[36]

The revamped CBCC took up a range of social and economic campaigns. Armed with a new slogan—"Building a Better Bedford Stuyvesant"—the council began to lobby for new housing, education, employment, health, and welfare services in the area. "Juvenile delinquency does not exist in a vacuum and has a vital relationship to the total spectrum of social welfare problems in the community," read a 1962 position statement, echoing the "root causes" analysis of the Youth Board and the PCJD. "The Council is now geared to address itself to any problem area where, it is felt, its efforts will help to bring about a better community."[37]

Following CBCC's reorganization, Chisholm drew up a list of pressing issues for 1963, which the full council subsequently endorsed. City officials had accused Bedford-Stuyvesant's leadership of being disorganized and diffuse; now CBCC would strive to make sure that the community spoke with one voice about planning priorities. Item number one was housing: Chisholm recommended that CBCC leaders meet as soon as possible with the mayor and the City Planning Commission to press for urban-renewal funds and programs to address "the total housing and public services picture of the community." Chisholm also urged CBCC to train its sights on educational reform, proposing to tackle overcrowded classrooms, inadequate special-needs programs, and appallingly low graduation rates. Finally, Chisholm called for federal, state, and local funds for a broad-based youth program modeled on those in Harlem and the Lower East Side. Following on these recommendations, CBCC assembled a number of issue-specific committees (labor, health and sanitation, youth services, urban planning and housing), each under the chairmanship of a prominent local citizen. Together, these committees would enable the council to initiate an "all-out drive" to remedy the "social ills" plaguing Central Brooklyn. To accomplish such goals, CBCC's leaders would learn to work inside the city bureaucracy while simultaneously taking to the streets to protest against it—a model of community action with great potential and great pitfalls.[38]

Neighborhood Revolts

Several developments in the city's political culture paved the way for CBCC's reinvention. It was a heady time. Reformers were mounting a political insurgency against Brooklyn's entrenched Democratic Party machine, which unfolded against the dramatic backdrop of a citywide reform movement. A wave of civil-rights protests washed over Kings County just as the national struggle was cresting. Meanwhile, neighborhood groups were bubbling up across the city, seeking to protect aging landscapes from rapacious developers and the bulldozers of the urban-renewal regime. These various revolts were in many ways intermingled, and in Bedford-Stuyvesant they came together under the auspices of CBCC.[39]

In 1961, Mayor Wagner made a historic break with Tammany Hall. Only eight years earlier, Tammany boss Carmine DeSapio had sponsored Wagner's accession to the mayoralty; in 1957, all four of the city's Democratic machines had united to help Wagner win election by a plurality of more than 920,000 votes—the largest margin in New York's history. But splits had begun to emerge within the Democratic Party, and in 1958 a reform wing led by Eleanor Roosevelt and Herbert Lehman broke with the regulars. The reformers hoped, in Lehman's words, "to free this city with one blow from the shackles of the boss system"; most immediately, this meant democratizing the Manhattan Democratic organization, long dominated by Tammany. By 1961, with reform clubs sprouting up all over the city, it became clear that Wagner would have to join them or else be seen as a tool of the bosses. DeSapio was a legendary figure who, with shaded glasses, impeccable hair, and tailored suits, seemed the very incarnation of backroom politics. But the Queens, Bronx, and Brooklyn machines were also formidable foes. Wagner, with one eye on future national campaigns, took them on in 1961 and beat them all. In so doing, he became the reform movement's unlikely factotum and triggered a reconfiguration of the city's political landscape. The Wagner of the 1953 and 1957 elections had drawn on a classic New Dealer's alliance; in 1961, he lost a portion of the white working class but pulled together a coalition made up of African Americans and Puerto Ricans, public-sector workers, left-leaning Jews, and intellectual elites. The reform movement stood for a brand of municipal liberalism that in many ways aligned with Wagner's beliefs. But it was an uneasy alliance. Many reformers found it hard to trust Wagner's sudden conversion to their cause—and the mayor was determined not to let them assume too much power.[40]

By 1962, there were forty-four reform clubs in the city. The most prominent were based in Manhattan neighborhoods, but there were eight clubs in Brooklyn, eight in Queens, and seven in the Bronx. Reformers planned to contest district leaderships in each one, and several candidates hoped to unseat machine-backed candidates for statewide office. Brooklyn's reform movement had two wings. In Brooklyn Heights, South Brooklyn, and Park Slope, a newly arrived group of white professionals and intellectuals took on patronage-dispensing clubhouses that were supported by working-class white ethnics. In Central Brooklyn, the movement was also led by a fledgling middle class—except that there the Democratic reformers were largely African American and were attempting to build an independent base of black political power.[41]

The leader of this latter group was Thomas R. Jones, a diminutive yet imperious attorney. Jones gave voice, in his rousing speeches, to the reform movement's idealistic impulses. Born in 1913 to Barbadian immigrants, Jones spent his early childhood living in an area of South Brooklyn later known as Boerum Hill, where Jews, Poles, Italians, and West Indians lived side by side. In the 1920s, Jones's family moved to Hancock Street in Bed-Stuy. His father, a podiatrist, was a Garveyite who helped organize the rising numbers of African American homeowners in Bedford-Stuyvesant into block associations. During the Depression, the young Jones began practicing law out of a Fulton Street storefront, working mostly with labor groups and block associations. During the Popular Front years, he represented Communists and victims of police brutality; he also became active in the New York Youth Congress, a leftist organization, and claimed the radical actor and singer Paul Robeson as a personal friend. After serving as a rifleman in World War II, he returned to Brooklyn and felt the sharp sting of bigotry. When he attempted to join the Democratic club in his home district, he was referred instead to the "colored club." The episode launched Jones's decades-long crusade against Brooklyn's Democratic Party regulars. In 1948, he supported the American Labor Party's presidential candidate, Henry Wallace, and ran (unsuccessfully) for a judgeship on the ALP ticket. Then, in the early 1950s, he teamed with Wesley Holder and Shirley Chisholm to found the upstart Bedford-Stuyvesant Political League.[42]

Jones slowly built up his political network until, in 1959, he again joined forces with Chisholm to launch the Unity Democratic Club. Though led by African Americans—and, especially, by second-generation West Indian immigrants—the UDC was proudly integrated. Jones and his allies dismissed previous efforts by the Kings County Democratic machine to broaden black voting power; they saw the first elected black Brooklynite, Assemblyman Bertram Baker, as a token. Unlike Baker, the new reformers would challenge the regulars head-on. The Unity Democrats raised their profile in Bed-Stuy through dogged street-level organizing and by helping people address day-to-day concerns. They offered advice on how to buy homes without falling prey to unscrupulous lenders. They supported the efforts of Reverend Milton Galamison and the Brooklyn NAACP to desegregate public schools, and they teamed with civil-rights groups to boycott companies that refused to hire black employees. Jones pledged to "run the carpet baggers out of the community" and posed as a neo-populist defender of "people against power, men against money." In 1962, with Eleanor Roosevelt campaigning on his behalf, Jones took on incumbent Sam Berman for the 17th Assembly seat and won.[43]

Jones's victory in the Assembly race temporarily energized Bed-Stuy reformers keen to see the civil-rights struggle translate into formal political power. "A political cloud lifted in our community" was the assessment of Ernesta Procope, an *Amsterdam News* columnist and insurance broker. Ruth Goring, a CBCC stalwart who rode Jones's coattails to election as co-district leader, explicitly tied the election to parallel campaigns to bring improved government services to Central Brooklyn. "Walk through the streets of Bedford-Stuyvesant and see why," she told the *Amsterdam News* when asked why she ran for office. "Look at our youth, the unemployment . . . and the elderly, and see why. Look at the political structure. They gave us nothing." Yet electoral politics could scarcely address the full range of injustices and deprivations facing Brooklyn's African American population. Even as the Unity Democrats were laying siege to segregated clubhouses in Kings County, activists were massing their forces for the most concerted assault on racial discrimination in New York City's history.[44]

New York activists in the early 1960s drew their inspiration from events unfolding in the South; many registered voters in Mississippi, rode Greyhounds into Alabama, and marched on Washington. But the city's civil-rights mobilization was far more than an appendage of the Southern effort. New York activism during the high tide of the freedom struggle tapped into a decades-long tradition of black protest. Harkening back to

"Don't-buy-where-you-can't-work" campaigns of the 1930s and 1940s, Brooklyn activists in the 1960s mounted a string of boycotts against businesses accused of unfair practices: Sealtest Dairy, Ebinger Bakeries, White Castle, and A&P supermarkets, among other firms. To an extent, Brooklynites felt empowered because they had the law on their side. New York had strong anti-discrimination legislation, and the city's congressional delegation included a peerless group of civil-rights champions, including Representatives John Lindsay and Emmanuel Celler, Senator Jacob Javits, and, above all, Harlem's Adam Clayton Powell. The liberal Republican Nelson Rockefeller, ostensibly a supporter of civil rights, became governor in 1959. Increasingly, Brooklyn-based activists could also tap into various access points to the state; the men and women who led street protests were simultaneously working within the structures of city government to secure resources for their neighborhoods. Jones and the UDC picketed Jim Crow workplaces while also working their alliance with Wagner and the Manhattan-based reform movement to penetrate the political system. Reverend Gardner Taylor of Concord Baptist Church simultaneously collaborated with the Congress of Racial Equality (CORE) on direct-action campaigns, marched alongside Martin Luther King Jr., and served as Wagner's main surrogate in Bedford-Stuyvesant in the wake of the mayor's split with the Democratic regulars.[45]

The ties linking Brooklyn activists to elected politicians meant that direct-action campaigns often ended in negotiation and compromise rather than attack dogs and fire hoses. Such negotiated settlements sometimes stole the thunder from more radical voices eager to highlight systemic inequalities. In the summer of 1963, activists tied to CORE and various church groups staged a month-long direct-action campaign outside the site of Downstate Medical Center in Brooklyn, a state-funded hospital project being built by Jim Crow construction crews. Pickets demanded a quota system to provide construction jobs for blacks and Puerto Ricans; hundreds of protestors went to jail. The campaign grabbed headlines but also exposed splits within Brooklyn's civil-rights coalition. For a time, dozens of ministers—led by Sandy Ray and Gardner Taylor—supported the struggle, spouting fiery rhetoric and drawing as many as 6,000 congregants to rallies. Though generally not radical in their political leanings, the preachers of Bedford-Stuyvesant "set aside their moderate approaches and became revolutionaries," in the words of historian Clarence Taylor. "Revolution has come to Brooklyn!" Taylor preached at one event. "The protest will be peaceful, but if the ruling white power structure brings it about, our blood will fill the streets." But when Rockefeller offered to sit down and negotiate, the churchmen hammered out a compromise with the governor, who pledged to enforce anti-discrimination laws and combat racism in the construction industry. The resolution disappointed many activists. Radicals from CORE accused the ministers of selling out their constituents in exchange for token concessions.[46]

As evidenced by the Downstate protests, the grievances of New York's African Americans and their white allies concerned not unjust laws but unequal allocation of resources. New York's elected officials had almost to a man pledged allegiance to the cause of civil rights. But activists wanted more than rights. They demanded a fair share of state largesse: hospitals, housing, public-sector jobs, urban-renewal monies. Nor would resources alone be sufficient; by mid-decade, activists in Bed-Stuy and other Brooklyn communities were waging a prolonged struggle for the power to *control* those resources.

Brooklyn's freedom struggle depended on the union of forces often seen as irreconcilable: integrationists and separatists, radicals and moderates. This mirrored a broader inclination among activists in the urban North who, as historian Thomas Sugrue has written, were "improvisational with their strategies and ideologically inconsistent." An emblematic figure was Robert Palmer, who replaced Maude Richardson as president of CBCC in 1961. Palmer, a chiropractor, was perhaps best known for running, unsuccessfully, for a State Assembly seat in 1960, as a Republican. He also ranked among the leaders of the Brooklyn chapter of the Congress of Racial Equality. In the early 1960s, CORE had more than fifty chapters in cities across the country, and the organization had gained international fame for organizing the Freedom Rides. Palmer chaired the Brooklyn group and hosted meetings at his home, bringing together a small but focused group of Jewish and black activists. The group launched a series of direct-action campaigns, attacking housing discrimination, Jim Crow workplaces, and all-white construction sites while also organizing tenant strikes among the area's poorest citizens. Brooklyn CORE was particularly successful at gaining press coverage through confrontational protests that, according to historian Brian Purnell, "attracted media attention and embarrassed intransigent powerbrokers into negotiations or concessions." That strategy made Brooklyn CORE a model to follow for young militants around the country in the mid-1960s—though the chapter's increasingly

New York Governor Nelson Rockefeller meets with a coalition of Bed-Stuy
ministers on August 6, 1963, to discuss discrimination at the construction site of
the Downstate Medical Center in Brooklyn. Seated with Rockefeller are
Milton A. Galamison and Gardner C. Taylor; Walter Offutt, William A.
Jones, W. G. Henson Jacobs, and Benjamin J. Lowry look on. *August 6, 1963.*
Associated Press

radical tactics wound up alienating older, more moderate members, including Palmer.[47]

At the height of his involvement with CORE, Palmer also sat on the executive board of the Bedford-Stuyvesant Neighborhood Council, an affiliate of CBCC. The Neighborhood Council was a consortium of about
ninety block associations that had been founded during the 1930s to promote interracial unity and quality-of-life improvements in the area. The
organization spoke mostly for and to homeowners, organizing them to
plant trees, run cleanup drives, and clear empty lots. The group emphasized individual responsibility for neighborhood conditions, encouraging
each citizen to take pride in his or her home and block. But this didn't stop
the Neighborhood Council from lobbying city and borough officials for
stepped-up police protection, improved public transportation, and regular
garbage collection. The latter issue—trash—was a particular point of contention in Brooklyn throughout much of the 1950s and 1960s. In 1962,
CORE led a memorable campaign to improve city garbage-collection

services in Bedford-Stuyvesant, in which activists dumped trash on the steps of Brooklyn Borough Hall. "Taxation without sanitation is tyranny!" went the rallying cry.[48]

Palmer's activism suggests the difficulties of distinguishing radicals from moderates in Brooklyn's freedom struggle. The Bedford-Stuyvesant Neighborhood Council reflected the concerns of the area's aspirational black middle class; Brooklyn CORE in the early 1960s included Communists and soon became an incubator of Black Power thought. For Palmer, it made sense to work within both groups, to restore tranquility on brownstone blocks while also tackling the structures of racial oppression. The balancing act could last only so long: by 1962, CORE's left-wing faction had written Palmer off as an "NAACP type" who preferred negotiations to the confrontational tactics the group had come to favor. But Palmer's eclectic commitments no doubt underpinned his election as CBCC president in 1961. In the early 1960s, CBCC provided a space in which activists of various political leanings could come together, even as it also reflected the complex partnerships linking Bed-Stuy's grassroots activists to the state.[49]

Neighborhood Conservation

The overlapping movements of the early 1960s—political reform, civil rights, block-level organizing—helped inject an element of participatory democracy into New York's civic life. Adding to the tumult was a citywide uprising against the urban-renewal program that had been transforming the landscape under master builder Robert Moses. Using federal funds released by the Housing Act of 1949, Moses had uprooted hundreds of thousands of New Yorkers and turned broad swathes of the city into dust. By the late 1950s, grassroots groups were pushing back. In 1958, the mothers of Greenwich Village, with Jane Jacobs at the helm, defeated Moses's plans to ram a highway through Washington Square. A year later, the Cooper Square Committee, a grassroots group on the Lower East Side, rose up against the city's slum-clearance plans and produced a community-initiated redevelopment plan, the first of its kind. All over the city, citizen groups felt empowered as they confronted previously unresponsive power structures and demanded more say in determining the shape of physical landscapes. Though some neighborhood activists opposed urban renewal altogether—and, in Jacobs's case, rejected the very premises of urban planning—others were keen to see urban renewal proceed, as long as it was done in consultation with neighborhood groups.[50]

The latter stance characterized many activists affiliated with CBCC. Slum clearance had disproportionately affected African Americans, who, in New York as in cities across the country, characterized urban renewal as "Negro removal." Many Central Brooklyn residents had settled there after experiencing firsthand the shattering effects of urban renewal, and many lived in fear of bulldozers. But Moses's Slum Clearance Committee had taken little interest in Bed-Stuy. CBCC leaders saw the urban-renewal program as a potential funding source—one from which their community had been frozen out. In the early 1960s, they feared decline as much as displacement. Optimistically, they gambled that urban-renewal monies could help revive their neighborhood. "The Bedford-Stuyvesant area needs any help it can get," the *Amsterdam News* commented in 1963.[51]

Many of the homeowners who made up the core of CBCC's leadership group had originally moved to the area in the 1940s and 1950s because they valued its elegant blocks, refined social life, and tranquil appearance. The number of such places where African Americans could aspire to buy homes was severely circumscribed, thanks to redlining and countless acts of cruelty and intimidation meted out by unwelcoming white neighbors.[52] In Bedford-Stuyvesant, beautiful homes were available, they were relatively cheap (despite blockbusting and predatory lending), and, increasingly, they were inhabited not by hostile whites but by welcoming blacks eager to build a nurturing, family-friendly community. Bed-Stuy residents were happy to live far from the bustle, overcrowding, and social strife of Harlem. By the 1960s, however, many feared that social conditions and class hatreds in their backyards were coming to approximate Harlem's. Not only did crime, school overcrowding, and absentee landlordism stimulate their impulse toward social justice; such conditions also risked damaging real-estate values and making their beloved community unlivable. The challenge lay in convincing government officials that Bedford-Stuyvesant was especially deserving of attention at a time when countless neighborhoods in New York and across America were facing what Mayor Wagner called "crises of an unprecedented kind, and of an unprecedented severity."[53]

The reorganization of CBCC, and its subsequent growth, reflected the political savvy of its leaders, who learned to convey the energy of a social movement while playing bureaucratic politics. At the same time, their actions revealed their desperation. In 1963, Bed-Stuy's leadership class felt increasingly besieged and bewildered. Even as the civil-rights campaign was gaining steam, residential and educational segregation in Brooklyn was hardening. Mortgage capital was nonexistent except at usurious rates—a crushing burden for homeowners who needed refinancing so they could renovate aging Victorian buildings. City services—fire and police protection, sanitation, schools—seemed to be declining as fast as whites were decamping. Poverty and crime were spreading. Among CBCC activists, sincere concern for poor neighbors was intimately related to a concern for their own welfare. Their own blocks might be neat, affluent, architecturally rich, and organized—hardly "slums," in other words. But there was nothing to prevent "slum conditions" from stalking them and their children. "The middle-income group is the backbone of any society, minority, or community," asserted an *Amsterdam News* editorial aimed at drawing government aid, "and . . . Bedford-Stuyvesant is fast becoming a one-income area."[54]

Thomas R. Jones offered a typically candid assessment of these fears in a 1967 speech. Speaking to a group of white businessmen and politicians, Jones affirmed his faith in the work ethic of the neighborhood's residents. Recalling his own father's pride in "buying house," he explained that Bed-Stuy homeowners in the 1930s, 1940s, and 1950s "struggled for this, and because of these struggles and the home ownership, they have been able to maintain a pride and dignity which is unparalleled, I think in America." Bed-Stuy still boasted a large number of professionals, intellectuals, and artists, Jones pointed out, and it didn't face the "poisonous and degrading problems" that beset Harlem, where a "trickery and hustler attitude" reigned. According to Jones, a large middle class was waiting for opportunities to better itself and would enthusiastically embrace programs to revitalize the neighborhood. Yet "a widening gap between working people and those who are disillusioned and discouraged" was emerging. Jones added, "I want to say candidly that I couldn't go into the streets when the recent riots took place, because they would have thrown me into the sewer."[55]

Bed-Stuy activists had to walk a fine line when describing neighborhood conditions to outsiders and demanding urban-renewal funds. Dramatizing the deterioration of their neighborhood and the "blight" in their midst could help draw the attention of policymakers, along with new funding opportunities. On the other hand, efforts by outside authorities to label the neighborhood a "slum" or a "blighted area"—and, later, in the 1960s, a "ghetto"—could be read as veiled slurs that suggested a generalized decline of public morality, order, and social status among all local residents. The "slum" designation also carried the taint of slum *clearance*.

Elsie Richardson and other activists affiliated with CBCC maintained a pragmatic ambivalence when it came to urban renewal. They frequently complained that Bedford-Stuyvesant had been denied access to a plentiful pool of federal funds; they insistently asked city officials why no projects were planned for Central Brooklyn, even as tens of millions of dollars were being spent elsewhere in the city. Indeed, it was the City Planning Commission's decision in 1962 to table plans for urban renewal in Bedford-Stuyvesant that provided the trigger for CBCC's reorganization. At the same time, fear of Moses's bulldozers ran deep. Though CBCC leaders generally welcomed low-income housing developments at a time when majority-white areas of the city rallied to block them, they also opposed clearance and high-rise towers. Richardson could speak from personal experience about the ravages of slum clearance, and she firmly opposed any efforts to tear down structurally sound buildings. When CBCC leaders invoked urban renewal, they emphasized things like scattered demolition of abandoned structures, rehabilitation of dilapidated but structurally sound brownstones, and improvements to public transportation. CBCC also hoped renewal monies could fund vest-pocket parks, health centers, and even a community college somewhere in Central Brooklyn.[56]

For Richardson, the "shortchanging" of Bed-Stuy when it came to urban renewal was a civil-rights issue. "Minorities want first-class neighborhoods with first-class citizenship," she wrote to Wagner in a 1965 letter requesting urban-renewal funds for Central Brooklyn. Urban renewal, as Richardson saw it, could allow Stuyfordites to regain control of their environment by eliminating "the hundreds of burned-out and abandoned buildings which spread blight and decay throughout the rest of the community." In a 1967 statement prepared for hearings held by the City Planning Commission, she compared the aspirations of Bed-Stuy residents to those of white New Yorkers in working-class communities like Sheepshead Bay and Middle Village. "[The] people of Bedford-Stuyvesant don't like slums either; *we* don't want crime; *we* don't want too many high-rise buildings; *we* don't want over-crowded schools; *we* want effective police coverage; and we want *all* the recreational space we can get."[57]

110

Others opposed urban renewal outright, fearing that, once begun, it would lead to indiscriminate demolition no matter what community members might say. That was the opinion held by Martha Ross Leigh, a CBCC housing expert who also sat on the board of directors of the citywide Citizens Housing and Planning Council, an influential policy group. "I feel that this is a typical so-called 'grey area' in terms of city problems and as such may be in line for serious consideration by the planning commission and housing boards," Leigh said of Bed-Stuy in 1961. "But large numbers of the houses, while obsolete in terms of original uses, are well-designed, structurally sound and certainly capable of sustained use for a long time if the desirable social climate can be maintained. Urban renewal projects are not called for in the main here."[58]

The cautious attitude of many Brooklyn homeowners was summed up in an August 1962 *Amsterdam News* headline: "Urban Renewal—Yes! But Don't Change Face of Area, Residents Plea." The "residents" in this particular context were leaders of the Brower Park Civic Association, a group made up mostly of homeowners in the area of Crown Heights bordering the Brooklyn Children's Museum. In 1961, the City Planning Commission had proposed a program of urban renewal in the area, only to reverse course the following year. The Brower Park Civic Association—a CBCC affiliate group—welcomed the prospect of renewal, but with three caveats. They asked that home-improvement loans be offered to homeowners at low interest rates, that small property owners be given access to the same kinds of tax abatements offered to large developers who sponsored renewal projects, and that rent-control restrictions be eased. These demands reflected the interests of homeowners keen to strengthen their foothold in a rapidly changing area, even if it meant raising rents. Finally, they insisted that the "basic character of our community" be preserved in any renewal scheme. "We don't want to be thrown out of the community in the process."[59]

Such demands dovetailed with a rising movement against Moses's brand of urban renewal. Cautiously, Wagner fostered a shift in the city's policies. In 1959, he unveiled the Neighborhood Conservation Program, under the supervision of the Housing and Rehabilitation Board. (Wagner first floated the idea in 1954, the same year that saw passage of a federal Housing Act requiring that community participation play an important part in any future urban-renewal plans.) The aim of neighborhood conservation was to preempt slum clearance by "saving" targeted areas from becoming "all-out slums." Instead of demolishing dilapidated buildings, the program would enforce housing codes and provide neglectful landlords with incentives to renovate. To head the effort, Wagner called on the reformer and civil-rights activist Hortense Gabel, whom the *Times* described as "the only white person in the Wagner administration who really has a close relationship with the Negro community."[60]

The neighborhood-conservation approach was not unique to New York. The first such program had emerged in Chicago's Hyde Park neighborhood, where the municipal government had partnered with energetic block groups to maintain real-estate values in the face of demographic change and infrastructural decline in the early 1950s. The National Association of Real Estate Boards had also embraced the concept of conservation, launching a "Build America Better" campaign to lobby local governments for public improvements to streets, sewers, and schools; rehabilitation or demolition of dilapidated buildings; and rezoning of empty lots. After Congress passed enabling legislation in 1954, similar programs emerged in Detroit, Cleveland, Cincinnati, and other cities. James Rouse, a mortgage banker known for his rehabilitation work in Baltimore, also promoted the idea of inner-city revitalization through an organization named American Council to Improve Our Neighborhoods, which received the backing of the Ford Foundation.[61]

In 1959, Wagner declared that the city would launch "community action programs" in select neighborhoods as part of a "massive attack on slum conditions." The first interventions unfolded in small Manhattan tracts that generally covered four or five street blocks and two avenue blocks. These were the places the Ford Foundation called "gray areas": neighborhoods in transition, where groups of newcomers—mostly blacks and Puerto Ricans—mixed with white residents who had been there for a generation or two. In such enclaves, industrial activity hummed alongside schools and playgrounds, and townhouses pressed up against warehouses. The city pledged to prevent such places from turning into "slums" by working with settlement houses and property owners to rehabilitate run-down buildings. The pilot project unfolded in a section of Chelsea on the west side of Manhattan; the area had once been known for its quiet elegance, and the city focused on brownstone rehabilitation as a way to lure back middle-class residents.[62]

Though scanty funds ($125,000) supported the first year's efforts, the neighborhood-conservation approach marked a break with old ways.

Echoing Wagner's Community Planning Boards and the Youth Board's community councils, the new rehabilitation effort promoted citizen participation in planning. The emphasis on rehabilitating historic buildings also reflected the ideas of activists such as Jane Jacobs, who published her landmark assault on urban planning, *The Death and Life of Great American Cities*, in 1961. With the Neighborhood Conservation Program, the city government implicitly acknowledged the point that Jacobs and her fellow block-based organizers were making: that in an era of middle-class flight, Victorian townhouses could provide a counterweight to the allure of the suburbs.[63]

Such an intervention seemed plausible by 1960. Wagner was moving—slowly—to rein in Moses, and the "power broker" soon lost control of the notorious Committee on Slum Clearance. The new thinking about neighborhood development was encapsulated in a report submitted to Wagner in March 1960 titled "Building a Better New York." Its author, Anthony Panuch, suggested a sweeping reorganization of the city's housing and urban-renewal bureaucracies and called for "a vigorous program" of new housing in deteriorating business districts, where few residents would have to be displaced. "Don't tear down desperately needed, structurally sound tenements," Panuch wrote. One result of Panuch's report was the creation of a new Housing and Rehabilitation Board, which aimed to lead "a more orderly rebuilding of the city." Placed under the chairmanship of J. Clarence Davies (a former real-estate man), the board also included Robert C. Weaver, a staunch critic of the city's urban-renewal programs and a future secretary of the federal Department of Housing and Urban Development under President Johnson. In the early 1960s, New York policy elites would arrive at something of a post-Moses consensus. The new urban-renewal regime, historian Christopher Klemek argues, "appeared politically well entrenched, relatively progressive, and responsive to both elites and average citizens—at least rhetorically."[64]

Yet the conservation approach, in its hostility to "slums," shared certain assumptions with the slum-clearance approach it was ostensibly dislodging. Cooperation among city agencies, settlement houses, and landlords was often forged at the expense of tenant groups, according to historian Joel Schwartz. The program's emphasis on overcrowding and "slum conditions" could easily lead to displacement. Despite official estimates that only 633 people were displaced by conservation programs between mid-1960 and the end of 1962, a study carried out by the Metropolitan Council on

113

Housing in 1963 found that over 1,400 families, 95 percent of them blacks and Puerto Ricans, had been turfed out of their homes to alleviate "congestion." Tenant groups also expressed alarm at news of Laurance Rockefeller's efforts to turn the Neighborhood Conservation Program into a for-profit scheme through an outfit named the Conservation Renewal and Rehabilitation Fund. "Neighborhood Conservation means the green light to real estate speculators who would like to turn Chelsea into another Yorkville or Greenwich Village," was how the Chelsea Tenant Council put it.[65]

Brooklynites also weighed the benefits of the new approach. In Crown Heights, the Brower Park Civic Association embraced conservation, demanding that the city enforce building codes and provide tax abatements for home-improvement programs. Tenants, meanwhile, complained that such measures would inevitably mean higher rents. Those fears made sense in an area where renters often lived on the top floors of owner-occupied townhouses—especially since homeowners were advocating loosened rent-control laws on the grounds that tenants should "carry their share of the costs" of renovations. "We want the code enforced, and we want community renewal," the Brooklyn Tenants Welfare Council said in 1963, "but we don't want the tenant to pay for the landlord's improvement."[66]

Despite murmurs of opposition, the idea of neighborhood conservation was popular among the homeowners who made up CBCC's leadership group. Maude B. Richardson had first petitioned Hortense Gabel for conservation funds shortly after the program was announced in 1959. In 1962, Central Brooklyn activists renewed their attempts to bring neighborhood-conservation funds to the area, and CBCC's reorganization that fall helped bring city agencies to the table. By that time, the Neighborhood Conservation Program had begun to draw federal funds and was focusing on "social renewal" in addition to physical renewal. Where conservation projects had once sought to save "sound" neighborhoods from deteriorating, the new effort, dubbed the Area Services Program, would strive to reverse the tide of "slummification" in enclaves where poverty and physical blight were the rule rather than the exception. The language used to justify the new program echoed the ideas of epidemiologists. As an official from the Neighborhood Conservation Program put it in 1963, addressing a CBCC meeting, "area services" were designed to "hold the line [and] minimize contagion to adjoining areas."[67]

Responding to this mandate, city officials conducted building inspections, slapped landlords with summonses, and rehabilitated aging buildings. Meanwhile, they "saturated" small areas with counseling and social services such as "study clubs" for children living in SROs buildings. Among the city agencies involved were the departments of Buildings, Health, Fire, Police, Sanitation, Welfare, Education, and Water Supply, along with the Youth Board and the Commission on Intergroup Relations—in Wagner's words, "an effective complement of social, educational, and health services." In some neighborhoods, Area Services officials petitioned local businesses to open up more jobs for minorities; in Bedford-Stuyvesant, Wagner allowed the Area Services office to serve as an employment center for young blacks eager to join the construction trades in the aftermath of the Downstate protests.[68]

This new thrust made the Neighborhood Conservation Program all the more appealing to the men and women of CBCC. For one, it dovetailed with their vision of scattered rehabilitation rather than large-scale urban renewal. Further, the program promised to bring in a wide array of city services—as would be needed if CBCC were to launch an "all-out drive" to remedy the "social ills" of Bed-Stuy. City funds for physical renewal as well as social services could help boost the efforts of local homeowners to preserve their blocks while also uplifting the less fortunate in their community. "Deterioration and blight plague several sections of our community," read a March 1963 report authored by John L. Procope, who chaired CBCC's Committee on Housing and Urban Planning and would later become the publisher of the *Amsterdam News*. Procope was a realtor and insurance broker for an agency named E. G. Bowman, which had been founded by his wife, Ernesta, and specialized in $25 fire- and home-insurance policies sold to Bed-Stuy residents unable to gain credit from mainstream banks.[69] The firm also offered financing for brownstone rehabilitation, and Procope, wearing his CBCC hat, argued that the predominance of brownstones in relatively good condition made wholesale urban renewal undesirable. However, code enforcement, rehabilitation, and ramped-up social services—the hallmarks of the Neighborhood Conservation Program—seemed attractive. Notably, Procope and CBCC also called for selective slum clearance in the area surrounding Tompkins Park, where "a few Old Law tenements" still stood.[70]

On February 7, 1963, representatives of the Department of City Planning and the Department of Housing and Rehabilitation, which oversaw neighborhood-conservation projects, appeared at a CBCC board meeting to lay out possible programs for Bedford-Stuyvesant. Members of CBCC's Housing Committee were asked to choose among three zones that had been recommended for renewal by Raymond & May Associates, an urban-planning firm. (One of the firm's partners, George M. Raymond, was a professor of urban planning at the Pratt Institute in nearby Clinton Hill, and he would begin assisting CBCC as an unpaid consultant the following year.) They opted for the area immediately surrounding Tompkins Park—the same spot that had lent its name to the Brooklyn Council for Social Planning's gang-outreach initiative fifteen years earlier. It remained one of Brooklyn's poorer enclaves, though fewer of its buildings had been left to decay than in some other areas proposed for rehabilitation. Around 15 percent of residences were owner-occupied, and a similar number were SROs. The area also included a mix of different types of housing, with fewer long rows of tidily matching brownstones than in Stuyvesant Heights or Crown Heights.[71]

In March, Wagner unveiled plans for an Area Services project in a twenty-two–block area surrounding Tompkins Park. To run it, he called on Darwin W. Bolden, a lawyer who had previously worked with the Harlem NAACP and Brooklyn CORE and who would later become executive director of Bed-Stuy's official War on Poverty agency. The *Brooklyn Eagle* heralded the initiative as a "massive redevelopment program," though its initial undertakings were small-scale. Headquartered in the Bedford Avenue YMCA, where CBCC held its meetings, Bolden hoped to compel landlords to bring buildings up to code while also helping locals with welfare, health, and schooling issues. He hired a full-time community organizer and six full-time city inspectors, who scoured the area for violations of the city's building code. By August 1963, the inspectors had reported 4,426 violations. Delinquent property owners were given a chance to comply voluntarily; Bolden also invited them to air their own grievances in person. Early on, this approach scored a measure of success, with reports that 1,000 violations were fixed within six weeks of being flagged.[72]

Meanwhile, Bolden encouraged local residents to document price gouging in local stores. He also worked with the Bed-Stuy Neighborhood Council and its local block associations, who energized a community cleanup drive. In 1963, 3,000 tons of debris disappeared from the area's streets, and activists used Area Services funds to plant trees, install

window boxes, and fence in empty lots. The activity marked the beginning of a long-term redevelopment program in the Tompkins Park area,
financed by the city but conceived by local activists such as Almira
Coursey and Herbert Von King. From 1964 on, Coursey, a teacher, was
instrumental in lobbying the city on behalf of Bedford-Stuyvesant residents through the Tompkins Park Committee, an affiliate of CBCC
supported by Area Services. By the late 1960s, new facilities included the
iconic Kosciuszko swimming pool (designed by Morris Lapidus), a band
shell, an indoor performance space, Little League fields, and a community
center.[73]

If the Neighborhood Conservation Program in Manhattan had represented a hedge against white flight—and, to some extent, a way of removing
the poor blacks and Puerto Ricans around whose presence the discourse
of white flight was euphemistically constructed—in Bedford-Stuyvesant
it represented an intervention against *black* flight. By the mid-1960s, New
York's policy elites and neighborhood activists alike had reason to worry
that the black middle class might abandon the city as whites were doing.

Wagner's right-hand man, Paul Screvane, expressed such fears in public
and tied them to the city's efforts to work alongside middle-class outfits like
the CBCC. Screvane lauded CBCC for giving voice to "the quiet side, the
respectable side" of Bedford-Stuyvesant and helping to maintain "the character and dignity which attracted home-buyers" to Brooklyn in decades
past. "We hear much about the white middle class moving to the suburbs.
This phenomenon pertains to the Negro middle class as well," Screvane
told a CBCC meeting while campaigning to replace Wagner as mayor in
1965. "I know that it is the objective of the citizens of Bedford-Stuyvesant
to build a community to hold its home-owners and its businessmen. This
is an objective which agencies of the City Government share in common
with groups and organizations in Bedford-Stuyvesant." In other words, the
Wagner administration not only acknowledged CBCC's claims to be a representative group and a responsible broker within black Brooklyn, but the
city also endorsed the council's self-definition as a bulwark against the departure of the borough's black middle class. That made CBCC an interesting choice as the de facto organizer of War on Poverty initiatives in
Bed-Stuy. Though its organizers earnestly took on the charge of fighting
poverty, they also believed that to save Bed-Stuy they would need to save
the middle class.[74]

A Central Brooklyn Coordinating Council poster, circa 1963. "Your organization can help place this star by joining forces with other members of the CBCC," reads the thought bubble pointing to the young man. Inscribed on the steps are several community aspirations: "an aroused and alert citizenry," "adequate schools," "sufficient housing," "recreational facilities," "cultural institutions," "elimination of juvenile delinquency," "strengthening family ties," "adequate social services," "adequate public utilities," and, at the top, "total community participation." The ultimate goal hovers above the star: "A Better Bedford Stuyvesant."

"A Militant Spirit"

The reform insurgency, the civil-rights struggle, and the revolt against the urban-renewal regime together gave CBCC a new vocabulary with which to define community grievances and petition governments for resources. Increasingly, they used that vocabulary to dramatize the link between racial discrimination and economic inequality while also pushing for programs that might help transform the local economy. One area of particular concern for CBCC was unemployment. In early 1963, CBCC leaders began putting increased pressure on Wagner to address the problem of jobs, especially among youths, in Bedford-Stuyvesant. They stressed the urgency of the situation, demanding an end to surveys, studies, and speeches. "This is a powder-keg that can blow up anytime," the *Amsterdam News* opined of Bed-Stuy's jobless population. "And even more, we are wasting good youthful fiber, everyday, which could be turned into vital citizenry who could be a credit to their country instead of jailbirds. So please Mr. Mayor, no surveys. Just action."[75]

On February 8, a diverse group of Bed-Stuy leaders converged on City Hall to meet with Wagner and his top assistant, Julius Edelstein, along with Commissioner of Labor James McFadden. The Brooklynites included Shirley Chisholm, Walter Pinkston, Assemblymen Bertram Baker and Thomas R. Jones, and a half-dozen others, among them a Jewish delegate from Crown Heights, Stanley Leyden, and a Hispanic activist, the Urban League's Raymond Rivera. That these notables came together under the CBCC banner was an indication of the council's increasing reach. By defining themselves as a "united front" in negotiations with the city government, they were putting forth a new vision of the political power that could flow from their community. Jones, Chisholm, and company requested that the city's Department of Labor open a service center in Bed-Stuy to coordinate on-the-job training and run study programs for people preparing to take high-school equivalency tests. Wagner agreed, and by June he was set to place a Labor Office on Fulton Street in the heart of the neighborhood. Among its signature initiatives would be a "Job Talent Corps" to help recent graduates find work. The department also promised to investigate allegations of workplace discrimination. A modest beginning, perhaps, but the office affirmed the premise that there was a role for the city to play in helping black Brooklynites obtain "basic educational skills, basic worker's skills, and good jobs."[76]

Even so, controversy erupted when it emerged that Commissioner Mc-Fadden had tabbed a resident of Westchester County, Charles Fields, to run the office. McFadden had neglected to run the choice past any of Bed-Stuy's leading politicos. (Perhaps he assumed that Fields, who was black, would prove acceptable on the basis of his skin color.) CBCC leaders greeted the news with scorn. "I am sick of this kind of attitude of the powers that be making decisions for us without consulting us," Thomas Jones objected. Joseph Anderson, the chairman of CBCC's Committee on Labor, declared it "a very definite slap in the face of the Bedford-Stuyvesant community." Added Anderson, "This is another example of planning for us and not with us. A very undemocratic process of democracy." Even the arrival of much-needed city services was now not enough to placate Bedford-Stuyvesant's leaders. What they wanted, increasingly, was *power* over how those services would be dispensed because, in Chisholm's words, "we know this community best."[77]

Once the furor died down, Mayor Wagner visited Bedford-Stuyvesant on July 1, 1963, to preside over the opening of the new Labor Office. The ribbon-cutting ceremony demonstrated that CBCC could extract concessions from the city government through negotiations and soft pressure. Wagner's speech also offered proof that the national civil-rights movement, which was intensifying across the country, was helping to set the mayor's agenda. Only two weeks earlier, President Kennedy had submitted his civil-rights bill to Congress; the bloody Birmingham campaign and the assassination of Mississippi activist Medgar Evers had captured national headlines that spring. "The alarm bells have been sounded, North and South, for the government—all levels of government—to act and act now to remedy the conditions of discrimination, segregation and deprivation which have so long been the lot of so many of our fellow-Americans," Wagner said. To the mayor, recent protests offered "dramatic evidence of what might be called the Spirit of '63. It has been a militant spirit, a vigorous spirit, a fearless spirit," the mayor said.[78]

For all that militancy and vigor, CBCC continued to pursue its old goal of controlling deviant youth behavior in Bedford-Stuyvesant. The funds flowing to the antidelinquency programs in Harlem and the Lower East Side inspired Brooklyn activists to push for government-funded youth programs on their own turf. In December 1962, CBCC's Youth Services Committee redoubled its efforts to obtain federal and city funds. Led by an attorney named William Chisholm (no relation to Shirley), CBCC activists set up a series of meetings with government officials and social scientists active in the juvenile-delinquency field. These included Deputy City Administrator Henry Cohen; Leonard Stern of the PCJD; professors at Brooklyn College, including eminent sociologists Charles Lawrence and Clarence Senior; and staffers from Mobilization for Youth and HARYOU.[79]

The meetings began to pay off in the "militant" summer of 1963. In July, a CBCC delegation huddled with Wagner at City Hall and extracted from the mayor a promise that he would fund a more muscular antidelinquency program in Bed-Stuy. Then, on August 14, Robert Kennedy alighted in New York for another impromptu tour. This time the attorney general toured the PCJD projects in Harlem and the Lower East Side. ("He was hatless, without so much as a briefcase," a dazzled *Times* reporter wrote.) Having observed in action remedial-reading centers uptown and vocational-training programs downtown, Kennedy sat down to chat with representatives of CBCC, who proposed to import some of MFY's programs across the East River. According to the Brooklynites, Kennedy pledged his "support and cooperation" for a federal antidelinquency program in Bed-Stuy. The PCJD would never get around to funding that effort; within six months, most such initiatives would be folded into the War on Poverty. But CBCC's leaders took heart from Kennedy's promise and began planning a new project.[80]

A first step was "Operation Pipeline," an outreach program to solicit feedback from locals about what kinds of programs CBCC should be pursuing. In particular, the council hoped to hear from young people, who were urged to speak their minds in person either at the Stuyvesant Community Center or to the Youth Board. (In a similar vein, Kenneth Clark had actively tried to tap into the streetwise expertise of Harlem's teen gangs while conceiving of HARYOU.) Thomas Jones, meanwhile, was convening public meetings and drawing up plans of his own for a comprehensive delinquency program. But Jones had action—not research—in mind, and he warned that CBCC should steer clear of theory-based demonstration programs in the PCJD mold. "We have had enough studies of unemployment, bad housing, juvenile delinquency," he said in August 1963. "Now we need a program. We are all well aware of the problems that exist in our community. It is our goal to get immediate help and extra money." The root cause of those problems—"three centuries of prejudice and discrimination"—was clear as day to Jones. It didn't take a scholar to make that diagnosis.[81]

4

War and Rumors of War

> If the War on Poverty means anything, it is a statement that we
> must look, not just to the poor—but to the whole cloth too—and
> even to the loom. The whole fabric of our society must be re-
> woven, and the patterns we must weave are patterns of justice,
> opportunity, dignity, and mutual respect.
>
> —SARGENT SHRIVER, 1966

utlook for '64: A War on Poverty"—so read the headline in the *Wash-*
ington Post on January 1, 1964. It had been less than six weeks since the
assassination of President John F. Kennedy. Camelot was dead, the New
Frontier a distant horizon. Lyndon B. Johnson, the garrulous Texan whom
few saw as presidential, now slept in the White House. New Year's celebra-
tions in the nation's capital had been muted. But as bleary-eyed liberals
stepped to their doorsteps that morning, they found heartening news.

"The fledgling Johnson Administration, true to Democratic Party in-
stincts, again has stolen a march on the Republicans by uncorking an
easily grasped mass appeal issue," the *Post* reported. "The issue is the continued poverty of millions of Americans in a land of plenty." Despite the
much-trumpeted triumph of affluence since World War II, some 30 million Americans—a fifth of the population—still lived in households
earning less than $3,000 a year, the government's official poverty threshold.
What liberals described as "the paradox of poverty amid plenty" offered a
political opportunity, which Johnson intended to pursue. "Such a program
is likely to enhance Mr. Johnson's political standing among some groups
where his initial appeal might be less than Mr. Kennedy's was—Negroes,
liberal intellectuals and industrial workers fending for jobs," the *Post* predicted. "And the antipoverty package is one that will carry a Johnson
stamp—not a re-label from the Kennedy administration."[1]

The director of the federal Office of Economic Opportunity, Sargent Shriver, visits Brooklyn's first official Community Action Agency, Bedford-Stuyvesant Youth in Action, circa 1965. *"New York City War on Poverty, 1965: A Report to the Citizens of New York," Bedford-Stuyvesant Youth in Action*

Seven days later, Johnson stood before a joint session of Congress and delivered his first State of the Union address. Around the country, millions of living-room eyes gazed nervously at grainy black-and-white television screens. The president—receding hair slicked back past floppy ears, too-small head perched atop hulking 6-foot-4-inch frame—lacked the breezy, youthful elegance of his predecessor. But as he took the podium to speak, Johnson looked dignified and vital. He began on a somber note. "I will be brief," he said, softly, "for our time is necessarily short and our agenda is already long." He continued in measured, almost hushed tones, carefully eschewing flights of rhetoric that might ring dissonant in the subdued chamber. His proposals, too, came wrapped in moderate packaging: Johnson opened by announcing a $500 million rollback in federal spending, which would bring the budget down to $98 billion for the coming fiscal year.[2]

And yet Johnson that day put forth a fresh, sweeping vision of American life. Though the speech was particularly short for a State of the Union address, clocking in at a mere sixteen minutes, the president offered more than a sober exhortation for a grieving country to unite. He promised the most ambitious domestic agenda since the New Deal. Ted Sorensen, John F. Kennedy's former speechwriter, had drafted most of the text, but two dozen others had offered edits and contributions. "That State of the Union message was probably rewritten more times, by more people, than any Kennedy speech, with the exception of the October 22, 1962, speech during the Cuban missile crisis," Sorensen later wrote. Fittingly, the final draft contained something for everyone. Budgets would shrink even as programs would proliferate; peace would be achieved, at home and abroad. Johnson exhorted lawmakers to pass a series of measures that taken together would extend the protections of the American welfare state to those groups the New Deal had left behind.[3]

It would be another four months before Johnson began affixing the "Great Society" label to his domestic programs. But he was already making his intentions clear:

> Let this session of Congress be known as the session which did more for civil rights than the last hundred sessions combined; as the session which enacted the most far-reaching tax cut of our time; as the session which declared all-out war on human poverty and unemployment in these United States; as the session which finally recognized the health needs of all our older citizens; as the session which reformed our tangled transportation and transit policies; as the session which achieved the most effective, efficient foreign aid program ever; and as the session which helped to build more homes, more schools, more libraries, and more hospitals than any single session of Congress in the history of our Republic.[4]

It was an astonishing list of priorities. And LBJ wasted no time getting to work. The former Senate majority leader made clear from the start that he would honor the slain president by passing laws JFK had proposed but a recalcitrant Congress had refused to approve. (Johnson would later remark that he had tried to "take the dead man's program and turn it into a martyr's cause.") First up was the series of tax cuts Kennedy had first proposed—and Congress had rejected—in 1963. More ambitiously, Johnson

would take up the issue of civil rights, which Kennedy had cautiously embraced during the final months of his life.[5]

But if the civil-rights bill and the tax cut were the major pieces of unfin-
ished business left over from the Kennedy administration, it was the poverty program that was to be Johnson's signature domestic initiative. As a
society, the United States had achieved prosperity unequaled in human
history—but few Americans were in a self-congratulatory mood. Johnson,
who fancied himself a friend of the underdog, sensed that if ever the country's middle classes might be asked to sacrifice for those left behind, that
time was now, in the wake of tragedy. The war against poverty could be
sold as the moral thing to do—a campaign designed as much to uplift
people's spirits as to fill their pockets. This would be an integral part of
building a Great Society in which "men are more concerned with the
quality of their goals than the quantity of their goods."[6]

Johnson, of course, was a politician through and through. He hoped the
War on Poverty would prove a political winner in an election year. It would
be hard for Republicans to oppose the initiative without seeming callous;
it also promised to win over minority groups and Northern elites otherwise
predisposed to distrust a Southern Democrat in the White House. But
Johnson knew that he ran the risk of alienating hard-working Americans
who struggled to make ends meet and suspected that social programs targeting poor people were wasting their tax dollars. So it made some sense
to speak of the campaign against poverty as a war. To declare war on poverty was to bind social programs to patriotic sentiment. To declare war on
poverty was to conjure up images of national unity, wholesale mobilization, and collective action. To declare war on poverty was to assert that the
campaign could be won.[7]

"This administration today, here and now, declares unconditional war
on poverty in America," Johnson said in his State of the Union address.
The language—martial, uncompromising, urgent—would haunt LBJ in
later years, as critics accused him of boosting expectations with grand
promises he could never hope to fulfill. On January 8, 1964, though, it
fit the country's mood. Or so Johnson hoped. To be safe, he hedged his
bets. The War on Poverty would include a welter of programs "obviously
not for the poor or the underprivileged alone": universal health care for the
aged, enforcement of minimum-wage laws, federal aid to public schools,
and a beefed-up program of unemployment insurance. In other words,

the campaign against poverty would benefit society at large. To woo business groups, Johnson tied the poverty program to tax cuts and repurposed the old New Deal argument that social-welfare programs would boost workers' purchasing power and thus spur economic growth. To those worried about government waste, LBJ promised to turn the unemployed into taxpayers and coax the poor off welfare. This latter point was key to the Texan's political calculus. Self-help would become a byword of the War on Poverty; poor people would be offered not cash but opportunity. "A Hand Up, Not a Handout," went the official slogan. As LBJ's appointee to run the War on Poverty, Sargent Shriver, began work that February, Johnson offered a simple bit of advice: "No doles!"[8]

All this undeniably carried what the *Washington Post* called "a Johnson stamp." Still, the poverty program featured no shortage of "re-labeling." Johnson's idol, Franklin D. Roosevelt, was another inveterate foe of doles. The War on Poverty repackaged popular New Deal initiatives, such as the Civilian Conservation Corps, which paired relief with moral uplift and job creation. Johnson often appropriated the language of the New Deal in selling the poverty program, as when he referred to "our fellow citizens who are ill-clad, ill-fed, ill-housed" in his announcement that Shriver would run the new Office of Economic Opportunity (OEO). A more proximate influence for the War on Poverty was the work that had gone on during the Kennedy administration; the most innovative idea embedded in the program—the community-action principle—was handed down from the President's Committee on Juvenile Delinquency.[9]

The new program also reflected influences from outside Washington, DC. Long before LBJ officially launched the War on Poverty, many of its foot soldiers had been mobilizing in neighborhoods around the country. In Bedford-Stuyvesant, the antipoverty programs implemented in 1964 and 1965 harkened back to the rich exchange of ideas that had unfolded among municipal policymakers and grassroots activists in the previous two decades. The Central Brooklyn Coordinating Council, which had emerged in the late 1950s to run city-funded delinquency programs, was the group called on in 1964 to create Brooklyn's first Community Action Agency under the rubric of the War on Poverty. Given federal support for the empowerment of local communities, it was only natural that CBCC should become the mouthpiece for Bedford-Stuyvesant. Energetic, outspoken organizers like Elsie Richardson and Shirley Chisholm had built up experience in the practice of linking neighborhood groups to policy-

makers, and they had spent years thinking through solutions to the intensifying urban crisis. The poverty warriors who set to work in Bedford-
Stuyvesant in 1964 also included many of the preachers, lawyers, social
workers, and homeowners who had led community activism in previous
years. While they adopted an analysis of poverty in line with that emanating from academics and federal policymakers, they made sure to weave
in concerns that reflected the unique character of their neighborhood.

Rediscovering Poverty

In 1958, economist John Kenneth Galbraith famously declared the United
States "the affluent society." By the time Kennedy took office in 1961, however, the triumph of affluence was beginning to seem a little less decisive.
The economy continued to expand, to be sure, and the steady migration
of middle-class urbanites into suburban dreamlands continued apace. Yet
if the Eisenhower years enshrined the mythology of abundance in the
American psyche, they were also years of relative economic stagnation.
Minor recessions hit in 1953–1954, 1958, and 1960–1961. From 1933 to 1952,
two decades of unprecedented Democratic Party dominance, the American economy had grown at an astounding average annual rate of 6 percent;
during the Eisenhower years, GDP growth averaged only 3 percent. The
unemployment rate, which neared 25 percent during the 1933 nadir of
the Great Depression, reached a postwar low of 2.5 percent in early 1953,
as Harry Truman was vacating the White House, but crept back up to
7 percent by the time Kennedy became president in 1961. Meanwhile, a
dramatic transformation was unfolding in the sectorial makeup of the
economy. Between the end of World War II and 1970, the fraction of Americans working on farms declined from 17 percent to 3 percent; white-collar
jobs, meanwhile, increased from 31 percent of total employment to 47
percent. Increasingly, American workers were providing services instead of
producing goods.[10]
   In 1960s New York, the economy was becoming "more and more biased
against the preservation of a stable and honorable family life for wage
earners," as Daniel Patrick Moynihan, then the assistant secretary of labor,
put it in 1964. Employment in the city's manufacturing sector reached a
high point in 1959, when 963,000 New Yorkers held factory jobs; by 1964,
close to 100,000 of those jobs had disappeared. What blue-collar jobs remained tended to pay less than they once had. Whereas in 1950 hourly

earnings in New York City's manufacturing sector ranked tenth among U.S. cities, by 1960 New York had dropped to thirtieth. A 1959 study found that the average weekly wage among New York's factory workers was $83, compared with $117 in Detroit, $110 in Pittsburgh, and $107 in Cleveland. That same year, Mayor Wagner called attention to "sweatshop conditions" in New York's garment industry and proposed a 25-cent hike in the state and federal minimum wage, to $1.25. The city's minimum wage reached $1.50 by 1964, but 25 percent of New York families and 44 percent of single individuals were making do on incomes below the poverty line.[11]

The city was in a paradoxical position. The local unemployment rate remained low—the mayor announced in August 1964 that it had dipped to 5.1 percent—but job growth in the city owed almost exclusively to the dramatic spike in government spending that had occurred under Wagner's watch. The Bureau of Labor Statistics reported in 1964 that there had been "no net increase whatsoever" in private-sector employment in New York City between 1958 and 1963. The exception that proved the rule was the construction industry, where robust job growth had partly been fueled by government spending on urban renewal and the 1964 World's Fair. As manufacturers moved en masse to suburbs and the Sunbelt, technological innovation further reduced the need for blue-collar laborers. New Yorkers who remained were left to fret that their city was built on shaky economic foundations. "This revolution of automation, like a raging flood, is crumbling all the smaller dikes on its path," Wagner said in 1964.[12]

Nationally, the Kennedy-Johnson years were boom times. GDP growth averaged 5 percent a year between 1961 and 1969, while unemployment dipped below 4 percent in 1966 and stayed there through 1969.[13] Yet the early 1960s also witnessed a new sensitivity to urban poverty among journalists, social scientists, and policy elites. Galbraith's *The Affluent Society* (1958) and Gabriel Kolko's *Wealth and Power in America* (1962), among other works, dramatized the economic inequality that endured in an age of abundance. But no book made a greater impact than Michael Harrington's *The Other America*, a tightly written yet emotional 1962 study of the country's "invisible poor." Harrington, a socialist and freelance journalist, had spent the early 1950s working among homeless alcoholics on the Bowery in Lower Manhattan. In *The Other America*, he recounted his visits to Americans in various other "pockets of poverty"—Appalachian farms, California migrant camps, urban ghettos—as well as those individuals whom prosperity had forgotten, including most notably the aged.

Harrington offered vivid descriptions of life on the margins, tugging at heartstrings and stirring consciences in a way that recalled Jacob Riis's *How the Other Half Lives*, which had dramatized poverty in the 1890s. The book became a surprise best-seller.[14]

Beyond gripping reportage, Harrington exposed his readers to a new body of social-scientific knowledge. *The Other America* argued that poor people were not merely Americans who lacked money; rather, they lived in what was, for all intents and purposes, a different civilization. This interpretation reflected Harrington's reading of the "culture of poverty" thesis put forth by anthropologist Oscar Lewis. For Lewis, who had carried out much of his research among slum dwellers in Mexico, the poor were ensnared in a multigenerational pattern of unemployment, ignorance, and hopelessness. Though structural factors (discrimination, automation, capitalist exploitation) had helped create the conditions in which poverty emerged, once the poor were poor they became caught in a "vicious circle." Because parents were poor, their children would likely go to failing schools and lack motivation to succeed; even if they did thrive, they would face dim job prospects upon graduation. In turn, *their* children would grow up poor, too. As Harrington put it: "Poverty is a culture in the sense that the mechanism of impoverishment is fundamentally the same in every part of the system. . . . There are people in the affluent society who are poor because they are poor; and who stay poor because they are poor. To realize this is to see that there are some tens of millions of Americans who are beyond the welfare state."[15]

The culture of poverty thesis would later come in for intense criticism, especially after it became embedded in the program design of the War on Poverty. With its emphasis on the self-perpetuating aspects of lower-class lifestyles, Lewis's thesis was easily co-opted into arguments that poor people were to blame for their own poverty and deserved to be disciplined and shamed into changing their behaviors. But that had hardly been the initial thrust. Historian Alice O'Connor writes that for Harrington, Lewis, and their ilk, "the culture of poverty was more than an explanation for persistent disadvantage; it offered a dissent from postwar optimism about the solvent of economic growth, and a dire warning about the consequences of failing to act." Yet as a new body of what O'Connor calls "poverty knowledge" coalesced in the early 1960s, the emphasis on cultural conditions tended to preclude discussions of structural inequalities. Thus, Harrington unwittingly laid the basis for a federal assault on poverty that emphasized individual remediation rather than changes to the political economy.[16]

Harrington's work struck a chord in the White House. On the campaign trail in September 1960, Kennedy had promised that if elected president he would task himself with "wiping out poverty here in the United States." Five months earlier, he had been moved by the grinding rural poverty he encountered while contesting the West Virginia primary; later, his brother would alight in some of the country's most benighted neighborhoods as part of his work with the President's Committee on Juvenile Delinquency. These emotional encounters with misery primed both Kennedys to accept arguments that fighting poverty was both a moral and political imperative. Mounting pressure from the civil-rights movement to address the economic demands of African Americans—half of whom lived below the poverty line in 1960—reinforced the point. But it was *The Other America* that gave the Kennedys a conceptual apparatus with which to make sense of the suffering that had so moved them in the hills of Appalachia and the ghettos of New York City.[17]

Prior to 1962, the Kennedy administration had pursued a battery of programs that took on various manifestations of poverty and unemployment. These included aid to depressed rural areas, manpower training, a higher minimum wage, an early version of food stamps, expanded housing for low-income families, and public-works projects. (Congress rejected other proposals to provide health care for the aged and create a Department of Housing and Urban Development.) And yet, according to James L. Sundquist, the deputy undersecretary of agriculture and a key member of the group that began to explore the issue of poverty in 1963, Kennedy's various programs "were striking only at surface aspects of what seemed to be some kind of bedrock problem, and it was the bedrock problem that had to be identified so that it could be attacked in a concerted, unified, and innovative way." It was *The Other America* that, in Sundquist's recollection, "defined the target for Kennedy and supplied the coordinating concept—the bedrock problem, in a word, was 'poverty.'"[18]

The Kennedy administration's "rediscovery" of poverty marked a turning point in the history of federal efforts to assist the downtrodden. By naming the problem, Harrington raised the possibility that something might be done to solve it. Though a socialist, he deftly appealed to liberal sensibilities—and, in so doing, reintroduced wealth inequality into the national conversation. That was no small feat, given the sclerotic state of the American

left in the wake of McCarthyism. Federal policymakers' newfound interest in poverty paved the way not only for the programs lumped under
the War on Poverty rubric but also a slew of social-welfare initiatives—
Medicaid, Medicare, food stamps, health clinics, and educational reforms, among others—that benefited the poor and the middle class alike
and, taken together, contributed to the halving of poverty rates during
the 1960s.

Of course, government officials were hardly ignorant of poverty's persis-
tence before Kennedy read *The Other America* (or at least Dwight Mac-
Donald's summary of it in *The New Yorker*). In New York, the "invisible
poor" had inspired significant policy innovations throughout the 1950s and
early 1960s. At the height of the Cold War, liberals were sometimes reti-
cent to speak explicitly of poverty, but there were many ways of talking
about economic want and social inequality that didn't involve using the
actual word *poverty*. Housing officials were more likely to invoke blight,
overcrowding, and unsanitary living conditions; architects of gang-outreach
programs spoke of delinquency, family breakdown, unemployment, and
discrimination. In 1950s New York, terms like "slums" and "multi-problem
families" denoted a set of intertwined social and cultural conditions similar to what the word "poverty" evoked in the 1960s. The conditions the
New York City Youth Board had tackled in the early 1950s, which the Central Brooklyn Coordinating Council took up in the late 1950s, and which
the city's Neighborhood Conservation Program attacked in the early 1960s,
together constituted something called "poverty." The Northern civil-rights
movement, too, addressed inequality and deprivation by focusing on the
socioeconomic consequences of racism: mass unemployment, slumlords,
price-gouging merchants, failing schools. In Bedford-Stuyvesant, local
residents hardly needed to rediscover poverty in 1962: they were surrounded
by it. Among social workers and activists like Kenneth Marshall, Walter
Pinkston, Archie Hargraves, and Elsie Richardson—all of them active in
the struggles of the 1950s, all of them antipoverty crusaders during the
1960s—poverty often was left unnamed not because it had been forgotten
but because it was so widespread that it was taken for granted.

What was new in the 1960s was the set of ideas that emerged about
how culture intersected with poverty. Taken literally, the word "poverty"
denotes an economic condition: a lack of wealth, a lack of money. But
poverty was rediscovered not as a matter of economics but as a social, psychological, and ethnic condition. In some ways, the "culture of poverty"

thesis assumed a policy function in 1960s Washington similar to the "root causes" understanding of juvenile delinquency in postwar New York. It acted as the entry wedge for a reform agenda aimed at altering social and political structures.

In December 1962, Kennedy asked the chairman of his Council of Economic Advisors, Walter Heller, to begin gathering facts on poverty and to lay out blueprints for a possible antipoverty program. A devoted Keynesian, Heller was a forceful advocate of tax cuts aimed at stimulating economic growth, but he recognized that growth alone would not be enough to lift the "other Americans" out of their misery. Heller had been receiving advice from Robert Lampman, a former University of Wisconsin professor who had joined the staff of the Council of Economic Advisors under Kennedy. Lampman's work in the late 1950s had focused on the connections between economic growth and the low-income population. He found that poverty rates had declined rapidly since the end of World War II, and he argued that "a more aggressive Government policy could hasten the elimination of poverty and bring about its virtual elimination in one generation."[19]

The influence of the President's Committee on Juvenile Delinquency, and especially of its flagship project, Mobilization for Youth, was widely acknowledged. The PCJD's executive director, David Hackett, argued that the campaign against teen crime had much in common with the incipient campaign against want. Hackett was the first to propose using community action as a key tool in the War on Poverty. Another major point of emphasis of the poverty program would be on preventing people's "entry into poverty." This implied extra efforts at reaching young people and enhancing their ability to access "opportunity structures." The government would also strive to accelerate the exit of older individuals from poverty and to alleviate hardships endured by those unable to escape poverty—but the primary focus would be on youth.[20]

Only days before his death, Kennedy met with Heller and made it clear that he would throw his weight behind a poverty program of some sort within the coming year. Small groups of administration officials had met repeatedly for brainstorming sessions about the poverty program since the spring of 1963, but the outlines of the initiative remained blurry. Most insiders agreed that youth programs and community action would be the central components of the coming "attack on poverty and ignorance," to use Heller's words. On November 23, less than forty-eight hours into his presidency, Johnson met with Heller and told him to press on with the effort. "That's my kind of program," LBJ said, to Heller's surprise. "Go ahead. Give it the highest priority. Push ahead full tilt."[21]

"It Must Be Won in the Field"

The architects of the federal War on Poverty envisioned it as a series of local skirmishes. "Poverty is a national problem, requiring improved national organization and support," Johnson said in his first State of the Union address. "But this attack, to be effective, must also be organized at the State and the local level and must be supported and directed by State and local efforts. For the war against poverty will not be won here in Washington. It must be won in the field, in every private home, in every public office, from the courthouse to the White House." Johnson had come of age during the New Deal as the Texas coordinator of the National Youth Administration. He understood as much as anyone the possible benefits of local initiative and creative federalism; he also recognized the potential for parochialism and local obstructionism.[22]

Contrary to Johnson's pronouncement, many key battles in the War on Poverty were in fact won in Washington. Some national policies designed to reduce inequality and reinforce the social safety net required little local planning. Food Stamps, Medicare, tax cuts—these were conceived and debated by federal policy elites and would turn out to be effective antipoverty measures. But the coming attack on poverty, Heller told Johnson on December 20, 1963, would also take aim "at specific local areas of poverty" while combining federal funding and supervision with "well-organized local initiative, action, and self-help." The most immediately visible and controversial aspect of the War on Poverty was the Community Action Program, which took as its mission the empowerment of poor people and the transformation of their neighborhoods. Through community action, poor people and their representatives would exercise "maximum feasible participation" in the planning and implementation of local antipoverty programs. Like the New York City delinquency experiments of the 1950s and early 1960s, many Community Action Agencies initially focused on youth programs, seeking to tackle the "barriers to opportunity" embedded in local landscapes.[23]

No place in the country was quicker to mobilize than New York City, which had been readying itself for the War on Poverty for almost two decades. Since the postwar years, governing elites and neighborhood activists alike had stressed the connections between youth crime, racism, and unemployment, arguing that delinquency ought to be addressed with community-based policy innovations and not merely stepped-up law enforcement. Mayor Wagner himself had been declaring war on various manifestations of poverty throughout his three terms in office. In 1957, Wagner had promised an "intensive fight" on juvenile delinquency in poor neighborhoods; in 1958, he had unveiled a "massive new attack on slums"; and in 1961, he had declared "all-out war on the forces of crime, slum blight, and poverty" on Manhattan's West Side. A 1963 study of child services commissioned by the mayor had called for a "war against poverty and discrimination." Amid this flurry of martial rhetoric, the leader of the city's Liberal Party, Alex Rose, facetiously nicknamed the mayor "Fighting Bob."[24]

In the weeks following Kennedy's killing, as word of the planned federal antipoverty initiative spread, Wagner prepared to launch a poverty program of his own. A hot topic of conversation among the mayor and his aides was unemployment. In July 1963, Wagner had inaugurated his Council on Expanded Economic Opportunity and Training. Among other things, the seven-member body oversaw Job Orientation in Neighborhoods (JOIN), a $3 million job-training program for youth financed jointly with the federal Department of Labor. JOIN offered guidance, basic-skills training, and on-the-job training. According to official estimates, the program had placed only 6,000 people in jobs by the end of 1965—a small number in view of the rapid loss of industrial jobs in the city at the time. But the initiative foreshadowed the War on Poverty in that it attempted at once to train young people for employment in the emerging sectors of the urban economy, and to do so in a way that was sensitive to local needs.[25]

Increasingly, Wagner warned about the need to reach out to unemployed New Yorkers—especially young African American and Puerto Rican men, who experienced the highest jobless rates. In 1963, after years of inaction, Wagner pledged to take on segregated construction unions, and he asked the private sector to help workers develop the skills they needed to flourish in a changing economy. One idea floating around in late 1963 was to stage a public-works program with a focus on training young people for jobs in the new, service-oriented economy. But it was unclear how any city government, even one as large as New York's, might find the resources for such an initiative. Perhaps the new federal poverty program would help.[26]

Another reason for Wagner to be enthusiastic about the War on Poverty was that it promised to move people off welfare and into jobs. By 1964, New York was experiencing a "startling" rate of increase in its welfare expenditures. As of 1964, the number of welfare cases in the city was reported to be growing by 5,000 per month; Wagner announced that fall that the city could no longer afford to foot the bill for welfare payments. The city was in a bind: New York in the early 1960s was rapidly losing blue-collar jobs at the same time that the dropout rate was rising and large numbers of unskilled workers were settling in the city. Under Wagner, the city government itself filled a good part of the employment gap. The city budget rose 70 percent to $3.4 billion during Wagner's second and third terms; by 1965, some 382,000 people—more than lived in the entire state of Wyoming— were working in civilian government jobs in New York City, and 250,000 of them received their paychecks from the municipal government. Such government growth exposed Wagner to intensifying pressure from business and real-estate interests to lower taxes and cut back on social-welfare programs. The 1963–1964 city budget was the first to feature the kinds of accounting tricks that would come home to roost during the fiscal crisis of the 1970s. To avoid having to provide "perpetual dole," the mayor urged his charges to come up with creative solutions to the new configurations of poverty and unemployment in the city.[27]

As planning for the War on Poverty unfolded behind closed doors in Washington, Wagner supporters were floating trial balloons regarding the mayor's own future. Almost immediately after Kennedy's death, speculation arose that Wagner might run as LBJ's vice-presidential nominee in 1964. No matter that "Fighting Bob," once game to defend the common man and overhaul city government, seemed increasingly detached as crisis after crisis buffeted his city. Political wisdom at the time held that the next VP should be a Northern liberal, preferably a big-city Catholic. Front-runners included Peace Corps director Sargent Shriver, Governor Pat Brown of California, Senators Eugene McCarthy and Hubert Humphrey, and of course the slain president's younger brother. Wagner, who had been mulling a run for Senate in 1964, also fit the bill. The rumors intensified when Johnson invited Wagner to sit in the presidential gallery for his November 27, 1963, address—known as the "Let Us Continue" speech—before a joint session of the Congress. On December 20, Wagner traveled to Washington for a one-on-one meeting with LBJ, and the Wagner-as-VP story became front-page news.[28]

New Yorkers, tiring of their three-term mayor, responded by flooding the White House with hundreds of anti-Wagner letters during the weeks following the Kennedy assassination and again in the summer of 1964, when rumors again bubbled up that Wagner might be the Democrats' VP candidate. The letters expressing the most outrage came from Democrats who now threatened to bolt the party. "Wagner's name on the ticket will mean the loss of my vote and of my many democratic friends," wrote one school librarian. "But Wagner's name on the ticket will delight my Republican friends."[29]

Still, the mayor's accomplishments translated easily onto the national stage at a moment of liberal ascendancy. He had served three terms at the helm of the nation's largest city. Under his watch, City Hall had dramatically improved its relations with municipal employees and begun collective bargaining with unions. New York had added unprecedented numbers of public-housing units and schools, and the City University system had been consolidated. Wagner had brought about the city's first rezoning in almost a half-century and passed a new city charter. Yes, the budget had exploded under his watch, with spending doubling from $194 per capita annually to $396; yes, Wagner had often procrastinated when faced with difficult decisions; and yes, increasing numbers of New Yorkers worried that the city was on the verge of a period of devastating decline. But as the *Times* put it soon after the assassination, "Mayor Wagner has an impossible job—one that would strain the capacities of a superman. The Mayor is no superman, but in his slow, tenacious way he has done much to improve New York City's government." To top it off, the Wagner family name occupied a position of almost unrivaled prominence in the liberal pantheon.[30]

Wagner disclaimed such talk, publicly scolding surrogates who campaigned on his behalf during what was meant to be a national period of mourning. (Only eighteen months later, Wagner announced his retirement from politics, emotionally exhausted from raising two sons while caring for a wife dying of lung cancer.) What, then, had Wagner discussed with Johnson during the December 20 parley at the White House? "We need to tackle this whole question of poverty," was how Wagner summed it up. During the same visit, Wagner and his aides met with Labor Secretary Willard Wirtz and his assistant, Daniel Patrick Moynihan, to talk about the incipient poverty program and job-retraining initiatives. On January 7, 1964, a day before Johnson made his official declaration of war,

Wagner garnered front-page headlines by announcing that the city was preparing to tackle poverty "in its many local manifestations" and that he hoped the New York programs might "be helpful in providing a pattern for the federal government." The same day, the city's Labor Department announced that it would be holding a major conference under the banner of "Hope vs. Poverty."[31]

On January 16, a week after Johnson's official declaration of war, the mayor laid out his own vision of the emerging antipoverty drive in an uncommonly long and moving address to the City Council. The speech, titled "Poverty and Unemployment," was notable for its endorsement of the "culture of poverty" thesis. "The fact is," Wagner declared, "that a portion of our population which lives within sight and sound of the rest of us, actually inhabits almost a different world—a submerged world of utter, abject, grinding, hopeless poverty. The New Yorkers to whom I refer are not only poor; they are impoverished. They are stricken, paralyzed and disorganized by poverty. Many of them are at the same time disfigured by the permanent scars of racial discrimination, oppression, and degradation."[32]

People born into such deprivation, Wagner warned, were "social dynamite" waiting to erupt. The situation was particularly "corrosive and explosive" because of the extreme contrasts between wealth and poverty on display throughout the city. And those contrasts, Wagner insisted, took on added poignancy "when mixed with the experience of racial discrimination and the current eruption of revolution against it." So how did the mayor hope to defuse the situation? Most of his ideas echoed the kinds of initiatives his father supported during the New Deal: public-works programs to employ the jobless, increased and improved public-housing construction, increasing the minimum wage (a longtime Wagner cause), and youth camps for dropouts. Vocational training, too, figured prominently; Wagner offered up the JOIN initiative, then being launched in Bedford-Stuyvesant, as an example of the type of youth-employment program that might help in the antipoverty campaign. Conspicuously missing from the address was a plug for community action, which would soon emerge as the centerpiece of the federal poverty program. But federal efforts to promote citizen participation in planning echoed past efforts by various city agencies—the Youth Board, the Neighborhood Conservation program, Community Planning Boards—to open policy dialogues with grassroots groups.[33]

As the federal government mapped out its assault on poverty, Wagner took to trumpeting the amount of money his city was spending to address "conditions approximating poverty." Annual outlays lumped into this category totaled more than $725 million. It was a gargantuan tab for any municipal government—if also a slightly misleading way of tallying up the figures. Of that money, some $305 million was dispensed in welfare checks and $260 million went toward hospital care for citizens lacking health insurance. Another $102 million was spent on youth programs, including Mobilization for Youth, which by 1964 was receiving almost $5 million from the city.[34]

Wagner's early endorsement of the president's program promised to put New York at the vanguard of the Great Society. "He was the mayor who was most willing to try the Great Society programs," the chief advisor to Lyndon Johnson on domestic affairs, Joseph Califano, would recall decades later. "Part of what he did was empower minorities." Wagner had a long record of promoting African Americans in city government, supporting anti-discrimination laws, and partnering with community organizations, though his alliance with the city's leading black activists would deteriorate during his final two years in office. The new campaign against want—which the *Amsterdam News* went so far as to call the "Johnson-Wagner War on Poverty"—was meant, in part, to reestablish Wagner's support of neighborhood groups in minority neighborhoods. Yet the mayor's characterization of poor New Yorkers—and especially racial minorities—as "stricken," "paralyzed," "disorganized," and "disfigured" would have lasting, unintended consequences.[35]

Opening Shots

It soon became clear that the bulk of Wagner's antipoverty initiatives would target New York's predominantly African American and Hispanic neighborhoods. At the time the War on Poverty was declared, unemployment rates for black workers were half again as high as for whites; for Puerto Ricans, they were twice the rate for whites. Minorities made up 19.5 percent of all New York City families but accounted for 37 percent of all families making less than the federal poverty threshold of $3,000 per year. The portrait of minority poverty was even grimmer when one took into account that black and especially Puerto Rican households were larger and younger, on average, than were white ones. It meant one thing to live on $3,000 a year as a retired couple but quite another when there were four children to feed and clothe. With thousands of low-skill manufacturing jobs, especially in the garment and food-processing industries, fleeing the city every year, the situation threatened to worsen. For African Americans, whose mobility was seriously hampered by the geography of racism, it was much harder to follow the jobs out of town, as their white working-class neighbors were increasingly choosing to do. Nor was education a foolproof solution: while 29 percent of white college graduates earned $10,000 or more per year, this was true for only 7 percent of nonwhite college graduates.[36]

On the other hand, optimists could point to growing evidence that many African Americans in New York were moving out of poverty and into middle-class lifestyles. For instance, more than 60 percent of employed black women in 1940 were domestic workers, but that was true of just 20 percent in 1960. With the city undergoing its metamorphosis from a predominantly industrial economy to one anchored by finance, insurance, and real estate, the share of female black professionals in the city doubled; the percentage of clerical workers rose from 2.4 percent to 18.9 percent. Similar increases were observed among black men, among whom the share of low-wage factory workers was decreasing. Further, poverty rates among African Americans in New York were significantly lower than elsewhere in the country. Census figures from 1960 revealed that half of all African Americans were poor; by comparison, 27 percent of black families in New York counted as impoverished.[37]

Few places in the city were better acquainted with the phenomenon of grinding poverty coexisting side by side with rising expectations than Bedford-Stuyvesant. Though Harlem was the most famous "ghetto" in America, Bed-Stuy had by the early 1960s become home to more black people. Harlem, wrote Harrington in *The Other America*, "is not the most depressed" black community in New York. "That honor belongs to Bedford-Stuyvesant." Segregated classrooms left the average Bedford-Stuyvesant eighth grader more than two years behind the city average in reading; in 1963–1964, only 1 percent of seniors at the local high schools graduated with averages high enough to qualify them for city colleges. (Many upwardly mobile families sent their children to private schools or to selective public high schools outside Bedford-Stuyvesant.) Meanwhile, studies found that 30 percent of all houses in Bedford-Stuyvesant could be described either as "dilapidated" or "deteriorating." Despite catastrophic infant-mortality rates, local mothers received less prenatal instruction and care than in any other area of the city. Rates of venereal disease were four times higher than for the city as a whole. According to the 1960 census, Bedford-Stuyvesant families earned a median income of $4,487—26 percent lower than the citywide figure and only 150 percent of the federal poverty threshold. One study estimated that given the high costs of living in New York City, a family of three would qualify as "poverty stricken" if it took in less than $4,390. If such calculations were true, then close to half of all Bed-Stuy families must count as poor. On the other hand, a study conducted at mid-decade estimated that 10 percent of local families earned $10,000 or more each year.[38]

Bedford-Stuyvesant continued to house a substantial population of professionals, but deindustrialization made unemployment a worsening problem. In 1965, it was estimated that joblessness in Bed-Stuy had reached 8.3 percent, including 11.6 percent for men—at a time when the national figure was fluctuating between 4 percent and 5 percent. Further, according to one study, "most jobs Bedford-Stuyvesant residents hold lack stability or job security." The Navy Yard, which two decades earlier had made Brooklyn a magnet for thousands of black job seekers, locked its gates in 1966. The high price of consumer goods in Bedford-Stuyvesant further exacerbated its residents' economic troubles. Better-quality clothing cost less in downtown Brooklyn than in Bedford-Stuyvesant, and food retailers in Bed-Stuy charged significantly more for staple products. Black Brooklynites blamed racism for these discrepancies: a 1966 study found that whites owned 70 percent of the businesses on Fulton Street, Bedford-Stuyvesant's main shopping thoroughfare, along with 78 percent of all large businesses in the area. Meanwhile, despite the efforts of neighborhood activists, youth crime in Bed-Stuy had increased 150 percent in the decade ending in 1962, leaving the neighborhood with a juvenile-delinquency rate twice as high as that for the city as a whole. A 1965 opinion survey conducted in the relatively affluent enclave of Stuyvesant Heights found juvenile delinquency to be the most commonly invoked problem in the area. People of all classes feared that their community was breaking down.[39]

It made sense, then, for the opening shots in New York's new War on Poverty to be fired in Bedford-Stuyvesant. On January 16, 1964, immediately after delivering his poverty speech to the City Council, Mayor Wagner announced that he was asking the Central Brooklyn Coordinating Council to carry out a major study of youth problems in Brooklyn, with an eye toward launching a "comprehensive youth demonstration program" later in the year. CBCC received an initial grant of $39,500, administered through JOIN, but the group could look forward to greater funding if it put together an ambitious action plan.[40]

By 1964, CBCC inhabited a unique political space. The consortium had expanded to include more than fifty civil-rights organizations, churches, social clubs, block associations, and fraternal orders. Though CBCC continued to serve as a conduit for new government programs in Bedford-Stuyvesant, its organizers had grown increasingly frustrated with funding delays on a number of fronts. The group brought together vocal, forward-thinking activists like Elsie Richardson; budding politicians like Shirley Chisholm; and respected professionals, including physician Cecil Gloster. In early 1964, the group hired a new executive director, the Trinidadian-born Donald Benjamin, whose knack for conciliation and skills as a grassroots organizer paved the way for further expansion of CBCC's membership; by 1966, over one hundred organizations would be loosely affiliated under the council's tent. The group's leaders had picketed Jim Crow in Brooklyn and beyond; many had mounted the barricades to support the Unity Democratic Club's insurgency against the Kings County machine. Meanwhile, they had developed an analysis of their community's socioeconomic landscape that drew attention to the linkages among poverty, unemployment, failing schools, poor housing, and discrimination. But the issue of youth crime remained the surest route toward persuading policymakers to put up substantial funding.[41]

CBCC's Youth Services Committee had obtained a $26,000 grant from the Youth Board in November 1963 in order to hire a full-time executive secretary, research consultants, and office staff. Darwin Bolden, a lawyer who had set up the city's Area Services program in Bed-Stuy, came on to direct the project. The January grant, Bolden said, "was the consummation of efforts undertaken by the CBCC beginning in 1960 to develop a program for youth services in this area." With the wind in its sails, CBCC prepared to engage in the type of theoretical work and planning that had characterized Mobilization for Youth's efforts on the Lower East Side. Rather than oversee that work directly, the council spun off a new community-based organization called Bedford-Stuyvesant Youth in Action (YIA) under Bolden's direction. Upon the announcement of CBCC's new initiative, the executive director of the Youth Board, Arthur Rogers, commented that it was "just another indication that the Youth Board has recognized the stability and the potentials of the Council's leadership, and we know that through such leadership the 'little man' will find a medium of expression."[42]

YIA would soon grow into a multi-faceted community agency, drawing millions of dollars each year to implement a slew of War on Poverty initiatives in Bedford-Stuyvesant. In 1964, however, its leadership was drawn almost exclusively from CBCC's network of local activists. These men and women were generally well-educated, politically connected, professionally successful, and most often owners of their own homes. Few were wealthy, but by the standards of 1960s Bedford-Stuyvesant, they qualified as an elite. In 1964, all twenty seats on the Youth in Action board of directors were filled by college graduates, and three-quarters held advanced degrees. By contrast, only 5.4 percent of the Bedford-Stuyvesant adult population had attended college, and 0.3 percent had done graduate work.[43]

William Chisholm, a lawyer who had formerly chaired CBCC's Youth Services Committee, became the chair of YIA's board. He was joined by another lawyer, Garvey Clarke, and a judge, Franklin Morton. Ministers H. Carl McCall and William Jones also assumed leadership positions in the new organization, and several other preachers, including Milton Galamison, soon joined the board. Two physicians, Cecil Gloster and Robert Palmer, both past chairmen of CBCC, also joined. Other Youth in Action directors included John Procope, the real-estate and insurance broker who had chaired CBCC's Housing and Urban Renewal Committee and would later become publisher of the *Amsterdam News*; Russell Service, the head of the Bedford branch of the YMCA; Sydney Moshette Jr., a young probation officer and the son of a prominent Fulton Avenue real-estate broker; and Johnny Parham Jr., a twenty-seven-year-old who had led lunch-counter sit-ins in his native Atlanta before moving north to head up Brooklyn's chapter of the Urban League. Women, many of them leading CBCC organizers, also got involved; the most prominent were the indefatigable Elsie Richardson, social worker Anne W. Pinkston, and an IBM employee named Louise Glover. All but one of the original directors was black. (The sole white board member was Sylvia Shapiro, a schoolteacher, though a white sociologist, Don Watkins, also joined the YIA board later in 1964; both would stay in their posts through the early 1970s, long after most of

Youth in Action's founders had moved on.) Puerto Ricans, despite making up a growing segment of Bed-Stuy's population, took no seats on the board, though they would figure more prominently in later years. In short order, a slew of elected officials would also join the board, including State Assemblywoman and former CBCC spokesperson Shirley Chisholm; William Thompson, a judge who later gained election to the State Senate; Albert Vann, a teacher and future New York State assemblyman; and Thomas Fortune, a future district leader and state assemblyman.[44]

This accumulation of social and political prestige on the new agency's board was significant for several reasons. Youth in Action, like CBCC, would spend much of its early years rallying political support as it waged repeated battles for funds that always seemed meager and slow to arrive. One of its main goals was to organize Bedford-Stuyvesant and build political power among a largely disempowered constituency. This mission dovetailed with the ongoing efforts of reformers like Shirley Chisholm and Thomas Jones to build a durable, black-led reform coalition within the Democratic Party. Further, the presence on YIA's board of civil-rights leaders like Galamison and William Jones lent star power and organizing clout to the group's efforts. These ministers yoked the energy and hope associated with the freedom struggle to the new fight against poverty. Their role was all the more relevant at a time when national protest leaders were becoming increasingly vocal about the interrelationship of poverty, racism, and political disempowerment. As the Harlem-based activist Bayard Rustin put it in 1965, "the very decade which has witnessed the decline of legal Jim Crow has also seen the rise of *de facto* segregation in our most fundamental socio-economic institutions. At issue, after all, is not *civil rights*, strictly speaking, but social and economic conditions."[45]

That said, there was something dissonant about putting a self-selected group of doctors, lawyers, preachers, and teachers in charge of poverty policy. These men and women had organized tirelessly on behalf of black Brooklynites of all classes, and they were well positioned to speak for the community during negotiations with the power structure. But none belonged to the area's low-income majority. Where were the custodians, the cashiers, the shelf stockers, the laid-off seamstresses? Where were the single mothers on welfare? As Youth in Action became the foremost War on Poverty agency in Brooklyn, more and more voices in Bedford-Stuyvesant began to demand that poor people have their say.

Dark Ghetto or Competent Community?

Youth in Action's first step was not action but study. Having hired a group of social scientists as research consultants, the agency embarked on an exhaustive survey and demographic study of Bedford-Stuyvesant. Led by executive director Darwin Bolden, YIA planners consulted extensively with staffers from Mobilization for Youth and Harlem Youth Opportunities. Just as importantly, they read what the intellectual architects of those programs, Richard Cloward and Kenneth Clark, had written, and attempted to apply their insights to Brooklyn. Youth in Action's program was to be rooted in theory: the new agency would attempt to chart, in painstaking fashion, the relationship between youth crime and poverty.[46]

For that reason, the founding of YIA was not unanimously welcomed in Bed-Stuy. The new funding stream represented a triumph for CBCC, to be sure, but the announcement that YIA's first move would be a study was met with "fireworks, disagreements, misunderstandings, and outright withdrawal from participation and cooperation of many of our leaders, political and civic," in the words of CBCC's Almira Coursey. Why such skepticism? None wanted another study of Bedford-Stuyvesant. "We've been studied, studied, and nothing has been done for us," was how Coursey summed up local feeling.[47]

Events soon changed the equation. On July 16, 1964, a white police lieutenant in Harlem shot and killed a fifteen-year-old African American, James Powell. The officer, Thomas Gilligan, claimed to have acted in self-defense after Powell had attacked him with a knife. Harlemites didn't buy it. That night, the Congress of Racial Equality led a march on Harlem's 26th Precinct house, where demonstrators met a wall of policemen in riot gear. Some marchers hurled bricks and bottles at the cops, who responded by firing shots in the air and beating whoever came too close. What ensued was a weeklong outpouring of rage and grief that spilled over the East River into Brooklyn and then migrated upstate all the way to Rochester. Marauding gangs smashed store windows, took whatever they could grab inside, and torched the rest. By the time tempers cooled, the police had made more than 450 arrests. Hundreds of stores sat smoldering; more than a hundred people were injured. The mayor, vacationing on the Spanish island of Majorca, was sufficiently alarmed that he cut short his holiday and flew home. He landed at Kennedy Airport looking tanned and "grim-faced," in the *Times*'s assessment. City Council President Paul Screvane, who filled in as acting mayor while Wagner was gone, blamed the violence on "fringe groups, including the Communist Party." But the response to Powell's killing was no nihilistic outpouring: it expressed a widespread feeling of anger and injustice among the city's African Americans. Amid the violence, CORE, led by James Farmer, had organized large demonstrations demanding that the city act against police brutality, hire more black police officers to work in Harlem and Bed-Stuy, and form a civilian complaint review board to oversee the NYPD.[48]

The uprising kicked New York's War on Poverty into high gear. On July 29, two weeks after the killing of James Powell, Wagner announced that the city would be creating between 18,000 and 20,000 new jobs within government agencies, most of them for unemployed sixteen- to twenty-one-year-olds with few skills. Each new worker would receive training, either through the soon to be launched federal Job Corps or through some more traditional form of workplace apprenticeship. Wagner's personnel director, Theodore Lang, instructed the 100-odd department heads and deputies assembled at City Hall to "roll up your sleeves and get to work." For the moment, such talk represented little more than a lofty aspiration. But it gave skittish city officials a talking point when asked what they were doing to avert further unrest. "This program must succeed," said Welfare Commissioner James R. Dumpson, an African American who had been a detached worker among Harlem gangs in the late 1940s, "or we can look forward to something more awful and more terrible than anything we have seen so far."[49]

Critics of the War on Poverty in years to come would tar it as a "riot-insurance program." Johnson, in an election year, felt compelled to rebrand the War on Poverty as "a war against crime and a war against disorder," as he put it on October 16, the same day he swore in Shriver as head of OEO. The riots of July 1964 were also on the minds of the people crafting Brooklyn's new poverty program. Youth in Action's leaders believed that what they'd witnessed on the streets of Bedford-Stuyvesant was a direct response by underprivileged youths to poverty and discrimination. Once again, they urged government officials to act on their promises to end poverty and discrimination. On July 26, Wagner approved a second municipal contract with Youth in Action, this one for $223,000. Notably, the federal government was not yet on the scene; though Youth in Action would later draw federal funds as Bed-Stuy's official Community Action Agency, enabling legislation for the War on Poverty didn't clear Congress until later that summer. Anticipating Johnson's shift in emphasis that fall, Wagner explicitly tasked YIA both with fighting poverty and with pre-empting unrest. "Not only must we ensure law and order in all sections of our city," he said in announcing the grant, "but we must take effective and comprehensive action to relieve the basic causes of poverty, unemployment, and other ills which trigger violence and lawlessness." Screvane added, ominously, that the city would be "heading for very, very, serious trouble" unless it addressed the root causes of poverty. The need for social control justified new social policy.[50]

Youth in Action immediately switched gears. For the first six months of the agency's existence, its skeletal staff had been compiling data on delinquency in Bedford-Stuyvesant, hoping to get a few targeted programs up and running later in the year. Now, Youth in Action would be on the front lines of the nationwide crusade to address poverty, unemployment, and urban violence. The new grant destined for the group's coffers testified to the success of CBCC in convincing the city government to act in Bedford-Stuyvesant. But it also reflected the sense of urgency in the air that summer.

Youth in Action's program proposal, submitted to the city in August, grappled with the usual "problem symptoms" of juvenile delinquency: alcoholism and drug addiction, unemployment, and a high dropout rate. But it drew particular attention to the violence being perpetrated by and against Brooklyn's black youth. On April 21, 1964, for instance, several black teenagers, while returning from the funeral of a slain classmate, had tussled with Jewish schoolchildren at the United Lubavitcher Yeshiva. On Memorial Day weekend, several violent clashes had exploded on Brooklyn subways, resulting in a tense confrontation between the police and a group of black youths. African American boys who commuted to Park Slope's John Jay High School, one of a shrinking number of integrated schools in Brooklyn, had endured a series of beatings at the hands of Italian American teen gangs. The July uprising followed hard on the heels of these incidents.[51]

Youth in Action's architects argued that the rioting testified both to the effects of poverty and to the "cult of color" permeating American society. According to the program proposal put together by Bolden and his staff, racism had caused young African Americans to develop "a sense of impotence and inferiority which tends to destroy aspirations and develops a feeling of being locked in a prison from which escape is rare." The children of Bedford-Stuyvesant grew up in a "televised arena of open violence and conflict between black and white Americans"; their parents, meanwhile, struggled to make ends meet while facing discrimination by unions and employers. According to YIA's board chairman, William Chisholm, the only way to preclude further uprisings was for local communities and governments alike to work toward "alleviating the smoldering feeling of powerlessness." YIA would seek to uplift the youth of Bedford-Stuyvesant by boosting their self-esteem, involving them in community action, finding them summer jobs, and teaching history. "Negroes and Puerto Ricans *do* have a past, which not only includes slavery but, also, a rich reservoir of heroes, culture, and artistic achievement," the YIA proposal stated.[52]

Youth in Action's planners also took pains to emphasize that while Bedford-Stuyvesant was "a community in crisis," it was far more than a "slum-ridden, tension-torn, gang-infested, black ghetto." They took particular exception to press portrayals of Bed-Stuy as "just another Harlem, but a little bit worse." While careful to lay out in detail the many indicators of social strife and poverty in the area, they also stressed the community's diversity and resourcefulness. As YIA's initial proposal pointed out, large swathes of the neighborhood featured "many fine tree-lined streets with solid, substantial middle-income brownstone buildings, a large residential leadership group, many institutions with great strength and wealth, some private schools catering to the children of middle income Negro families." Though Bed-Stuy was suffering from a slew of problems that were weakening the community from within *and* without, YIA posited that those problems were "not necessarily insoluble." All told, Bed-Stuy had reached "a crossroads between physical rehabilitation, social renewal, and resurgence of a vital, positive community life—or an acceleration of the process of deterioration, stagnation, waste, helplessness and hopelessness."[53]

To carry out the research program mandated by the new grant, YIA hired a City College sociology professor, Joseph Bensman. Wisconsin-born, Bensman applied a heavily theoretical perspective to his investigation of Bedford-Stuyvesant. A major influence was his colleague at City College, Kenneth Clark, who had founded HARYOU in 1962. Clark had famously testified about the psychological effects of racism in the *Brown v. Board of Education* case, and he had spent years working with his wife, Mamie, at the Northside Center in Harlem, which provided mental-health services. Clark's study of delinquency in Harlem resulted in a landmark 1964 document titled "Youth in the Ghetto: A Study of the Consequences of

Powerlessness and a Blueprint for Change." (Clark would later revise the study's findings in a scholarly book titled *Dark Ghetto: Dilemmas of Social Power*, and the agency even released a comic-book version aimed at teenagers.) Clark's ideas reflected what Alice O'Connor has termed the "self-consciously behavioral, psychological drift" that informed early theories of community action. Harlem was a "sick" community, Clark argued, and its young people in particular suffered from psychological deficiencies born of racial discrimination, poverty, and family breakup. Penned in, despised, and demoralized, they could not resist the lure of instant gratification. But outside forces weren't insurmountable. Clark believed that Harlemites, though in need of government-financed remediation, could also empower themselves through community action, especially by targeting education and jobs for youth.[54]

According to YIA documents produced under Bensman's watch, the "pathology of the ghetto" that Clark had turned up in Harlem was equally palpable, and equally damaging, in Central Brooklyn. In a Youth in Action planning document dated January 20, 1965, Bensman argued that the root of almost every problem facing Bedford-Stuyvesant youth could be found in "the heritage of slavery, and subsequent segregation, discrimination, and exploitation in a ghetto community." Slavery, Bensman claimed, had destroyed black families, and the subsequent onslaught of segregation and workplace discrimination had conspired to disempower and emasculate black males. Black women, compelled to become breadwinners as well as caregivers, had struggled to devote enough time to their children; it was no surprise, then, that these children had failed to develop what the YIA planning document dubbed the "creative capacity, habits, personality, and motivation" needed to succeed. The youth of Bedford-Stuyvesant, especially males, also lacked self-esteem, role models, and career aspirations. As a result, they dabbled in "forbidden, malicious, negativistic, hedonistic activities" and, following the example of their parents, gave up on pursuing opportunities outside "the framework of the ghetto." All told, YIA posited that the youth of Bedford-Stuyvesant were caught in a "self-defeating vicious cycle." Though racism initially closed off opportunities, these young people responded in ways that closed off even more.[55]

This was the "culture of poverty" analysis taken to its logical conclusion. In its analysis of black poverty's historical roots and condescending tone toward black working-class culture, YIA's analysis foreshadowed the controversial 1965 report penned by the Department of Labor's Daniel Patrick

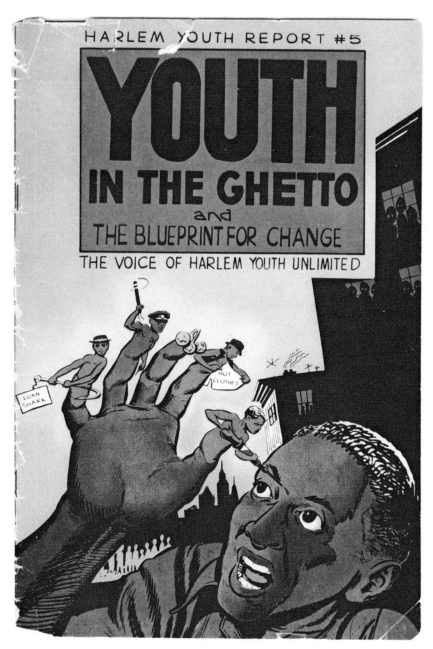

The comic book version of "Youth in the Ghetto," a 620-page report and program proposal issued by Harlem Youth Opportunities Unlimited (HARYOU). The group, led by Dr. Kenneth Clark, was started as an antidelinquency program and later received War on Poverty monies.

Moynihan and titled "The Negro Family: A Case for National Action." While calling attention to the socioeconomic legacies of racism, the YIA report seemed also to pin the blame for youth misbehavior on the deficiencies of black families. Such lines of analysis, in the words of historian Michael Katz, "patronized the poor by reinforcing stereotypes of empty, childlike incompetence." They also laid a shaky theoretical foundation for an agency meant to empower a disempowered community. Youth in Action proposed to lift up "large groups of disabled persons, poverty-stricken, ghettoized, and segregated from the opportunities of the general society." But how could one expect to rally people to community action while at the same time telling them they were incompetent, damaged, and pathological?[56]

One answer lay in the "opportunity theory" of Richard Cloward and Lloyd Ohlin, which had provided the theoretical framework for Mobilization for Youth. CBCC had emerged out of the same set of Youth Board programs as had the Lower East Side experiment, and the Brooklynites drew inspiration from MFY's success at accessing funds from diverse sources. The programs YIA proposed early on reflected the Cloward-Ohlin influence. Remedial education, mental and physical health facilities, leadership training, a neighborhood "Youth Council," even coffee houses—all these were seen as potential "barrier eradicators." By giving young people a stake in running these programs, YIA would help them build self-esteem and broaden their horizons. Similarly, the Brooklyn agency hoped to foster an "effective Negro leadership corps" by training talented youths in leadership techniques, African American history, and community organizing. That new generation of leaders, the agency hoped, would in turn rededicate itself to the removal of "discriminatory bars to employment opportunities." Only then would it become possible, as YIA's chairman, William Chisholm, wrote in 1964, "to arrest the tide of human waste and youth deterioration rampant in this community."[57]

Scholars of the War on Poverty have often presented its theoretical underpinnings as a fatal flaw in the overall design. Michael Katz, for instance, argues that the emphasis on remedying deprivation through new opportunities was incompatible with a supposedly "unconditional" struggle against poverty, since it foreclosed any discussion of wealth redistribution. The poverty planners, according to Katz, "wanted to give everyone a chance to compete, unhindered by the accident of birth, for the sweet rewards of success. No approach to poverty could be more conventional, or

more American." A further criticism of the War on Poverty is that it ignored the political economy of inequality. According to Alice O'Connor,
the Community Action Program treated poverty as "a problem that could
be addressed without recourse to structural measures such as targeted job
creation, without seriously upsetting the political status quo, and without
explicitly mentioning race."[58]

But Youth in Action also demonstrated that it was possible for Community Action Agencies to straddle the fence, to pay lip service to the theoretical language of cultural deficiency while at the same time calling for
practical measures to create jobs and combat segregation. In fact, many
within YIA disagreed with the ideas the agency advanced under Bensman.
According to Don Watkins, the Brooklyn College sociology professor who
sat on YIA's board, policy discussions within YIA committees and at board
meetings tended to focus not on the supposed cultural deficiencies of
Bedford-Stuyvesant but on issues related to jobs and the political economy
of racism. The activists who had toiled for years on picket lines, in political
clubhouses, and at late-night CBCC meetings probably did not believe
that slavery had left them with "a world view such that self-improvement,
acquisition of skills, both manual and symbolic, is deemed senseless," as
one YIA document held. Most community planners were prepared to
endorse the culture of poverty analysis because it replicated the social-
scientific discourse the agency needed to produce in order to justify its
existence to city and federal funding bodies.[59]

Meanwhile, YIA planners were thinking about how they might use their
new agency to attack structural inequities in the urban economy. From the
start, the agency focused much of its energies on the problem of jobs. YIA
proposed to open up employment opportunities for African Americans,
young and old, by fighting workplace discrimination (especially in the construction unions), as well as offering remedial education and job-training
programs. The newly employed, it was assumed, would enjoy newfound
self-esteem and pride and offer examples for others. For all their talk about
ghetto pathologies, Youth in Action planners clearly targeted the political
economy of segregated urban space as a crucial factor in perpetrating poverty. "Provision for economic opportunity is the *sine qua non* of any long-
term program for breaking the vicious cycle," one YIA planning document
declared. Neither self-esteem, motivation, the desire to acquire new skills,
or the ability to defer gratification, according to YIA, could occur without
the "promise and actuality of opportunity." Thus, the agency's first priority

must be to increase the employability of Bed-Stuy's young people by educating them and training them for the new economy while also fighting
racial segmentation in the job market. Later, YIA itself would become a
major employer in the community, providing work experience to hundreds
of young people.[60]

The task of implementing this ambitious agenda fell to YIA's executive
director, Darwin Bolden, who brought relevant experience to the job.
Having previously worked as a field secretary for CORE in Harlem, Bolden
had arrived in Bedford-Stuyvesant in 1963 to head up the Area Services
initiative, launched under the auspices of the city's Neighborhood Conservation Program. In many ways, Bolden's work at the helm of YIA was a
continuation of what he had done with Area Services. By early 1965, he'd
hired a staff that included eight professional researchers, six secretaries,
and five neighborhood workers, including a former Mobilization for Youth
organizer, Carlos Russell. The agency began holding town-hall meetings,
soliciting the participation of local leaders, and setting up a youth advisory
council. Meanwhile, researchers combed the sprawling district street by
street, sounding out the opinions of block associations, church groups,
school administrators, and civic groups ranging from the Wynn Center
Drum & Bugle Corps to the YMCA Luncheon Club.[61]

Youth in Action's final set of program proposals, titled "Planned Intervention to Halt and Reverse the Vicious Cycle," appeared in March 1965.
It theorized a program that would simultaneously attack the "root causes"
and the "symptoms" of delinquency by folding antidelinquency efforts into
a comprehensive antipoverty program. The programs YIA proposed to
launch catered mostly to youth: a remedial education program for young
mothers; a youth leadership-training institute; a 2,800-person chapter of
the Neighborhood Youth Corps, which was meant to provide teens (mostly
male) with paid work experience while encouraging them to stay in school;
a homework-study program for 390 fourth graders; cultural arts education;
and Head Start, an innovative daycare program for low-income children.
Crucially, all these programs would not only provide badly needed social
services but also, in their implementation, open up a slew of new jobs in
the community.[62]

YIA's proposals clearly built on the work CBCC had been doing in
Bedford-Stuyvesant in past years. But the new agency was staking out new
ground. By wrapping its efforts in the theoretical language of the federal
antipoverty effort, YIA put itself in a curious position. Though it didn't in

fact receive federal funds during its first year of existence, YIA nonetheless attempted to imitate the language and techniques of those agencies that did. The premise was that target communities were disorganized, apathetic, damaged, and powerless to change their circumstances. And yet Bedford-Stuyvesant, far from a disorganized, apathetic place, was a highly organized community. (The same was of course true of Harlem and countless other neighborhoods targeted by federal policies.) Its class structure and ethnic diversity put a lie to blanket statements about life in "the ghetto." Many Bedford-Stuyvesant residents were vocal, well-connected activists who had been practicing community action for years. Through CBCC, they had struggled to preserve the character of a neighborhood they saw not as a pathological mess but as a threatened space needing protection.

Accordingly, YIA never failed to point out that Bed-Stuy held within it "great strengths which if constructively utilized can eradicate the community's weaknesses." In effect, the agency proposed a division of labor among Bed-Stuy's different class groups. To begin with, the area's middle class would extend a helping hand to the "upper lower class who are striving to overcome the shackles of poverty and prejudice"; this latter group, in turn, would use YIA as a means of improving its condition and providing positive "ego models" to the very poor. In keeping with its focus on youth, the agency would launch a "cultural development project that will expose the deprived child to middle-class values." Meanwhile, the area's "reservoir of middle-upper class Negroes" would help build an "interdependent relationship" between Bedford-Stuyvesant and the rest of American society. Such "constructive" community action, if it led to the emergence of new, dynamic leaders from among the ranks of the area's low-income groups, would provide the next generation of young people with an example of problem resolution and, it was hoped, shatter their apathy. This, as YIA planners saw it, would eventually help restore to the community "a sense of its own strength . . . that may lead to continuous and persistent attacks on segregation, exploitation and poverty wherever it occurs." In this sense, YIA was pursuing political objectives similar to those of Thomas Jones, Shirley Chisholm, and the Unity Democratic Club. As one planning document put it, the Bedford-Stuyvesant community needed "a decision making role in . . . policies that directly affect this community."[63]

The fledgling antipoverty program, then, did not merely reflect theories being dreamed up and handed down by social scientists and bureaucrats.

"We are not happy with our lot, nor are we contented with the 'culture of the poor' theory held by some sociologists," was how Elsie Richardson put it. In Bed-Stuy, Richardson and others drew from a long tradition of community organizing. They conceived of the new federal struggle as a tool for achieving old goals: attacking segregation, coping with an unequal political economy, mobilizing the political power of African Americans, and, especially, preserving community stability.[64]

Counterattack

On August 20, 1964, the same day Youth in Action submitted its initial program proposal to the Wagner administration, the War on Poverty became law. The Economic Opportunity Act, which passed the House of Representatives on April 8, cleared the Senate on August 11 and met the president's pen nine days later. Some $785 million was appropriated for fiscal year 1965, which had begun on July 1, 1964. At the time, one in five Americans lived in poverty; for all the attention paid to urban poverty, more than half of the country's poor people lived in rural areas. Women headed close to 50 percent of all poor households, and OEO found that some 38 percent of households headed by the aged were living in poverty.[65]

At the outset, Johnson conceived of a War on Poverty that would include educational funding, medical insurance, and urban revitalization. But it soon became clear that when administration officials invoked the "poverty program," they were referring to the various initiatives administered by the Office of Economic Opportunity (OEO), the new agency headed by Sargent Shriver. This rhetorical shift would rob the War on Poverty of precious political capital; Medicare and Medicaid helped bring about dramatic reductions in the official poverty rate, especially among senior citizens, but they scarcely merited mention in conversations about the War on Poverty. The White House insisted that the poverty program was about promoting economic *opportunity*, not redistributing wealth. And given the focus on opportunity, it made sense for most War on Poverty programs to target youth. One popular OEO program was the Job Corps, which was modeled on the Civilian Conservation Corps of the New Deal and offered a two-year program of vocational training and on-the-job experience for young women and (mostly) men, aged sixteen to twenty-one. A related experiment, the Neighborhood Youth Corps, provided summer jobs for high-schoolers and work training for potential college students. Upward

Bound, a work-study program, sent money to institutions of higher learning (some 663 were funded in the first year) to underwrite part-time jobs for students. Head Start, launched in 1965, offered free education for poor preschoolers. Finally, Volunteers in Service to America (VISTA) operated as a domestic Peace Corps, harnessing the idealism of young people. Some OEO initiatives targeted adults. The Work Experience Program, for instance, employed "heads of families" on welfare, and the Adult Basic Education program provided literacy training.[66]

The Community Action Program, meanwhile, was designed to funnel federal funds directly to ad hoc coalitions of social-service agencies, settlement houses, community activists, and poor people. Youth in Action, along with MFY and HARYOU, served as prototypes. Each Community Action Agency, according to a 1964 planning document, would provide "a means whereby a community can look *anew* and *comprehensively* at the problem of poverty. It enables the various local agencies and citizens to plan *together*, and from their pooled experiences and diverse perspectives, to find new and more effective ways to reduce poverty." This was a tall order, and the process of solving problems through community action was by design unpredictable and difficult to control. At the very least, federal planners hoped the new agencies would coordinate fragmented social services and guard against "the assumption that Uncle Sam will now solve their problems."[67]

In New York, Mayor Wagner greeted the federal antipoverty apparatus with skepticism. A frustrated official working in the embryonic OEO wrote in August 1964 that "New York has not begun to plan, has not begun the preliminaries to planning; and there is no sign of a beginning. . . . New York's 'planning' thus far is totally unacceptable to us; and [the] city is far behind others." In fact, New York had for years been waging its own campaign against poverty. If anything, the Wagner administration was guilty of excessive planning and excessive preliminaries to planning—and insufficient implementation. Having preempted the federal poverty program by setting up the shell of New York City's initiative, Wagner expected leeway in determining how to spend OEO monies. As the Economic Opportunity Act wound its way through Congress during the summer of 1964, Wagner's top advisor, Julius Edelstein, repeatedly insisted to federal officials that he saw no need to modify New York's existing programs. "New York has its own poverty program," Edelstein would say. "We spend $800 million a year on it."[68]

It soon became clear to OEO officials that Edelstein and Paul Screvane, the City Council president whom Wagner tabbed to oversee the city's attack on poverty, had no intention of following the directives emanating from Washington. New York City officials were suspicious of Sargent Shriver's new superagency, especially as OEO rolled out the Community Action Program. The community-action model may have been a fresh concept on the national stage, but it had been playing out in a variety of New York City experiments for a decade.

Wagner's wariness was understandable. The mayor presided over an unsteady electoral coalition and a Democratic Party on the verge of implosion. Wagner's break with the machines in 1961 had gained him some goodwill among African Americans, Hispanics, and liberal Jews but had also lost him many working-class whites. Since then, the tone of the black freedom struggle had grown more urgent and the scale of protests had intensified. In February 1964, Milton Galamison and the NAACP led a massive student boycott of the city's public schools to dramatize increasingly segregated classrooms. That summer, CORE threatened to block all access points to the World's Fair as a way of protesting the paucity of jobs made available there for African Americans. Wagner's racial liberalism, though sincere, was limited. As historian Clarence Taylor points out, the mayor felt comfortable sitting down and bargaining with "an established black leadership." But he struggled to respond to grassroots protest movements that accused the city of systemic racism. A champion of organized labor, Wagner was loath to take on the construction unions or otherwise alienate the white working class—though minorities demanded that he do just that so they could gain equal access to schools, jobs, and housing. Increasingly the mayor gave the appearance of acting against discrimination while in fact doing just enough to avert unrest.[69]

Once a champion of community planning in poor neighborhoods, Wagner reacted with alarm as the radical implications of the new federal policies became clear. In setting up the various government agencies related to the poverty war, Wagner had turned to tried-and-true institutions of urban progressivism: labor unions, social workers, settlement houses, and the NAACP. But many of these institutions were in fact changing their outlook in the new era of federally funded urban social work. That was especially true for settlement houses, for which the Community Action Program signaled impending obsolescence. Embedded in the "Johnson-

Wagner War on Poverty" was a new politics fundamentally at odds with Wagner's vision of social change.[70]

Mobilization for Youth, in particular, tested the mayor's commitment to the new politics. Wagner had been the experiment's first patron, but as funds poured in from the Ford Foundation and the federal government, MFY had moved away from its settlement-house roots and taken on a more explicitly political function. In addition to providing social services, small-business grants, and legal aid to the poor, the group had begun organizing Lower East Side residents to launch rent strikes, picket the welfare bureaucracy, and confront City Hall. The agency had also begun to reflect the alienation of its increasingly Puerto Rican constituency, helping to organize direct-action campaigns that linked the Puerto Rican and African American civil-rights struggles. In early 1964, MFY faced Wagner's ire for helping Galamison and Bayard Rustin organize the school boycott, and for collaborating with CORE on direct-action campaigns. In effect, the Lower East Side agency had made the transition from one model of community organizing to another. In the 1950s, it had ostensibly embraced the Clifford Shaw model pioneered in Depression-era Chicago, by which communities organized for the sake of increasing internal cohesion, competence, and social control. By the early 1960s, MFY's style of community organizing echoed that of Saul Alinsky, who sought to empower communities to take on outside power structures in pursuit of greater resources. The Shaw model, Wagner could abide; Alinsky, not so much.[71]

Controversy engulfed MFY during the summer of 1964. The trouble began with the *Daily News*, which lobbed accusations of Communist infiltration against the agency, leading the city to suspend funds and launch an investigation. The tabloid's redbaiting was based on bogus evidence, but that didn't stop city officials from attacking the agency. At the same time, Mobilization's founding director, James McCarthy, found himself accused of shoddy bookkeeping and possibly fraudulent expense accounts. Further accusations followed: that MFY had distributed leaflets supporting Robert F. Kennedy's campaign for the U.S. Senate (partisan activity that was forbidden in government agencies); that Richard Cloward had been improperly paid a full-time salary while remaining on the payroll of Columbia University; and that MFY staffers were organizing riots. No evidence of systematic wrongdoing turned up. But McCarthy and Cloward both quit the project, and MFY was well on its way toward becoming a cautionary tale about the dangers of assailing the system from within.[72]

In Harlem, meanwhile, Kenneth Clark's youth agency had become embroiled in an unwinnable political fight. Congressman Adam Clayton Powell Jr. had insisted that if federal funds were to arrive in his district—as they had been for two years, via the President's Committee on Juvenile Delinquency—he would have control over them. Powell had thrown together an agency named Associated Community Teams and had pushed for a merger with Clark's Harlem Youth Opportunities. Even more distasteful than the ensuing acronym (HARYOU-ACT) was the way in which Powell shunted Clark aside and set about converting the demonstration program into a patronage mill. Wagner, who had often clashed with Powell, tried in vain to beat back the congressman's power play. But the mayor was in a bind: Powell in 1964 was at the height of his influence, and the antipoverty bill then before Congress became law thanks to Powell's labors as chairman of the House Committee on Health, Education, and Welfare.[73]

This confluence of events—intensifying protests, the radicalization of Mobilization for Youth, and the power struggle in Harlem—may have convinced Wagner that he was witnessing the first eruptions of the "social dynamite" he had warned against in January. The city started reining in its fledgling community-action agencies. On July 1, 1964, Screvane announced that Mobilization for Youth, HARYOU-ACT, and Youth in Action required "further study" and would henceforth be funded on a "week to week" basis. Three weeks later, the uprisings in Harlem and Bed-Stuy convinced Wagner to increase Youth in Action's funding tenfold. But a precedent had been set: the mayor would keep a watchful eye over the community agencies and might pull the plug on them at any time.[74]

After Johnson signed the War on Poverty legislation into law in August and OEO began disbursing money around the country, it became all the more clear that Wagner, like Powell, had no intention of letting the federal government fund experiments on his turf unless he could exercise a measure of control over them. Wagner's solution was to have all OEO funds flow through municipal coffers. Most Community Action Agencies around the country incorporated as private nonprofits and received funds directly from OEO. But in New York City, the municipal government itself was the delegated Community Action Agency. All federal monies destined for agencies like Youth in Action first passed through the hands of the city's antipoverty bureaucracy, to be doled out by Screvane. This gave Wagner veto power over where—and when—Community Action Agencies would germinate in the five boroughs.[75]

The city's main policymaking body, the Council Against Poverty, initially targeted sixteen neighborhoods designated as "poverty areas." In thirteen of these areas, so-called Community Progress Centers set up shop with the help of settlement houses, religious charities, civil-rights groups, and other local organizations. Once armed with government monies, these groups would be tasked with holding elections in which local residents could elect board members. In the remaining three areas, the preexisting agencies—Mobilization for Youth, Harlem Youth, and Youth in Action—were to coordinate community action and spend the relevant government monies. As the local agencies got off the ground, representatives from each were to join the Council Against Poverty, thus vaguely satisfying the federal mandate that the War on Poverty unfold with the "maximum feasible participation" of the poor.[76]

The citywide council soon ballooned to seventy members, most of them representatives of the same religious groups, settlement houses, government agencies, and local reform coalitions that had directed juvenile-delinquency policy in earlier years. The poor themselves were slow to take a seat at the table. For instance, in 1965, the representatives of Youth in Action on the Council Against Poverty were three veteran CBCC leaders—Cecil Gloster (a doctor), William Chisholm (a lawyer), and Almira Coursey (a teacher)—as well as Dorothy Orr, a social worker who had recently become YIA's executive director. Further, Wagner set up an agency, the Antipoverty Operations Board (APOB), which controlled city antipoverty funds and dispensed community-action monies by a different mechanism that circumvented the Council Against Poverty. The APOB, which controlled $30 million a year, was made up exclusively of Wagner appointees and tapped into traditional patronage networks. With federal funds being routed through the Council Against Poverty, the APOB allowed the city to continue to finance its own poverty war alongside the federal one.[77]

New York's funding structure was deliberately engineered to put City Hall in control of community action. Having two separate funding streams for the poverty agencies gave Wagner a measure of control that most other mayors were initially unable to exert. According to Bertram Beck, the executive director of Mobilization for Youth after 1964, Wagner's setup, had it been preserved, might have ensured "greater stability, greater productivity, with less excitement and less involvement of poor people." But Wagner's attempts to suppress the radical tendencies of Community Action Agencies ended up undercutting their most basic functions. By forcing

CAAs to report to two different sets of bureaucracies, Wagner made it difficult for those agencies to set organizational goals and plan ahead—especially since city planners often disagreed with federal bureaucrats about what community action should mean. In early 1965, OEO withheld $10 million destined for New York because of Wagner's refusal to abide by the federal "maximum feasible participation" directive.[78]

In Bedford-Stuyvesant, the plodding poverty bureaucracy ground Youth in Action to a halt. Having fostered the agency's creation amid high hopes and apocalyptic fears, the city planted a series of hurdles in the way of its development: overlapping jurisdictions, confusing regulations, and an agonizingly slow and opaque process of releasing funds. New York's War on Poverty was devolving into a skirmish, one pitting activists against bureaucracies.

5

Maximum Feasible Bureaucratization

> Everybody seems to be playing a little football with the money.
> We are saying if anybody is going to be playing football with
> the money, let the poor people spend the money. . . . We are
> probably the greatest experts on poverty. I don't think they
> taught poverty in the educational system, but all of a sudden
> everybody is a professional on poverty.
>
> —TIMOTHY VINCENT, 1966

On March 26, 1965, two weeks after Youth in Action submitted its comprehensive program proposal to city and federal authorities, the Bed-Stuy antipoverty agency hired a new executive director, Dorothy Orr. She was a surprising choice. A longtime resident of Westchester County and a professor of social work at Fordham University, she had no obvious ties to Brooklyn. Prior to being hired by YIA, Orr was probably best known to most Bed-Stuy residents, if they had heard of her at all, for her appearances in the society columns of the *Amsterdam News*. (She'd earned several honorable mentions in the paper's annual "Best Dressed Women in New York" roundup.) Described in the press as "pretty and petite," Orr would prove herself anything but a lightweight in her new job. Behind the sweet smile and neatly coiffed hair was a confident, forthright woman. Some Brooklynites saw her as an arrogant outsider; others welcomed her as an asset.[1]

Orr had begun her career as a caseworker among emotionally disturbed boys in the Westchester County town of Dobbs Ferry, and she brought with her a social-work professional's view of how community action should unfold. "The poor are being trained," she explained in 1965, "so they have an important role in implementing the program instead of it being just a handout." She also promised to infuse YIA with managerial competence;

This 1967 poster produced by Bedford-Stuyvesant Youth in Action encourages locals to "break the chains" of poverty and oppression and "take control of your community" by getting involved with the agency's activities. *Youth in Action Newspaper*

her starting salary of $17,500—the equivalent of $132,000 in 2015—reaffirmed her status as a top talent. An *Amsterdam News* profile opined that Orr "epitomizes simultaneously the essence of feminine gentility and the no-nonsense approach of the efficiency expert." (Later in life, she would cochair the Interracial Council for Business Opportunity and move on to Equitable Life Assurance, where she oversaw corporate social responsibility and affirmative-action programs.) But Orr's fondness for professionalism and order would be put to the test in Bed-Stuy.[2]

Youth in Action was rapidly developing a reputation for chaotic meetings, confused objectives, fiscal uncertainty, and rampant infighting. To an extent, that chaos was unavoidable, even intentional. The War on Poverty was, after all, an effort to organize the unorganized, empower the disempowered, and assail closed "opportunity structures." From its outset in 1964, the federal Community Action Program courted controversy thanks to the clause in the Economic Opportunity Act stipulating that antipoverty efforts must unfold with the "maximum feasible participation" of the poor. That mandate heralded a radical experiment in what Lyndon Johnson called "creative federalism." It also set the White House on a collision course with local governments. In many big cities, the War on Poverty brought about the spectacle of Democratic mayors openly fighting against a Democratic White House they accused of fostering rebellion among their (mostly Democratic) constituents. The unrest intensified as red tape held up the arrival of funds in poor communities like Bedford-Stuyvesant.

The Community Action Program tended to incorporate preexisting organizations, along with their old-guard leadership groups, into a new bureaucratic apparatus. That's what happened in Bed-Stuy. At the same time, the "maximum feasible participation" mandate also exposed elites to pointed challenges from community members who felt excluded from the new poverty-fighting institutions. Orr, for one, suspected that the traditional community leaders represented on YIA's board were not committed to empowering the area's low-income majority. They countered that *all* classes in Bed-Stuy would be uplifted and unified by effective community action. In launching Youth in Action, they pledged to mobilize "all forces of the community"—not only the poor but also "Negroes with middle-class values, ambition, and achievement," as YIA's chairman, William Chisholm, explained. But on whose terms should those forces come together? Orr, an outsider to Bed-Stuy, would soon find herself clashing with some of the neighborhood's most prominent citizens.[3]

163

By the time YIA's programs got up and running, an impatient community, fueled by the rebellious spirit of the mid-1960s, took the antiestablishmentarianism implicit in the federal program and ran with it. Beginning in the fall of 1965, Youth in Action's leaders engaged in a prolonged debate about the meanings of "maximum feasible participation." Protests proliferated; discontent simmered. Under the new administration of Mayor John Lindsay, those protests gave way to a high-minded yet confusing effort to foster grassroots democracy within the city bureaucracy. What remained obscure was what exactly "maximum feasible participation" was supposed to mean—and what it could accomplish. How would the *political* empowerment of the poor lead to their *economic* well-being? Was the point to give poor people decision-making power, or was it to give them jobs within city agencies? YIA, compelled from above to nurture democracy from below, slid deeper into turmoil.

Though political organizing took up a large portion of YIA's energies, the agency did manage to launch several popular programs. The most successful were those that offered constructive responses to an unresolved question at the heart of the War on Poverty: How could young African Americans be integrated into a changing urban economy? Interestingly, for all the talk and theorizing about wayward young men in Bedford-Stuyvesant, the most promising initiatives undertaken by YIA targeted women. Experiments like the Young Mothers Program and the Women's Talent Corps explicitly argued that the way to break the "vicious cycle of poverty" was to foster social mobility among mothers, especially single mothers. Though top-down in their conception, such programs in effect democratized the urban landscape by opening up new ways for black women to pursue their education and gain work.

"Like Pulling Teeth!"

By the spring of 1965, the national War on Poverty seemed to be steaming ahead. On February 17, President Johnson requested $1.5 billion to fund programs authorized by the Economic Opportunity Act in fiscal year 1966; the overwhelmingly Democratic Congress responded by releasing almost $2 billion. This figure doubled the amount appropriated in 1964. Of these funds, $825 million were earmarked for youth programs, $680 million for the Community Action Program, $300 million for work-experience programs, and $70 million for rural-poverty programs. The Office of Economic Opportunity (OEO), tasked with implementing the War on Poverty, planned to fund a Neighborhood Youth Corps 300,000 strong, a Job Corps with 80,000 enrollees, a college work-study program involving 145,000 students, literacy programs for 70,000 adults, and on-the-job training for 250,000 workers. Community Action Agencies were expected to spring up in 700 locations across the country. Optimism ran high in the nation's capital: OEO's director, Sargent Shriver, reckoned that poverty could be eradicated within a decade.[4]

Back in Brooklyn, though, frustrations were mounting. "Maximum feasible participation" had been promised, but what unfolded was maximum feasible bureaucratization. By the time Orr took charge of Youth in Action, in March 1965, the agency had spent more than a year diagnosing and cataloging the problems of its study area. Solutions lagged while paperwork piled up. "The war on poverty in Brooklyn has been anything but a war," Brooklyn Borough President Abe Stark declared on March 10. "It has consisted of sporadic skirmishes, which have made very little progress toward alleviating the effects of deprivation." The city's Council Against Poverty had so far allocated six times more antipoverty money to Manhattan than to Brooklyn, despite the fact that Kings County had twice as many people and a higher incidence of poverty. In response, Stark and several Brooklyn congressmen mounted an effort to bypass the municipal government and solicit Brooklyn's antipoverty funds directly from federal agencies. They struck out.[5]

Worse, it was beginning to look as if New York City would be frozen out of the federal poverty program altogether. Such was the obstructionism of Mayor Robert F. Wagner Jr., by then a lame duck in Gracie Mansion, that OEO temporarily cut off all community-action funds and ordered the city to heed the "maximum feasible participation" directive if it wanted funds released. In June 1965, Wagner joined the U.S. Conference of Mayors, led by Chicago's Richard Daley, in accusing OEO of "fostering class struggle" through its sponsorship of community action. That same month, Wagner announced he was reorganizing the Council Against Poverty to include representatives of the poor, and OEO agreed to release $9.2 million in delayed funds. But it wouldn't be the last time that bureaucratic maneuvering would deprive New York's neighborhood agencies of much-needed antipoverty monies.[6]

In the meantime, Youth in Action faced an agonizing budgetary process. It was a time that "taxed the patience of the community [and] the skill of the YIA staff," according to Orr, and resulted in "the mounting of community tension, particularly among the youth who became discouraged and hostile with the continued delay of funds."[7] The agency, after carrying out a painstaking fourteen-month study of Bedford-Stuyvesant, submitted the final draft of its comprehensive program proposal to the citywide Council Against Poverty on May 7, 1965. The proposal included a request for $5.2 million, but after a month-long review process, the council asked for a revised plan based on a budget half that size. On June 14, YIA submitted the new program proposals, which the council approved. Further foot-dragging ensued; for reasons that remained mysterious, the city put off forwarding the relevant materials to OEO. Once they did receive the proposal, the federal funders, already wary of anything stamped with the Wagner seal, refused to fund a comprehensive program in Bed-Stuy. Instead, OEO released a summer grant of only $440,351, effective July 1—though it took another three weeks for the City Comptroller's Office to get the OEO funds into Orr's hands. Finally, Bedford-Stuyvesant was receiving federal War on Poverty funds.

But those monies expired at the end of the summer, and Orr was forced once again to rely exclusively on city monies. On September 23, Wagner's Antipoverty Operations Board, which maintained a separate War on Poverty apparatus funded exclusively by the city, awarded YIA a $2.5 million grant—approximately the amount first discussed in May. But only $600,000 of that amount was released, and that did not occur until late October. In the interim, YIA depended on emergency bank loans to cover payroll. Meanwhile, YIA submitted a revamped (and wildly optimistic) budget proposal calling for $25 million in expanded programs; at Christmas, the agency was still waiting for a response. On December 29, OEO asked YIA to recompute budgets by January 3, causing a mad scramble and forcing increasingly irritated YIA staffers to cancel New Year's plans. On January 7, 1966, YIA re-signed a contract with the city that approved the release of $1.9 million originally granted the previous September. But, on January 31, YIA's budget was again put on hold, and municipal funds didn't arrive until March 10. A federal grant of $838,759 was finally approved in April, but it wasn't until June 1966, almost two and a half years after Johnson and Wagner had jointly declared unconditional war on poverty, that both the federal and city governments were simultaneously supporting the Bedford-Stuyvesant agency with substantial funds. Shortly thereafter, it came to light that some $10 million of the federal antipoverty allotment to New York City had gone unspent because administrative chaos and bureaucratic delays had rendered action impossible. The Head Start program, which promised to provide free early-childhood education to low-income families, was a particularly poignant example. By the time OEO released $6.5 million in Head Start funds destined for New York, less than $4 million could actually be spent because the city had failed to brief local agencies on health and safety standards required of buildings that housed preschools. In Bed-Stuy, only three of the fifteen Head Start centers that had been in the works passed inspection by June 1966.[8]

"The year was eaten up in review," YIA's fiscal director, Owen Hague, complained in August 1966. "We couldn't spend more than half the money we eventually got. It was impossible to hire, let alone run a program." A handbill from early 1966 was more blunt: "Getting Money for YIA Was Like Pulling Teeth!" In Bed-Stuy, alienation grew among even the most idealistic of reformers. That it had taken two and a half years to begin acting on the grand promises of January 1964 struck them as a cruel joke—especially considering that the Central Brooklyn Coordinating Council had been among the first grassroots organizations in the country to propose ways of implementing the antipoverty campaign.[9]

By 1966, a gust of change had blown into the mayor's office. John Vliet Lindsay presented himself as a compassionate, earnest, sleeves-rolled-up kind of reformer. Promising to infuse a declining city with wit, vigor, youth, and creativity, he brought with him a band of young idealists eager to storm City Hall. "He is fresh and everyone else is tired"—that had been his campaign's motto in 1965. For seven years, Lindsay had represented Manhattan's Upper East Side, the so-called Silk Stocking District, in Congress. While he was not wealthy himself, he seemed the epitome of moneyed ease. Tall, stylish, and handsome, he exuded noblesse oblige. Though a Republican, Lindsay embraced Great Society liberalism even as his party was flirting with Goldwater conservatism. According to a former aide, Richard Aurelio, Lindsay "had an obsessive interest in racial justice and civil liberties." As a congressman, he supported Medicare, civil rights, and federal aid to education. Later, haunted by the Watts riots of 1965, he became one of the foremost national spokesmen for an analysis that linked urban conflagrations to black poverty and the legacies of racism.[10]

Lindsay arrived in office on January 1, 1966, and was greeted with a twelve-day transit strike that inflicted lasting damage on his credibility.

He soon found himself snowed under by the pressures of what he called "the second toughest job in America." Yet Lindsay began his mayoralty with the earnest belief that he might "reformulate city government and make the city into a laboratory for Great Society social policy," in the words of historian Vincent Cannato. A centerpiece of this vision was Lindsay's plan to revamp the antipoverty program and get OEO monies flowing into the city's poorest neighborhoods. This wasn't a selfless wish: Lindsay hoped to solidify a tenuous political coalition that united the left-wing intelligentsia, philanthropic foundations, business elites, the civil-rights leadership, and low-income minorities. He believed he could do so by championing the antipoverty effort. New York's corporate class, along with the foundations they oversaw, supported antipoverty programs as the best bet for avoiding urban chaos, while many African American leaders used such initiatives to consolidate new power bases.[11]

Even before he swore the oath of office, Lindsay solicited the opinions of experts, including Michael Harrington, author of *The Other America*; Assistant Secretary of Labor Daniel Patrick Moynihan; economist John Kenneth Galbraith; and Richard Boone, former national director of the Community Action Program. On December 5, 1965, a month after the mayoral election, Lindsay announced the formation of a fourteen-person task force to review the city's poverty program. He named the former in-spector general of OEO, William Haddad, to chair the group, and the task force held a series of public meetings around the city, at which Lindsay often presided. Once in power, Lindsay kept showing his face in poor neighborhoods; it was a calculated political strategy, but one that revealed the mayor's genuine sensitivity to the problems of ordinary people. That won hearts and minds. "I loved him to death," Elsie Richardson would later remark. "He felt that the people in the community knew what their problems were, so he expected them to be able to solve their problems."[12]

Lindsay aimed to show that New York could "lead the nation in the war against poverty." The rhetoric was familiar, but whereas Wagner had allowed a gaping chasm to yawn between words and actions, Lindsay intended to follow through. Once in office, he hired well-known urbanist Mitchell Sviridoff to overhaul the city's antipoverty programs. Together, Lindsay and Sviridoff would seek to reinvent the municipal bureaucracy and ease tensions between (and among) city agencies and neighborhood groups. Not only would their reforms promote community involvement at all levels of decision-making. They would also unwind the red tape that was choking substantive action in places like Bedford-Stuyvesant. At least that was the idea. But Lindsay couldn't act fast enough. Despite his support for community organizations, in early 1966 he bore the brunt of rising anger about the direction the War on Poverty was taking.[13]

A Social Movement of the Poor

In view of Bedford-Stuyvesant's large population and glaring needs, the meager funds being released made it difficult to launch significant service programs. YIA staffers and some board members decided to capitalize on the discontent caused by the funding deficits to raise political awareness in the community. YIA spent much of early 1966 organizing community action, though not necessarily of the sort the OEO had in mind. For the preachers and social-work professionals who oversaw much of YIA's work, political organizing in the War on Poverty held out the promise of unifying Bedford-Stuyvesant across potentially divisive age and class lines. Yet much of the frustration targeted at outside authorities would soon be diverted inward.

The increasingly restive mood surfaced on February 3, 1966—the day before Robert Kennedy's first tour of Bed-Stuy. With John Lindsay himself in attendance, Youth in Action supporters packed the auditorium of P.S. 3 on Jefferson Avenue for a meeting of the new mayor's antipoverty task force. Among other demands, they asked the city to provide better police protection, traffic lights, health clinics, and daycare centers in Central Brooklyn. Isaiah Lewis, a twenty-one-year-old high-school dropout employed by YIA as a community-outreach worker, then riled up the crowd with a screed against the poverty program's architects.[14]

"I can't speak the big words you all sling around, but I know about poverty because I live in it," said Lewis, who described himself as an "intellectual mau-mau." Johnson and Lindsay, he said, were "pseudo-liberals" who had delivered promises in bundles but copped out whenever it came time for real action. The assembled crowd responded with calls of "That's right!" and "Tell it like it is!" Lewis continued: "They think they can just throw a little money in here and hope the natives. . . ." He trailed off, but some in the crowd finished his sentence for him: "Don't get restless!"[15]

Lindsay seemed to have an appetite for such meetings. Two weeks after his confrontation with Isaiah Lewis in Brooklyn, he faced jeers at a meeting of his antipoverty task force in Harlem and then was serenaded with calls

169

of "Watts! Watts!"—a reference to the recent uprising in Los Angeles. As he walked to his car, a group of local youth leaders accosted him, chanting "Where's the bucks, John?" That same week, a group of YIA representatives traveled to Washington, DC, to solicit funds from OEO officials and politicians, including Representative Emmanuel Celler of Brooklyn's 10th District and the senior senator from New York, Jacob Javits. At one point during a meeting with a Community Action Program official, the irascible Isaiah Lewis rose, with tears in his eyes, and warned, "I'm getting madder and madder. I can't return to Brooklyn and tell the poor people to wait for hope. Can you tell a starving man to wait?" Javits promptly took up the issue with OEO's director, Sargent Shriver. In view of the "long and disturbing delay" caused by the now-departed Wagner administration, Javits explained, he felt YIA's application for OEO funds should be expedited.[16]

Dorothy Orr looked on proudly, if with some worry. YIA's executive director approved of the political consciousness her agency was nourishing among its "articulate and well-informed" community-leadership trainees, including Isaiah Lewis. "The Task Force Meeting was an excellent demonstration of the potential and capacity of the 'poverty stricken' to respond," Orr reported to her board. "There was a new sense of self, an awareness of their political power. . . . The total atmosphere within YIA presently is one which reflects a resurgence of drive, ambition, and restlessness to have knowledge; to get training and to 'join the great society,'" she added. Orr believed that the only way for Bed-Stuy to extract concessions from the federal and city bureaucracies was to get mad and get organized. "Bedford-Stuyvesant residents know and feel strongly that it is not a community of decadence, apathy, or lack of drive," she wrote in 1966, "Rather it is a community that has a history of fierce pride, concern, and a will to 'overcome.' The problem is not one of indifference; it is one of lack of opportunity, lack of funds, and lack of cooperation from the world outside." Yet Orr also believed that only an alliance between the area's middle class and its low-income majority could bring about meaningful social change. By the spring of 1966, she perceived a widening rift between the middle class and a new generation of leaders who fused the language of Black Power with grassroots organizing and pressure tactics borrowed from street gangs.[17]

The most prominent of these leaders was Robert "Sonny" Carson. A former member of the Bishops gang who had also served in the Army and worked as a drug dealer, Carson emerged in the mid-1960s as one of the most divisive public figures in Brooklyn. He took control of Brooklyn

CORE in the summer of 1966, just as the Black Panther Party was coming together in Oakland and Stokely Carmichael of the Student Nonviolent Coordinating Committee was adopting the slogan "Black Power." Under Carson's leadership, Brooklyn CORE repudiated its past as an integrationist group dedicated to nonviolent direct action. Fusing street theater and no-nonsense oratory, Carson preached black pride, community self-determination, and self-defense in the face of police brutality. He overtly disrespected the bastions of middle-class authority in Bedford-Stuyvesant. He was brash and bombastic, and he flaunted his criminal affiliations. Though he held no official position within the local antipoverty apparatus, no group could afford to ignore him. He wielded special influence within YIA: he was known to crash the agency's meetings flanked by a posse of armed followers, whom journalist Jack Newfield described as "proud, goateed, and very masculine." Carson would soon earn national notoriety for his role in the Ocean Hill–Brownsville school controversy, which resulted in a citywide teacher strike and significant racial strife. In 1975, he would go to jail for kidnapping—but not before seeing his autobiography turn into an acclaimed film. As historian Brian Purnell sums it up, "His face, of the younger, militant, uncompromising black man, was the new image of black leadership in the nation at that time."[18]

Younger activists, including Isaiah Lewis, gravitated toward Carson and CORE while also taking paid positions with YIA's community-organizing arm. Though employed by the state, they challenged the very legitimacy of the government and denigrated the bureaucratic apparatus that structured the poverty fight. They even disclaimed a role as "representatives" of the poor. "We *are* the poor," one "mau-mau" was quoted as saying in 1967. "Maximum feasible participation means me, baby."[19]

In the eyes of such young men, both the civil-rights movement and the War on Poverty had failed. Segregation persisted, and life in "the ghetto" seemed to be getting worse, not better. The generation of moderate, middle-class leaders who had erected the antipoverty apparatus in places like Bedford-Stuyvesant seemed toothless at best. For years, black liberals had waited on Wagner to put money where his mouth was; now they vested their hopes in Lindsay. What good was their leadership if they couldn't convince their liberal allies in government to throw some change their way? Orr warned the YIA board that hostility toward "community systems" was growing among Bed-Stuy's citizens. She urged traditional leaders to seek a rapprochement with the "indigenous population" by delivering benefits, however small, as quickly as possible. But they could do little without adequate funding—and funding depended entirely on the whims of city and federal decision-makers.[20]

Absent such funding, there was nothing to do but organize. Led by a new chairman, Reverend William A. Jones, Youth in Action's board aimed to reassert its legitimacy by capitalizing on local discontent and raising political awareness in Bedford-Stuyvesant. Jones, who replaced William Chisholm as chairman in early 1966, was a charismatic figure beloved in Bed-Stuy for his civil-rights activism and easy demeanor. Born in Kentucky, Jones was the son and grandson of ministers. During the early 1960s, he became a close ally of Dr. Martin Luther King Jr. and made his name by coordinating the New York chapter of King's Southern Christian Leadership Conference; later, he would head the New York branch of the Operation Breadbasket campaign, another King initiative. Since 1962, as pastor of Bethany Baptist Church, Jones had preached to a congregation of 5,000 and led a series of high-profile boycotts, marches, and protests. As an orator, Jones had few rivals. He stood 6 feet 5 inches tall, weighed 265 pounds, and had a booming baritone to match. He was also known for his warmth, charm, and sense of humor. When asked how he was doing, he would often answer, with a smile: "Jumping up and down and calling it progress." At the close of YIA board meetings, which usually stretched long into the night, he would go around the room and make sure everyone had a ride or a safe route home. "The hawks are out tonight," he would quip. It was easy to forget he was only thirty-one years old.[21]

Jones, like many among his cohort of black ministers in the mid-1960s, used the War on Poverty as a stepping stone from the picket lines to the state apparatus. With fellow churchmen Carl McCall and Milton Galamison, he was among the first wave of YIA board members; Jones would be succeeded as board chair by Reverend Walter Offutt, his colleague in the Bethany Baptist pulpit. In the early 1960s, Bed-Stuy's ministers had "sacrificed their comfortable positions as power brokers," in the words of historian Clarence Taylor, by leading school boycotts, picket actions, and the Downstate Medical Center protests. Yet they quickly recaptured those positions by tying themselves to the expanding welfare state. Beginning in 1964, they gambled that the achievement of long-cherished community goals would be possible within the new institutional settings the federal War on Poverty created. They quickly found themselves playing an inside-outside game. Jones and Offutt spent years simultaneously struggling for funds and influence within the bureaucratic world of poverty policy while at the same time trying to shore up their legitimacy among increasingly restive flocks.[22]

Jones made it clear that the War on Poverty was a direct extension of the civil-rights struggle. As Youth in Action's funding crisis dragged on, Jones sponsored the formation of a new group, dubbed the Citizens Committee for the Preservation of Youth in Action, which, unlike the agency itself, could devote itself exclusively to protesting delays in the disbursement of city and federal funds. Jones also convened a series of town-hall meetings at which Bed-Stuy residents were invited to air their complaints face to face with representatives from city agencies. At one of these meetings, on April 1, 1966, with upward of 600 people attending, YIA officials encouraged representatives of the "indigenous population" not only to pose questions but also to run the meeting. The following month, YIA began issuing official "memberships" to local residents, with an eye toward forming neighborhood planning boards. Jones claimed that 21,000 locals signed up within a fortnight.[23]

In effect, Jones was using the new agency to build a social movement of the poor. If the city chose to stand in his way, he would use this expanding grassroots network as a political weapon in the fight with City Hall. On June 17, 1966, Jones led a rally at Fulton Park in Bed-Stuy, which he had organized to protest the $1.5 million discrepancy between the money YIA had been promised and what it had received. Posters read: "Red Tape is keeping our children from having a full Head Start program in Bedford-Stuyvesant. Let's cut it!" Addressing the crowd, Jones thundered that the city's treatment of YIA amounted to "an insidious attempt to bring about the ultimate demise of Youth in Action."[24]

Though Jones underestimated Lindsay's desire to devolve power to low-income communities, he rightly sensed the way the political winds were blowing in Washington. Support in Congress for the War on Poverty had waned dramatically, and Lyndon Johnson himself was turning against a program that seemed to be causing more than its share of controversy. In a letter to Lindsay, Jones pinpointed a central problem of much of the War on Poverty: the curse of high expectations. "It will be difficult to interpret to a community, just becoming mobilized to seek solutions to their problems, such a solution," he wrote of the administration's plan for yet another reorganization of the community-action agencies. The funding delays, Jones told the mayor, had increased citizens' hostility toward government, which imperiled YIA's basic goal of "redirecting the angry and destructive feelings of residents into constructive channels."[25]

Orr, meanwhile, was taking the community grievances of Bedford-Stuyvesant all the way to Washington, DC. Ever committed to maximum feasible participation, YIA's executive director continued to push radical youth leaders to the forefront of what she saw as a grassroots crusade for community empowerment. When invited to testify before the Senate Sub-committee on Labor and Public Welfare on June 24, 1966, Orr demurred, presenting Timothy Vincent as the agency's spokesman. Dynamic and outspoken, Vincent had served in the Air Force and toured with the Harlem Globetrotters before returning to Bed-Stuy and starting a softball league meant to bring together teens from different turfs. According to YIA's newsletter, he had "earned a special place in the hearts and minds of the youth of this community" by organizing sports activities and running the Youth Leadership Institute, which mobilized and provided job training for young men aged seventeen to twenty-three, especially those who were referred to as "hard-core dropouts." Speaking to the most powerful legislative body in the land, Vincent laid out what was becoming a familiar litany of complaints. YIA had not received federal funds in almost nine months. Only a small portion of the funds requested were being provided by the city government. When such funds were released, it was on a sudden and ad hoc basis and was accompanied by threats that the monies would be withdrawn if unspent by arbitrarily imposed deadlines. Of the funds appropriated in 1965, the better part had been earmarked "to keep the young fellows cool" through the summer. Other monies repeatedly got bogged down in confusing bureaucratic channels. As for the poor, they stood by powerlessly, organizing to no avail, pursuing maximum feasible participation in a hoax, and growing angry and cynical.[26]

"It has been our observation that there is a general air of discontent among the grassroots segment of the community," Vincent said, "because only token efforts have been made toward elimination of adverse conditions affecting them: unemployment, poor housing, substandard city service, health welfare, and police." According to Vincent, it was getting harder and harder for YIA's supporters to justify their program of reforming the system from within. In talking to young people on the streets of Brooklyn, he had heard the questions a hundred times: "What is happening, baby? Do they really mean business?" Now was the time for the feds to show that they did indeed mean business. "When we get back to Bedford-Stuyvesant, we would like to have the cold cash," Vincent concluded.

The cold hard cash finally landed in Youth in Action's coffers in the summer of 1966. By October 1966, YIA had received a total of $2.55 million in funding, of which $1.57 million came from the city and the rest from OEO. The debate about maximum feasible participation took on a new dimension as the agency started expanding its staff. During the 1966–1967 fiscal year, YIA devoted 42 percent of its total budget to trainees and aides and spent another 22 percent on clerical staff. Poverty work paid well: vacancies advertised by YIA in November 1966 included associate director of administration ($18,000 per year, or the equivalent of $130,000 in 2015), executive assistant for external affairs ($13,000), Community Action Group work training specialist ($11,000), assistant director of home work study ($10,000), consumer education specialist ($10,000), and cultural arts specialist ($7,500). Such administrative positions, by and large, were occupied by educated professionals. But YIA recruited the bulk of its staff from among what it called the "indigenous population" as a way of simultaneously providing on-the-job training while dispensing services. Unemployed locals with few skills were often hired as "Community Action Neighborhood Workers," who earned an hourly wage of $1.50 or $2. They staffed service centers and took charge of publicizing YIA's programs—and dramatizing its funding shortfalls—at street level. If its board represented the middle-class leadership of Bedford-Stuyvesant, the Youth in Action staff in effect came to represent the "maximum feasible participation" arm of the agency. This produced a bitter series of power struggles.[27]

Orr believed that the agency's survival hinged on incorporating poor people into YIA's decision-making processes. This meant holding community meetings, laying the groundwork for neighborhood-board elections, and recruiting gang members into youth-leadership programs. To these organizational efforts, she appended a redistributive philosophy. "The war on poverty is a war which calls for a redistribution of power, responsibility, and participation by all people in the economic, political, and social structure of our country," she wrote. "The vested interest of the middle class, the professional, the politician, the businessman must be touched in this process. The shift of power does not come easily or without active and angry resistance."[28]

Orr hoped to focus YIA's energies on the political empowerment of young, poor African Americans. Yet she saw controversy and conflict as beneficial if and only if they could be "redirected into appropriate and productive channels" within mainstream American political life. She differed with YIA's middle-class board not so much on ends but on means. Orr hoped that "the poor, the professional, the wealthy, the politician, etc. can merge on a policy-making, program-planning, and implementation level so as together to alleviate some of the basic core problems of poverty in the community."[29]

It was a nice idea. But Orr herself repeatedly butted heads with the agency's board and the established community leadership. As YIA gained traction, she felt that the Central Brooklyn Coordinating Council was jealously seeking to undermine an agency it had once controlled. After a particularly heated meeting on September 1, 1965, which the *Times* described as a "brick-throwing brawl," Orr charged that hecklers affiliated with CBCC had tried to incite a riot and were preaching "a kind of community action that is oriented toward violence." CBCC's executive director, Donald Benjamin, countered that Orr was a power-hungry outsider with no knowledge of the community. Elsie Richardson, meanwhile, penned a stern open letter recounting CBCC's long history and pointing out the absurdity of Orr's charges. No matter—such incidents tarnished YIA's image and embarrassed community leaders. In the aftermath, Almira Coursey, a CBCC stalwart who also sat on the YIA board, tried to smooth over the rift, calling on all "to join hands to see that Bedford-Stuyvesant becomes the garden spot of our metropolis that we have long hoped for." But tensions persisted. In April 1966, YIA chairman William Chisholm accused Orr of mismanagement, while Orr replied with allegations that the board was trampling on administrative privileges. The dispute blew up in a fiery shouting match at an April board meeting, which led Chisholm to resign. Two weeks later, Milton Galamison, who had been serving as interim chairman, followed suit. In submitting his resignation from the board, Galamison explained, somewhat cryptically, that "there was nothing more I could do for an agency that resists constructive help."[30]

By the summer of 1966, the situation had become untenable. Following yet another clash with the board on September 23, Orr quit. (She would soon take a job as executive director of the Harlem Youth Opportunities Unlimited agency.) She was followed by the agency's well-respected treasurer, Owen Hague, and a dozen employees from YIA's fiscal department. In an interview with the *Times* following his resignation, Hague accused the YIA board of reflecting a middle-class outlook divorced from the concerns of poor Stuyfordites. According to Hague, board intransigence had frozen poor people out of YIA's decision-making process and was thus preventing the agency from reaching out to the most "hard-core" delinquents. In other words, YIA was unable to implement maximum feasible participation and was thus "committing a fraud on the public."[31]

From the standpoint of YIA's middle-class leaders, nothing could be further from the truth. Board members had organized block associations, mobilized the mass movement against segregation, and spearheaded protests for improved schools, sanitation, and welfare services. They had taken the lead in Bed-Stuy's poverty program, to be sure, but they insisted that their poor neighbors were equal and willing participants. "The Board has not shown a lack of concern for the poor," William Jones wrote in an October 3 letter to the commissioner of the city's Community Development Agency, George Nicolau. "The Board is not middle-class oriented. In fact, the 'indigenous' are well represented and their voices are distinctly heard in all matters pertaining to policy in this agency." As proof, Jones listed six "indigenous" board members, all women. He also took pains to point out that YIA's representative on the Council Against Poverty, Oliver Ramsay, was a sanitation worker who lived in public housing—which ostensibly made him a fitting representative of Bed-Stuy's "indigenous" population. But Jones's use of the term "indigenous" obscured as much as it revealed. As a euphemism for "poor people," it turned economic want into a class-blind abstraction with vague connotations of racial solidarity. Yet only some members of the community were held up as proof of maximum feasible participation in action. If the "indigenous" were truly leading the antipoverty effort, then why should Jones—a well-established preacher— need to highlight their participation? And if only poor people were "indigenous," did that mean middle-class folks were interlopers? The answers remained unclear.[32]

Moving Mountains

Jones's efforts to broaden YIA's base of community support dovetailed with an ongoing reorientation of city policy under Mayor Lindsay. By mid-1966, the poverty program was in deep trouble. The *Times* ran an article in June under the headline "Kafka and Poverty," in which city officials were quoted comparing their workplace to the "maze-like government" portrayed in *The Trial*. Yet change was afoot. The man tasked with saving New York's

War on Poverty, Mitchell Sviridoff, delivered his long-awaited report in late June, and he called for nothing less than a total reorganization of the city's social-service bureaucracy. "We must move mountains," he proclaimed. "Very courageous," commented Dorothy Orr.[33]

Sviridoff had begun his career on the assembly line in a New Haven aircraft-parts factory and eventually rose to become president of the Connecticut AFL-CIO. In 1962, he had helped to launch Community Progress, Inc., a New Haven antipoverty program that received funding from both the federal government and the Ford Foundation's Gray Areas program. Two years into the War on Poverty, Community Progress employed some 1,500 people and drew such generous funding that Sviridoff had become nationally known as a "genius at organization" who was "magic at getting money." People from community organizations all over the country, including CBCC, traveled to New Haven to see the miracle in action. Yet Sviridoff himself was unimpressed with the federal antipoverty fight. "We speak of the War Against Poverty, but we're not fighting it like a war," he opined in mid-1966, "for we would never ration our ammunition in the battlefield as tightly as we are allocating resources to the fighters against poverty. It would be a national scandal."[34]

In his report, Sviridoff laid out a grand vision: the city should strive to provide every citizen with a job, an education, and access to city services. More concretely, he proposed to create more efficient management structures while allowing for greater participation of the poor in the poverty program. To oversee the transformation, he called for a new mega-agency, called the Human Resources Administration, which would absorb the city's Department of Welfare and the Youth Board, as well as new agencies spawned by the War on Poverty. The disbursement of federal community-action funds would stay in the hands of the Council Against Poverty, but a new Community Development Agency would act as the administrative arm of the relevant bureaucracy. The old Antipoverty Operations Board, by which Wagner had controlled a separate stream of antipoverty funds, would be abolished, thus pooling city and federal funds.[35]

Lindsay accepted Sviridoff's recommendations, and the New Haven man became head of the new Human Resources Administration. One of his first pieces of business was to reinvent community corporations like Youth in Action—or, rather, to have them reinvent themselves. According to Sviridoff's guidelines, such agencies would reconstitute as nonprofit "community corporations" and give up responsibility for direct services such as job training, remedial education, and family planning. Instead, they would focus on issuing program guidelines, coordinating area-wide services, and spinning off delegate agencies to carry out on-the-ground initiatives. Sviridoff stressed that each community must tailor its corporation to local needs. YIA and other local groups would be given more autonomy in dispensing funds, but first they would have to prove that they were "broadly representative of the community" by holding elections.

"Community action is an evolving and dynamic concept," proclaimed the new guidelines issued by the reorganized Council Against Poverty. "The instruments which will operate community action programs should be similarly evolving and dynamic." Accordingly, the governing boards of community corporations should be ever-changing entities; city regulations mandated that "at least part of the boards" should be up for renewal every year. In theory, the constant infusion of new blood was conducive to a robust, democratic exchange of ideas and would guard against control by what Sviridoff called "a closed clique which excludes many elements of the community." In practice, such turnover also ended up destabilizing community groups like Youth in Action.[36]

Sviridoff's reforms had contradictory effects. On the one hand, they signaled the mayor's seriousness about injecting political capital into the poverty program and petitioning OEO for increased monies. At the same time, there was something inherently contradictory, even disingenuous, in dictating participatory democracy from above, despite Lindsay's stated desire to empower poor people. In the short term, Sviridoff's reforms exacerbated the contradictions that were already undermining New York's antipoverty programs. As Bertram Beck, former head of Mobilization for Youth, would later explain, "On one hand, the complex nonfunctioning, citywide bureaucracy was made even more complex and, on the other hand, there was a direct transfer of power to the neighborhoods which found themselves frustrated by the malfunctioning, citywide structure."[37]

In response to the new mandates, Youth in Action embarked on a complex process intended to bring the agency closer to the "indigenous" population it was meant to be serving. In its new guise as an umbrella agency, YIA would be tasked with picking and choosing from among a slew of local program proposals and rewarding innovative approaches with funds and political cover. YIA would also initiate a "spin-off" process by which many of the agency's functions would be handed off to a network of five neighborhood boards, each serving a subsection of Bedford-Stuyvesant.

YOUTH IN ACTION, MONTHLY NEWSPAPER JULY 1967 PAGE 5

Candidates For
Bedford-Stuyvesant Community Corp. Hit
The Campaign Trail

A page from the *Youth in Action* newspaper showing candidates in the community-corporation elections of 1967. *Courtesy Bedford-Stuyvesant Youth in Action*

The boards were designed to foster local initiative and "self-help" by tailoring services specifically to the local population. (For instance, the heavily Hispanic area of northern Bedford-Stuyvesant would offer services in Spanish as well as English-language remediation classes.) In addition, each board would help to ensure representation of block-level concerns during meetings of the central YIA board. The neighborhood boards were also meant to develop new sources of leadership at street level and to act as bulwarks against corruption. YIA showed it meant business in the fall of 1966 by sending out a small army of trainees to canvas each area "on a block-to-block basis" and recruit candidates for the boards. This amounted to an ambitious plan to breed participatory democracy in an area housing almost 400,000 people. But excessive devolution of decision-making power intensified the problems the community corporation was facing in its efforts to coordinate area-wide policies.[38]

YIA's transformation into a "broadly representative" community corporation was overseen by Orr's replacement in the executive director's office, Walter Pinkston—the same man who as a Youth Board worker in the late 1950s had helped to spur the formation of the Central Brooklyn Coordinating Council. Sviridoff's guidelines recommended that the "spin-off" process be complete by December 31, 1966, but YIA took the better part of eight months. Committee meetings, planning and training workshops, public hearings, and community-planning sessions unfolded sporadically from September to March. Full elections did not take place until May 20, 1967.[39]

By February 1967, Youth in Action had forty board members, of whom sixteen were classified as members of the "target population" (a new euphemism for poor people). Thirteen of those sixteen were women, many of them mothers. At a time when the National Welfare Rights Organization was heralding the arrival of low-income black women as a national political force, Youth in Action reflected a similar impulse. Still, the group strove for even greater representation. The May election saw seventy-five new members join YIA's board—fifteen from each of the five subareas into which Bedford-Stuyvesant had been divided the previous year. The vote followed two weeks of campaigning and months of preparatory efforts that monopolized meetings and occupied a large portion of staffers' time. Of the 154 candidates running for 75 positions, few had any experience working in government. In an effort to preserve an element of stability, it was decided that the outgoing board could select a dozen "at-large" directors for the new community corporation. This latter group included politicos like Thomas Fortune and Shirley Chisholm, along with longtime directors Sylvia Shapiro (a schoolteacher), Don Watkins (a professor of sociology at Brooklyn College), and Oliver Ramsay, who represented Bed-Stuy on the citywide Council Against Poverty. Still, most of Youth in Action's institutional memory had vanished.[40]

All told, only two of Youth in Action's twenty original board members remained. The group had cycled through three executive directors and three chairmen in three years. Absurdly, the board had ballooned to eighty-seven members. (By comparison, only ninety-four people sat in the New York State Senate and the New York City Council *combined* in 1967.) Most new directors had no experience at all running organizations. Those who did felt compelled to pass motions calling on their colleagues to respect Robert's Rules of Order. Meetings often descended into chaos anyway, despite the best efforts of the chairman, Walter Offutt, to maintain decorum. Instituting community control had become enormously time-consuming—and YIA would have to do it all over again less than a year later, when OEO ordered a further reorganization prompted by a congressional amendment to the Economic Opportunity Act, which required that boards of designated community-action agencies have no more than fifty-one members, of which at least one-third were to be drawn from the "target population."[41]

As YIA was converting into a community corporation, it was also struggling to expand its staff and launch programs. The sudden infusion of substantial grant monies after two years of delays was welcome in Bedford-Stuyvesant, of course, but it also destabilized an agency that was devoting so much energy to its own reorganization. YIA was also facing increasing scrutiny from various federal and city oversight bodies. An evaluation carried out by Sviridoff's Human Resources Administration in February 1967 found that the Brooklyn agency had failed to develop systematic objectives or formulate long-term goals. According to the report, those failures owed in part to the "atmosphere of urgency surrounding the War on Poverty," which had inspired YIA to launch a variety of experimental programs without adequate planning.

Management, too, posed a significant challenge. By 1967, YIA had 300 full-time and contract personnel in addition to some 1,300 training aides. Many new staff had been recruited from among Bedford-Stuyvesant's "target population" of poor young people, especially dropouts. The idea was to put money in people's pockets while simultaneously providing on-the-job training, dispensing services, and mobilizing community energies. In an economically depressed district, using antipoverty funds for make-work projects made sense, especially given YIA's earlier attentiveness to the problem of jobs in Bed-Stuy. But getting the new recruits up to speed necessitated what the HRA report called "a step-by-step, trial-and-error approach"—a tough thing to pull off in an atmosphere of urgency. As a result, administrative oversight suffered. Records were poorly kept, program functions overlapped, and, most worrisome, opaque accounting procedures offered signs of rampant incompetence and possible fraud.[42]

The Office of Economic Opportunity, after conducting a separate investigation, drew even harsher conclusions. A scathing report issued in May 1967 declared YIA to be rife with hidden agendas and undermined by the competing goals of various factions. As a result, administrative chaos reigned. According to OEO, various people on YIA's payroll weren't working, and the aide-training program was being used to reward cronies. All told, the Brooklyn agency had become a case study in the perils of launching community action in a time of unrest. YIA, the OEO report stated, "is a classic example of a program that was pulled together very rapidly amidst a crisis with a mandate to spend a lot of money, to employ large numbers of people, and to keep the ghetto 'cool'. All of the inherent strengths and weaknesses of such an approach to meeting the needs of the community are present in the YIA program."[43]

This was particularly true in the neighborhood centers, according to the report. The centers' directors complained of having no say in hiring decisions; none of the centers had any trained social-work or management professionals on staff. Unsurprisingly, budgets, minutes, and other basic files seemed to be missing. In the case of Area 2, which had roughly equal populations of African Americans and Puerto Ricans, ethnic strife was crippling YIA's street-level work. Most of the training aides, who hailed from among the low-income population, seemed neither to be learning any specific skills nor moving into permanent jobs. The one agreed-upon function for the neighborhood centers was to engage in community organizing—but to what end?[44]

The agency's flaws, when highlighted by oversight agencies, appeared damning. But they resulted in part from efforts to comply with the mandates set out by those same outside agencies, which had earlier complicated YIA's efforts by withholding promised funds. Much confusion arose directly from efforts to ensure maximum feasible participation in Bed-Stuy. It was hard to put forth a comprehensive vision for Central Brooklyn's transformation while also making a fetish of ultralocal decision-making. It was even harder to run a competent agency while also serving as an employment service for high-school dropouts, gang members, and the long-term unemployed. The OEO report from 1967 found that there were no college graduates or experienced managers on staff at any of the neighborhood centers. This was, to some extent, a good thing, because it meant more money was left over to pay low-income residents and it left more room for poor people to make decisions about the program. On the other hand, the absence of expertise made it hard for YIA to fulfill its training objectives and help aides graduate into permanent jobs.[45]

While challenged from the grass roots, YIA was also hampered by the constraints it faced from above—funding delays, forced reorganizations, and overlapping supervisory bodies. For two years, the agency operated on the assumption that its existence was imperiled. When funds finally arrived, heated disputes erupted over how to spend them. In a resource-starved community of 400,000 people, $6 million was hardly enough to alleviate poverty. But it *was* enough to touch off vicious power struggles. It didn't help that YIA services were being dispensed from some thirty-three locations around Bedford-Stuyvesant. Such decentralization kept staff in touch with the street, but it also increased the difficulty of directing them toward a common goal.[46]

Sviridoff's reforms, ostensibly an exercise in participatory democracy, had the effect of devolving decision-making structures to the point where concerted programmatic innovation became impossible. Decentralization tended to strip elites of their authority and to invite contestation at every step of the process—as Lindsay was finding out. The more time YIA spent on bureaucratic reorganization, the more time it spent on political infighting and the less it spent on fighting poverty. And that, in turn, generated further community tensions. Added to these tensions were the continuing federal efforts to enforce maximum feasible participation in local community-action efforts by withholding funds if the mandate was not met. In Bedford-Stuyvesant and around the country, many wondered whether the entire exercise had been engineered deliberately to distract poor Americans and give them a false sense of hope. The lead story in a 1966 newsletter published by Mobilization for Youth summed it up: "Maximum Feasible Participation: A Hope or a Hustle?"[47]

Of Young Mothers and Talented Women

Despite the uncertainty that clouded the first three years of Youth in Action's existence, the agency managed to launch a number of programs. "Miraculously," the OEO report stated in 1967, "some good is being accomplished." The agency's first funded programs included a Medicare alert service to help senior citizens register for the new federal healthcare program, an eight-week job-training course with the New York Port Authority, and consumer-action drives to protect Bedford-Stuyvesant residents against unfair business practices. Of the eighty-six Head Start centers up and running in Brooklyn by mid-1966, thirty-five were in Bedford-Stuyvesant and Crown Heights. By 1968, Youth in Action was funding the second-largest Head Start program in the city, surpassed only by the Board of Education itself. As the first program to provide free, nonparochial pre-school classes to low-income children, Head Start proved enormously popular, not only in Brooklyn but also in cities around the country. In a similar vein, YIA also ran after-school study programs for local children whose parents worked long hours.[48]

During the 1967–1968 fiscal year, Bedford-Stuyvesant—the most populous of any New York City "poverty area"—received $6.4 million of the $33.5 million in community-action funds doled out by the New York City Council Against Poverty. These monies were distributed, via Youth in Action, to an array of programs, many of which were greeted enthusiastically in Central Brooklyn because they created jobs and offered valuable services—and, allegedly, kept the streets calm. The Manpower Service Center, operated under YIA auspices, advertised that it had "over 1,000 jobs available," including positions within the local bureaucracy and on-the-job training opportunities elsewhere. The Bed-Stuy chapter of the Neighborhood Youth Corps promised to provide teenagers with paid work experience while encouraging them to stay in school. Beginning in 1968, Youth in Action also funded the efforts of historic preservationists who were uncovering traces of the lost village of Weeksville, where freed slaves had settled in the nineteenth century; teenagers from the Youth Corps and from Timothy Vincent's Youth Leadership Institute were recruited to participate in digs. Meanwhile, YIA's consumer-education program was earning praise for its efforts to prove that "the poor pay more" and for mobilizing low-income women to wage a new form of pocketbook politics in the service of the poor. Youth in Action was also planning a Legal Services program that would help familiarize victims of police brutality with their rights, provide legal counsel to indigent residents, advocate for tenants' rights, and train a corps of neighborhood legal aides. Like Head Start, Legal Services was a national program initiated by OEO that would prove among the most popular and enduring initiatives undertaken during the War on Poverty.[49]

Of all the programs initiated by Youth in Action, it was the Young Mothers Program that earned the most praise. Young Mothers arose from the efforts of Olga DeFreitas, a one-woman whirlwind of activity who had previously taught at Brooklyn College. A social worker who valued case-work at a time when many in her profession were pursuing systemic change, DeFreitas believed she could help transform Bed-Stuy by touching individual lives, one at a time. One of her admirers wrote of DeFreitas that "she can be arrogant, stubborn, and authoritarian, but most often, she is caring, warm, and sympathetic." Armed with a small YIA grant, as well as money garnered through door-to-door fundraising, DeFreitas in late 1965 began operating out of a Salvation Army basement. Her goal was to provide training, counseling, remedial education, and prenatal care for pregnant teenagers. Many of these women came to DeFreitas from families unable or unwilling to support them through their pregnancies. All had dropped out of high school once they discovered they were pregnant.[50]

Underlying DeFreitas's work was a theoretical analysis that echoed Youth in Action's diagnosis of the "culture of poverty" in Bedford-Stuyvesant. According to a 1965 study, a quarter of all Bed-Stuy babies were being born out of wedlock. That statistic, which would continue to rise in subsequent decades, represented for reformers like DeFreitas what youth-crime figures had signified to Maude Richardson and Archie Hargraves a decade earlier: a harbinger of social breakdown. As DeFreitas and other YIA planners understood the issue, the spike in out-of-wedlock births owed partly to the legacies of racism and partly to the mores of the rural South and the Puerto Rican countryside, which postwar migrants had brought with them to Brooklyn. "For the Negro girl," one YIA study opined, "the impact of segregation, the social and economic status of the Negro, the plantation view of the Negro woman as a sexual target, the discomfort of living in a ghetto and the lack of parental role models all contribute to promiscuous and superficial relationships with men." As much as black and Puerto Rican men found it difficult to penetrate "the mainstream of the metropolitan community," unwed mothers from these groups faced "additional social stigma" that made it hard for them to participate in the social and economic life of the community. "Without help she and her children can be caught in the web of economic dependency and a life of poverty," the YIA study argued. According to the agency's findings, most young mothers themselves had been raised in environments of "psychological deprivation" and often in single-parent homes. "In Negro homes the absence of a stable paternal and masculine figure heightens the sexual insecurity of adolescence for the young Negro woman," a YIA document explained. This allegedly made young women more likely to become pregnant as a way of proving their womanhood or otherwise establishing a role in society. Their infant children, in turn, were almost certain to become ensnared in the cycle as they aged. Thus, the increasingly prevalent pattern of out-of-wedlock births testified to the "social and emotional pathology" prevalent in Bedford-Stuyvesant.[51]

Given such deep-rooted pathologies, what could be done to help the young mothers of Bed-Stuy? DeFreitas began by enrolling pregnant girls between the ages of fourteen and eighteen in a daily program of study and training. The first group of forty-five officially began classes in the spring of 1966, in a space provided by Milton Galamison's Siloam Presbyterian Church on Jefferson Avenue. Six hours a day for fifteen weeks, the expectant mothers got down to the studies they had been forced to abandon when they got pregnant. They also received sex-education classes, prenatal training, and in-house nursing services. (Some of the young mothers had already given birth once, and they were invited to bring their first child to classes with them.) In addition to an academic curriculum designed to help students reenter high school at a higher grade level, the program also featured a number of elective choices, from "History of La Négritude" and "Minority Group Heritage" to "Electives in Sewing" and "Fashion and Grooming." Students could also sign up for remedial tutoring and skills training for a future trade.[52]

For their efforts, the young mothers received not only training but also small cash payments. DeFreitas took pains to emphasize that stipends were not paychecks. Rather, they were conditional grants—paid out at a rate of $1.50 per hour of class attended—to be used in support of babies. DeFreitas also made it clear that stipends could easily disappear. According to house rules, the penalties for showing up late to classes, which started promptly at 8:50 A.M., were, for a first offense, the loss of two hours' stipends; for a second offense, the loss of a full day's stipend; and, for a third

The cover of "Welcome to Young Mothers," a 1967 brochure published by Bedford-Stuyvesant Youth in Action. "We believe that there is new life for you here," new recruits read on the first page. "A new life of womanhood, motherhood, and responsibility." *Courtesy Bedford-Stuyvesant Young Mothers Program*

offense, a "conference with Ms. DeFreitas." Students were also fined twenty-five cents for swearing and fifty cents for "disrespect," enforced by a peer group named the Big Sisters Club.[53]

DeFreitas endeavored to inculcate "self-discipline" and to make young women "economically independent"—goals that resonated with long-cherished American ideas about the wellsprings of individual freedom and autonomy. Indeed, the Young Mothers Program subscribed to a philosophy of self-help and bootstrap individualism that was typical of the early War on Poverty. A 1965 Youth in Action planning document explained that the community-action effort embraced "the philosophy that the individual must be taught, trained and given the knowledge to act independently in a free society." The Young Mothers Program fit squarely into this ethic. Its expressed goal was to help teenage mothers "move out into the mainstream, confident of their ability to provide emotional and economic security for their children." As DeFreitas put it in 1967, "We have done what the Office of Economic Opportunity expects of the antipoverty effort, by proving what can be done for a community through self-help." Such language would've been music to Lyndon Johnson's ears. "No doles" indeed.[54]

The Young Mothers Program, then, was pitched as an attempt to rescue teenage mothers and their children from "a web of economic dependency" and to wean them from their welfare checks. At a time when African Americans across the country were repudiating the "culture of poverty" analysis, largely in response to Daniel Patrick Moynihan's controversial report on the black family, the program seemed to internalize the analysis of black families as damaged, disempowered, and pathological. But Olga De-Freitas was working at street level; her ultimate goal was to empower black women. If conservative in some ways, the Young Mothers Program was also innovative on several fronts. Reaching out to pregnant teenagers and encouraging them to envision future careers flew in the face of contemporary norms. In normalizing the idea of single motherhood in Bed-Stuy and offering to those mothers the tools for their future advancement, the program offered an implicit critique of the very line of thinking it seemingly endorsed—namely, that the decline of the nuclear family was what was condemning black communities to poverty and disintegration. Moreover, DeFreitas petitioned OEO to approve biweekly stipends for any girl with a strong attendance record and "a desire for self-help." Given the societal disdain in the mid-1960s for teenage mothers, the program ran a considerable political risk by asking taxpayers to pay the girls a salary to attend school.[55]

Focused and tightly managed, the Young Mothers Program flourished. Working on promises of an annual $224,000 grant, DeFreitas hired ten staffers in 1966; that number would climb to thirty-five the following year. She could soon boast of hundreds of graduates who had been successfully reintegrated into the educational system. By late 1967, 175 women were enrolled in what had become a twenty-week program that included a counseling service, free lunches, prenatal care, infant and postnatal care, and job training. The program's success inspired a group of community activists, led by educator Almira Coursey, to raise funds for a daycare center, where young mothers could leave their babies while they studied or attended on-the-job training. The program also drew the attention of the *Times*, which published a florid account of the December 18, 1966, graduation ceremony for 110 young mothers. "A sustained chord sounded the piano in the packed and hushed auditorium of Public School 21 in the

Bedford-Stuyvesant section of Brooklyn, a signal for 110 girls to rise to their feet at a special graduation ceremony," the paper reported. "The girls, between the ages of 14 and 18, did so heavily, and as they rose they smoothed their maternity dresses."[56]

Decades later, former Bed-Stuy poverty warriors would point to Young Mothers as one of Youth in Action's signal accomplishments.[57] What was perhaps most notable about the program, aside from the individual lives transformed, was that it demonstrated the potential of creative federalism. DeFreitas had little use for maximum feasible participation as an organizing tactic, but her end goal, in keeping with YIA's overall thrust, was to democratize life in Bed-Stuy by helping an outcast group reintegrate into the social fabric. As the Bed-Stuy newspaperman and politico Andy Cooper commented in the mid-1970s, DeFreitas had "substituted love, compassion, and understanding for near-hate" and, in the process, "saved 5,000 souls." The Young Mothers Program offered real opportunities for advancement to women, both as staffers and as recruits. But the initiative's dependence on uncertain funding streams left it vulnerable, and the program would fall on hard times in the 1970s.[58]

Another farsighted War on Poverty initiative that began serving Brooklyn women in 1966 was the Women's Talent Corps (WTC), a program to train low-income women for jobs in the social-service bureaucracy. Like Young Mothers, WTC emerged from the initiative of one woman; it was neither a direct outgrowth of Youth in Action's own programming nor an idea conceived by federal poverty planners. It sprang from the creative mind of Audrey Cohen, a well-off white woman who was also a civil-rights activist and educational reformer. In the late 1950s, while still in her twenties, Cohen had founded Part-Time Research Associates, a group that employed well-educated housewives to carry out social-science research. Its clients included the McKinsey consultancy, AT&T, the State Department, and Governor Nelson Rockefeller. In the early 1960s, Cohen turned her attention to finding work for low-income women. Her central insight was that as the country's core economic activity shifted away from manufacturing, the social-service professions could become an important source of jobs for women living in deindustrializing cities. Cohen observed that New York City lacked trained workers to staff the growing health, education, and social-welfare sectors. "In the field of community service there exists a shortage of jobs, as well as a short supply of professional and non-professional workers to fill them," she wrote in a 1965 request for antipoverty funds. "If our efforts are to be directed forcefully against the conditions of poverty, new jobs in community and social agencies must be developed and persons presently unemployed or underemployed must be recruited and trained for them," she added.[59]

The key, Cohen decided, would be to recruit low-income women, with or without high-school diplomas, to train for paraprofessional positions in understaffed social-service professions. This would fight poverty on two fronts. First, "meaningful, socially useful jobs" would provide poor women with an alternative to welfare by offering both job training and placement. Second, once employed, those women would act as "bridges" between poor people and the hospitals, schools, social-work agencies, health clinics, legal-services centers, and daycares they depended on. Of course, this vision implied widespread "institutional change." Many of the jobs Cohen envisioned did not yet exist, and it would be necessary to convince social-service and governmental agencies that creating such jobs would serve a social good.

In 1965, Cohen pitched her idea to the federal Office of Economic Opportunity and held a series of meetings in the Bronx, Harlem, Brownsville, and Bedford-Stuyvesant to rally support among the local Community Action Agencies. She received crucial help from Preston Wilcox, a Columbia University professor and Harlem community activist. Mobilizing Wilcox's connections in various community organizations, WTC used direct-action tactics to convince OEO to put up the funds necessary to launch the program. Meanwhile, Cohen set about testing her assumption that public institutions, especially schools, "could be persuaded to incorporate the new community service functions into their existing job structures, creating new positions." After months of lobbying efforts carried out by Cohen, school principals, and the United Federation of Teachers, the city's Board of Education agreed to create a variety of new paraprofessional positions.[60]

One strength of the program lay in who was doing the training. Cohen, departing from her experience with Part-Time Research Associates, planned to call on underemployed yet highly educated women with expertise in the social services to fill this role. Wilbur J. Cohen, under-secretary of Health, Education, and Welfare, wrote, "This project, by making use of professionally trained women, not now employed, to train disadvantaged women for jobs . . . provides one method of obtaining manpower to staff anti-poverty programs."[61] Audrey Cohen also tapped into the new institutional networks created by the War on Poverty. Local antipoverty agencies referred applicants for the Talent Corps and pledged to hire graduates as interns, research assistants, social-work aides, and legal secretaries. Youth in Action hoped the program would help find jobs for currently unemployed Bedford-Stuyvesant women in welfare agencies, neighborhood houses, health clinics, daycare centers, legal-service centers, churches, schools, and recreational centers. "The non-professional woman will be trained in the field in her own neighborhood," a Youth in Action memo explained.[62]

Of the first group of forty trainees to take classes at the WTC's institute in Lower Manhattan, almost all were unemployed at the time they were chosen to participate. Many had never finished high school. More than half were single mothers, and 90 percent were black or Puerto Rican. All were living on incomes below the poverty level. The $2-an-hour stipend they received for attending lectures and participating in internships was a valuable resource in and of itself. (Program coordinators earned $4 an hour.) Even more valuable were the jobs waiting for them upon completion of the educational program. Of the first seventy-five students to graduate in 1966–1967, most immediately took jobs created specifically for their cohort. The lion's share of Brooklyn women who graduated from the WTC in the late 1960s would take up jobs as teacher's aides in city schools.[63]

The Women's Talent Corps, planned for women by women, represented a creative use of state resources to quietly advance the goals of the feminist movement. It also facilitated the entry of African American women into government jobs, which, as Michael Katz has observed, ended up being one of the lasting legacies of Great Society programs in cities around the country. Equally significant was the fact that the Talent Corps explicitly repudiated the culture of poverty thesis:

> The training program reflects a basic philosophy about the "teachability" of uneducated people. It assumes that the "culture of poverty" does not affect the attitudes of most of the low-income groups in New York City, and specifically not of the women enrolled in the Women's Talent Corps program. Rather . . . trainees subscribe to the basic cultural values of the U.S. and strive for the same goals as other Americans. It assumes that these women are ready and able to become the "new careerists" of the future. What they need is help in developing and focusing their latent talents, rather than major restructuring of their attitudes toward society.[64]

By 1968, the Talent Corps had a backlog of close to 2,500 applications. The program, Cohen wrote, had "tapped an artesian source of competent, ambitious, aroused, forgotten women." No place in the city had as many paraprofessionals staffing its schools as Bedford-Stuyvesant, where Youth in Action continued to help screen candidates for WTC and place them once they had completed their training. The increasing number of paraprofessionals in local schools was especially significant. Their presence helped "reshape and democratize" relations between the community and the educational bureaucracy, according to historian Nick Juravich. At a time when nine out of ten teachers—and nearly all administrators—in the city's public schools were white, a cohort of black and Hispanic women was suddenly arriving in classrooms. Most of these women were mothers, and most of them were active members of the communities in which they now worked. Thanks to the recruitment efforts of agencies like YIA, the majority of paraprofessionals citywide were placed in schools within ten blocks of their homes; according to a 1969 study, 85 percent regularly encountered students and their families outside the classroom. These were women who wanted to be teaching in the poor, minority neighborhoods that white teachers often fled at the first opportunity. As such, they offered a unique kind of support to local students and functioned as de facto brokers between schools and the streets surrounding them. Many paraprofessionals went on to become teachers in their own right; by 1978, more than 1,500 had made the leap in schools across the city. The WTC model proved so successful that in 1970, the City University of New York launched a teacher-education program targeting paraprofessionals. Cohen, meanwhile, founded the College for Human Services (later renamed the Metropolitan College of New York) to give WTC an institutional structure.[65]

This quiet, unheralded aspect of the War on Poverty helped democratize the educational system, create jobs, and enhance the status of African American women. One enduring critique of the War on Poverty is that it focused more on psychosocial remediation than on creating the kinds of jobs that were needed to offset the storm of deindustrialization that was set to ravage American cities.[66] No doubt, efforts to promote job growth were insufficient, but efforts there were, and many of them did in fact help open up new, white-collar sectors of the urban economy to minorities who might otherwise have been condemned to unemployment or part-time, menial jobs. A similar premise underlay the Women's Talent Corps: government agencies that were devoting increasing resources to fighting poverty through social work and income support could further that fight by becoming job creators themselves.

Olga DeFreitas and Audrey Cohen showed that select programs, if shepherded along by strong leaders with a clear vision of what they were seeking to accomplish, could succeed in the War on Poverty. Both Young Mothers and the Women's Talent Corps offered cash incentives and valuable training to their enrollees. Favorably covered in the press, the programs also received strong support from both local activists and War on Poverty funding agencies. Not coincidentally, neither initiative made much use of community action, though sporadic protests helped pressure governments to release funds. That said, both DeFreitas and Cohen did benefit from the existence of Community Action Agencies, whose institutional framework helped connect local residents with the new resources being offered to them. Another notable aspect of these programs was that they explicitly targeted women, especially mothers. That ran counter to the gendered discourse that had dominated the long War on Poverty. Dating back to the postwar gang initiatives, ideas about poverty and its root causes had been crafted around young males and their criminal activities; women had largely been ignored. Yet female reformers like Dorothy Orr, Olga DeFreitas, and Audrey Cohen understood the importance of making the War on Poverty work for women. Programs like Young Mothers and the Women's Talent Corps expanded the educational opportunities of young women and helped launch their careers in a rapidly changing urban job market. These were forms of maximum feasible participation in their own right.

Things Fall Apart

Even as these successes were unfolding, Youth in Action was on the brink of imploding. In the spring of 1967, the antipoverty bureaucracy cracked down. Findings of managerial incompetence within the embattled Brooklyn agency led to the imposition of "special conditions" by both the federal OEO and the city's Council Against Poverty. Reverend H. Carl McCall, a onetime YIA board member who now chaired the Council Against Poverty, threatened to withdraw funds from YIA unless it systematically evaluated its programs and staff and completed the "spin-off" process by which YIA programs would be delegated to other local groups. In the interim, the agency would not be permitted to hire any staff or fund new programs without approval from both city and federal authorities. After three years of planning, waiting, and restructuring, the agency now found itself being humiliated.[67]

Meanwhile, internal factionalism was hampering YIA's ability to establish goals and communicate them to the public. Several rival camps had emerged within the agency's orbit. The board, led by Walter Offutt, formed one camp, which accused executive director Walter Pinkston and the professional staff surrounding him—a second camp—of gross mismanagement.[68] Pinkston in turn blamed YIA's woes on a group of disaffected staffers within the agency who were allied with Sonny Carson and the street radicals of Bed-Stuy. This third camp included many neighborhood workers and youth leaders drawn from among the "indigenous" population; their grievances included low pay, poor working conditions, and a lack of benefits such as paid sick days and vacations.[69]

Throughout the late 1960s, the agency staggered from one crisis to another. Board meetings were routinely disrupted by protesters, professional agitators, and ordinary citizens wanting to air their grievances. Added to this was the challenge of maneuvering within a complex set of municipal, state, regional, and federal regulations that even the most seasoned planners—never mind employees hired off the welfare rolls—found difficult to navigate.[70] Naturally, staff at delegate agencies used their positions to build constituencies and employ friends. In an era of capital flight, the jobs created by the poverty programs were valuable resources. Any one of these factors might have caused Youth in Action's failure, and their accumulation pretty much guaranteed it.

A public board meeting on August 9, 1967, gave a glimpse of things to come. The meeting, held in the auditorium of P.S. 21, was called to inform the community of YIA's recent activities. It quickly devolved into a political slugfest. The opening round involved the dispensation of part-time jobs in the Neighborhood Youth Corps. Such jobs were valuable currency in the marketplace of neighborhood influence, but a board member, Carson Wright, explained that only 2,400 of 3,600 available positions had been filled for the summer. When Wright blamed incompetent staffers for mishandling files and recommended that board members be allowed to handpick new recruits, a group of irate youths rushed the stage, led by Timothy Vincent, director of YIA's Youth Leadership Institute. After a long shouting match and some near-scuffles, the meeting moved on to a discussion of financial reports. Those, too, were explosive. As Ralph Ward,

YIA's bookkeeper, delivered the figures for Head Start, a woman in the audience rose and impatiently asked what had happened to $4,000 allocated for "parent activities." That provoked yet another outbreak of tumult. Again, the meeting resumed, only to devolve once more into chaos when a young woman grabbed the microphone and demanded to know where YIA's money was being spent. At this point, Vincent barged onto the stage for the second time and demanded to know what the agency was doing with "all the money." This prompted CORE's Isaiah Lewis, who, like Vincent, was on the YIA payroll, to accuse Pinkston—his boss—of fraud. Further screaming, swearing, and sweating ensued. The meeting eventually broke up, amid chaos, at 10:30 P.M.[71]

Community action was undeniably at work—but the community was taking action against itself. Similar stories played out across the country. The "maximum feasible participation" mandate inspired activists to organize, agitate, and dream big. It also split communities into rival camps scrapping for pieces of a pie much smaller than initially expected. Sviridoff would look back decades later and conclude that the War on Poverty had "succumbed to an 'empowerment' fetish." According to the architect of New York's antipoverty bureaucracy, "years were lost while groups fought over their place in the hierarchy, scarcely remembering what it was they wanted control over, or why." Three years into the War on Poverty, the social transformation envisioned by Lyndon Johnson, and by Dorothy Orr, seemed a long way off.[72]

The Community Action Program had originally been conceived as a tool for "achieving maximum institutional change," as one planner put it. But there were contradictions lurking in the weeds. On the one hand, communities were held to have been damaged by the legacies of segregation, poverty, and blocked opportunities; on the other, they were assumed to possess within them sufficient intellectual resources and political clout to take on the structures that were supposedly blocking their opportunities. Communities were judged to be disorganized, lacking in competence, and rife with pathologies; nonetheless they were expected to promote self-help through effective organization.

The men within the Kennedy-Johnson administration who came up with this theoretical framework can be forgiven for their inconsistencies. The civil-rights movement had shown just how potent the organizing power of the oppressed could be; in 1964, as the War on Poverty was ramping up, the Mississippi voting-rights drive was providing an object

196

lesson in what "local people" could accomplish when they came together. Further, the War on Poverty was crafted at a historical moment when formerly marginal groups around the globe were finding within their own communities the strength, intellectual leadership, and moral authority to take on structures of authority. Such developments clearly affected the architects of the Great Society.[73]

For all that, community groups like Youth in Action were necessarily limited in what they could accomplish. Focused on their own neighborhood, Bed-Stuy activists only had power to achieve "maximum institutional change" over the institutions they already controlled. That resulted in internal struggles to influence YIA itself. In small ways and for brief moments, the activists of Bed-Stuy managed to beat the odds and launch successful programs that helped individuals and empowered the community. Teenage mothers finished high school, learned skills, and gained a sense of dignity. Unemployed women gained footholds in the social-service professions and democratized access to schools. Toddlers went to school while their mothers worked. Meanwhile, Youth in Action hired hundreds of staffers from among its "indigenous" population, providing valuable jobs and, for some, skills training. But there was little the people of Bedford-Stuyvesant could do to counter the larger forces that came to be arrayed against them. "The task of social reconstruction has been delegated to the Community Corporation," Sonny Carson wrote in Youth in Action's monthly newspaper in August 1967. "But who takes care of the immediate problems of Black people? Who cares when they are driven to delirium by the many bureaucratic processes one has to penetrate in order to acquire one's rights in this great metropolis?"[74]

Even the most successful YIA initiatives found it hard to manage bureaucratic hurdles and overcome the lack of basic resources in Bed-Stuy. The Young Mothers Program, for instance, was waylaid by a seemingly mundane problem: inadequate classroom facilities. In 1967, the Board of Education refused to accredit the program on the grounds that its cramped, shoddy quarters constituted an unsuitable educational environment. In response, Olga DeFreitas began a frantic search for a building in which to house the program, but the best option she could find was an abandoned church on Monroe Street in need of "a vast amount of renovating and face-lifting." Help would eventually come from a coalition of DeFreitas's many admirers around Bedford-Stuyvesant, and the popular program got its building in 1971. But, in 1977, DeFreitas was indicted on charges of fraud and embezzlement connected with an abandoned building she had rented for the Young Mothers Program in 1969, during its search for a permanent home. She was eventually acquitted—she had been an unknowing dupe in a real-estate fraud orchestrated by a friend of hers—but her career lay in shambles. "I'm finished caring," she said.[75]

The discrepancy between Lyndon Johnson's soaring rhetoric and the limited resources at the disposal of community groups—as illustrated by Olga DeFreitas's search for a classroom—bred disillusionment and cynicism. What exactly was community action meant to accomplish? Were agencies like Youth in Action vehicles for community empowerment and policy reform or were they institutions for controlling restive populations? Carson, for one, dismissed YIA and other "organizations created to handle the many social needs and grievances of the Black citizens" as thinly veiled efforts to "pacify, train, analyze, propagandize and organize depraved areas to make them more contiguous [sic] with the rest of American society."[76]

The policy genealogy of the War on Poverty could certainly be read in a way that vindicated Carson's claim. It was undeniable that the community-action approach had emerged from efforts to tame young criminals, and that policymakers' quest to uncover the "root causes" of juvenile delinquency took on a greater urgency in the mid-1960s, following the urban uprisings. But the story of community action was not only the story of elite intentions. The residents of "depraved areas" had not merely been acted on; they had acted, and their demands had been heard. What Carson dubbed "the grievances of Black citizens" had been articulated, clearly and forcefully, by a leadership group intent on increasing its power through the welfare state.

The Community Action Program, at its heart, was a political mechanism designed to link communities in need with the people possessing the knowledge and resources to do something about those needs. Hence the emphasis on *empowering* the poor. The poverty warriors in Washington, DC, not only predicted that this process might lead to political clashes; they embraced that possibility. As one of them wrote in a 1964 memo:

A central mechanism which creates such unaccustomed bedfellows (as those possessing the problem and those with the power to do something about it) and then plans to engage in action seeking changes in organizations rather than (or in addition to) individuals, *must produce conflict*. The community action program shakes up existing arrangements and demands a rethinking of traditional definitions of the problem. Such conflict must be anticipated. It is not only normal but indicative that key community forces are finally dealing with problems which have become all too "invisible."[77]

Conflict, then, would be a necessary and proper part of community action. But how could the energies unleashed during such conflicts be harnessed and then diverted into substantive policy reforms? That remained something of a mystery. But as Youth in Action was floundering, the citizens of Bed-Stuy were preparing to launch a new experiment in community development.

6

The Power to Act

We must maintain our commitment to act, to dare, to try again.
The plight of the cities, the physical decay and human despair
that pervades them, is the great internal problem of the American nation, the challenge which must be met.

—ROBERT F. KENNEDY, 1966

Close to a thousand people packed the auditorium of Public School 305 on Monroe Street on December 10, 1966. They were there for the plenary session of the Central Brooklyn Coordinating Council's third annual conference about the War on Poverty—but nobody expected to hear much about the roiling controversy surrounding Youth in Action. On the agenda was something bigger: the opening of a new front in the poverty war. It had been ten months since Elsie Richardson first met Robert F. Kennedy, and the community's plea for help had not fallen on deaf ears. Since then, Kennedy's staff had worked closely with CBCC on blueprints for the revitalization of Bedford-Stuyvesant. Now, the senator had chosen the CBCC conference as the occasion to go public with his new community-development initiative.[1]

As Richardson strode to the podium to open the proceedings, the crowd jostled for position in the back of the hall and craned their necks expectantly at the star-studded entourage Kennedy had brought with him. Seated behind Richardson were local bigwigs—Thomas R. Jones, Lucille Rose, and Ruth Goring—and a battery of powerful elites: Kennedy, of course, along with John Lindsay, Senator Jacob K. Javits, investment banker André Meyer, and Robert C. Wood of the federal Department of Housing and Urban Development. In the front row facing Richardson sat Brooklyn's three black Assembly members—Shirley Chisholm, Samuel Wright, and Bertram Baker—and behind them waited hundreds of Bed-Stuy's grass-roots activists.[2]

200

Elsie Richardson of the Central Brooklyn Coordinating Council addresses the crowd assembled at P. S. 305 on December 10, 1966, when Robert F. Kennedy announced the founding of twin Community Development Corporations in Bedford-Stuyvesant. Sitting behind her in the front row are André Meyer, Thomas Jones, Kennedy, Jacob Javits, John Lindsay, and Robert C. Wood. *Central Brooklyn Coordinator*

Richardson, true to character, refused to hide her ambivalence about the sudden onslaught of political capital in her community. She also made sure the citizens of Bed-Stuy took center stage. For every outsider that graced the rostrum, Richardson summoned a local personality—a minister, a block organizer, a clubwoman. First up was State Senator William C. Thompson, a Bed-Stuy native, whom she commanded to "direct a charge to the city, state, and federal officials seated here today." Thomson promptly did just that, but also threw in a joke about "a Jew, an Italian and a Negro," delivered in heavy Brooklynese, which brought the house down. "That's our boy," Richardson replied, laughing. Then she proceeded to read, slowly, from an article in the previous day's *World-Journal Tribune*.[3]

"'As a first step in curing the social and economic ills of Bedford-Stuyvesant, Brooklyn's teeming *ghetto*,'" she read, her voice dripping with irony as she stressed certain words, "'the city must find—quote—*someone* who can coordinate whatever federal and state help is available—end of quote. This was the opinion of Senator Robert F. Kennedy after he toured the ghetto last winter, peering into its *abandoned* buildings and talking to its *downtrodden* people.'"[4]

Richardson paused for dramatic effect, letting the audience's hesitant chuckles turn into a torrent of guffaws. Cackling sardonically herself, she set the broadsheet aside and resumed in a dead-serious tone. "Actually," she said, "this served as a reminder to me of our February meeting. I really had not given too much thought to what took place that day, since, frankly, I didn't have the time. We find here in Bedford-Stuyvesant that you do what you have to do at a specific moment and then you have to move on to the next problem." The message was clear: Kennedy had a lot to learn about the "teeming ghetto" he was proposing to transform, and support for his project would be conditional.[5]

And yet Kennedy shared much of Richardson's thinking about the past, present, and future of Bedford-Stuyvesant's War on Poverty. Disillusioned with the Community Action Program, the senator believed that too much time had been spent promoting participation, empowerment, and political conflict. Going forward, urban programs should funnel capital into poor neighborhoods, encourage business initiative, foster home ownership, and— most importantly—create jobs. In his speech, Kennedy promised that the new project would "combine the best of community action with the best of the private enterprise system."[6]

To carry out that ambitious mandate, Kennedy announced that he had brought together an unprecedented coalition linking the blocks of Central Brooklyn to the boardrooms of Lower Manhattan. Supported by some of the country's top urbanists and foremost financiers, the new Bed-Stuy initiative would circumvent the kinds of funding difficulties, bureaucratic obstacles, and political pressures that were hampering agencies like Youth in Action. Or so Kennedy hoped. "The power to act," he said in his speech, "is the power to command resources, of money and mind and skill; to build the housing, create the social and educational services, and buy the goods which this community wants and needs and deserves." In Bedford-Stuyvesant, nothing was yet assured—but the combination of community competence, private investment, and public power was promising. "If we here can meet and master our problems," Kennedy said, "if this community can become an avenue of opportunity and a place of pleasure and excitement for its people, then others will take heart from your example, and men all over the United States will remember your contribution with the deepest gratitude."[7]

In the meantime, how to set about reinvigorating Bedford-Stuyvesant? The whiz kids on Kennedy's staff were bursting with ideas; the businessmen had their theories, too. But the people of Bedford-Stuyvesant had themselves spent years thinking about how to stem capital flight, promote home ownership, and create jobs for the restless, unemployed youth of the area. Although Kennedy's initiative was bold in its embrace of private-sector support, the new project gathered together a familiar group of Brooklyn organizers and politicos. After all their painstaking efforts to set up community-run antipoverty programs, the activists affiliated with CBCC were loath to let outsiders dictate the terms of participation in Bed-Stuy's latest policy experiment.

Since setting up YIA in 1964, CBCC had continued its search for "comprehensive" solutions to Bed-Stuy's problems. Though supportive of YIA's initial programs, Richardson and her colleagues saw them as insufficient. Beginning in 1964, they enlisted urban planners from the nearby Pratt Institute for Design to help devise new approaches to urban renewal, business development, and brownstone preservation. This kind of thinking represented the other side of the War on Poverty. Where the Community Action Program had sought to revitalize Bed-Stuy's psychic resources, the new Community Development Corporation would strive to repair its physical resources.

Advocacy Planning for Brooklyn

The Pratt Institute for Design sits in Clinton Hill, a quiet enclave of Brooklyn on the northwestern edge of Bedford-Stuyvesant. Founded in the late 1880s, the school's elegant campus stands as a testament to a bygone era when industrialists such as Charles Pratt, director of the Standard Oil Trust, flocked to the area. By the mid-1960s, Clinton Hill's stately row houses and high-ceilinged mansions had grown decrepit. Meanwhile, the great engine of working-class life in the neighborhood, the Brooklyn Navy Yard, was shutting its gates. Seemingly overnight, the area's white majority cleared out. Against this backdrop of poverty and disinvestment, Pratt, which offered degrees in art, architecture, and urban planning, emerged as a clearinghouse for new ideas about how cities might be revitalized. It was there that the trail was blazed for Kennedy's journey into Brooklyn.[8]

In 1963, the chairman of Pratt's Department of City Planning, Professor George M. Raymond, founded an institute he called the Pratt Center for Community Improvement.[9] The hopeful name belied deep frustration. Raymond, a partner in a prominent urban-planning firm, had long worked as a consultant to the New York City Planning Commission and had helped design dozens of urban-renewal projects up and down the East Coast. But his career had hit a roadblock. The neighborhood revolt against urban renewal, along with the 1961 release of Jane Jacobs's *The Death and Life of Great American Cities* (which Raymond judged "regrettably slanted"), put planners in a tough spot. Jacobs had not only undermined their wisdom and expertise but had vociferously denounced the very existence of their profession. With her followers proliferating and becoming increasingly strident, Raymond concluded that it was becoming "almost impossible to make progress because of serious friction between the city and neighborhood groups."[10]

In fact, Raymond himself had been criticizing New York's urban-renewal efforts for years. He had decried the city's refusal to create "well-planned, integrated residential neighborhoods"; he thought there had been insufficient follow-through in neighborhood-rehabilitation programs; and he worried that public housing was descending into "deadly project monotony." In the heyday of Robert Moses, he had advocated the involvement of non-elites in urban renewal. In 1962, Raymond was already invoking the idea of "maximum community participation" in planning, foreshadowing the language of the Economic Opportunity Act.[11]

But in the era of Jacobs, Raymond suddenly found himself running to keep up. He had experienced the backlash firsthand in 1962, when he collaborated with citizen groups and city officials to come up with an urban-renewal plan for a slice of Brooklyn just south of Atlantic Avenue. This was an area mostly inhabited by Brooklynites of Italian and Irish descent, along with a growing group of Arab Americans. But a new wave of "brownstoners" had begun to settle there too, spilling out of Brooklyn Heights and into the poorer precincts of what was then known (rather imprecisely) as South Brooklyn. Eager to lend their new stomping grounds a whiff of historical cachet, they had renamed it Cobble Hill. The newcomers— white, middle-class, creative types—were instinctively suspicious of government-sponsored urban renewal, and Jacobs helped them mobilize against the plans drawn up by Raymond and supported by the area's old-guard community organizations. The project was eventually scuttled.[12]

What bothered Raymond was not merely that his plans had gone for naught but that those plans had been carefully drawn up "in response to the community's own initiative," only to be iced by a "few articulate groups" who rejected urban renewal altogether. Raymond accused those groups of blindly following Jacobs's lead and stampeding their neighbors into rejecting much-needed services. Raymond supported community participation, but it would be dangerously undemocratic to give self-styled community advocates veto power over the kinds of citywide planning decisions needed to modernize infrastructure and preserve what Raymond called the "social balance." Citizens with no grounding in land-use regulations or housing laws could easily make bad decisions or have their opinions diverted into routinized channels. "It is to be hoped that the forces unleashed by recent revolts against specific renewal proposals will be brought under control before they succeed in undermining the very principle of delegation of power by the people and their faith in democratic processes," Raymond wrote in the inaugural issue of *Pratt Planning Papers*, a journal he founded in 1962. Raymond also worried that cynical politicians, sensing which way the winds were blowing, were chanting participatory slogans as a way to defuse challenges to the established political order. Citizen participation was being elevated into an end in itself—at the expense of tangible improvements to residential neighborhoods. All told, Raymond wrote, "meaningful citizen participation . . . is almost impossible to achieve."[13]

That's where Pratt's new Center for Community Improvement came in. Raymond and his students would arm "legitimate, broadly representative citizens' organizations"—as opposed to special-interest groups—with the tools they needed to make smart planning decisions. In so doing, they would show that planners and grassroots activists were not natural antagonists but potential allies. Done correctly, planning could harness the impulse toward participatory democracy and all the while improve neighborhoods. It was a powerful idea in sync with the time and place—and it anticipated the fusion of policy expertise and grassroots energy that Robert Kennedy would aim to achieve in Bed-Stuy.[14]

Raymond's new center sprang to life with a grant of almost $100,000 from the Rockefeller Brothers Fund, earmarked for a demonstration program aimed at educating poor communities on how to use government agencies. Raymond assigned his star graduate student, Ron Shiffman, to canvass Pratt's backyard in search of community partners. Shiffman's outlook, it turned out, differed from his teacher's in significant ways. ("George made the mistake of hiring me to do the project," he would joke decades later.) Raymond was an old-style Progressive who hoped to educate communities about planning so they would ultimately be more amenable to the advice of experts. Shiffman, meanwhile, was a man of the New Left who foresaw a process of mutual learning. He had grown up in a family of Russian Jewish immigrants in the Bronx, and he was fresh to Brooklyn. Only twenty-six, he had marched in civil-rights protests and had met some of the Bed-Stuy activists, including future CBCC executive director Donald Benjamin, on a bus ride from Harlem to the March on Washington. Shiffman thought planners should offer technical expertise—statistical analysis, mapping—and tips on how to navigate bureaucracies, regulations, and zoning ordinances. But they shouldn't pretend to know what was best for local people. To give the voiceless a voice, planners must instead listen, collaborate, and advocate. In Bed-Stuy, Shiffman discovered a landscape alive with ideas, organizations, and political ferment. "The community groups were the leaders," Shiffman would later say, "and we were just helping them think things out."[15]

This approach put Shiffman at the forefront of a fledgling movement that would soon become known as "advocacy planning." The concept was formalized in a 1965 article by planner Paul Davidoff in the *Journal of the American Institute of Planners*. Davidoff addressed the basic dilemma facing planners in the mid-1960s: "Urban politics, in an era of increasing government activity in planning and welfare, must balance the demands for ever-increasing central bureaucratic control against the demands for increased concern for the unique requirements of local, specialized interests. The welfare of all and the welfare of minorities are both deserving of support: Planning must be so structured and so practiced as to account for this unavoidable bifurcation of the public interest."[16]

This analysis applied not only to urban renewal but also to social-welfare provision. In many ways, it encapsulated the difficulties the Community Action Program was just beginning to face. For Davidoff, it was imperative that planners explicitly spell out their values and advocate "courses of action" that exemplified those values. Planners should stop portraying themselves as value-neutral technicians devoted only to physical change. Instead, Davidoff urged them to support the struggle against racial discrimination and economic inequality by lending their expertise to poor communities. Fairer cities could be built, as long as planners took the time to teach ordinary citizens about the complex decisions that affected their lives—and, just as importantly, if planners provided space for those citizens to voice their concerns. Yet Davidoff, like Raymond, maintained that citizen participation was not an end in and of itself. "The difficulty with current citizen participation programs is that citizens are more often *reacting* to agency programs than *proposing* their concepts of appropriate goals and future action," he wrote. In effect, Davidoff wanted the planning profession to follow the lead of the various other professionals who had enlisted to help fight the War on Poverty: sociologists mapping out demonstration projects, social workers fostering community action, lawyers staffing Legal Services offices, and nurses working in neighborhood health clinics.[17]

The Pratt Center's work was also inspired by Paul Ylvisaker of the Ford Foundation. In the late 1950s, Ylvisaker had called for an urban equivalent to the rural-extension agents that land-grant colleges had long assigned to work with farmers in the surrounding areas. Ford followed up with an experimental program of "urban extension" run through several universities around the country. The federal government would endorse urban extension in the Higher Education Act of 1965, and in 1966 the Pratt planners received a modest federal grant of $15,000 for their urban-extension work. The idea of urban extension struck a chord with the Pratt planners because it assumed that academics had a responsibility to serve the communities in which they worked.[18]

The first group to step forward and request Pratt's help was called Church Community Services. Run out of the Bedford Avenue branch of the YMCA, where CBCC held many of its meetings, Church Community Services coordinated the social-outreach endeavors of various black churches in Brooklyn. The group was led by H. Carl McCall, a young clergyman from Boston, who would later chair the Council Against Poverty under Mayor Lindsay. It also included some of Bed-Stuy's most visible civil-rights leaders, notably Milton Galamison and Sandy Ray. The ministers group took on many campaigns, including voter registration, political education, and youth programs. Members also partnered with a coalition of Harlem ministers to plan a summer youth-outreach program that received city and federal antipoverty funds in 1965. But what McCall and his fellow churchmen asked of Raymond and Shiffman was help in retaining Bed-Stuy's shrinking middle class.[19]

The issue of urban renewal loomed in the background. In the post–Robert Moses era, New York's urban-renewal program was no longer synonymous with "Negro removal." Some Bed-Stuy activists, including the ministers who approached Raymond and Shiffman, believed that renewal needn't mean demolition: it could instead fund the rehabilitation of historic districts, action against slumlords, aid to homeowners, and much else. Such activists saw renewal as the best hope for injecting government funds into their neighborhood at a time when private capital was drying up. Yet most Brooklynites, including many poor people who had been displaced themselves, continued to regard urban renewal as a symbol not of a benevolent state but of an overbearing, destructive one. According to Shiffman, "There was a lot of fear."[20]

In 1964, both the hopes and the fears were justified. That April, the City Planning Commission announced that it was done atoning for past sins. Selective slum clearance would resume—but this time with a human face. According to the *Times*, the new program "would tear down some of the worst slums without tearing apart the lives of the occupants. In part, the program would mean a return to the bulldozer—the only way of dealing with the hard-core slums, in the opinion of most experts. But . . . that would be buffered by a wide range of techniques for relocation and social aid developed in recent years." The city chose three majority-black areas, including a section of Bedford-Stuyvesant surrounding Fulton Park, as testing grounds for the new ideas. "In these areas," the Planning Commission announced, "blight and deterioration are so advanced that much of the recommended renewal treatment is likely to be redevelopment." To people living around Fulton Park, that sounded an awful lot like slum clearance. They began to mobilize.[21]

The men of Church Community Services also opposed the Fulton Park plan, but for slightly different reasons. As they observed to the Pratt planners, demolition would displace people from the renewal area just south of Fulton Street into nearby Stuyvesant Heights, which by 1965 was starting to show "evidences of severe blight . . . even along the east–west streets, which, until recently, had managed to remain fairly immune to decay." They predicted that the influx of low-income residents into an affluent but jittery enclave would end up "tipping the balance toward its deterioration" and send the remaining professionals packing. The group commissioned a team of Pratt students led by Shiffman, by now an assistant professor, to conduct a housing survey around Fulton Park, with an eye toward designing alternatives to the city's demolition-focused renewal plan. The overall objective, in Raymond's words, was "to demonstrate how a core city community can be conserved, rehabilitated, and renewed, by saving the best part of each neighborhood, and by giving the stable leadership of the community an incentive to remain and improve their housing." But the young, white Pratt surveyors received a cold welcome. The issue of urban renewal touched a raw nerve in Central Brooklyn. "We very quickly encountered a lot of opposition," Shiffman would recall.[22]

That opposition was voiced through a group called the Fulton Park Community Council, which represented local tenants and homeowners of modest means. These people worried less about the flight of Stuyvesant Heights's bourgeoisie than about seeing their own blocks obliterated by bulldozers. Many were women who opposed the all-male ministers group, and especially the Pratt planners, as patronizing outsiders who had no right to speak for them. They pointed out that few of the ministers lived in the area slated for renewal. Led by the voluble Elsie Richardson, whose house on Prospect Place sat just south of the renewal zone, the Fulton Park Community Council demanded help in halting the city's plans.[23]

The Pratt men counseled patience. Despite the sordid history of "negro removal," Raymond insisted that a well-thought-out urban-renewal program was "the community's best available chance of launching it on a course toward the changes it so obviously needed." Among the potential benefits, the city had mooted the idea of building a community college on cleared land near Fulton Park. The locals balked. "Because of the city's almost incredibly poor and insensitive performance in recent years," Raymond and Shiffman would write in 1967, groups like the Fulton Park Community Council "were suspicious of the renewal program and were highly skeptical of the city's motivation."[24]

The Fulton Park Community Council by itself wielded little clout, but as an affiliate of CBCC, the group could tap into a much larger federation of activists, including Elsie Richardson herself. And the Pratt men were listening. They proceeded with the study for Church Community Services—which resulted in a 1965 report titled "Stuyvesant Heights: A Good Neighborhood in Need of Help"—but Shiffman especially was keen to help CBCC come up with an alternative to the city's plans. As it turned out, the drama surrounding Fulton Park would last two decades. Under pressure, the city agreed first to modify its plans, then it delayed implementation for several years, and then it changed directions again before ultimately proceeding with construction on a piecemeal basis. But, as Elsie Richardson would insist, Fulton Park was only a small piece of the puzzle.

Urban Renewal Renewed

While the protests surrounding Fulton Park were picking up steam in the summer of 1964, CBCC was in the midst of launching Youth in Action. If this undeniably represented a coup for CBCC, none saw it as a final solution to the problems of Bed-Stuy. In the early 1960s, CBCC activists like Elsie Richardson, Shirley Chisholm, and Robert Palmer had worked toward varied goals: improving failing schools, desegregating workplaces, attracting urban-renewal monies, rehabilitating depressed blocks, combating youth crime, and strengthening black political power. By 1964 they had achieved a measure of success on several fronts—yet they worried that "uncoordinated, piecemeal attempts at social and physical renewal" would ultimately fall short. Thus, even as they were launching YIA, Richardson and company were laying the groundwork for a "comprehensive" program of government-funded community revitalization.[25]

A common historical argument about the War on Poverty is that the social-scientific theory embedded in the Community Action Program ultimately limited the range of policy outcomes. According to this line of thinking, poverty planners' understanding of economic want as a cultural condition foreclosed the possibility of tackling inequalities embedded in the political economy. Unemployment and systemic racism were ignored in favor of less tangible goals such as community cohesion and the transformation of youth behavior. Such flawed theoretical premises, combined with the overheated rhetoric of the president and OEO, led to great disillusionment.[26]

The problem with this interpretation is that it overlooks the openness of policy dialogue at the local level. There was nothing to prevent grassroots groups from doing two or more things at once. They could adapt social-scientific discourse to fit their own needs, simultaneously launching juvenile-delinquency programs *and* pursuing efforts to create jobs and fight discrimination. The very fact that a War on Poverty had been declared encouraged activists to think big, to push beyond simply implementing the programs being sponsored by OEO and the city agencies. This was supposedly an unconditional fight, so why settle for a youth-oriented Community Action Agency? From the perspective of CBCC's activists, the drive to remedy Bed-Stuy's psychosocial ills must be supplemented by efforts to tackle physical problems. If anything, the War on Poverty should attack both simultaneously.

Beginning in 1964, CBCC worked closely with the Pratt planners in an effort to articulate a new vision of community-led urban renewal. The pivot point for this partnership was Elsie Richardson. In 1964, Richardson was emerging as the most forceful voice within CBCC and as its most energetic organizer. Her prominence reflected a changing of the guard in Bedford-Stuyvesant, a shifting mood. Richardson didn't hail from an established family or from the ranks of the striving professional class. Nor did she harbor political ambitions, in contrast with Maude Richardson, Robert Palmer, Shirley Chisholm, and other CBCC leaders. Instead, Richardson made her name as an activist by organizing tenants at Albany Houses, the Crown Heights public-housing project where she and her family lived in the early 1950s. She first came to CBCC as a representative of Stuyvesant Community Center, which had been launched in the 1940s with funds from the Brooklyn Council for Social Planning and later received Youth Board monies to perform outreach work in the projects. By the 1960s, Elsie and her husband had become homeowners. In the early 1960s, she dedicated the bulk of her activism to block associations and to CBCC's Housing and Urban Planning Committee, of which she became chair in 1964. She also served on the executive board of the PTA at P.S. 83, which her children attended, and she eventually became a vice-president of the citywide United Parents Association.[27]

Richardson approached problems with the straight-ahead, forthright manner of a working mother who had no time to waste on halfway measures. She sometimes stunned men, especially powerful ones, by refusing to flatter them. Often enough, she issued orders instead. Unlike her friend Shirley Chisholm, another famous straight-talker, Richardson had little patience for political niceties. On the public stage, she was relentless, even domineering. But at street level, people knew her as a community builder who blessed her neighbors with magnificent smiles and remembered everybody's birthday.

As Pratt's Ron Shiffman began navigating Central Brooklyn's array of block associations and civic groups, he encountered Elsie Richardson everywhere. The two soon struck up a working partnership that would turn into a lifelong friendship. Fifteen years Shiffman's senior, Richardson took the young planner under her wing and mentored him in the subtleties of community organizing. Shiffman's task in Bedford-Stuyvesant was to educate the locals, but he learned from Richardson a lesson few outsiders in the 1960s were prepared to comprehend. "Elsie Richardson taught me that

CBCC leaders meet with Brooklyn Borough President Abe Stark and planners affiliated with the Pratt Institute in 1965. From left: Lucille Rose, Donald Benjamin, Shirley Chisholm, Stark, Nat Parrish, Elsie Richardson, Ruth Goring, and Ron Shiffman. *Youth in Action Newspaper*

Bedford-Stuyvesant wasn't a ghetto," he later recalled. "It was a community." Meanwhile, Shiffman lent her his professional insight whenever she asked for guidance. (She had a habit of calling him at 6:30 A.M. the morning after CBCC meetings, just so they could keep the conversation going.) "He has served as my right arm," she declared at the meeting unveiling Kennedy's project. "When we sit in meetings, I'm fine until it comes right down to the technicalities, and when it does, I simply turn around and I look for Mr. Ron Shiffman."[28]

In researching Stuyvesant Heights, Shiffman concluded that any plan for the revitalization of the area must take all of Bedford-Stuyvesant into account, not merely its middle-class brownstone blocks. That squared with the vision put forth by Richardson and other CBCC leaders such as Lucille Rose, Louise Bolling, and Ruth Goring. As the collaboration deepened, Shiffman relied on CBCC's congenial executive director, Donald Benjamin, to help him defuse tense situations and offer expert advice without seeming domineering. Shiffman joined the boards of both CBCC and, briefly, Youth in Action. The Pratt men took dozens of Brooklyn activists, including the CBCC leadership group, to New Haven and Baltimore, two cities that had earned national attention for their urban-renewal programs and neighborhood-conservation techniques. Shiffman and Richardson invited city, state, and federal officials to join community leaders in conversations about what lay ahead for Bed-Stuy. The Pratt men, Richardson would later recall, "taught us a lot about organizing the community."[29]

Shiffman and Pratt also helped CBCC develop its media strategy. In 1965, the council began airing a radio series called "Lifeline," which broadcast in fifteen-minute segments on Saturday nights and Sunday mornings on the local station WWRL. (Subjects included the poverty program, urban renewal, youth programs, and the history of Bedford-Stuyvesant.) Also in 1965, CBCC started publishing a monthly newspaper with a print run of 10,000. The *Central Brooklyn Coordinator* provided news and views about housing, poverty, and policy. Along with the *Youth in Action* newspaper, which began publication in 1964, the *Coordinator* provided neighborhood news to a community that had previously relied on the Brooklyn edition of the Harlem-based *Amsterdam News*. As a self-consciously activist publication, the *Coordinator* focused on improving the image of Bed-Stuy in the press and "changing the 'jungle' image which has been plastered all over Bedford-Stuyvesant." At the same time, CBCC activists appropriated the "ghetto" trope in the pages of the *Coordinator* and wielded it to their advantage. While pointing out the absurdity of Bed-Stuy's ever-changing boundaries, they pushed those boundaries outward as a way of dramatizing the area's needs. The inaugural issue of the *Coordinator*, dated August 16, 1965, called Bedford-Stuyvesant "the largest Negro ghetto in the country" and informed readers that it contained "just under a half million (500,000) people," along with 378 vacant lots, 346 abandoned buildings, and 56 burned-out buildings. Two months later, the *Coordinator* put Bed-Stuy's population at *over* half a million people—perhaps the most expansive estimate of the neighborhood's size ever put to print.[30]

Another facet of this strategy was to invite policymakers and urban scholars from across the city to join Bed-Stuy activists in reflecting on the challenges of urban redevelopment. On November 21, 1964, CBCC and Pratt co-hosted the first of several annual conferences about the War on Poverty. Some 500 people attended, including activists from around the five boroughs and representatives of sundry city and federal agencies. They joined a series of workshops, brainstorming sessions, and panels about how to revitalize Bed-Stuy and what role governments should play in that process. The result was a hodge-podge of proposals, some eminently practical and others wildly ambitious.[31]

The conference also gave CBCC a platform for the release of a working paper titled "Program for Total Rehabilitation and Renewal of Bedford-Stuyvesant and Central Brooklyn Area." The paper had been drawn up by CBCC's Housing and Planning Committee, which Richardson chaired, with Shiffman's help. It laid out for the first time CBCC's vision of "comprehensive" community development. Block-by-block organizing would be a key component, as would Youth in Action's programs. But the time had come for bricks-and-mortar projects that would create jobs. CBCC proposed to demolish burned-out buildings, clean up vacant lots, plant trees, maintain sidewalks, and create vest-pocket parks on abandoned land. Brownstone-renovation projects would also be a focus; on select blocks, a certain number of abandoned townhouses would be rehabilitated and transformed into social-service centers or, in some cases, new housing for large families. Crucially, each of these projects would create jobs. Builders contracted to work in the community would receive incentives to hire young, unemployed black men and use the building sites to train them in the construction trades. Thus did CBCC propose to address the problems of jobs, skills, physical blight, and wayward youth, all in one shot—in other words, to marry the New Deal and the Great Society.[32]

These proposals reflected the emerging belief that historic housing stock could anchor redevelopment efforts. One reason Bed-Stuy was often labeled a slum in the 1960s was because such a high proportion of its buildings (91 percent) were built before 1939. As one 1965 study put it, "The age of these buildings is directly representative of their quality. Thirty percent of the buildings in the area are categorized as deteriorating or dilapidated." The Central Brooklyn brownstoners flipped this equation on its head. They concurred that age was directly representative of quality, but insisted the older the better. Dilapidation was something to be embraced as a challenge. Older buildings could be romantic, and they could be beautiful. Victorian townhouses offered tradition, continuity, sophistication, and community. They need not necessarily send the creative classes fleeing the city limits.[33]

In some ways, this thinking lined up with the brownstone-revitalization movements that were unfolding in nearby neighborhoods of Brooklyn at this time. "In a kinetic modern city," historian Suleiman Osman has written, "brownstones were anchors, their heavy facades giving new white-collar workers a sense of rootedness and permanence in a transient urban environment." The brownstoning ideal, as Osman shows, was particularly attractive among white, countercultural types. In Park Slope and Boerum Hill, for instance, groups of brownstoners were cleaning up parks and empty lots, planting trees, and restoring historic blocks, one façade at a time. Those activists shared many battles with the block-based activists of Bedford-Stuyvesant: against redlining, declining city services, and clubhouse politicians. Yet the white brownstoners harbored an antistate impulse that reflected their self-perception as pioneers in an "urban wilderness." The homeowners who formed the core of CBCC held no such romantic notions. They eyed the state warily. But given the speed with which *private* capital had fled their community since World War II, they also saw government—and especially the national Democratic Party—as a potential ally in the fight against further deterioration.[34]

"Public funds and public initiative to encourage private contribution will be essential if substantial total renewal is to take place," CBCC argued in its 1964 proposals. For instance, the city must push to integrate building-trades unions and to desegregate housing by enforcing open-occupancy laws. Municipal authorities would also do well to convert rehabilitated brownstones into public housing rather than placing more clients in already overcrowded highrises. More low-rent housing was needed, but it should be integrated into the fabric of middle- and high-income areas rather than concentrated in grim surroundings. Crucially, CBCC also called on governments to address the legacy of redlining, demanding that "plentiful loans, on liberal terms, be made available to homeowners and small landlords to rehabilitate their property." If large financial institutions refused to cooperate, the community could create a "rehabilitation pool" from public funds and savings cooperatives to stimulate development and investment in Bedford-Stuyvesant.[35]

This kind of thinking, articulated at the very outset of the federal War on Poverty, offered evidence that the activists of Bedford-Stuyvesant were fighting on several fronts and had been for some time. Taken together, the CBCC proposals represented a set of assumptions about Bed-Stuy that would prove appealing to Robert Kennedy two years later. Rather than seeing apathy and pathological behavior as the chief obstacles facing the community, CBCC emphasized joblessness and the inaccessibility of investment capital. They argued that the presence of a relatively large group of homeowners could be a source of strength and stability, and that Bedford-Stuyvesant's building stock, made up in large part of stately, sturdy brownstones, offered a leg up in the rehabilitation game. That this analysis was presented at a "War on Poverty" conference demonstrates the complexity of the thinking that was unfolding at the local level. It also shows that the War on Poverty was not so much a fixed set of programs legislated in 1964 (and doomed to fail soon thereafter) but a process that inspired local activists to think through new ways of accessing state resources, despite the limitations of governmental action.[36]

Shiffman, Richardson, and their allies in Brooklyn were hardly alone in promoting a model of neighborhood action that aspired to tackle physical, social, and economic rehabilitation simultaneously. In 1963, for instance, the Citizens Housing and Planning Council of New York (whose high-powered board of directors included George Raymond) asked Mayor Wagner to fund a demonstration program in Brownsville aimed at achieving "total community development" by harnessing both public and private resources.[37] Grassroots activists around the country were also experimenting with such initiatives. The best-known effort was led by Reverend Leon Sullivan of Zion Baptist Church in North Philadelphia. Through a for-profit corporation named Progress Investment Associates, Sullivan's group began building low- and middle-income housing in the mid-1960s and in 1968 erected the first black-owned shopping center in the country. Another Sullivan initiative was the Opportunities Industrialization Center, which offered training for young African Americans and put them to work on local construction projects. The Philadelphia experiments caught the attention of the Ford Foundation, along with Kennedy.[38]

Such ideas were also beginning to percolate up to other federal policymakers. In October 1965, President Johnson appointed the Task Force on Urban Problems, which proposed what was baptized as the Demonstration Cities program. Later renamed Model Cities, this was an effort to wield overwhelming resources in a select number of depressed urban areas. In effect, Model Cities functioned as Lyndon Johnson's rejoinder to mounting criticism of the Community Action Program. The program placated mayors by sending federal funds not to community groups but to municipal governments. Each city was given considerable leeway in designing its own "comprehensive solutions" to physical decay. Generally, programs focused on physical rehabilitation, new housing, and infrastructure projects, though some Model Cities programs also emphasized youth programs and social services. That said, federal guidelines dictated that citizen participation be a key component of the planning process, thus making Model Cities of a piece with other fronts in the poverty war.[39]

Similarly, in 1966, New York's Council Against Poverty stressed that community corporations should focus not only on community action and antipoverty activities but also education, housing, jobs, and physical planning. Later, the council defined its twin goals as "to eliminate the *physical* blight of poverty neighborhoods as well as the human deterioration of the people who inhabit them." This, the council argued, justified including middle-income neighborhoods among the city's target areas in the War on Poverty (which numbered twenty-six in 1967 as opposed to sixteen two years earlier). Blight ultimately affected the poor and non-poor alike, and arbitrary boundaries could not always be drawn between "deteriorated" and non-deteriorated areas.[40]

CBCC's proposals, then, emerged amid a broader shift in thinking among policy elites, who were taking a fresh look at urban problems in the mid-1960s. But the specific proposals the Brooklynites advanced in 1964 were ahead of the curve, and they made barely a ripple. Partly, this neglect owed to the strong emphasis poverty planners were still placing on juvenile delinquency; it also reflected the institutionalization within OEO of opportunity theory and the "culture of poverty" thesis, both of which stressed the psychosocial roots of urban problems. Most importantly, Bedford-Stuyvesant activists lacked the political clout needed to effect major policy changes. The struggle to gain urban-renewal funds, which had been ongoing since the late 1950s, proved that point, as did the eighteen-month fight to gain funds for Youth in Action.[41]

Members of CBCC's Urban Planning and Housing Committee met repeatedly with lawmakers and policy experts over the course of 1965, but they failed to win real support for their proposals. Shiffman and Richardson became so adept at leading tours of Bed-Stuy that they developed different routes to tell different stories about the neighborhood, depending on the visitor. ("There was one tour where you could drive along the east–west blocks and see nothing but nice brownstones," Shiffman later recalled, "and another where you would drive north–south and see nothing but advanced decay.") Activists continued to push for a redrawing of congressional district lines in Central Brooklyn, where gerrymandering had so far kept white Democratic regulars in power. But that campaign wouldn't bear fruit until 1968, when Chisholm became Brooklyn's first black member of Congress. In the meantime, local leaders bitterly complained that Harlem had become the "glamour ghetto" and was drawing more than its fair share of urban-renewal and poverty funds, thanks to the outsize influence of Congressman Adam Clayton Powell Jr. "We get the feeling that many officials think that the only place for large-scale programs which affect Negroes is in Harlem," stated an editorial in the first issue of the *Central Brooklyn Coordinator*. "We are amazed that some of the best intentioned people have given only lip service to our needs and constant pleas. When we compare the programs which have been put into Harlem and look for their counterpart in Bedford-Stuyvesant, we are shocked to find that Bedford-Stuyvesant is very much underserved." CBCC activists continually emphasized that Bedford-Stuyvesant was as big, as diverse, and as complex as many major cities, and it should be treated as such. None of it changed the equation. "We were rebuffed constantly," Shiffman recalled. "We didn't have political power." A patron would have to be found.[42]

Tribune of the Underclass

As 1965 drew to a close, Robert F. Kennedy was completing his metamorphosis from jutted-jaw anticommunist to what historian Arthur Schlesinger called the "tribune of the underclass." This was no sudden transformation. Kennedy's reputation as a "tough guy" and a ruthless political operator was well-earned: he had ferreted out communists for Joseph McCarthy, fought Jimmy Hoffa during the McLellan Committee hearings, and, in the words of historian Joseph Palermo, "unleashed his innate aggressiveness in political combat" while promoting his brother's political ascendancy. Yet a strong sense of moral purpose underscored such episodes and carried through to his late-career crusades. From his time as attorney general, Kennedy encouraged alliances between the powerful and the powerless, between neighborhood groups and the federal government.[43]

Kennedy, like his brother, had been deeply touched in the early 1960s by Michael Harrington's "other America" thesis (though it's unclear whether they ever read the book) and by visceral encounters with human misery in the coal country of Appalachia and on the streets of New York City. Through the President's Committee on Juvenile Delinquency (PCJD), he sponsored early community-action experiments in Harlem and on the Lower East Side. Kennedy and his acolytes, principally his friend David Hackett, the executive director of PCJD, also helped design the War on Poverty. According to Richard Boone, a PCJD staffer who later oversaw the federal Community Action Program, Kennedy's "representatives on the anti-poverty task force were the strongest champions of maximum involvement of the poor."[44]

In the realm of civil rights, Kennedy's tenure as attorney general, from 1961 to 1964, proved transformative. The Kennedys entered office keen to hold together a tenuous electoral coalition, having squeaked past Richard Nixon by the narrowest of margins in the 1960 presidential election. The brothers pledged to pursue the goals of the black freedom struggle, and they were cognizant of the political clout wielded by urban black votes. Through the first year of their administration, their engagement with black activists primarily reflected political concerns. But the attorney general was forced to take a stand because of the controversy over James Meredith's admission to the University of Mississippi. By the end of 1962, the younger Kennedy had fashioned himself the strongest civil-rights advocate within the administration's inner circle, though the Justice Department frequently rebuffed pleas for federal protection from embattled Southern activists, and the attorney general also authorized the wiretapping of Martin Luther King Jr. that same year. The president himself held the movement at arm's length through the first half of 1963, a time of mounting protest and grotesque reaction. It was not until June, with less than six months to live, that he finally unveiled the landmark civil-rights bill that would eventually meet Lyndon Johnson's pen in July 1964. While his brother prevaricated, Robert Kennedy had begun to earn praise among influential African Americans. "We still believe that Robert Kennedy has the right idea and the courage of his convictions, the determination to bring the force of law to bear on the civil rights dilemma," Jackie Robinson wrote in his "Home Plate" column in the *Amsterdam News*. "We hate to admit it, but we are not convinced that the Attorney-General's brother has the same courage, although he may have the same convictions."[45]

The younger Kennedy, like the country, was forever transformed on November 22, 1963. His brother's assassination touched off a period of grief and reassessment. Reporter Jack Newfield, a confidant and biographer, has described this period as a moment of inner turmoil similar to what most people encounter in adolescence. RFK seemed to reemerge from his post-assassination crisis a born-again existentialist. He tore through the works of Camus, quoted liberally from Aeschylus, and increasingly adopted the language and tone of the New Left as his own. One biographer has written that Kennedy in his final years was "always on the lookout for real-life existential heroes"—Cesar Chavez, for instance.[46]

Robert Kennedy also maintained a mistrust of Lyndon Johnson that verged on loathing. In their personal and political temperaments, the two men were dramatically different, and they had developed a strong mutual antipathy during John F. Kennedy's lifetime. Following the assassination, Kennedy viewed Johnson as a usurper; Johnson saw Kennedy as a threat. Yet, in early 1964, both men agreed on the importance of bringing the dead president's major domestic initiatives to fruition. To Kennedy, the War on Poverty was a major component of that legacy, despite Johnson's efforts to brand it with his own presidential stamp.[47]

Johnson's special assistant, Jack Valenti, once mused that, "In every area where the poor, the black and the uneducated suffered indignity and neglect, President Johnson and Bobby Kennedy thought alike." On a broad ideological plane, that was true. But their assessments of what should be done to address that suffering—and what was politically feasible— diverged substantially as the War on Poverty unfolded. Kennedy's distaste for Johnson disposed him to challenge the foundations of Great Society liberalism. But neither did he bow reverentially before the ghost of FDR. Indeed, Kennedy distrusted bureaucracies and was hostile to the kind of centralized, alphabet-soup planning he associated with the New Deal. "The inheritance of the New Deal is fulfilled," he declared in 1966. "There is not a problem for which there is not a program. There is not a problem for which money is not being spent. There is not a problem or a program on which dozens or hundreds or thousands of bureaucrats are not earnestly at work. But does this represent a solution to our problems? Manifestly it does not."[48]

Kennedy's thinking about poverty in 1964 reflected some of the ambiguities lurking within the new federal program. In a letter to Johnson written on January 16, 1964, he warned against "building another level of government" in the form of an antipoverty superagency, complaining that existing poverty programs were "always planned for the poor—not *with* the poor." This explained his emphasis on self-help and his endorsement of the community-action experiments taken up by the PCJD. But Kennedy foresaw that local obstructionism would hamstring the War on Poverty, and he urged Johnson to ensure cabinet-level coordination in planning durable, centralized, and "comprehensive" programs in the fields of education, employment, housing, retraining, health, and welfare. That the drive for community self-help might run at cross-purposes to centralized planning was a lesson waiting to be learned.[49]

Kennedy's opinions on such matters were also expressed by one of his most trusted surrogates, David Hackett. The PCJD boss strongly opposed the creation of an executive "super-authority" to administer the poverty program because, as he wrote in early 1964, it "would impose a layer of administrative authority between the President and the Cabinet officials reporting directly to him and suggest a downgrading of Cabinet authority." Like Kennedy, Hackett may also have been irked by the idea of the Johnson White House taking full ownership of a program the late president had initiated in the final months of his life. Given the tendency of Kennedy and his entourage to conceive of the poverty program as a direct descendant of the PCJD programs, they thought themselves better equipped than anyone else in the federal government to oversee the community-action approach that would be at the new program's core. Indeed, in the weeks that followed the assassination, Hackett hoped that the attorney general would be picked to chair a cabinet committee overseeing the antipoverty effort, with an executive director (a post Hackett presumably coveted) and staff reporting directly to him.[50]

Another contradiction resided in the widely accepted idea that, as Kennedy put it in a 1964 speech, "the impoverished American lives in a crippled community." Like most elite poverty warriors, Kennedy believed that "the ghetto" was a place that crushed individual initiative and "stifles and exploits people." Yet he insisted that the best way to promote self-help was to foster local responsibility. On June 26, 1964, Kennedy testified before Congress in favor of the Economic Opportunity Act. In particular, he praised community-action programs, which, he said, would lead to "long-range and far-sighted programs—based on the belief that local citizens understand their communities best—based on the conviction that they will seize the initiative and provide sustained vigorous leadership." But if poor communities were "crippled," as Kennedy suggested, how could they possibly solve all their problems on the basis of self-help?[51]

Kennedy himself had expressed doubts from the start. In 1964, he wrote Johnson that unless the poverty program was carefully planned at the federal level, it "could actually retard the solution of these problems." As a good New Frontiersman, Kennedy held an optimist's faith in the ability of experts to solve social problems. But he would sour on the War on Poverty as newly minted agencies bogged down in bureaucratic processes while urban political machines kicked into gear to co-opt community action. By the time he was elected to the Senate in 1964, Kennedy had already begun to explore new ways of fighting poverty. On the campaign trail, he pledged to introduce legislation that would help "break the tragic pattern of decayed neighborhoods, slums, and poverty" by providing improved housing and good jobs for those whom automation had shunted from the industrial economy.[52]

Increasingly, Kennedy expressed concern that American cities were becoming vistas of despair. In the worst neighborhoods, he remarked, poverty was an affliction that could not simply be calculated in dollars and cents. To live in dismal surroundings, to sleep in rat-infested rooms, to shop in shoddy grocery stores, and to feel the sting of government neglect, indifferent principals, and hostile cops all factored into what it meant to be poor. Kennedy also sought to draw connections between poverty and racism. In his June 26, 1964, testimony, he warned that, "The fight for civil rights will not be won merely by ending discrimination. It does little good to give a child the right to attend school outside the slums if he has no carfare to get there. Fighting discrimination requires that we also fight the effects of discrimination."[53]

From 1965 onward, much of Kennedy's thinking about poverty developed in concert with a "brilliant and imaginative" young assistant named Adam Walinsky. A former Marine who routinely worked 110-hour weeks, Walinsky took on all manner of portfolios in the senator's Washington, DC, office. Like his boss, he was brash, idealistic, and possessed with an almost messianic urge to save America. He relentlessly pushed Kennedy to denounce the Vietnam War and support civil rights and antipoverty programs. He penned the bulk of the speeches that made Kennedy an aspiring spokesman for the poor and the dispossessed. Even in interoffice memos, Walinsky's zeal came through. America was "slipping," he told his boss in 1966. "I have the sense that everywhere, people feel themselves and their world spinning off into chaos, unable to affect the course of events; and . . . the cities, the center of our nation, are going down the drain, seemingly irreversibly."[54]

From the outset of the War on Poverty, Walinsky had emphasized the importance of job creation and physical rebuilding. In July 1964, he wrote a combative *New Republic* article critiquing the Economic Opportunity Act for its emphasis on opportunity, training, and pilot programs. According to Walinsky, poor people would stay poor as long as the middle-class majority wanted them to stay poor. And at a time when many in the middle class suspected that their security and status might soon be threatened by automation and urban strife, they were unlikely to support for long a program meant to lift the poor to their level. Any government program aimed at easing class distinctions, Walinsky wrote, "will encounter resistance which increases in direct proportion to its size and probable effectiveness." If anything, the War on Poverty had thus far provoked relatively little backlash, according to Walinsky, because it had deliberately steered clear of challenging middle-class assumptions about the origins of wealth and poverty. "Thus its concentration on opening up the opportunity structure could be used to justify inaction on government employment programs tailored to large numbers of the un- and under-employed," he wrote.[55]

Walinsky believed that only a massive public-works program would solve unemployment. Even at a time of rapid macroeconomic growth, Walinsky called attention to "the depression-level unemployment rates that still prevail among the urban poor," which he called the "master problem" that all antipoverty programs, including community action, should address.[56] Such ideas proved influential after the Watts riots of August 11–16, 1965, which provoked an overwhelming police response that left thirty-four people dead. Some of Kennedy's closest aides felt that Watts marked the moment when he finally began to put his brother's assassination behind him. The senator was among the first national figures to speak sympathetically about the residents of Watts, and he offered a stern rebuttal to the parade of politicians lining up behind ex-President Dwight D. Eisenhower to blame the violence on what Ike termed "a policy of lawlessness."[57]

"The law to us is a friend, which preserves our property and our personal safety," Kennedy told an all-white gathering in Spring Valley, New York, on August 17:

But for the Negro, the law means something different. Law for the Negro in the South has meant beatings and degradation and official discrimination; law has been his oppressor and his enemy. The Negro who has moved North with this heritage has not found in law the same oppression it meant in the South. But neither has he found a friend and protector. . . . The laws do not protect them from paying too much money for inferior goods, from having their furniture illegally repossessed. The law does not protect them from having to keep lights turned on the feet of children at night, to keep them from being gnawed by rats. The law does not fully protect their lives— their dignity—or encourage their hope and trust in the future.[58]

Later that fall, Kennedy visited Watts and chatted informally with its residents. Again and again, they told him that the main problem facing them was the lack of jobs. By that point, he had already concluded that the flames of discord were being fueled by crisis-level unemployment. This was not only a black problem, he argued in his August 17 speech: Watts embodied a national failure to come up with ways to give poor, jobless people a real stake in the decisions that affected their daily lives. Thereafter, jobs would be his "highest priority," according to staffer Peter Edelman.[59]

In advancing this "root causes" diagnosis, Kennedy deliberately positioned himself to the left of mainstream political discourse. Yet he also anticipated the emerging right-wing critique of the Great Society. "A way must be found to stop this waste of human resources," he said in his post-Watts speech. Bulging welfare rolls and the necessity of an increased police presence were a "financial drain on the rest of the community," according to Kennedy. "Our slums are too expensive," he added. Though Kennedy in the final years of his life positioned himself as a close ally of the poor and the downtrodden, he retained a paternalist streak. As late as 1966, he remained convinced that "fundamental social change" would necessitate "the integration of the slum Negro into the ethos of private property, of self-government, of *doing* what is necessary instead of asking the government to do it," as he wrote to his old friend McGeorge Bundy, who had just left his post as LBJ's national security advisor to become president of the Ford Foundation. The implication—that "the slum Negro" was lazy and dependent on handouts from others—would not have gone over well in Bedford-Stuyvesant had Kennedy voiced it in public.[60]

That said, Kennedy exhibited great personal growth during his brief time as a U.S. senator, and many poor minorities were swayed by his heart-felt commitment to the pursuit of justice and equality. After Watts, Kennedy grew increasingly obsessed with the "urban crisis," and already in the summer of 1965 his staffers were reflecting on how they might intervene in a New York ghetto to be determined at a later date. In August 1965, the chief of staff of Kennedy's New York office, Thomas Johnston, coauthored a confidential memo with David Hackett, the director of the PCJD, warning that Bedford-Stuyvesant and Harlem could go the way of Watts, despite ongoing summer programs and attempts in each neighborhood to spark community action. Hackett and Johnston observed that the un-fulfilled promises of the Great Society were exerting a radicalizing effect in black neighborhoods; action must start soon. Foreshadowing the broad-based coalition Kennedy would ultimately forge in Brooklyn the following year, they called for a tripartite commission uniting labor, civil rights, and business leaders to deal with problems of both Harlem and Bedford-Stuyvesant.[61]

Two weeks after the eruption in Los Angeles, Kennedy asked Walinsky and another young aide, Peter Edelman, to begin charting a new antipoverty approach. Edelman had previously worked under the top civil-rights lawyer in Kennedy's Justice Department, Burke Marshall, and the senator asked him to examine segregation in Northern cities. Walinsky, meanwhile, set to work fleshing out his proposal for a massive program of urban reconstruction, with job creation as its core aim. Their work resulted in a trio of speeches Kennedy delivered on successive days in January 1966. The addresses, as Kennedy biographer Edward Schmitt has astutely observed, "blended liberal and conservative ideas in a communitarian vision." That vision would animate Kennedy's new urban agenda in the months to come.[62]

The first speech, delivered on January 20, 1966, to a luncheon of the Federation of Jewish Philanthropies, was mostly Edelman's work, and it called for a renewed federal push to combat segregation. Blacks must be given the freedom to live where they wished, Kennedy argued in the speech; the ghettos must eventually be dismantled. Otherwise, "we can expect continuing explosions like Watts." The speech fell flat, as Edelman later recalled: "Walking into a chicken à la king lunch at the American Hotel in New York and standing up and giving this very long, very serious, very heavy speech really threatening all of them . . . it was just a bomb, and he was really very irritated with me afterwards."[63]

The following day brought different results. Kennedy spoke at a conference in Harlem hosted by the Manhattan borough president, Constance Baker Motley. The address, drafted by Walinsky, was tailor-made for the audience, which included a good portion of New York's black elite. Kennedy touched on themes at once conservative, liberal, and visionary. He lamented failing schools, daily injustices, and declining job opportunities; at the same time, he decried a welfare system that was breeding dependency, sapping individual initiative, and destroying families. He demanded that policymakers "stop thinking of the people of Harlem . . . as liabilities, idle hands for whom some sort of occupation must be found. Let us think of them instead as a valuable resource, as people whose work can make a significant contribution to themselves, their families, and the nation." That contribution would be to rebuild American cities. Kennedy argued for a brand of community action in which bricks and mortar would supplement social services, leading to "a total effort at regeneration within the entire slum community." Kennedy insisted that jobs in such areas must go to the people who lived there. Programs should aim to create neighborhoods in which residents would take pride. This could mean offering condominium ownership to the people who had helped build them or enlisting the participation of locals in rehabilitating sound building stock.

But what about the costs of such a program? Kennedy never quite answered the question. He believed much of the funding could be recouped by phasing out inefficient urban programs and banking on the diminution of welfare payments. But the private sector must also lend a hand. Kennedy called for "active participation of the business community in every aspect of the program," and he thought universities and labor unions could help with on-the-job training. In short, Kennedy's vision implied "an effort to mobilize the skills and resources of the entire society, including above all the latent skills and resources of the people of the ghetto themselves, in the solution of our urban dilemma."[64]

The White House was not about to embrace a massive new poverty program, especially one pitched by Johnson's nemesis. Model Cities, which also aimed to rebuild urban areas, was already in the works, and Congress began considering relevant legislation in early 1966. On January 26, 1966, Johnson himself promised to promote large-scale urban renewal married to local energies, declaring it "the year of rebirth for American cities." The president's speech touched on many of the themes Kennedy was emphasizing in his own speeches that week, and it echoed some of the arguments put forth by CBCC members in years past. "I propose that we combine physical reconstruction and rehabilitation with effective social programs throughout the rebuilding process," he said. But Model Cities would turn out to be a deeply flawed program. Originally conceived by a task force led by Robert C. Wood, it was meant to be a demonstration program (overseen by the Department of Housing and Urban Development) that dedicated huge sums to a small number of cities. But after Congress got its hands on the bill, the cities involved ballooned from thirty-six to sixty-three; by 1968, 138 cities had received a green light. Given tight budgets for the overall program, there was never enough money to go around. Though some smaller cities were able to make good use of what funds they got from Model Cities, the program in New York City accomplished little in the way of building. Part of the problem was that the city cut up its slice of a pie that was inadequate to begin with. Activists from Brooklyn, led by CBCC, were able to convince the Lindsay administration to fund not one but three Model Cities project areas: Harlem, the South Bronx, and Central Brooklyn. The latter area was then further subdivided into sections covering Bed-Stuy, Brownsville, and East New York. Though ambitious plans for school construction, new housing developments, and infrastructure projects were unveiled, funding available for the program was "one-twentieth of what was needed to make it effective," according to Walter Thabit, a planner who had helped design Model Cities plans for East New York.[65]

Even before the Model Cities debacle, Kennedy had come to the conclusion that the main obstacles hampering the poverty fight were bureaucratic and political. At a time when many Americans were turning against government solutions to socioeconomic problems, Kennedy still believed the state could be a force for good—so long as power was removed from sclerotic big-city machines, the chaotic structures of the OEO, and, most importantly, President Johnson. Though disillusioned with the way the War on Poverty had thus far unfolded, the senator nonetheless hoped to find a way of salvaging and institutionalizing the commitment the federal government had made to fight poverty. He thought Americans could still be rallied to that campaign and that he might forge a bipartisan, biracial coalition around it. However, the escalation of American intervention in Vietnam—which Kennedy now opposed—all but guaranteed that federal antipoverty funding would remain severely limited in the years to come. For any new approach to succeed, Kennedy believed, the private sector would have to participate.

At the same time, Kennedy clung fast to the idea that antipoverty programs should harness the energies of the poor themselves. Following the scandals that had besieged the Community Action Program, few national figures were prepared to defend the "maximum feasible participation" mandate. Kennedy, though, refused to blame poor people for the failures of community action. As he saw it, the poverty program had suffered from too little funding, too little community participation, and too much bureaucracy. On January 23, 1966, the day after he delivered the third of his three poverty speeches, Kennedy summoned Walinsky and Edelman. "Now listen," he said. "I don't just want to talk about this. I want to do something about it."[66]

"To Hold the Middle Class"

Bedford-Stuyvesant's activists shared much of Kennedy's diagnosis of what had gone wrong to that point in the War on Poverty. Many within the CBCC orbit had spent the first two years of the War on Poverty simply trying to pry loose enough government funds to get projects off the ground. Now they were seeking not only to launch new kinds of programs but also to find new funding sources. "The crumbling of the anti-poverty constituency's power over the bureaucracy caused many people to look for new means of financing independent programs," Geoffrey Faux, an OEO official in the 1960s, later wrote. "One such means, the possibility of generating independent funds for anti-poverty programs, provided a partial reason for the attractiveness of community-based economic development." As Faux suggests, people long involved in local antipoverty programs expressed doubts quite similar to those of Kennedy and his staff—though they were not yet speaking the same language.[67]

Following the trio of speeches, Kennedy turned his attention to Bedford-Stuyvesant. Pratt's Ron Shiffman had heard from a friend on the City Planning Commission, philanthropist Elinor Guggenheimer, that Kennedy was shopping around for a neighborhood in which to launch an antipoverty experiment, and he reached out to Kennedy's office. Soon Kennedy aides were traipsing through Central Brooklyn, meeting with activists and surveying the area's political and economic landscape. The terrain seemed promising. On February 4, 1966, Kennedy alighted in Bedford-Stuyvesant, met Elsie Richardson, and explored the area's streets. The former attorney general was no stranger to the landscapes of urban poverty or to the frustration that smoldered there. What impressed him in Bedford-Stuyvesant was the cadre of leaders who greeted him. Richardson, Thomas Jones, Louise Bolling, Ruth Goring, Lucille Rose—they were impassioned, impatient, and angry. They were also educated, ambitious, and striving. For all their apparent radicalism, they sought to foster community strength and stability through reform, not revolution. "These were people who believed in homeownership and education and raising families," a future president of the Bed-Stuy Restoration Corporation, Colvin Grannum, would later comment. "They bought into America and what some people would call 'conservative values.'" Despite his ire at being criticized so openly by CBCC leaders, Kennedy could understand their frustration. He decided to make Bed-Stuy the place where he would implement his vision.[68]

Kennedy asked Thomas Johnston to team up with Pratt and CBCC and draft designs for a new poverty program. Johnston, a thirty-year-old from Kentucky who had worked in advertising, ran the senator's New York office, where a kinetic, chaotic atmosphere prevailed. Kennedy's staff included a cohort of bright, highly motivated men in their twenties and early thirties: Edelman, Walinsky, and Johnston, plus Carter Burden and Earl Graves. Ideas bounced around like super balls. Egos competed for the senator's attention and affection. Overlapping responsibilities accumulated. Johnston oversaw the Brooklyn project, but Graves—a Bed-Stuy native and the sole African American on Kennedy's staff—became the on-the-ground fixer.[69] Walinsky continued to supply strategic advice and grand visions, devoting half his time to the Brooklyn project. He and Johnston traveled widely during the spring and summer of 1966, researching experiments in urban redevelopment and, in Jack Newfield's description, "picking the brains of black militants, university urbanists, Federal administrators, journalists, mayors, foundation executives, millionaires from the banking and business communities."[70]

Like Shiffman, Richardson, and the Brooklyn activists, the Kennedy team had come to believe that the keys to urban revitalization lay in creating jobs and building affordable housing—and that the two issues should be addressed in tandem. The senator did share a basic premise with the CBCC group: that young, unemployed African Americans, especially men, ought to be given skills and jobs, and that community-led efforts to build housing and infrastructure could fulfill that purpose. Crucially, all involved agreed that their efforts must at once nourish feelings of community empowerment and convince the area's nervous homeowners not to pack their bags. "Again and again," remarked a Ford Foundation researcher who carried out dozens of interviews with local activists and Kennedy staffers in the late 1960s, "the recognition to involve the hard core was coupled with urgent pleas to 'hold the middle class.'"[71]

On February 22, members of CBCC's housing committee, joined by Shiffman, met with Kennedy's people at the senator's office near the United Nations. The Brooklynites had done their homework. They showed up armed with a thirteen-point program that reflected their long-term priorities and demonstrated a familiarity with Kennedy's recent thinking. Their vision included stepped-up government programs as well as community-based initiatives. They asked that Bed-Stuy be designated an "Urban Demonstration Area" under the fledgling Model Cities program, and they asked for an immediate amendment to the federal Housing Act earmarking urban-renewal funds to Central Brooklyn. They foresaw setting up a nonprofit Community Development Corporation, which would allow CBCC to administer privately funded rehabilitation efforts as well as government-sponsored renewal efforts in the area. In the latter category, they emphasized the renewal of the Fulton Park area (which remained in limbo), the demolition of abandoned buildings, and the construction of a community college. The Brooklynites also proposed that contractors hired to work on the projects be obliged to employ integrated crews; that Bed-Stuy entrepreneurs be provided with seed monies to set up construction firms; and that local residents receive training in the building trades, urban planning, architecture, finance, real estate, and social services. Finally, CBCC proposed to set up cooperatives that would pool local resources to compensate for the lack of available mortgage capital and insurance in Bed-Stuy. The overarching goals would be to build more and better housing, set up job-rich industrial facilities, and rehabilitate declining brownstones.[72]

Such ambitious aims captivated Kennedy and his staff. The senator began to make frequent trips to Bedford-Stuyvesant, often flying up from Washington just to attend planning meetings about the new project. "It took a lot of energy," recalled Edelman, who remembered Kennedy sometimes traveling to Brooklyn twice a week in 1966. "It was quite hard work." Kennedy agreed to help set up a new community-development initiative, dubbed the Bedford-Stuyvesant Renewal and Rehabilitation Corporation (R&R). He asked Richardson and the chairman of CBCC, Lionel Payne, to lay the groundwork. (Payne worked as a city housing inspector and was also among the leaders of the Paragon Progressive Credit Union.) The local notables they assembled came mostly from within the CBCC orbit. Indeed, Kennedy's staff worked with CBCC as their exclusive conduit to Bedford-Stuyvesant's grassroots activists through the fall of 1966, insisting that all parties keep the project a secret and that only an intimate group surrounding Richardson and Shiffman contribute directly to the planning process.[73]

There were good reasons for secrecy: Kennedy feared that any publicity about his work in Bed-Stuy would raise hackles in Harlem; that it would force him into a close collaboration with Mayor Lindsay, whom Kennedy saw as a lightweight; that it would leave the senator vulnerable to accusations of pursuing personal glory in the ghetto; and that it would touch off a flurry of pork-barrel politics in Congress. The Brooklynites were so committed to accommodating Kennedy's wishes that Lindsay was kept in the dark about the project until October, eight months after the first policy discussions between CBCC and Kennedy's staff. When Lindsay finally did find out (from Kennedy himself), he assigned his top poverty man, Sviridoff, to act as a liaison but otherwise agreed not to interfere. Senator Javits knew even less about the details of Kennedy's work in Bedford-Stuyvesant; he later claimed that the first time Kennedy personally briefed him about the project was only days before he publicly announced its launch, in December 1966. That said, press reports surfaced in October that Kennedy and CBCC had been collaborating on creating a Community Development Corporation that would, in Thomas Jones's words, "bring private enterprise, foundations, and government into a multi-million dollar program for the good of our most neglected area."[74]

For the CBCC activists, frustrated by the "interminable lag between promise and performance" in Bed-Stuy, Kennedy's interest held out the tantalizing prospect of action. As planning progressed behind closed doors in weekly meetings, Richardson, Rose, Payne, and their allies assumed that Kennedy's project, once it evolved from plans to action, would also remain their project. Having lost control of Youth in Action a year earlier, the CBCC leadership intended to turn the Renewal and Rehabilitation Corporation into an institution through which to consolidate their clout. "That was clearly seen by the Coordinating Council as their entity," H. Carl McCall later recalled. "They really felt that that was what they ought to dominate." But their faith would turn out to be misplaced. By the summer of 1966, Kennedy had grown concerned by what he saw as an increasingly difficult political environment. Against the backdrop of Youth in Action's funding woes, and with radical sentiment growing more palpable in the community, Kennedy staffers working in Bedford-Stuyvesant—particularly Johnston and Graves—fretted about the political risks of making CBCC their sole partner. Would CBCC be able to manage community sentiment? Was the group as representative as it claimed to be?[75]

Graves suggested that Kennedy call on Thomas Jones to see if he would help steer the project. Jones, who as leader of the Unity Democratic Club had defeated the Kings County Democratic machine in 1962, had since taken a position as a Civil Court judge. The former assemblyman was widely respected in Bedford-Stuyvesant, and he remained a keen political operator. Though he had confronted Kennedy following the senator's tour in February, he knew nothing about the emerging renewal plan. That appealed to the Kennedy people, who thought the judge embodied the kind of neutrality, competence, and political integrity they hoped would define the new project. But Jones was not without enemies in Bed-Stuy. Few of the main movers within CBCC thought he shared their interests, and they were taken aback when the senator proposed that the judge chair R&R. When Kennedy insisted, they accepted—grudgingly.[76]

Around the same time, Kennedy set Walinsky to work on drawing up a legislative framework for the new poverty initiative. With the federal Office of Economic Opportunity under attack, largely because of the chaos surrounding the Community Action Program, Kennedy thought a new set of institutions would have to be devised in order to salvage the federal commitment to fighting poverty and providing for the disadvantaged. But he was also concerned lest the new, neighborhood-based approach turn into a balkanized mess, with every city trying to get a piece of the pie all at once—a fate that befell the Model Cities program as it wound its way through Congress. As a start, Kennedy called for federal creation of nonprofit Community Development Corporations, which would wield both government funds and private monies to "carry out the work of construction, the hiring and training of workers, the provision of services, and encouragement of associated enterprises."[77]

A new political coalition would also have to be forged. As a first step, Kennedy cemented his alliance with Javits, New York's senior senator. A moderate Republican, Javits had been working on legislation for something called the National Technical Assistance Corporation, which would tap private-sector funds and talent and put them to work on "ghetto problems." Walinsky and Javits's assistant, Robert Patricelli, decided to team up on a bill that would combine their pet projects. The vehicle for turning their vision into policy was an amendment to the Economic Opportunity Act of 1964—the War on Poverty law. Kennedy and Javits quietly spirited the amendment through the Senate in November. Title I-D, known as the Special Impact Program (SIP), took as its premise that previous efforts had done too little to create jobs or involve private enterprise in the fight against poverty. The Kennedy-Javits program would fund "comprehensive" approaches to urban development, laying special emphasis on business development, construction, and job growth. The senators proposed that the new program be run out of the Department of Labor and not OEO, ensuring that the entire federal antipoverty apparatus—and, in New York City, the municipal poverty bureaucracy—would be frozen out of the funding process. (As it turned out, oversight of SIP and the Community Development Corporations it funded was transferred to OEO beginning in 1968.) An initial appropriation of $75 million passed the Senate, but the House of Representatives later cut that figure to $50 over two years, of which the largest share, $7 million, would be destined for Bedford-Stuyvesant.[78]

The new community-development effort was conceived to supplement rather than replace existing Community Action Agencies. Projects receiving SIP funds were directed to cooperate with cities and CAAs to "train and employ area residents to assist in economic, social, and physical rehabilitation of the areas." SIP also promised to put local activists in touch with deep-pocketed donors who, in Jones's words, "could unlock the doors and break the logjams that were keeping us from achieving democratic rights."[79] Kennedy remained convinced that the project would falter unless it gained private-sector support. It would fall to him to secure meaningful commitments not only from philanthropies—the Ford, Astor, and Rockefeller foundations—but also from the city's financial elites. Yet, for all the talk of private-sector involvement that surrounded the Kennedy initiative, the $7 million in SIP funds earmarked for Bedford-Stuyvesant in 1967 would dwarf the contributions made by either foundations or the business community. And despite the subsequent arrival in Bed-Stuy of an all-star cast of urbanists, architects, and corporate leaders, the ideas that would define the project there emerged from the discussions undertaken in 1966 among Kennedy staffers, CBCC activists, and the Pratt planners.[80]

A memo drafted that September by Raymond and Shiffman summarized the major ideas being put forth by the community group. Among other things, the CBCC-Pratt alliance was calling for a mortgage cooperative to assist potential homebuyers and underwrite home renovations; seed money for the bonding of small local construction firms; new retail facilities to be run as community cooperatives and used for on-the-job training; the establishment of industrial on-the-job training programs at the Brooklyn Navy Yard; brownstone-rehabilitation programs that would "add grace and character to the area"; the establishment of a four-year college and a two-year community college in the area; construction of a cultural center and a hospital; and the demolition of abandoned buildings deemed beyond repair, to be replaced with a network of parks, study centers, health clinics, and child-care centers. Finally, they called for redistricting to create a majority-black congressional district in Central Brooklyn. An internal memorandum in Kennedy's office shortly thereafter endorsed most of Raymond and Shiffman's proposals, many of them reiterated word-for-word.[81]

So there was agreement on the basic ideas. But implementation posed a different—and more pressing—problem. By the close of 1966, it was becoming clear that the great liberal surge that had birthed the Great Society was waning. Disaffection with Johnson's agenda contributed to historic Republican gains in the midterm elections, when forty-seven congressional Democrats were voted out of office and right-wing governors were elected from Georgia to California. Watts and other episodes of urban violence were also offering whites an excuse to turn away from efforts to aid blacks. Meanwhile, the president was wasting increasing blood and treasure in Vietnam. The acute sense of crisis that prevailed on the streets of Bed-Stuy also pervaded the thoughts of Kennedy and his aides. They were in a race against time; would Brooklyn be the next city to burn? "The point is not to have more meetings or talk or exchange of views, all of which I suspect are surplus goods in the ghetto," Walinsky wrote to his boss in the fall of 1966. "The point is to build an organization which . . . will begin to make demonstrable progress toward rebuilding Bedford-Stuyvesant, hiring people, training, educating, etc."[82]

The people of Bed-Stuy, too, were hungry for progress. On December 10, 1966, they seemed finally to have found what they were looking for. Even as Kennedy stood before the community, announcing an unprecedented commitment to the revitalization of Bed-Stuy, many assumed the senator was using them for future political gain. But the real possibility that he might endow the area—or, more likely, certain groups in the area—with unprecedented political and fiscal capital motivated people like Jones and Richardson to lay aside their suspicions. For years, CBCC had pursued what Raymond dubbed a "wise, restrained, and methodical search for the right levers of power." Now Kennedy's very presence validated the ideas of CBCC and its allies at the Pratt Institute.

The endorsements quickly piled up. "It is a very important experiment . . . and I'm here to insulate this effort from political implications," Javits promised. The city offered its full cooperation, as did the federal government. Further, Kennedy announced that the Ford Foundation had promised $750,000 in grant monies. The *Times* opined on December 11 that the Bed-Stuy project could become the country's "most exciting endeavor to give the people in racial ghettos meaningful participation in reviving their decaying neighborhoods." The *Amsterdam News* was exultant: "Santa Arrives in Boro 15 Days before Christmas," blared one headline. Jackie Robinson, in his *Amsterdam News* column, called the new program a "giant step in the right direction." Even Elsie Richardson was heartened. "A new day has dawned in Bedford-Stuyvesant," she told the audience at P.S. 305. As of December 10, 1966, the rest of America was watching the battle for Bed-Stuy unfold.[83]

7

Whose Community, What Action?

> We cannot deny that there *was* movement on December 10, 1966. However we do not recognize a bit of evidence that anything is going to be different in Bedford-Stuyvesant in the near future. . . . I will not be satisfied until the *words* become *action.*
>
> —ELSIE RICHARDSON, 1967

I have a feeling this might turn out to be a very auspicious occasion," William Paley, the chairman of CBS, told some two dozen men assembled in his Manhattan boardroom on the evening of January 12, 1967. "This project that was initiated by Senator Kennedy is creating a good deal of interest and if all goes well, this might be the beginning of something very, very important."[1]

So began the inaugural board meeting of the Bedford-Stuyvesant Development and Services Corporation (D&S), the latest group to tackle the tangled web of poverty, disinvestment, and decay in "America's largest ghetto." The men Paley was addressing made for an unusual collection of poverty warriors. These were the best and brightest of American business and finance: André Meyer of the investment-banking firm Lazard-Frères, also known as the "Picasso of banking"; banker and former treasury secretary C. Douglas Dillon; the president of IBM, Thomas Watson Jr., whom *Fortune* magazine would later call "the greatest capitalist who ever lived"; George Moore, the president of First National City Bank; and Roswell Gilpatric, a partner at the Wall Street law firm of Cravath, Swaine, and Moore and a former Defense Department undersecretary in the Kennedy administration.[2] Brought together by Robert F. Kennedy, their task was to revitalize Bedford-Stuyvesant. These men had little experience fighting poverty or planning housing initiatives, yet they agreed with Kennedy that desperate times called for heroic efforts. The summer riots of recent years

236

Abandoned Bed-Stuy townhouse, 1968. This image was part of a special report published in *Life* magazine about the fledgling Restoration Corporation.
Photograph by Bob Gomel. The LIFE Picture Collection. Getty Images

had convinced them that something ought to be done for the city's most impoverished areas, if for no other reason than to avert urban chaos. And all agreed that the War on Poverty had been a disruptive and wasteful use of taxpayer dollars.[3]

Most members of the D&S board were Republicans who had serious doubts about the Great Society—and about Kennedys. But the junior senator from New York had managed to persuade them that their own time could be well spent fighting poverty and that they could play a crucial role in the rejuvenation of American cities. Their main mission was to unlock the kinds of private-sector grants and investment capital needed to create jobs and transform the urban economy in ways government could not. In addition, they must lend sound management principles to otherwise disorganized (and potentially corrupt) neighborhood groups. Such ideas resonated in the CBS boardroom. Kennedy himself admitted that when he talked about Bedford-Stuyvesant to his newfound allies, he "sounded like a Republican."[4]

Republican or not, remarkably similar ideas had been bouncing around in the Bedford Avenue YMCA, where the Central Brooklyn Coordinating Council held its meetings. Indeed, the new project Paley was heralding had grown out of a collaboration between Kennedy's staffers and the wing of CBCC led by Elsie Richardson. Kennedy made clear that the spirit of bottom-up reform would continue to inform his approach. But he worried that the fledgling Bedford-Stuyvesant Renewal and Rehabilitation Corporation (R&R) might devolve into yet another chaotic tangle of red tape. That was where D&S came in.

As Kennedy conceived of the new initiative, R&R, under the leadership of Thomas Jones, would take charge of program design and implementation while managing citizen participation in planning. D&S would kick in with logistical support, managerial acumen, and fundraising clout. The role of the businessmen was to ensure tangible, immediate results and shelter the project from the existing antipoverty bureaucracy. Meanwhile, Kennedy had signed up Edward Logue, known as the "top urban renewal man in the country," to provide policy expertise, along with celebrated architect I. M. Pei. "We have never seen a coalition . . . with such potential power," was the excited assessment offered by Mitchell Sviridoff, who had overseen the reorganization of the city's poverty bureaucracy the previous year.[5]

Potential power, yes—but how to exercise it was up for grabs. In the early months of 1967, the Kennedy project provoked a series of acrimonious, multisided debates about the contours of political power in Bedford-Stuyvesant. The central questions echoed the ones that were just then being asked of Youth in Action: Who should speak and plan for the community? On what terms should local people interact with political and economic elites? For that matter, was it even possible to speak of Bed-Stuy as a "community" anymore?

Within R&R, struggles for influence among different factions stoked rancor, rumor, and recrimination. Latent resentments of the power wielded by the area's "matriarchy" rose to the surface, and male influence-seekers launched devastating attacks on CBCC's female leadership group. Youth in Action, too, entered the fray, arguing that Kennedy was making an illegitimate and paternalistic end run around Bed-Stuy's democratically elected antipoverty agency. Radicals argued that a project premised on the support of corporate elites would unavoidably pursue conservative paths toward community economic development. Meanwhile, the very structure

Kennedy had devised to manage affairs in Bed-Stuy struck many as a symbol of the colonialist attitudes embedded in the enterprise. The point of having two corporations instead of one, remarked Franklin A. Thomas, who was drafted to lead the project in May 1967, was "to insure that at the first meeting of the board, if somebody said 'motherfucker,' the white guys wouldn't all get up and run."[6]

For Elsie Richardson and her allies in CBCC, the "power to act" would remain frustratingly conditional. Even at the height of their influence, they could easily be forced back into the shadows. The experts Kennedy brought with him were not about to sit back and take their cues from the black women of Brooklyn. On the contrary, Logue and his ilk viewed Bed-Stuy as an open laboratory in which to carry out "macro-scale" experiments in urban engineering. The project also carried serious political implications for the senator. Though Kennedy strenuously denied he was seeking political gain in Brooklyn, his aides were loath to let the locals lead. But with a presidential run looming, they suddenly found themselves scrambling to extinguish the flames of discord that threatened to engulf the project. For help, they turned to two men, Jones and Thomas, who incarnated managerial competence and defined themselves in contradistinction to the CBCC women—but who, in their way, also tapped into the tradition of middle-class reform that CBCC had represented.

Playing Politics

It was Kennedy's singular innovation in Bedford-Stuyvesant to figure out how words might become action, as Elsie Richardson put it. In Congress, Kennedy found a creative way to fund the Brooklyn project and to shelter it from the pressures bearing down on other federal antipoverty programs. Kennedy also brought with him close ties to the Ford Foundation, which provided critical funding and programmatic expertise from the outset. Meanwhile, the senator's courtship of Republicans Jacob Javits and John Lindsay lent the project impeccable bipartisanship credentials and provided its planners with valuable breathing room at a time when anti-liberal backlash was endangering the Great Society. Finally, Kennedy convinced business and financial elites to support the initiative and pledge the kinds of resources Bed-Stuy activists had desperately been pursuing since the 1950s.[7]

It was the latter commitment that seemed most improbable. Money was not enough; Kennedy wanted big names who would donate time, expertise, and political capital to the project. The key, according to Kennedy aide Thomas Johnston, was for the businessmen to "own the land, so that if it failed, it was their failure." For help, in the fall of 1966 the senator had turned to Meyer, a trusted friend and confidant to the Kennedy clan. The head of Lazard-Frères, according to David Rockefeller, was "the most creative financial genius of our time in the investment banking world," but he was excited to wield his creativity on something entirely different. Over the ensuing months, Meyer personally invested a great deal of time, money, and goodwill in the project. With his help and with an assist from a twenty-nine-year-old investment banker named Eli Jacobs, who had roomed with Johnston at Yale, Kennedy scheduled a whirlwind tour of Wall Street and Midtown Manhattan in October 1966. In a single day, he netted Paley, Dillon, Watson, Moore, Gilpatric, and the former head of the Tennessee Valley Authority, David Lilienthal, now a private consultant. (According to Jack Newfield, David Rockefeller was the only man to turn Kennedy down.) This group, a Kennedy aide wrote, would "assure prospective foundations and businessmen that this idea for aiding a sick community is sound. . . . Perhaps for the first time a slum community will not have to suffer from the lack of managerial and administrative competence."[8]

Other than Meyer, the businessmen greeted Kennedy with skepticism, if not scorn. As Republicans, most eyed the senator's leftward turn warily; like many New Yorkers, they saw him as a carpetbagger because he had never lived in New York as an adult prior to his run for the Senate seat in 1964. Benno Schmidt of J. H. Whitney and Company, a D&S board member, later remarked that "there was a large body of thought to the effect that Bob was arrogant, that he was unduly ambitious, that he was vindictive." Further, suspicions lingered as a result of President Kennedy's confrontation with U.S. Steel, which Schmidt and others saw as evidence of the Kennedys' hostility to business. But the senator's interest in Bed-Stuy came across as sincere.[9]

Kennedy knew he was unpopular in the business community, and he spun a simple message designed to invoke conservative values: "The basic purpose of the program is to create jobs. There isn't enough money to solve the problems of the ghettos. Private enterprise must be brought into this area." Otherwise, he warned, there would be chaos. That he had earned the seal of approval of liberal Republicans Lindsay and Javits (the latter of whom maintained especially friendly relationships on Wall Street) boosted his cause. Schmidt said that during his initial conversation with Kennedy, he explicitly told the senator that he had never supported a Kennedy ticket and would be more inclined to join an initiative headed by a New York Republican—be it Javits, Rockefeller, or, to a lesser extent, Lindsay. "Well, that doesn't make the slightest difference," Kennedy replied. "I am extremely anxious that this *not* be a Robert Kennedy project." According to Jacobs, a Republican who had "militantly opposed" Kennedy in 1964, "Kennedy's motivations could not be narrowly political, for the chances of failure in Bedford-Stuyvesant were far greater than the chances of success. I therefore saw his decision to become involved there as an act of political courage."[10]

Still, Kennedy remained a Kennedy. In 1966, he had yet to decide whether he would run for the presidency two years later. But everything Kennedy did and said carried political repercussions, and there were political opportunities to be exploited everywhere he went. In Bedford-Stuyvesant, people assumed that the senator's sudden interest in their plight reflected presidential aspirations. Since gaining his seat in the Senate, Kennedy had routinely taken up causes and made appearances more befitting of an aspirant to the Oval Office than a freshman senator from New York: touring Watts, speaking at the University of Mississippi, and visiting farm workers in California. Foreign trips—to South Africa, to Latin America—had garnered favorable media coverage. By the fall of 1966, however, his staffers were encouraging Kennedy to make Bedford-Stuyvesant the centerpiece of a long-term strategy leading up to a possible presidential run in 1968. Walinsky urged Kennedy to put off his next high-profile trip (preferably to the Soviet Union or China) until late 1967, "which would keep the memory of the trip fresh." In the meantime, Walinsky wrote, there was a "preferable alternative—a job which desperately needs doing, a job which only you can pull off, a job which will pay dividends to you and others for some time to come." And that job was to bring together a Community Development Corporation in Brooklyn.[11]

"If you make this work, it will be the 'Kennedy plan' everywhere," Walinsky told his boss, while also warning of the risks "in time, in sweat, and in the penalties for failure." The potential political advantages for Kennedy were manifold. To begin with, the project could be a first step in improving his relationship with the business community, which Walinsky dubbed a "sore." Further, his work in the heart of Brooklyn would help to shore up Kennedy's New York credentials and make him seem like less of a carpet-bagger. If the project succeeded, it would put Kennedy in a position to magnanimously share credit with Lindsay (who, Walinsky wrote, was "desperate for help") while at the same time drawing a favorable contrast between the bold new stroke in Bed-Stuy and the city's clumsy efforts to reorganize the poverty program. Drawing such a contrast was all the more important in light of Johnson's flagging commitment to OEO. "There is now a complete vacuum in the poverty leadership—black or white," Walinsky wrote. "You can seize the lead."[12]

Certainly, there were many in Brooklyn, on Wall Street, and in Washington, DC, who assumed Kennedy was using them to position himself for a presidential run. The *Washington Post* commented in September 1966 that Kennedy "seems to be making the healing of the slums a key plank in his long-range run for the Presidency." Robert Patricelli, the Javits staffer who worked most closely on the dossier, later opined that Kennedy was "playing Bedford-Stuyvesant for political advantage for all it was worth." There was also reason to suspect that Bedford-Stuyvesant was an extension of Kennedy's personal vendetta against Lyndon Johnson, who by 1966 had decided that his former attorney general was not only a "little fart" but also "the enemy."[13]

Despite it all, Kennedy was able to convince not only conservative financiers but also moderate liberals and black nationalists to join the emerging coalition in Brooklyn. His ability to sell the Bedford-Stuyvesant model in a variety of contexts offered what historian Karen Ferguson calls "a brilliant demonstration of his genius for coalition building." No doubt, there were many who signed on precisely for political reasons: Kennedy's star was rising, and it made sense to forge links with an inevitable presidential candidate. But Kennedy also possessed the rare ability to touch people's most heartfelt hopes, even as he tapped their deepest fears. His promise to cut the Gordian knot of the urban crisis simultaneously invoked hope and fear. Schmidt later explained that Kennedy's initial appeal rested on his insistence that "this was a problem to which we had to find some better solution [than the federal programs] or it would destroy the nation." According to Schmidt, there was "a very strong and almost universal feeling in business that the urban problem, the urban ghetto problem and the racial problem . . . must receive greater attention." Surely, this was an exaggeration—only four years later, Republican president Richard M. Nixon, the darling of the country's businessmen, would contemplate a policy of "benign neglect" toward black urban neighborhoods. But the mere fact that Kennedy was able to inspire such feelings made his project unique.[14]

Thinking Big

Despite Kennedy's careful attention to the politics of the new initiative, he almost blew it up by bringing Ed Logue on board. A headstrong planner, Logue was characterized in a 1969 Ford Foundation report as "brilliant, dynamic, impatient with what he deems unnecessary and irrelevant questions." Logue had gained fame for his renewal work in Boston and New Haven. More recently, he had completed an extensive study, commissioned by Mayor Lindsay, of New York City's housing programs. In early 1967, he was also working as a consultant to Cleveland's new African American mayor, Carl B. Stokes, who envisaged a massive urban redevelopment program in his city.[15] In his December 10 announcement, Kennedy explained that Logue had been hired by D&S to "take on a principal responsibility for the overall development effort, recruitment of staff, and preparation and execution of programs." That came as a surprise to community leaders, who had been under the impression that those were R&R's responsibilities. Even while retaining his planning and development job in Boston, Logue pledged to devote a quarter of his time to Brooklyn. He quickly began ruffling feathers.[16]

In January, Logue recruited well-regarded Philadelphia planner David A. Crane to help direct the project and also hired modernist architect I. M. Pei, public-works consultant William R. McGrath, and the planning firm of George M. Raymond, the director of Pratt's Center for Community Improvement and a former CBCC consultant. This high-powered group put twenty-odd draftsmen, researchers, engineers, and designers to work on a "physical development plan" for Bedford-Stuyvesant. The plan, first submitted in February and revised in April, proposed extensive surveys and research as a preliminary to launching urban renewal on a grand scale. Logue defined Bed-Stuy expansively. Boston's master builder claimed to be planning for more than 450,000 people in a 4,000-acre district, an area approximately the size of Manhattan from river to river, from 34th Street to 125th Street. And not even a domain that large could contain Logue's ambitions: he saw the Bed-Stuy project as the opening salvo in a much wider transformation of Brooklyn. All told, Logue touted his plans as "the largest scale and the most promising piece of physical development and planning work of its kind that has ever been undertaken anywhere in this country."[17]

As a first step, Logue commissioned Pei to design a network of superblocks, which would stand as the project's early signatures. The superblocks were meant to invoke urban oases: through traffic would be blocked, play-grounds and wading pools built, and green space privileged. Pei's goal, he told the D&S directors, was to "make Bedford-Stuyvesant a garden spot of Brooklyn" by "reclaiming" seventy-five acres of parkland at a total cost of $15 million. The architect also proposed to offset the superblocks with traffic "supergrids," which the architect said would speed traffic in and out of the area while separating cars from pedestrian walkways and parks. Impressed, the Astor Foundation donated $700,000 to build the first two such spaces, which Pei hoped would eventually number several dozen; Astor also pledged $300,000 to Logue's broader plans.[18]

The centerpiece of Logue's vision was "a multi-story lineal pattern com-plex" along a long corridor of Fulton and Atlantic avenues—a $40 million project complete with sunken highways, office towers, and rerouted rail lines. The corridor plan, designed by Crane, called for "satellite cores" at each end, including commercial and community centers, as well as a "core" in the middle, where various educational, government, and office build-ings would be clustered together. To carry out this vision, along with Pei's proposed network of pedestrian walkways and green spaces, Logue esti-mated that 10 percent of all buildings in Bedford-Stuyvesant would have to be "cleared."[19]

In some ways, Logue's sweeping vision encapsulated everything Jane Jacobs decried about urban renewal in 1960s New York: top-down planning, the destruction of old buildings, and the isolation of residential areas from commercial ones. But Pei presented superblocks as a means to Jacobsean ends. "Now our endless, endless streets are basically parking lots," Pei told the *Times* in March 1967. "The superblocks will give the community a focus it now lacks. They should foster block organizations, self-reliance, and pride. The social idea is definitely more important than beautification."[20]

The planners, then, hoped to give Bedford-Stuyvesant more than just a physical facelift. As Logue explained at a January 1967 meeting of the D&S board, he would integrate an array of cultural programs, educational initiatives, and health services into his plans for physical renewal. If he had his way, the twin corporations, D&S and R&R, would function as a "quasi-government" for an area that, according to Logue, was desperately lacking in effective political leadership. There was one small problem, however. As Logue admitted during a heated exchange with skeptical D&S board members, "It's quite clear that even as distinguished a group as this can't put something like that over in that community." On that score, Logue was right. The community leaders who caught wind of his plans saw them as hopelessly out of touch with local needs. Bed-Stuy's street life and block associations had long been a source of strength; new street designs parachuted in from Boston were hardly necessary to "foster" such activity. Further, as Logue no doubt knew, the citizens of Bedford-Stuyvesant were just then engaged in an energetic effort to set up a "quasi-government" through Youth in Action.[21]

The directors of D&S, though not especially concerned about the viability of Bed-Stuy's community organizations, worried that Logue's plans didn't include enough short-term, readily achievable projects. Visual identifiers of progress were crucial, they believed, in demonstrating the outsiders' seriousness and goodwill. "Just as a group of this sort inspires great hope," said Benno Schmidt, one of the most active board members, "nothing coming out of a group of this sort, by the same token, results in equally greater frustration." But Logue had no patience for baby steps. Nor did he wish to run his plans by R&R, which ostensibly spoke for the people of Bedford-Stuyvesant. Instead, Logue was quick to underline the subordinate position of the local group. According to the plans his team submitted in February, three types of "community liaisons" would work with planners in shepherding the project through its early stages: people from the City Planning Department, people from D&S, and people from the city's Human Resources Administration. Representatives from R&R—and of black Brooklyn more generally—were conspicuously lacking. George Raymond later said it had been "indisputably clear" from the start that Logue intended for the planners' contractual relationship to be with D&S and not with the community corporation. Logue was particularly keen to get Ford Foundation grants earmarked for exclusive D&S use, so that he could support projects of his choosing and avoid having to consult the community.[22]

During this time, the chairman of R&R, Thomas Jones, repeatedly found himself excluded from important meetings and often heard secondhand about decisions made on behalf of his group. Jones complained to Kennedy aides that D&S was "planning for the community without being in the community, without hearing from the community." A particularly egregious example was a policymaking meeting with Mayor Lindsay on March 3, 1967; among the ten men present to discuss community development in Bedford-Stuyvesant, there had been not a single African American. "Certain individuals in Harlem and Bedford-Stuyvesant have begun to raise questions about the role of the R&R Corp., and its chairman," Jones wrote in a memo to Kennedy's chief assistant in New York, Thomas Johnston. "It has been suggested that we will not be consulted except in a limited way." This was personally humiliating for Jones, and he warned that the dual-board setup was causing "unnecessary political damage" to RFK.[23]

Logue, keen to make the project his fiefdom, dismissed such concerns. "Logue came in and bowled us over," Jones recalled. "He was the expert and brooked no interference. We were supposed to accept the Gospel according to Saint Logue, and we weren't prepared to do that." Even Eli Jacobs, the investment banker who in 1967 served as interim executive director of D&S and who had no particular love for the community-planning process, found Logue's behavior repellent. "One of the premises of this project was community decision making, diffuse decision making, community participation, and clearly that was at variance with Ed's notion of how you deal with these problems," Jacobs recalled. "And therein were highly incendiary conditions." Logue even adopted a know-it-all tone when addressing the D&S board, and he reacted defensively to criticism. He sealed his fate during a tense meeting on March 19 when he clashed with directors and gave the impression of having cut corners in his work. Afterward, Kennedy took Jacobs aside and dropped the axe: "Get rid of Logue."[24]

It was easy to make Logue a scapegoat, but there were deeper reasons for the growing resentment and miscommunication between the business group and community representatives. Kennedy and his aides had never intended to let the locals dictate the pace of an initiative that held serious implications for the senator's reputation. Though they collaborated with CBCC and appropriated key ideas being floated by Richardson, Shiffman, and the R&R planning group, Kennedy's men were not keen to relinquish control over the project. One internal planning memo argued that the "massive infusion" of outside funds and expertise was "a kind of 'foreign aid' to the under-developed country of the ghetto." Not incidentally, one of the first firms Kennedy's office consulted was simultaneously working on economic development projects in Indonesia; Lilienthal, too, was recruited because of his expertise in third world development.[25]

If the ghetto was an underdeveloped country, then it stood to reason that the natives were ill-equipped to manage affairs on their own. The locals should be "provided as early as possible with a comprehensive development strategy," one planning memo stated. Johnston, the Kennedy aide responsible for managing the nuts and bolts of the Bedford-Stuyvesant project, agreed with Logue's contention that grants should be kept far from R&R's control. In early 1967, when the Astor and Ford monies arrived, Kennedy staffers ensured that the funds were cleared through the Pratt Institute and then sent on to Logue. "Do we now want to start them [R&R] spending money of this kind?" asked the writer of an unsigned memo that circulated among the Kennedy staff in late 1966. "I think not."[26]

Matriarchs against the Man

While the Development and Services Corporation debated the merits of macro-scale planning, the activists affiliated with R&R stewed impatiently. By early 1967, R&R had yet to hire any full-time staff, nor did it have access to a reliable funding source. "A lot of papers have been shuffled back and forth, a lot of phone calls have been made, a lot of telegrams have been sent, and a lot of meetings have been held," was how Elsie Richardson summed up the first month's work in the January 1967 issue of the *Central Brooklyn Coordinator.* That was standard fare for community groups— except this was a community group that was saddled with the charge of transforming urban America.[27]

Simmering impatience within R&R would soon explode into an all-out brawl. Most of the people involved shared an acute sense of urgency. In 1967, frustrations were mounting in Bedford-Stuyvesant, in African American neighborhoods around the country, and among left-leaning activists of all stripes. After years of racking up legal victories, black protest leaders looked around their neighborhoods and saw things getting worse. Residential segregation in Northern cities now seemed a greater threat than the likes of Bull Connor or George Wallace. The Vietnam War was sapping people's faith in the goodness of a president and a Democratic Party in which they had vested immense faith only three years earlier. As for the War on Poverty, optimism had soured; community-action groups, for whom maximum feasible participation was a legal requirement, were beginning to wonder what the point was with money so scarce. In April, Dr. Martin Luther King Jr. lamented that "the Great Society, with its very noble programs, in a sense has been shot down on the battlefields of Vietnam."[28]

So the stakes were high in Bedford-Stuyvesant. Having labored for years to attract government resources for community development, many local leaders saw Kennedy's commitment as their last, best chance to fulfill the promises of the Great Society. None wanted to blow that chance. But neither did they want to see rivals take credit for the project's success or turn it into a patronage stronghold. A multisided struggle for control of R&R erupted in early 1967, with the major fault line pitting Thomas Jones, its chairman, against a faction led by Elsie Richardson and allied with Shirley Chisholm.

The struggle reflected long-brewing tensions among the Brooklyn activists who came together episodically under the CBCC umbrella. By 1967, CBCC represented more than a hundred organizations. Its backers, at least on paper, included Central Brooklyn's most influential ministers (Milton Galamison, Gardner Taylor, William Jones), along with every black Brooklynite serving in elective office: State Senator William C. Thompson, State Assemblywoman Shirley Chisholm and Assemblyman Bertram Baker, City Councilman J. Daniel Diggs, Judge Franklin Morton, and Judge Jones himself. Given the group's clout, as well as its strict nonpartisanship, it made sense for Kennedy to entrust CBCC with the task of setting up the new community corporation. But Kennedy's staff also fretted about the CBCC's ability to speak as the unified voice of Bedford-Stuyvesant.[29]

Indeed, the core activist group within CBCC—composed mostly of women—was struggling to shore up its legitimacy. Youth in Action, not CBCC, now carried a governmental stamp of approval as the community's official antipoverty agency. Further, a rising chorus of radical, young—and mostly male—voices was transforming the tone of black politics, in Brooklyn and across the country. At such a time, CBCC's leadership group found it increasingly difficult to sell its reform agenda, which was predicated on working within the boundaries of the welfare state. Jones worried that R&R would face a similar crisis. After all, the group itself was an outgrowth of CBCC—and an unelected one to boot, conceived in secret at the behest of the white power structure. Jones, who had seen his share of political combat, didn't think the women of CBCC were strong enough to provide a community counterpart to Logue and the businessmen. He urged the R&R board to expand its membership from twenty to fifty; specifically, he wanted to complement the old-guard community leaders with union reps, Puerto Rican activists, and radicals from CORE and the African-American Teachers Association. But board members were skeptical of Jones's motives. The core of CBCC's leadership group—Elsie Richardson, Lucille Rose, Louise Bolling, Ruth Goring, and Lionel Payne—suspected that Jones simply wanted to dilute their influence by installing a group he could control. In theory, Richardson et al. were willing to broaden the board's reach, but at a time when Logue was running roughshod over community sentiment, their most pressing priority was to consolidate their strength and firm up their relationship with Kennedy.

Activists within R&R were also gearing up for a fight over who should direct the project. Jones, urged on by Kennedy staffer Earl Graves, was supporting Franklin A. Thomas, a deputy police commissioner of legal affairs in the Lindsay administration. Though born in Bed-Stuy, the thirty-two-year-old Thomas had no prior experience in community development. That didn't sit well with longtime activists, who lobbied instead for one of their own: Donald Benjamin, a congenial social worker who had recently stepped down as executive director of CBCC to lead the newly formed Brooklyn Small Business Development Opportunities Corps. Benjamin and his former assistant, Constance McQueen, who replaced him as executive director in 1966, had provided quiet leadership and organizational acumen at the moment when CBCC was becoming a political force. For that reason, there was "a tremendous amount of loyalty" to Benjamin within R&R.[30]

In the power struggle that ensued, CBCC's leadership group found its legitimacy contested from all sides, often in gendered terms. In many ways, CBCC's weaknesses stemmed from its greatest strengths. The council's tireless organizing efforts had allowed it to emerge as the foremost community group in black Brooklyn. Claims to representing the "total community" had made the group an attractive interlocutor for two generations of New York Democrats, from Mayor Robert F. Wagner Jr. to Robert Kennedy. CBCC also provided a useful venue for cementing alliances among Bed-Stuy's eloquent, ambitious, and politically astute leaders. But with so many organizations participating in it, CBCC was of necessity a loose coalition. CBCC had very little executive capacity—in 1965–1966 it had all of five staff members and only $56,000 in Youth Board funds at its disposal—and remained almost entirely dependent on the work of its volunteers and on help from the Pratt Institute. When latent splits came to the surface, it became difficult for any faction to legitimately speak for "the community"—especially as the fight for control over the Kennedy project heated up.[31]

Since the late 1950s, CBCC had drawn its organizing strength from the women who disproportionately ran its affairs. In a male-dominated society,

CBCC put forth a public image of itself—and, by extension, of Bedford-Stuyvesant—as being planned and run, in the main, by smart, forthright women who were self-consciously "unbought and unbossed," in the words of the most famous among them, Shirley Chisholm. Most were middle-aged, most were mothers, and their power base was deeply rooted in community networks: block associations, civic clubs, PTAs, churches, and families. Some in the community referred to them as the matriarchy. "Call us what you will," countered Lucille Rose, a prominent CBCC activist, "but it's been the women who have held families together, worked in churches and for the community." The CBCC women made sure the organization remained attuned to the everyday concerns of local residents by promoting what historian Brian Purnell has described as a "'feminine' rehabilitation agenda" focused on preserving and revitalizing houses and nurturing physical wellness.[32]

In the mid-1960s, some of the best-known activists within the CBCC orbit included Almira Coursey, a schoolteacher who sat on the boards of several War on Poverty agencies; Ruth Goring, a prominent reform Democrat who in 1964 went to work for the Brooklyn borough president; and Louise Glover, an administrative assistant at IBM who sat on the city's Commission on Human Rights. But the most prominent, aside from Richardson and Shirley Chisholm, was Lucille Rose. Born in 1920 in Richmond, Virginia, she moved to Brooklyn as a child. Her mother, a widow, ran a small restaurant and also worked as a seamstress to support her kids. Lucille helped out in the restaurant, joined the NAACP in her teens, and worked as a welder at the Brooklyn Navy Yard during World War II. She went on to earn a B.A. from Brooklyn College and a master's in Manpower Planning and Economics at the New School for Social Research. Elegant, endearing, and energetic, she had won the NAACP's "Miss Brooklyn" contest while in her twenties and would become known as the "Lady Dean of Black Politics in Brooklyn" in her fifties. In 1964, Mayor Wagner hired her to take over as director of Bed-Stuy's Department of Labor field office, and she oversaw the Neighborhood Manpower Service Center affiliated with Youth in Action. Thus began a long career in city government that saw her serve as the commissioner of employment and become, under Mayor Abraham Beame, the first black woman to hold the post of deputy mayor. Her resume was also dotted with a dizzying number of affiliations: block associations, the Salvation Army, St. Francis College, the Catholic Interracial Council, the New York Urban Coalition, the National Association of Negro Business and Professional Women, the One Hundred Black Women, and more.[33]

Rose lived in a three-story limestone house that she bought for $8,000 in 1942 and would occupy for the next four decades. What kept her in Bed-Stuy through thick years and thin, she said, were the brownstones and "the great sense of pride on our blocks." Together, Rose and Elsie Richardson encapsulated the twin poles of women's organizing in Bed-Stuy. In her public persona, Richardson put forth a vocal, sometimes confrontational brand of activism; Rose, on the other hand, pursued "quiet political influence." The *Amsterdam News* opined that her strength derived "not so much from politics as from the respect gained from her volunteer work in a myriad of civic and religious organizations."[34]

In years past, CBCC had maintained something of a separate-spheres structure. Despite the organizing efforts of Rose, Richardson, and Chisholm, women often receded into the background when key meetings with public officials took place.[35] That had changed by 1966. Led by Chisholm, who would soon carry her colorful brand of black feminism onto the national stage, the women of Bedford-Stuyvesant had stepped into the limelight. Though CBCC's president was a man (Lionel Payne), Richardson was the public face of the organization, and another woman, Constance McQueen, was the executive director. Dorothy Orr was at the helm of Youth in Action. When the R&R Corporation came together in the summer of 1966, women held eight of twenty seats on the board. Among them were government officials such as Rose and Goring, along with popular block organizers like Sybil Holmes and Louise Bolling. At the December 1966 event where Kennedy officially unveiled his new initiative, Richardson called on a half-dozen Bed-Stuy women to say a few words from the podium while the suited dignitaries waited patiently behind them onstage.[36]

This accumulation of female clout put men on the defensive. In the summer of 1966, Kennedy aides complained to Jones that the CBCC women were difficult to work with. Richardson, especially, struck them as unpredictable, stubborn, and insufficiently deferential. Years later, Jones recounted Kennedy telling him that he had "never been dealt with as rudely" as he had by "some of the women of Bedford-Stuyvesant." Perhaps Jones was being self-serving in his recollections, but it was clear that Kennedy and his staff—like most men of their generation—found it slightly discomfiting to work in close concert with women, especially black women.

251

This helps explain Kennedy's decision to hand over control of the project to Jones, whom he thought he could manage. But the judge himself was a prickly personality, someone who could at times be "impossible to work with," as Franklin Thomas put it. Jones had a tendency to invoke the most noble of principles while playing petty politics. Further, in Ron Shiffman's words, Jones "really had a problem with strong black women."[37]

Jones dismissed the women who dominated CBCC and were fighting for control of R&R as "middle-aged matriarchs." At times, he accused them of wielding undue power in a community desperately in need of masculine role models, whereas at others, he belittled them. "I don't know how some of them, you know, cooked a meal or took a child to school," he said in a 1971 interview. "They had all the time in the world." Responding to the campaign by Richardson, Rose, and McQueen to make Donald Benjamin the chairman of R&R, Jones dismissed Benjamin as a "ladies man." Kennedy aide Carter Burden later recalled that during the debate over the composition of R&R's board, Jones on a few occasions "just went berserk about [how] these women were cutting off his balls." The CBCC women, meanwhile, resented Jones for having interposed himself between them and Kennedy, whom they respected and whose patronage they coveted.[38]

In using such imagery, Jones was hardly alone: calls for black empowerment in the late 1960s were often imbued with a discourse of masculinity that bemoaned the outsize influence of women in black communities. This was true across the political spectrum, from Daniel Patrick Moynihan to Sonny Carson. Embedded in liberal poverty policy was the assumption that generations of young black men had suffered psychological damage because of the paucity of male role models—and the preponderance of domineering mothers—in their midst. Members of Bed-Stuy's political elite, too, echoed that analysis of female power in the community. "Perhaps the most brutal offense of whites against blacks was the psychological castration of our men," Reverend Gardner Taylor was quoted as saying in a 1969 Ford Foundation report. "And most of the men of leadership caliber that we did produce went to places which had status-carrying opportunities. Bedford-Stuyvesant is not such a place." That same Ford report concluded, based on extensive interviews of participants in the project, that Franklin Thomas's "towering attractive figure was ideal for a ghetto community starved for male images that reflect strength and leadership." In some ways, what was most exceptional about the gender dynamics at play in Bed-Stuy was not that the women got sidelined—that was par for the course—but that they had previously been able to wield as much power as they had through CBCC.[39]

If the battle for access to Kennedy brought Bed-Stuy's latent gender strife to the fore, it also reflected preexisting political rivalries. In 1964, Jones had announced he was retiring from the State Assembly to run for a Civil Court judgeship. The move was a bit of a mystery. Jones was a bright, ambitious politician, only two years removed from a bold campaign against the Kings County Democratic machine. The bench was no place to park political ambitions. Why, at the relatively young age of fifty-one, was he suddenly giving up his hard-won seat? His official explanation was that being a judge paid a better salary—money he dearly needed after running a self-financed campaign for the Assembly seat. Yet Jones had also painted himself into a political corner. In open conflict with Democratic regulars, he had come to doubt the viability of his Unity Democratic Club as a long-term political base.[40]

Kennedy's arrival in 1966 seemed to breathe new life into the judge's career. Jones, according to Franklin Thomas, was "an articulate visionary who espoused great dreams and hopes for black people . . . [and] at the same time a dispenser of patronage, a kind of ward leader." Jones retained a substantial following in Brooklyn, where memories of his work as a crusading lawyer and civil-rights leader remained fresh. His sudden proximity to Kennedy promised to make him the top dispenser of patronage in the area. Jones was conscious, however, that things could easily turn sour. Any whiff of corruption would destroy his reputation as a jurist. On the streets of Bed-Stuy, his alliance with the white establishment would be tough to defend—and it would spell political doom if the project flopped. Jones saw the "matriarchs" as a self-interested, parochial group whose unwillingness to compromise could scuttle the project. No doubt, he also worried about CBCC's close ties to Youth in Action, which was just the kind of poverty agency Kennedy derided. Jones believed that the new project must be inoculated from the "mau-mauing" that had come to define the Community Action Program. The new initiative must project an air of seriousness, fiscal probity, and respectability. "We must give the best people who are here in Bedford-Stuyvesant an incentive to stay here," Jones explained two years later. "If the people who take pride in their work aren't able to hold up their heads and don't get a chance to participate, if the last guy who shouts 'pig' and knows best how to goldbrick gets rewarded, then the good workers give up." But accomplishing that goal meant not so much shunning the likes of Sonny Carson and Isaiah Lewis as giving them a seat at the table of influence and carefully controlling their access to resources. "If you really mean business about a transfer of power, you need to work with people who can handle power," Jones said.[41]

And who exactly could "handle power"? Embedded in such statements, again, were jabs at the old-guard leadership affiliated with CBCC. In the esteem of Jones and his liberal patrons, the "matriarchs" were too weak and too parochial to keep pace with the macro-scale planning emanating from D&S. To an extent, that was true: Richardson and her allies in R&R suddenly found themselves sidelined in the early months of 1967, unable to begin implementing the programs they thought their collaboration with Kennedy had made possible. (The same, of course, was true of Jones himself.) "A new ballgame came to town," one Kennedy associate told a researcher for the Ford Foundation, "and the women were only good at the old one."[42]

Yet one of the Brooklynites best equipped to handle power in 1967 was Shirley Chisholm. The former CBCC vice-president was quickly emerging as a political force in Brooklyn. Back in 1962, Chisholm had rapped her knuckles raw canvasing for Jones. Their alliance had since frayed. In 1964, Chisholm inherited both the leadership of the Unity Democratic Club and Jones's State Assembly seat, which she then defended twice. By 1967, her star was rising thanks to her reunion with Wesley Holder, the political strategist who had once upon a time mentored both Chisholm and Jones within the insurgent Bedford-Stuyvesant Political League. As Chisholm made a name for herself in Albany, Holder helped build a clubhouse filled with passionate supporters, especially women. Brooklyn's electoral map would not be officially redrawn until 1968, resulting in its first majority-black congressional district. But the rapid growth of Bedford-Stuyvesant's black population, along with a court decision that ruled Brooklyn's gerrymandered districts unconstitutional, had put the writing on the wall. Everyone knew that Bed-Stuy would have a black congressman—or congresswoman.[43]

Jones may have been contemplating a run for Congress in 1967; if he was, he saw Chisholm standing in his path. He knew that the CBCC people were Chisholm people.[44] She had been actively involved in the group's expansion and had maintained friendships with organizers like Richardson. In 1967, CBCC, along with Youth in Action, spearheaded a group calling itself the Committee for a Negro Congressman from

Brooklyn, which later endorsed Chisholm during her ultimately successful run for Congress in 1968. (Jones, meanwhile, would sniff around and find little support for his congressional aspirations, either within his old political club or among his new patrons; Kennedy thought he would be more useful managing strife in Bed-Stuy than speechifying in Washington, DC.) It so happened that Kennedy was laying the groundwork for his Bed-Stuy experiment at the very moment of Chisholm's ascent—but he rarely consulted the woman who proudly called herself "the top vote-getter" in Central Brooklyn. That he had chosen Jones as his surrogate could only have added to her sense of being snubbed.[45]

Kennedy and his staff, unfamiliar with the internal political dynamics of Bedford-Stuyvesant, were surprised by the extent of the rancor their project provoked. The dispute over control of R&R exploded in March 1967. Franklin Thomas, Kennedy's pick to become executive director of R&R, provided the spark. While he was considering whether to take the job, Thomas joined several Bed-Stuy leaders on a group tour of New Haven, where Logue showed the Brooklynites some of his greatest hits from his time as the city's urban-renewal chief. During the trip, Thomas felt as if Elsie Richardson and the CBCC women went out of their way to make him uncomfortable, peppering him with pointed questions. Did Thomas have other masters? What was in it for him? What made him think he was qualified for the job? Back in Bedford-Stuyvesant, an hour-long job interview with the R&R board turned confrontational and bitter. Though Thomas had grown up in Bed-Stuy, the Richardson faction pegged him as an outsider when it came to community organizing. It hurt his cause that Jones—and, by extension, Kennedy—promoted him as the *only* acceptable choice for the job. Allegedly, Kennedy was furious when he heard about the interview. According to Thomas, the senator called Jones and advised him to shake things up. "I think you've got a hell of a problem in getting someone who has something to lose to come into this and take it on, given that kind of hostility that's there," Kennedy said. Earl Graves, Kennedy's point man in Bed-Stuy and a Jones backer, recommended that the senator's team stop trying to collaborate with those who opposed the judge. Following this advice, the Kennedy team instead began trying to split off the pro-Jones members of the board from the faction led by Elsie Richardson.[46]

Meanwhile, the CBCC activists were again growing impatient. More than a year had passed since Kennedy's tour, and few tangible improvements had come to Bedford-Stuyvesant. The struggle for Youth in Action was ongoing. In March 1967, the Lindsay administration announced that urban-renewal funds for Fulton Park had once again been put on hold. "We now no longer ask politely for assistance," Richardson wrote in a March 27 telegram to members of Brooklyn's congressional delegation, including RFK. "We demand that the years of effort and anguish which we have invested in the future of our community not be used as justification for denying us what is rightfully ours."[47]

Matters came to a head on the night of March 31, when the R&R board met to decide its future. Rumors swirled that the Richardson faction would move to unseat Jones and force a vote to elect Benjamin executive director. The judge, who may have been the one sowing the rumors in the first place, showed up ready for combat. He opened the meeting by demanding votes on four resolutions he assumed the members would reject: first, that the board be expanded to fifty people; second, that a meeting be held three weeks later to elect new members; third, that he be put in charge of compiling the slate of names to be presented for election at that meeting; and fourth, that no further meetings take place in the interim. On each point, Jones demanded two-thirds approval, by way of forcing the issue. The board duly voted them down. Jones resigned on the spot and stormed out.[48]

This turn of events came as a surprise to Kennedy. The senator's staffers had talked to Jones about pursuing a divide-and-rule strategy vis-à-vis the community board, but they were sideswiped by the manner of the judge's sudden exit. Neither Mayor Lindsay nor Senator Javits had any inkling that a split was imminent. With the project on the verge of collapse, Jones gained Kennedy's permission to form a new body called the Bedford-Stuyvesant Restoration Corporation. It was a risky maneuver, but Jones promised to bring half the old R&R board with him and to pull together a new coalition within days. Kennedy staffers scrambled through the night to gain telegrams of endorsement from Javits and the Lindsay administration. (Lindsay was away on business, and it was Mitchell Sviridoff who made the decision to lend the city's support to the Jones faction of the community group.) On the morning of April 1, Kennedy's office went public with the news of Restoration's founding and began a frenetic public-relations campaign. Jones, meanwhile, set about lining up community support.[49]

The birth of Restoration was a major blow to CBCC; though it would continue to influence antipoverty activities in Bed-Stuy, the coordinating council would never again exercise the same clout. The organization in many ways had outlived its usefulness; after all, black Brooklyn was now represented by several elected officials, and CBCC had spun off not one but two government-funded antipoverty agencies. But Jones's coup left many Brooklynites bitter. The "matriarchs," shunned and stunned, lashed out. At the moment of their greatest success, just as they were finally gaining access to Washington, outside capital, and the institutional levers of change, they suddenly saw it all "slipping out of their hands," in the words of Franklin Thomas. Beyond that, the manner in which they had been sidelined—a cynical political maneuver, seasoned with a dose of machismo—represented a violation of the brand of grassroots organizing they had patiently nurtured for years. Richardson, Rose, and their supporters began to arm themselves for a fight.[50]

Bed-Stuy Bedlam

In the spring of 1967, to Kennedy's dismay, his Bedford-Stuyvesant initiative again made front-page headlines from Capitol Hill to Clinton Hill—no longer as a grand urban experiment but as an exercise in just the kind of bare-knuckled urban politics Kennedy had promised to transcend. Clearly, the senator and his staff had misjudged the political terrain in Central Brooklyn. Not only did they overestimate the cohesiveness of CBCC and vest too much faith in Jones; they also misunderstood the complex gender dynamics that underlay local politics. Further, the Kennedy people failed to anticipate the backlash their project would provoke from Youth in Action and its supporters. Indeed, just as the new Restoration Corporation was launched, thousands of Bed-Stuy residents were mobilizing their energies for the community-corporation elections mandated by Sviridoff's reorganization of the citywide antipoverty program. Many Stuyfordites believed that Youth in Action should be the vehicle by which the community would pursue its political and economic self-realization. Suddenly, the new Restoration Corporation threatened to draw poverty funds away from YIA and its many delegate agencies. Meanwhile, the CBCC leadership faction led by Elsie Richardson vociferously opposed Jones's new group, accusing it of stealing their ideas and marginalizing the people who had made it possible in the first place.

From Richardson's perspective, there was little immediate satisfaction to be gleaned from seeing her ideas finally gaining official support and funding. The brand of place-based politics that CBCC had been practicing for a decade was not only about drawing outside resources but was also a way of ensuring that those resources were deployed in a way that reflected local preferences and control. Her definition of community was not merely a question of geography. (She lived in what she jokingly called the "Crown Heights section of Bedford-Stuyvesant.") It was enmeshed in questions of leadership, past exclusion, and aspiration. Would the enactment of her ideas henceforth depend on the good graces of Bobby Kennedy and his surrogates? Would the task of defining the terms of community participation fall to Thomas Jones and his allies in the white establishment? As Walter Offutt, chairman of YIA, asked soon after Restoration's founding, "Can an outside force enter into a community and dictate to it who its leaders should be?"[51]

On April 5, 1967, more than 800 people joined in a passionate protest rally organized by the rump Renewal and Rehabilitation Corporation. Led by Elsie Richardson, Lucille Rose, and Lionel Payne, the dissidents teamed up with Youth in Action's leadership to issue a petition denouncing Thomas Jones and calling for community elections to select the new Restoration Corporation's board. Rose framed the issue in stark terms: "Shall we choose our leaders," she asked, "or shall they be chosen for us?" The anti-Jones group hoped to gain a vote of confidence "from the man in the street." But the street was in a volatile mood. Who constituted the "we" in Rose's formulation? The old guard, fractured and weakened, had lost the power to speak for the community it claimed to represent.[52]

The rally took place at P.S. 305 on Monroe Street, in the same auditorium where, only four months earlier, all parties had gathered to hear Kennedy speak. On this night, many arrived carrying hastily scrawled signs:

> "The Black Cat Is Back, So Lookout Black Rats"
> "Go Home Mr. K., We Don't Need Your Kind of Help"
> "Black Power Is Black Togetherness and You're Not With Us, Uncle Tom Jones"
> "Stop Making Deals With Outsiders Against Your Brothers"

The protesters squeezed into every seat of the auditorium, spilled into the halls, and stood shoulder to shoulder in the cafeteria, straining to hear speeches over the school's P.A. system. The place crackled with intensity. In a fiery speech, Offutt warned of a "movement afoot to put Negroes in their place." When Mayor Lindsay's envoy, James Smith, rose to deliver a message of support for Restoration from City Hall, a cacophony of catcalls and sneering laughter sent him back to his seat. Then Timothy Vincent, the head of YIA's radical youth-leadership wing, took the floor to denounce CBCC itself, arguing that the newly elected neighborhood antipoverty boards—and not old-line community organizations—were the real repositories of democracy in Bed-Stuy. The speech devolved into a shouting match between Vincent and CBCC's chairman, Payne.

Even Richardson had lost the ability to command the stage. When she tried to speak, Sonny Carson and his followers from CORE shouted her down. The young men, cheered on by the audience, rushed the stage and seized the microphone. Richardson had no right to make demands on their behalf, they proclaimed. After all, she spoke for an unelected organization that had done nothing but spin off more unelected organizations and call it community action. Now CBCC was suddenly invoking the "man in the street"? What a hustle. The CORE activists called Kennedy a "colonialist" and Jones a "Tom," and they denounced the "black bourgeoisie [trying] to make it uptown on the backs of the brothers." But they also directed invective at the women of CBCC, whom they accused of "emasculating the community and denying us our models of black manhood." An *Amsterdam News* headline summed up the scene: "Bed-Stuy Blight Bedlam."[53]

The fight reprised familiar themes. Unfolding at the tail end of a years-long debate over what "maximum feasible participation" should mean in Bedford-Stuyvesant, the struggle over the Restoration Corporation again raised the issue of community control. Whose community was Bedford-Stuyvesant? And on what basis should local power be translated into action? While Logue was making grandiose claims about setting up a "quasi-government," thousands of local citizens had been participating in the drive to do just that, through Youth in Action. Per city and federal rules, YIA had duly applied and reapplied for grants, restructured its programs several times, and set up neighborhood boards. By the spring of 1967, the agency was holding elections in efforts to make community action as democratic as possible. YIA thus formed a crucial link in a governmental chain stretching from the block association to the White House. Clearly, the agency had serious flaws, and even its supporters expressed disillusionment with the War on Poverty. But in April 1967 all factions of YIA, including the radical youth wing led by Timothy Vincent and Isaiah Lewis, briefly came together to attack the fledgling Restoration Corporation as a bait-and-switch, even as they also contested CBCC's leadership.[54]

Seen from outside Bedford-Stuyvesant, such disputes could easily be dismissed as petty parochialism. But they took on special urgency as a new session of Congress debated whether to jettison the poverty program altogether. Protecting Youth in Action, warts and all, became an overriding goal for the people who had invested the better part of three years in building a community-run poverty program. They argued that YIA, having converted into a community corporation, was now the legal body charged with representing local sentiment and instituting poverty policy. Despite being starved for funds and political support, it was organizing community action with extensive participation by the poor. How dare Bobby Kennedy and a bunch of white businessmen waltz into Bedford-Stuyvesant and trump that effort?[55]

Leading the charge for Youth in Action was Walter Offutt. An associate minister at William Jones's Bethany Baptist Church, Offutt had inherited from Jones the chairmanship of the Bed-Stuy antipoverty agency. He was twenty years older than Jones, less famous as an activist, and politically moderate, yet he was also growing radicalized by what he saw as a betrayal of the poor in the War on Poverty. The son of a clergyman, Offutt had done graduate work at the University of Pennsylvania, graduated from Union Theological Seminary in Manhattan, and later married pioneering black lawyer and jurist Jane Bolin. Beginning in the late 1940s, he emerged as a figure of some national prominence, leading desegregation struggles in Kentucky before serving as the national church secretary of the NAACP. In the latter role, he quietly traveled the country to mobilize preachers for the growing assault on the legal edifice of segregation. By the late 1950s, Offutt had turned most of his attention to Harlem, where he organized voter-registration drives, lobbied for a new hospital, and publicized incidents of discrimination against black workers. In 1960, when some three dozen organizations—city agencies, civic groups, settlement houses, and politicos like Percy Sutton—came together in a CBCC-like organization to plan an assault on poverty and social disorder in Harlem, Offutt got involved. That effort sowed the seeds of what would in 1962 become HARYOU, though Offutt by that point had turned his attention to Brooklyn.[56]

Offutt's activism, while eclectic and sustained, was not particularly exceptional among his generation of African American ministers. Like Archie Hargraves, William Jones, Milton Galamison, Gardner Taylor, and many others, Offutt harbored hopes that the civil-rights movement might bring about transformational change through a tactical alliance with the northern wing of the Democratic Party. Helping to set up and run New York's version of the Great Society was a big part of that reform vision. As the politics of the black freedom struggle veered sharply leftward in the 1960s, Offutt started speaking a new language, talking class as much as race and promoting the political empowerment of poor people. Yet he continued to insist that the War on Poverty represented the best hope for African Americans.

In a March 1967 column in the *Youth in Action* newsletter, Offutt argued that, in a sense, all black Americans were poor. Few had sufficient wealth to avoid worrying about their next paycheck; almost all lived in close proximity to dire poverty. Even the black bourgeoisie must recognize the precariousness of their position, Offutt argued: "When we look at our unemployed neighbor we say prayerfully, 'there but for the grace of God go I.'" The poverty program had yet to evolve into anything more than a "skirmish," Offutt admitted—but where else but to government could communities like Bedford-Stuyvesant look for the desperately needed infusion of outside capital? "The poverty program must go on," he wrote. "If we destroy it, we destroy ourselves—and as dramatic as it may sound, this country."[57]

Many in Congress disagreed with Offutt's assessment and advocated pulling the plug on OEO. On May 9, 1967, Offutt appeared before the Senate Subcommittee on Employment, Manpower, and Poverty. Others appearing that day included Mitchell Ginsberg, commissioner of the city's Department of Welfare; Carl McCall, chairman of the city's Council Against Poverty (and a founding member of the YIA board), and a dozen other officials at various levels of the social-welfare bureaucracy. It was an explosive moment. That summer, Detroit and Newark would burst into flames. Brooklyn would stay cooler, but men like Offutt had grown concerned about the mounting anger they detected all around them.[58]

The poor of Bedford-Stuyvesant, Offutt explained, had been able "to get a taste of ice cream for the first time in their lives, to realize that in this democracy there is a chance to vote, there is a chance to find a better life, there is a great opportunity." Through the Community Action Program, thousands of Brooklynites had enrolled in Head Start and homework-study groups, in youth-leadership programs and the Neighborhood Youth Corps, in the Young Mothers Program and other family-planning initiatives, and in on-the-job training and consumer-education courses. More significant than the jobs created, as far as Offutt was concerned, was the fact that Youth in Action had stirred people from their apathy and begun to do just what the Community Action Program had been tasked with doing in the first place: encouraging self-help and community resilience among the poor and the powerless. Such people, Offutt wrote in a statement for the record, "held meetings, conferred, formed block associations, read reports, prepared reports, held elections and made plans. They expect these plans to come to fruition. To tell them now that those plans will come to nothing because no funds are available is to destroy months and months of long arduous work."[59]

"I am not here to make any threats," Offutt told Senator Joseph S. Clark of Pennsylvania, the chairman of the Senate subcommittee, "but . . . when you started this legislation, you started people from Tobacco Road to 115th Street in Harlem and Fulton Street [in Brooklyn] on a march that nobody will be able to stop." Offutt was hardly the kind of man who might have been expected to speak in the language of the incipient revolution unfolding within the country's poorest places. He was in his mid-fifties, an established preacher whose wife was a judge. But although he came from a moderate, integrationist current of black protest thought, in 1967 he spoke of the possibility of rebellion. "All this energy channeled into constructive planning can now only burst out in frustration, rage and disaster for this area," he warned.[60]

Part of the reason for Offutt's alarm was that Thomas Jones and Restoration were making what seemed to be a hostile takeover of the antipoverty space in Bed-Stuy. The day before Offutt's testimony, Jones had appeared before the same Senate subcommittee—on which Kennedy sat—and gave his own version of events. Misleadingly, he represented himself as the chairman of the "Bedford-Stuyvesant Community Corporation." Thus, when it was Offutt's turn to speak, the committee members announced that they had already heard all they needed to hear about community action in Bedford-Stuyvesant. Declining to hear the speech he had prepared, they limited his testimony to a few off-the-cuff remarks. It was clear that these senators would defer to Kennedy's judgment—to the detriment of Youth in Action. Offutt conceded that Jones was "blessed with the power that we do not have." But he also warned that it would cause a "great hue and cry from the target population" if YIA were dismantled as a result.[61]

Another erstwhile moderate who was turning to militant rhetoric was Walter Pinkston, YIA's executive director. Pinkston had spent the previous fifteen years employed by New York City's social-welfare bureaucracy. As a Youth Board employee, he had helped found CBCC in 1958 and had later served as its executive director before moving over to YIA. In August 1967, Pinkston wrote that in view of the "years of oppression, discrimination and other forms of second class status imposed upon the Afro-American" as well as the "deaf ears that have been turned toward the community by the superstructures of city government," there was no other conclusion to draw than that the "time has run out for appeasement." Pinkston himself disavowed violence, and he failed to spell out how his own government-funded agency might turn away from "appeasement." But his new rhetoric revealed how YIA's middle-aged, middle-class leadership group felt itself under threat, from within and from without.[62]

Restoration captured $7 million in federal antipoverty funds in 1967. Youth in Action, meanwhile, was undergoing a complex and disorienting process of democratic reinvention, all to prove itself a legitimate recipient of lesser funds. As it turned out, YIA would continue to draw federal and city funds into the 1970s, at one point becoming the city's best-funded Community Action Agency. Still, in 1967, the emergence of Restoration as a rival antipoverty agency struck reformers like Offutt and Pinkston as a violation of the implied social contract between the neighborhood and the state. That contract was structured around painstakingly laid-out participatory structures, funding channels, and ideas about community competence. Viewed from the perspective of Pinkston and Offutt, the Kennedy project offered proof that the debate over "maximum feasible participation" in the War on Poverty had been an elaborate charade.

Ironically, Kennedy's staff answered critics by appropriating the participatory language of the War on Poverty. In a letter addressed to CBCC chairman Lionel Payne on April 4, 1967, three days after the implosion of R&R, Thomas Johnston invoked "this principle of maximum involvement of all interested individuals and groups in Bedford-Stuyvesant"—a clear echo of the "maximum feasible participation" mandate. According to Johnston, Jones's breakaway corporation was necessary because the R&R board members had blocked meaningful community participation in the project by refusing to expand from twenty to fifty members. As it turned out, that was a red herring: a year later, the board had only twenty-two members, all of them handpicked by Jones and Kennedy, and the number in 1980 was just twenty-six—of whom only three were women. But Kennedy and his surrogates were keen to stake a claim for Restoration as the true repository of community aspirations in Bed-Stuy. As Johnston put it, community participation in planning was "clearly far more important than any other single issue or difference in personality in the entire development effort."[63]

A noble sentiment—but Restoration, with its unelected board and opaque corporate structure, seemed to incarnate little of the War on Poverty's participatory spirit. What had originated in the community's quest for resources was now the "Kennedy project." Community-based planning was giving way, in the name of efficiency, to a top-down development effort led by outside experts and shot through with paternalistic assumptions. In the process, Kennedy and his local surrogates had shunted aside and embittered some of Bedford-Stuyvesant's most dedicated, forward-looking female activists. And Restoration's very existence destroyed any remaining hopes, however slim, that Youth in Action might succeed in its arduous efforts to establish a democratic Community Action Program. By mid-1967, half a year after Elsie Richardson heralded a new dawn in Bedford-Stuyvesant, the community seemed destined, finally, to receive the infusion of resources it so desperately needed. But local leaders wanted more than mere resources; they wanted to control how those resources were spent and distributed. The new Community Development Corporation might yet satisfy those concerns, but not if it reflected the dreams of Ed Logue or Eli Jacobs. It would fall to Franklin Thomas to figure out how to run an efficient organization while also giving credence to community aspirations.

8

From the Ground Up

> We knew we had to get started immediately to demonstrate to
> the community that something different, something impor-
> tant, something new, something exciting was going to happen
> as the result of this partnership. And the people themselves of
> the community would be an integral part, not only in con-
> ceiving what would happen to their community but in the
> actual implementation of those ideas.
>
> —FRANKLIN A. THOMAS, 2008

When Franklin Thomas took the reins of the Restoration Corporation in the spring of 1967, Bedford-Stuyvesant was being invaded by an armada of outside experts. From California came Paul O'Rourke, a former health commissioner and OEO administrator, who delivered a report on health facilities in Central Brooklyn. New York University psychologist and educational reformer Frank Riessman was hard at work on plans to shore up the area's schools. Businessman Eli Jacobs was pushing for a massive new commercial center at Broadway Junction, where Brooklyn bordered Queens—a perfect spot, he thought, to draw shoppers from Long Island. Architect James Polchek was sketching designs for a supersized recreational and community center, and I. M. Pei continued to push his super-blocks. All reported to the Development and Services Corporation (D&S), the business group Robert F. Kennedy had put together with the osten-sible purpose of *advising* Restoration—which controlled no funds and had hired no staff. The planning juggernaut threatened to submerge local aspi-rations in a tidal wave of proposals aimed at saving the American city.[1]

Thomas, though, insisted that the people of Bed-Stuy wanted tangible progress, not grand visions. Kennedy was impatient for action too. Twelve months of planning had given way to twelve weeks of strife. By June 1967, six months after Kennedy had officially launched the Bed-Stuy project,

The executive director of the Bedford-Stuyvesant Restoration Corporation, Franklin A. Thomas, discusses rehabilitation projects in 1968. The map reflects an expansive definition of Bed-Stuy; the outlined area, including most of Crown Heights, housed approximately 450,000 people. *Photograph by Bob Gomel. The LIFE Picture Collection. Getty Images*

nothing of substance had been started, aside from one superblock. Mindful of the turmoil caused by funding delays in the Community Action Program, Kennedy worried that local enthusiasm for his initiative would soon evaporate. Those fears only intensified following Jones's acrimonious split with the R&R board. But Thomas turned out to be a masterful conciliator and a brilliant organizational tactician. Almost immediately, he began to lay out an alternative vision for Restoration that would ultimately help the corporation establish its legitimacy. Even if Kennedy's new surrogate had been inclined to follow the outsiders' blueprints, he couldn't have done so without losing support on the streets of Bed-Stuy. Instead, the new boss wanted to take up small-scale, easily achievable projects that would put Restoration on the map—literally.[2]

Restoration would start at street level. Its first major campaign under Thomas saw the corporation partner with block associations to carry out façade renovations on owner-occupied brownstones. The animating principle was that highly visible improvements to the area's housing stock were the surest path to building community cohesion and creating jobs. Brownstone renovations appealed explicitly to the local middle class, whose continued presence and investment in the area were seen by Restoration's leaders as bulwarks against community breakdown. Restoration also set its sights on long-term goals that promised both to empower individuals and to grow the local economy: amassing a cooperative mortgage-financing pool, nurturing local businesses, and building a shopping center.

Thomas's vision of community development grew out of the neighborhood's long tradition of reform. Like the Bedford-Stuyvesant Neighborhood Council in the 1950s, the Restoration Corporation hoped to unleash the energies of local block organizations and harness them for neighborhood-wide improvement efforts. Further, echoing CBCC, Thomas honed in on construction projects that might train the poor, the young, and the unemployed by putting them to work. Though business development was an important part of Restoration's mission, so were social services and street-level outreach programs that mimicked the ones launched by Youth in Action. In the late 1960s, Restoration even teamed up with its rival agencies to lobby for a college in Central Brooklyn. An idea first mooted by CBCC in the early 1960s and pushed forward by Youth in Action and Restoration, the college campaign temporarily united all community factions and offered an object lesson in both the possibilities and the limitations of the kind of reform politics that had been practiced in Bed-Stuy since the 1950s.

The byword of the college campaign was not community action but community *control*. The semantic shift, seemingly slight, signaled the increasing prominence in Bedford-Stuyvesant of ideas associated with the Black Power movement. The Restoration Corporation also reflected that new mood. Thomas and Kennedy actively courted Sonny Carson and Al Vann, radical voices who would help establish Restoration's legitimacy on the streets of Bed-Stuy. Such alliances mattered all the more because the Restoration Corporation was not a democratic organization. In its top-down style, it incarnated a new phase in the pursuit of black political power, focusing less on activating grassroots energies and more on building managerial capacity.[3] Yet Thomas also sought to incarnate the spirit of community control. From the start, he struggled to marginalize his white supervisors and tailor Restoration's programs to the wishes of local people.

Efforts at renovating crumbling brownstones, launching a college, attracting businesses, and unlocking mortgage capital each reflected aspects of the community's long-standing quest to win resources *and* control over those resources. By the late 1970s, Restoration stood at the height of its power, having scored numerous victories despite almost insurmountable odds. Yet, as the Bedford-Stuyvesant model began to spread across America, the accomplishments of the Community Development Corporation that started it all appeared to rest on increasingly shaky ground.

Return of the Native

Franklin Thomas was uniquely equipped to heal the wounds opened by the founding of Restoration. One of five children born to immigrants from Barbados, he had grown up poor in Bed-Stuy. His father, a laborer, died when Thomas was just eleven. From his mother, who toiled as a waitress and a housekeeper, he inherited the work ethic he would later credit for his successes. At Franklin K. Lane High School, the 6-foot-4-inch teenager became a star in the classroom and on the basketball court. Several colleges offered Thomas basketball scholarships, but at his mother's insistence he instead accepted an academic scholarship at Columbia. He joined the hoops squad anyway, becoming its captain and setting school single-season and career rebounding records that would still stand six decades later. Thomas then spent four years in the Air Force before returning to Columbia for law school. A whirlwind tour in government followed: a year with the Federal Housing and Home Finance Agency, followed by a brief stint as an assistant U.S. attorney for the Southern District of New York. By the time Kennedy alighted in Bedford-Stuyvesant, Thomas was working as the deputy police commissioner in charge of legal affairs.[4]

Thomas hadn't contributed to the planning effort that preceded Restoration's founding. Earl Graves urged him to join the project in late 1966, and he quietly attended several meetings with Kennedy and his businessman allies. Despite a personal request from Kennedy that he sign on as R&R's executive director, Thomas demurred. But as he watched the project unravel, he reconsidered. Kennedy assured the young lawyer that he would have his unconditional support, and several of the businessmen told Thomas they would "take care of him" should the project fail. After the founding of the reorganized Restoration Corporation, he agreed to take the helm. A new Cadillac and a salary of $30,000 a year helped smooth his transition.[5]

The Manhattan men saw Thomas as someone they could work with. Kennedy hoped to develop a new generation of leaders in Bed-Stuy—and Thomas seemed the embodiment of that goal. "Without Frank Thomas the project would not have gotten launched, wouldn't have been credible," Eli Jacobs later said. Only thirty-two, Thomas exuded gravitas that belied his youth. Tall, fit, and preternaturally composed, he spoke with a soft yet assured voice that somehow had the power to persuade even inveterate foes of his good intentions. He had the rare ability to roll out one perfect sentence after another, expressing his thoughts in complete paragraphs. He was a keen listener, too, constantly soliciting others' opinions and nodding gently as they spoke. Yet beyond the accommodating demeanor, Thomas possessed unshakeable confidence, a ferocious drive to succeed, and an underrated temper. A Ford Foundation study from 1969 described him as "a natural political leader who is able to relate equally well to a Sonny Carson and a Douglas Dillon." He was an ideal Kennedy type.[6]

Thomas was also a "counter-revolutionary"—or so said some of his detractors. If Restoration was an attempt to demonstrate that a new approach to community development could succeed, it was also an attempt to breathe new life into the dream of an integrated society. "What we were doing was consciously, openly, and aggressively asserting that the future for development was a future that involved black and white people working together," Thomas later recalled. "We were prepared not just to articulate that but to demonstrate that." Many black Brooklynites arched their eyebrows at such aspirations. Even Jones, the chair of Restoration's board, wondered whether his own efforts at accommodating the "ghetto" to the structures of American capitalism were holding back a revolution that must someday come. "For now, I'm trying to do what I can, where I am," a friend recalled him saying of his work with Restoration, "but I know that sooner or later I'll be useless, that they'll have to push me aside to advance further. . . . Am I helping my people or am I obscuring the true solutions to their problems?"[7]

Through the spring and summer of 1967, Thomas held a series of public meetings in which he heard a litany of complaints, smiled patiently, and politely yet firmly answered each one. He pledged to take "whatever steps are necessary" to reconcile the feuding factions in Bed-Stuy. (Mayor

Lindsay also helped to defuse tensions by calling on the commissioner of the city's Equal Employment Commission, Samuel Jackson, to carry out a community-wide mediation process that summer.) Thomas recognized that behind the overheated rhetoric and the talk of "Toms" lay a legitimate set of grievances about how policy had been implemented—and not implemented—in Bedford-Stuyvesant. He suspected that the likes of Oliver Ramsay, Lucille Rose, and Elsie Richardson resented Jones far more than they did Kennedy. Behind the scenes, Thomas and Earl Graves plotted ways of changing minds. From their perspective, the stranded members of R&R represented not only a political danger but also a wealth of expertise and leadership that would eventually have to be tapped if Restoration were to succeed. "They must be flattered, coerced, courted," Graves wrote to Johnston in May. Meanwhile, bigwigs like Gardner Taylor and Milton Galamison, who had until then remained on the sidelines of the R&R dispute, should be "courted through cocktails, lunches, private visits, phone calls from the Senator, etc."[8]

Thomas calculated that the anger sparked by Restoration's founding would subside once new federal funds began to flow into the community—as they did in mid-1967. After all, the parties to the dispute shared much in common. Franklin Thomas and Thomas Jones, Elsie Richardson and Shirley Chisholm—all had grown up in a multicultural neighborhood populated by a strong cadre of homeowners. All four were of West Indian descent and inherited strong political inclinations from their immigrant parents. All belonged to a reform-minded middle class, and all pursued social change through government structures. They held different opinions about how to negotiate with the outside establishment—about how to balance confrontation with cooperation, about how much trust to invest in the corporate sector—but they collectively articulated a common vision for Bed-Stuy's future, premised on the infusion of government resources to preserve the middle class and increase opportunities for their low-income neighbors. They had not yet given up on the Great Society. It was their "beautiful woman" as much as it was Lyndon Johnson's. And it was their bedrock commitment to reviving Bedford-Stuyvesant that made possible the program Thomas began to implement in 1967.

The remnants of the old R&R held together for a time. Richardson rallied support from influential locals like Thomas Fortune (leader of the Unity Democratic Club), William Jones, and of course Shirley Chisholm—all of whom nominally sat on the R&R board in 1967. Pratt's

Ron Shiffman continued to work closely with the group in drawing up urban-renewal plans, especially around the Fulton Park area. "We continue to have as our goal," Richardson wrote in July 1967, "the implementation of many imaginative, forward-looking, and, above all, constructive programs asked for and worked out by the members of our community through the years." Richardson would complain for years that the Kennedy people were appropriating as their own ideas that had sprung from within the community. She was right—but as time passed, dozens of ex-staffers and board members from CBCC, R&R, and Youth in Action found their way to Restoration. "I ultimately came to know all of the Central Brooklyn Coordinating Council people involved," Thomas later commented, "and they were supportive of the work of Restoration." Owen Hague, the former YIA treasurer, took up a similar position at Restoration; former YIA and CBCC leaders Timothy Vincent, Lucille Rose, Almira Coursey, Oliver Ramsay, and Cybil Holmes all joined the board. Meanwhile, Richardson, along with Lionel Payne and a handful of other CBCC activists, threw their efforts into the ill-fated Central Brooklyn Model Cities program, which never gained the funds to build on anywhere near the scale it had envisioned. By the late 1970s, Restoration would be the only game in town.[9]

In 1967, the challenge for Thomas, Jones, and Kennedy was not merely to patch things up among the neighborhood's veteran middle-class leaders. They also made a concerted effort to woo Brooklyn's black nationalists. In the long run, the most important of these men—and they were almost all *men*—was the leader of the African-American Teachers Association, Al Vann, who sat on the YIA board and would later spend three decades serving in various legislative offices. But the most renowned of Restoration's recruits was Sonny Carson, leader of the Brooklyn branch of CORE. In some ways, Carson was a natural ally for Kennedy. According to journalist Jack Newfield, "Kennedy's sympathies, with their bias in the direction of the young, the activist, and the powerless, were with the more militant sections of the black community." Both Carson and Kennedy were gifted in the art of political theater, and they understood each other's language. Like Bobby, Sonny was alienated, impulsive, and existential. Though already on the wrong side of thirty, Carson appealed most of all to the young, as did Kennedy. Most of all, Carson was a dealmaker. One minute he was dismissing the Restoration Corporation as a hustle cooked up by the black bourgeoisie and the white power structure; the next minute he was sitting down with Franklin Thomas to iron out the details of an alliance. Along with Al Vann, he agreed to join Restoration's board shortly after Jones split from the R&R group.[10]

Carson straddled the contradiction between cooperation and opposition that stood at the heart of early Community Development Corporations. As political scientist Kimberley Johnson describes this fundamental tension, "On one hand they were supposed to work with and within the pre-existing economic and political structure. On the other hand, they were meant to act as a sort of permanent opposition—a community's attempt to control its own destiny against 'outsiders.'" That contradiction was especially glaring in the case of Restoration. Clearly, the entire endeavor was premised on the support of foundations and corporate elites. As such, it was bound to articulate a vision of political and economic power that tended toward incremental reform. At the same time, Restoration would clearly flounder were it perceived on the streets of Bed-Stuy as the pet project of rich white men and their local puppets.[11]

Carson's decision to join Restoration's board instantly infused it with street cred. With the old-guard leadership up in arms, Carson was expected to legitimize Restoration among the young, politically radical males whom Kennedy and Jones alike saw as the future architects of black political power. "These are the people we have to reach," Kennedy said of Carson and his followers. "Some people may not like it, but they are in the street and that is where the ball game is being played." Carson, too, was eager to take a seat at the table of influence. In the summer of 1967, he parlayed the simmering frustration in Bed-Stuy into an unofficial position as Mayor Lindsay's conduit to the angry street. Though he called for the destruction of capitalism and swore that he did not "want anything to do with the white power structure as it is now," he was keen to negotiate from a position of strength. Carson talked the talk of black separatism and armed self-defense, but he walked the walk of community control. Community control was fundamentally about the relationship of black Americans to the state; it meant nothing if there were no resources to be controlled—and Restoration promised resources. Carson's embrace of the new Community Development Corporation signaled that community control could be pursued in a roundabout way, by first appearing to cede an element of control.[12]

Thomas, too, struggled to establish a modicum of community control within the institutional structure Kennedy had imposed on the project. He strongly objected to the sequestering of the community corporation from the businessmen's group, D&S, which maintained a substantial staff and continued to hire various outside consultants. "It was stupid to have a system operating that purported to be a partnership based on trust and confidence, but operated as though you had a father-son relationship, or a mother-daughter—whatever your choice is—master-slave," Thomas said in 1972. The structure was hardly accidental: Kennedy staffers had initially prevented R&R from accessing funds because they didn't trust the community group. But even after the creation of an entirely new entity—the Restoration Corporation—and even after placing it under the control of a handpicked executive director, Kennedy's team continued to fret that the corporation, because of local pressures, would be inclined to launch a slew of well-meaning initiatives that would lack coordination and follow-through. According to Eli Jacobs, "Tom [Johnston] had the feeling that you couldn't trust Restoration, that they were not at a level of financial sophistication and maturity that you wanted to trust them with grants." In part, this owed to previous episodes of financial mismanagement among urban programs, not least of them Bedford-Stuyvesant's own Youth in Action. It also arose from the prevailing image of Bed-Stuy as a damaged, leaderless community. "You might say there were residues of a colonial outlook," Jacobs said. "Benevolent colonialism, but colonial nonetheless."[13]

From the start, Thomas realized that few of the white men associated with the project believed that Bedford-Stuyvesant could come up with enough qualified people to run the Restoration Corporation efficiently and properly. The businessmen, Ed Logue—most seemed to think the job would be better done by whites, and they assumed Thomas Johnston himself would figure that out sooner or later. Kennedy, too, probably shared this notion. "I think he [Kennedy] realized that the application of the Negro to the higher levels or middle levels of the economic society was going to be very difficult," recalled Thomas Watson of IBM in 1970. "I don't think he thought for a minute that you could take the average Negro and compete against the average white person and come off with the Negro holding his own."[14]

Thomas refused to concede the point. He would do more than hold his own—he would take the lead. As he set about hiring his own staff in 1967, he demanded that funds flow directly into Restoration's coffers. He also embarked on a series of small-scale projects intended to put Restoration back in touch with the grass roots. As the corporation expanded its reach in the late 1960s, it would initiate programs that reflected local priorities more than they did the grand designs of outside consultants. Echoing the spirit of maximum feasible participation, Thomas emphasized that the *process* of community development mattered as much as the products that emerged from it. "If you want genuine knowledge-building, knowledge-transfer to occur," he later explained, "you have to encourage and enable people closest to the problem to participate in the process."[15]

By the early 1970s, critics alleged that D&S, merely by continuing to exist, was hampering the work of Thomas and his lieutenants. For instance, Geoffrey Faux, a former OEO official who penned a nationwide study of CDCs in 1971, argued that the dual-board structure "appears to limit both the independence of the Restoration Corporation and the extent to which it can serve as the black community's vehicle for economic development." Thomas himself chafed under the arrangement, which sparked several "knock-down-drag-out fights" with John Doar, the former civil-rights attorney who served as executive director of D&S. The business group finally phased out its staff in 1973 and assumed a purely advisory role. "Nobody's going to tell Frank Thomas and his board what to do if they don't want to do it," Doar acknowledged. According to Thomas, this represented a long-overdue recognition that Restoration's staff was by far the more competent of the two—a hard realization since, in Thomas's words, "ostensibly your purpose in being there is to bring guidance to the natives. The natives didn't need it."[16]

Brick by Brick, Block by Block

From the start, Restoration defined itself in contrast with the Community Action Program. Whereas Youth in Action hired social workers to oversee its staff and finances, Restoration hired lawyers and MBAs. Whereas YIA specialized in papering Bed-Stuy with incendiary, handcrafted posters, Restoration produced slick brochures. Restoration's newsletters were carefully edited and cleanly designed (complete with a monthly "box score" tabulating the corporation's achievements), whereas YIA publications abounded in typos. As Restoration ascended and YIA disintegrated, technocratic visions of progress replaced grassroots protests.

In some ways, YIA served as a cautionary tale for Restoration. The agency never did manage to balance its political and policy functions, or its dual mission of serving the poor while also empowering them. By the early 1970s, YIA was receiving $8 million a year in city and federal funds—more than any other Community Action Agency (CAA) in New York City. Its delegate agencies included a housing-development program, a job-placement center, a computer-education project, a community-owned supermarket, a senior citizens council, an auto service shop that doubled as a job-training program, various public-health initiatives, legal services, and even a bicycle-racing program. It was an ambitious agenda that appeared to fuse the War on Poverty's uplift mission with the beginnings of a program to cope with a changing urban economy. But forward thinking was soon trumped by old-fashioned politics.[17]

In the 1970s, Bed-Stuy's CAA turned into a patronage mill run by City Councilman Sam Wright and State Senator Vander Beatty, both of them African Americans closely tied to the now-inclusive Kings County Democratic machine. The two men together controlled an archipelago of community institutions: Wright's main power bases were the Ocean Hill–Brownsville school board and the Brownsville Community Corporation, and Beatty's was Youth in Action. Beatty orchestrated a hostile takeover of YIA in 1971, organizing a muscular get-out-the-vote campaign in the community-corporation elections. He gradually sidelined other local politicians with ties to the agency—among them Thomas Fortune of the Unity Democratic Club and Waldaba Stewart, a former YIA staffer who had won election to the state legislature—before installing his cronies in high places. One of those allies, Executive Director Maurice Chessa, was arrested in 1974 on charges of loan-sharking, illegal gun possession, and attempted murder; after being convicted, he served five years in jail. Youth in Action's chairman, a nightclub owner named Richard Habersham-Bey, was later found guilty of fraud and embezzlement. In 1975, federal agents raided YIA's offices and seized its records. Both the city and a federal grand jury launched investigations of the agency, and its funds were cut to under $4 million the following year. Wright wound up behind bars in 1977, and Beatty followed him six years later. (Both men were convicted on fraud charges that were not directly related to their work with Youth in Action.) Meanwhile, YIA was abolished altogether in 1978 by incoming mayor Edward I. Koch. The agency had gone through ten board chairmen and seven executive directors in its thirteen-year history; millions of dollars in public funds were unaccounted for.[18]

Restoration strove to neutralize the dual pressures that had hamstrung CAAs: the impulse toward participatory democracy emanating from below and the welter of bureaucratic constraints bearing down from above. This meant proceeding independently of city bureaucracies as well as the federal OEO—though Restoration and other CDCs would be officially merged with the federal War on Poverty in 1968. Thomas scrutinized every dollar his organization spent in its early years. "He was very conscious of the fact that if there was any kind of scandal, ballgame over," recalled Barron Tenny, who served as Restoration's general counsel under Thomas. "He signed every contract, he signed every check." Restoration also distinguished itself by carefully recruiting a nonelected board that would be stable, competent, and incorruptible. As one Restoration staffer put it in 1973: "The problem with the 'antipoverty' program to date has been the three-year tenures for the community members of the boards. This is seen by many as a sure road to failure, since by the time unsophisticated community residents begin to acquire some expertise and understand what the program is all about, they have to step down, to be replaced by an inexperienced board. This ensures that any such program will never come of age."[19]

For all that, it was undeniable that the War on Poverty had laid the groundwork for Restoration and the community-development approach it pioneered. Restoration was not only a reaction against Great Society liberalism but also a vindication of it. The efforts of CBCC and YIA to unify Bedford-Stuyvesant from within went a long way toward drawing Kennedy to Brooklyn. Through War on Poverty agencies, local activists had yoked new ways of thinking about community development to the spirit of the civil rights struggle, creating a new social movement dedicated to neighborhood revitalization. The ways in which Restoration went about community development reflected many of the assumptions about neighborhood change that had informed Bed-Stuy's long War on Poverty from the start.[20]

In 1967, Restoration began printing and distributing twenty-page booklets containing phone numbers and useful information about every imaginable government service in the area: how to apply for food stamps, whom to contact for legal aid, which agency to call about building-code violations, where to get prenatal classes, and so on. The corporation also funded a television show, *Inside Bedford-Stuyvesant*, which featured the voices of everyday people and sought to counter negative stereotypes perpetrated in the press about the "ghetto." An Opportunities Industrialization Center, run by Milton Galamison and modeled on the programs started by Reverend Leon Sullivan in Philadelphia, launched with $1.2 million in federal funds and attempted to provide job training to thousands of young people. Finally, Restoration opened a network of five neighborhood centers, which hired trainees from other programs as well as people whom the director of the centers, Benjamin Glascoe, described half-jokingly as the "least employable" elements of the community (ex-convicts, drug addicts, sundry misfits). Together with social workers and paraprofessional counselors, the recruits offered the kinds of street-level services that the Youth in Action neighborhood centers had been designed to provide: advice on how to navigate the welfare bureaucracy, youth counseling, and tenant advocacy. They also ran sanitation drives, mobilized block associations, organized baseball leagues, and spearheaded clothing drives. This was the essence of community action—minus the political protests.[21]

In its infancy, Restoration had no trouble accessing funds. The Department of Labor provided an initial grant of $7 million, to be disbursed on a monthly basis. The Ford Foundation donated $1.65 million by October 1968; other foundations, banks, and corporations put up over $2 million more. As Thomas took control of the project and pushed back against the visions put forth by Logue, Jacobs, and the big thinkers, he gained more and more support from within the community. He was being pushed, too—to respect the spirit of community control. The cynicism surrounding Restoration's birth made it the object of widespread suspicion, if not outright hostility, on the streets of Bed-Stuy. Despite Kennedy's personal popularity, the project was easily dismissed as a top-down effort. Locals balked at the brand of progress being promised by Logue and the outside experts. As a 1968 report put it, "residents who came together at community meetings were no longer impressed by long-range sophisticated plans for improving their community." After years of unfulfilled promises, and with the ravages of urban renewal still fresh in many minds, what they wanted was not macro-scale planning but rather targeted improvements that would improve their lives immediately.[22]

Restoration started small. Early on, Thomas favored projects that would accomplish multiple objectives at once. Given the hotly contested political space Restoration was occupying, Thomas was keen to create jobs and mobilize grassroots energies. In the summer of 1967, Restoration hired the Center for Urban Education to oversee a survey of community attitudes in Bedford-Stuyvesant. After years of telling outsiders they had been "studied to death," in Elsie Richardson's words, few in the neighborhood thought another study was needed. But this was a study with a twist: it was also a jobs program. Eighty young recruits received training in planning, organizing, and surveying techniques. Many of these trainees later took jobs as paraprofessionals working at Restoration's neighborhood-outreach centers or within Youth in Action. The study itself found that "decent housing" was the top priority for local people, followed by jobs, "better schools," and clean streets. That came as no surprise—a slew of studies had come to similar conclusions. But the very process of conducting the survey put Restoration in direct contact with more than 3,000 households, all the while creating jobs. That offered a solid basis for further action.[23]

Though Bed-Stuy residents ranked housing at the top of their priority list, Restoration lacked the resources to build new residences on a significant scale. In any case, the Central Brooklyn Model Cities program, which operated separately from Restoration, was just then being set up with federal and city funds, and it envisioned building 70,000 new units and rehabilitating 16,000 more. (Such goals would turn out to be wildly optimistic.) Instead, then, the corporation focused on the more modest goals of rehabilitating existing buildings, lending an air of stability to the neighborhood, and promoting home ownership. The process started with the Community Home Improvement Program (CHIP). Launched in June 1967, CHIP was the signature Restoration program. In one fell swoop, it addressed several paramount concerns expressed by local residents: youth crime, unemployment, dilapidated housing, poverty, a frayed sense of community, and filthy streets. It also tapped into deep wellsprings of local pride by evoking the decades-old efforts of block associations to rebuild from the ground up.[24]

The simple idea behind CHIP was to recruit young, unemployed men and put them to work fixing up façades. Homeowners were asked to chip in $25 for the repairs and to pledge that at some future date they would hire local contractors to perform interior renovations that matched the value of the essentially free renovations their exteriors had received. (A Special Impact Program grant of $500,000 funded activities in the summer of 1967, and the Rockefeller Foundation contributed a further $250,000 for 1968.) The recruits, working under the supervision of a select group of craftsmen, would learn specific skills and gain work experience. At the end of the summer, those who stuck it out would be provided with referrals to employers willing to hire them for permanent jobs. The model resembled some of YIA's on-the-job training programs, and it also harked back to CBCC's Teens in Industry program of the late 1950s.[25]

The Restoration Corporation also justified the program in language reminiscent of the early War on Poverty. For instance, in discussing the causes of unemployment in Bed-Stuy, one Restoration report argued that beyond a generalized scarcity of jobs that matched the skills of the local labor pool, "the problems of unemployment also result from years of frustration and lack of opportunity for many minority group citizens. . . . Failure to experience success and reward from work destroys those values and motivational forces which ordinarily encourage people to meaningfully participate in our work-oriented society." Presented in this light, the reasoning behind CHIP echoed aspects of the "opportunity theory" put forth by Richard Cloward and Lloyd Ohlin in 1960. Training in home-improvement skills for the "hard-core" young men of Bedford-Stuyvesant would act as what Cloward and Ohlin had called a "barrier eradicator." Not only would CHIP create jobs; it would also provide young men with "the opportunity to experience steady, full-time and rewarding work that contributes to one's personal well being and to one's environment."[26]

In July 1967, Restoration hired twenty-eight craftsmen—painters, masons, ironworkers, carpenters, and landscapers. The craftsmen, half of whom were union workers and many of whom had previously been unemployed, were trained and evaluated based on teaching ability, communication skills, and their potential as supervisors. The corporation then enrolled 294 trainees, of whom three-quarters had not completed high school and 90 percent were unemployed. As some dropped out of the program, others were recruited; in total, 430 people received some on-the-job training by December, most for periods of six weeks or more. Deciding where to put all these trainees to work wasn't easy. Thomas insisted that the first blocks to receive attention would be ones already organized into formal block groups. The assumption was that owner-occupants were most likely to become active participants in revitalization efforts. Through block associations, Restoration hoped to mobilize enthusiasm among homeowners and use façade renovations as a springboard for other beautification efforts. But the effort initially met with indifference. On the first street selected for improvement, the leader of the block association had to wage a spirited publicity campaign and host a block party before he could convince any of his neighbors to fork over $25 to Restoration.[27]

Once work got started there, however, the program was a hit. "There is something about getting on a scaffold and seeing the work completed that is almost magical," Thomas later reflected. All it took was a stroll to the grocery store, bar, or Laundromat for people to see what was happening. On weekends, teens enrolled in the program would bring their families to newly restored blocks so they could show off what they had been working on. Restoration took care to brand its efforts. One stipulation of the program was that each house receiving CHIP renovations would have to place two green garbage pails painted with Restoration's logo out front. With Restoration pouring about $1,000 into each house it took on, the corporation's employees soon found themselves deluged by calls, letters, and petitions from homeowners who wanted CHIP to refurbish their homes. Restoring nineteenth-century masonry, ironwork, and sculptural details was painstaking, expensive work; through CHIP, local homeowners could get it done for pennies on the dollar. By the end of 1967, more than 200 block associations had contacted Restoration about the program, and 71 had submitted written requests for assistance.[28]

The bulk of these applications came from the affluent heartland of Stuyvesant Heights—Decatur, Halsey, MacDonough, and Macon streets— though some of the first blocks to be rehabilitated were in the poorer area surrounding Tompkins Park. "Every day we are besieged with requests," the secretary of the block association for Macon Street between Ralph and Howard avenues wrote on September 27, 1967, adding that she hoped to "get the checks mailed in to you as soon as possible." The Hancock Street Neighborhood Association, founded by Thomas R. Jones and his father (who remained its president in 1967), sent a letter announcing that it was "deeply interested in your program of refurbishment and renovation." The 129 Community Block Association (representing Quincy Street between Lewis and Stuyvesant avenues) had collected dozens of signatures on a petition declaring local homeowners "quite ready, able and willing to accept whatever help we can and may obtain from the Bedford Stuyvesant Restoration Corporation."[29]

Through CHIP's work in 1967, Restoration linked up with long-established networks and evoked a tradition of neighborhood pride. The home-improvement program echoed the efforts of the Bedford-Stuyvesant Neighborhood Council to beautify the area during the 1940s and 1950s, and it gave new energy to block associations whose leaders might have been losing faith by the late 1960s. On blocks where no associations had

The Restoration Corporation at work. *Restoration Newsletter*

previously existed, residents banded together, printed their own statio-nery, and fired off letters to Restoration, accompanied by dozens of signatures. "Dear Sir," one letter read, "We are a newly organized block association, namely 'The Hancock-Lewis-Stuyvesant Block Association.' We are aware of the program for home improvement, whereby for a nom-inal sum of $25 a homeowner can have the outside paint and trim done on his home by young men hired for this purpose. We have observed the im-provement this has made in Halsey Street, and we would like to take advan-tage of this program." Even tenants got in on the act, petitioning landlords to sign up for the program on blocks with low owner-occupancy rates.[30]

The home-improvement program soon gained such popularity that Res-toration held an annual lottery—which itself became a major community event—to decide which blocks would be next in line for the treatment. Publicity around the lottery in turn spurred the formation of more block associations. The job-placement component of the CHIP program was less successful, at least initially. Resistance by unions posed a problem, whether because of discrimination or perhaps because of Restoration's propensity for doing business with nonunion subcontractors. Most trainees did manage to find jobs, but few graduated into well-paying construction jobs. The forty companies that offered placements to CHIP graduates ranged from the Hudson Hotel to the Ocean Casket Company to the Doubleday Book

Shop to the Brooklyn Jewish Hospital. But only a third of the jobs obtained by the first batch of trainees paid more than $90 a week.[31]

Nevertheless, CHIP earned Restoration significant goodwill in the community. The program inspired upbeat press coverage and signaled that Bed-Stuy was an attractive place in which to invest and lay down roots. As planned, small-scale, highly visible projects had allowed Restoration to build its legitimacy at the grass roots. Façade improvements made for brilliant publicity because they lingered for all to see, long after the work crews had moved on. CHIP also showed that Restoration was at least beginning to address three of the four aspirations that local residents had articulated in the 1967 community survey: better housing, jobs, and clean streets. These projects would soon be supplemented by more ambitious efforts to renovate entire buildings that had been gutted by neglect and abandonment and to market them for a new generation of Bed-Stuy brownstoners. (CHIP also dovetailed with a push by preservationists to landmark a section of Stuyvesant Heights, which would bear fruit when the city's Landmarks Preservation Commission designated a historic district there in 1971.) In the meantime, however, Restoration turned its attention to the fourth key community concern: education.[32]

A College in the Streets

In the quarter-century following the *Brown v. Board of Education* decision, nothing energized the black freedom struggle the way schools did—and nothing so galvanized efforts to maintain white supremacy. Few issues proved as combustible, and few issues proved as resistant to comprehensive solutions. Brooklyn in the 1960s was a central battleground for struggles over education. Kings County had some of the worst-performing schools in the largest school district in the country, and local activists staged a series of high-profile campaigns for educational reform. Most such campaigns focused on the public schools, but activists also sought to democratize access to higher education by bringing a college to Central Brooklyn. What had once seemed like a far-fetched idea suddenly became possible in the late 1960s, thanks in good measure to the agencies that had helped wage Bed-Stuy's long War on Poverty—CBCC, YIA, and Restoration. But what kind of a college would it be, and who would run it? Those were hotly contested questions, especially given the battles for community control that were raging elsewhere in the city at just that moment.

At the time, catastrophic failure rates prevailed among young African Americans attending the city's public schools. A 1965 report drafted by Don Watkins, a Brooklyn College professor and a member of Youth in Action's education committee, observed that integrated classrooms were disappearing at a rapid pace and that black students were dropping out at alarming rates. Those who stayed in the public schools were falling far behind their white counterparts. In 1962–1963, for instance, the average sixth grader in Bed-Stuy read at a level 1.4 years behind the national norm; eighth graders lagged 2.2 years behind. Not one of the fourteen junior high schools in the area had taught its eighth graders to read at a level on a par with the average *sixth grader* in middle-income, predominantly white areas of the city. "One may well ask whether the Bedford-Stuyvesant children are becoming functional illiterates as they pass through the public schools," Watkins wrote in his report.[33]

In the 1960s, ninth graders in the city's public schools were awarded either an academic diploma or a "certificate," depending on their grades. Only students receiving the academic diploma automatically became eligible to attend an academic high school—as opposed to a technical or vocational school—and only students at academic high schools were eligible to apply to the city's public four-year colleges. In 1964, only 52 percent of Bed-Stuy ninth graders earned academic diplomas, whereas the figure for ninth graders elsewhere in Brooklyn was 81 percent. Among the Stuyford teens who did manage to qualify for academic high schools, few used them as a springboard to higher education. Whereas 65 percent of graduates from academic high schools citywide went on to study in colleges or technical institutions, only 26 percent of seniors surveyed at one academic high school in Bed-Stuy had even *applied* to such institutions. All told, at most, 2 percent of the Bed-Stuy youngsters who attended public high school graduated with the qualifications to attend the four-year city colleges. Watkins summed it up: "The educational profile of Bedford-Stuyvesant youth reveals a tragic waste."[34]

These grim realities inspired various responses. In 1964, a long struggle to desegregate New York City schools, led by Bed-Stuy's Milton Galamison, culminated in a boycott that saw 270,000 students stay home from school for a day. That same year, two Brooklyn middle-school teachers, Al Vann and Les Campbell (who later changed his name to Jitu Weusi), founded the Negro Teachers Association, which soon changed its name to the African-American Teachers Association (AATA) and began lobbying the city to hire more black teachers and principals.[35]

Failing schools led many African American reformers, both in and out of the school system, to embrace the idea of "community schools": spaces in which black parents could exercise an element of control over their children's education and maintain a dialogue with sympathetic teachers and administrators. In 1967, Mayor Lindsay and the Ford Foundation provided funds for an experimental, community-controlled school board in Ocean Hill–Brownsville, a district on the southeastern edge of Bedford-Stuyvesant. Made up largely of low-income African American parents and supported by the AATA, the community board soon clashed with the white-dominated United Federation of Teachers. Repeated efforts by the board's parent-appointed administrator, a black educator named Rhody McCoy, to take control of curriculum, budgets, and hiring practices met with union resistance. The dispute reached a boiling point in the fall of 1968 after McCoy fired nineteen white, tenured teachers. A series of strikes ensued, as teachers across the city rallied to the defense of their fired colleagues and the local board dug in its heels. The conflict, which led to the ultimate defeat of the community-control movement, looms in popular memory as a watershed moment in the history of New York City. Historian Jerald Podair, among others, has argued that it represented the rupture of the old New Deal coalition, a shattering of the hallowed alliance between left-liberal Jews and blacks. Yet the strike was as much a symptom as a cause of disillusionment with liberalism.[36]

McCoy and the community board were almost universally supported in Bedford-Stuyvesant, and the ultimate defeat of the community-school experiment rankled the community. But as the Ocean Hill–Brownsville conflagration was attracting national attention in 1968, local activists were quietly waging another campaign for community control of educational resources. This second struggle focused on bringing a college to Central Brooklyn, and it involved many of the same players who had been active in Bedford-Stuyvesant's long War on Poverty. CBCC first dramatized the issue in the mid-1960s, Restoration generated creative ideas about how the college should be structured, and Youth in Action helped organize grassroots support for the campaign. According to Don Watkins, the college campaign was "a catalyzing element in the community" that brought together "the Tom Jones types and the street." If the multitudinous factions in Bedford-Stuyvesant could agree on anything, it was that fixing failing schools was intimately related to fighting poverty and saving Bed-Stuy.[37]

Indeed, the federal War on Poverty had launched several programs that promised to alleviate the effects of educational segregation. For a time, Galamison chaired Youth in Action's education committee, and the agency took up a variety of remedial efforts directed at different stages of the educational system. Head Start catered to preschoolers, homework-study workshops helped elementary-school students, the Young Mothers Program reached out to high-schoolers, and the Women's Talent Corps served adults. Meanwhile, the citywide Council Against Poverty mandated in 1968 that 20 percent of all community-corporation funds be dedicated to "education action." Still, it would take years for such measures to make a difference. In the meantime, an entire generation of black Brooklynites was being condemned to what Jonathan Kozol, in reference to the Boston school system, dubbed "death at an early age." Surely more than 2 percent of black students in the public schools possessed the intellectual skills to attend college. Instead of waiting for the entire school system to shift so that such students could earn the proper credentials, it made sense to unlock more opportunities for them to attend college, regardless of qualifications. In the 1970s, the City University of New York (CUNY) would launch an open-admissions regime that followed this line of thinking. But open admissions were not yet a reality in the mid-1960s.[38]

Instead, activists in Central Brooklyn decided that what was needed was a college in their area. Appropriately, CBCC launched the campaign. In January 1964, the city's Board of Higher Education announced that it was seeking a location in Brooklyn for a new school, to be named Kingsborough Community College. News soon broke that the college would likely be built in the coastal community of Manhattan Beach, on the former site of a U.S. Air Force base. Tempers flared. CBCC organizers decried the fact that the new college would be built in a mostly white neighborhood that took more than an hour to access by subway from the heart of Bedford-Stuyvesant. Instead, they argued, the college should open in a place where it might serve the borough's black population—and where the attendant jobs and retail development would make an especially strong impact. Insurance broker John L. Procope, chair of CBCC's Urban Planning and Housing Committee, urged organizations and individuals affiliated with CBCC to write to city officials and speak out on the issue at public meetings of the city's Site Selection Board.[39]

The Bed-Stuy activists hoped that a college would help compensate for decades of educational segregation. Many also saw it as a tool for the cultural enrichment of a community in desperate need of ennoblement and a sense of self-worth. "We want another cultural institution in Bedford-Stuyvesant," said Thomas Jones, then still a state assemblyman, at one meeting in February 1964. "A massive dose of culture and education and new things should be given to people who have been deprived of opportunities." A week later, at an epic nine-hour hearing, Reverend Walter Offutt, future chairman of Youth in Action's board, argued that the decision to place Brooklyn's newest community college in Manhattan Beach would reinforce patterns of segregation. "Gentlemen, you're not kidding anybody," he jabbed at Borough President Abe Stark and City Comptroller Abe Beame, both in attendance. "Segregation comes from well-planned, calculated efforts. In order to satisfy the educational needs of both black and white children and keep this school from being racially segregated, I implore you to build it in Bedford-Stuyvesant." In response, a Brooklyn College dean quipped, "Why send students to areas of degradation and blight?" His comments touched off an uproar among the assembled African Americans, who bristled at such characterizations of their community. Still, the college ended up in Manhattan Beach.[40]

CBCC pushed forward with its advocacy for a college in Central Brooklyn. Working with Pratt's Ron Shiffman, CBCC integrated the college into proposals for stimulating economic development and drawing businesses to Bedford-Stuyvesant. In October 1966, Borough President Stark announced his support for CBCC's demand that the Fulton Park urban-renewal plan include a college with both a regular curriculum and remedial programs that would "enable the under-educated and the dropouts to have a second chance." In the meantime, CBCC and Pratt were launching the Central Brooklyn Neighborhood College, an innovative, if somewhat quixotic, experiment in educational reform. Nicknamed the "college of the streets," it was designed as a cooperative institution with a flexible curriculum, no entrance requirements or fees, and no degree-granting capacity. Its goal was to radically expand access to higher education among African Americans while nurturing educational innovation.[41]

The college of the streets opened its doors in time for the spring 1967 semester, with a student body of 150. Enrollees included gifted high-schoolers, unemployed dropouts in their twenties, and middle-aged laborers who had never had a chance to attend college. Classes took place in church basements, community centers, storefronts, and whatever rooms the Pratt Institute could spare; Youth in Action also provided space and logistical help.

Students chose from among twenty-eight course offerings, ranging from traditional Humanities to African History to Computer Science. One class devoted to the history of Bedford-Stuyvesant helped lead to the discovery, in 1968, of historic Weeksville, whose excavation was then funded by Youth in Action and the Model Cities program. The all-volunteer faculty included professors from Pratt, New York University, and Long Island University, as well as journalists, photographers, and writers. Some students learned job skills, some gained high school equivalency diplomas, and others used the Neighborhood College as a springboard for acceptance to CUNY. Various classes also piggybacked on existing War on Poverty programs; for instance, the Neighborhood College sent English professors from Pratt to teach reading and writing to women enrolled in the Young Mothers Program. Several other community groups—including the Tompkins Park Area Services office and Community Action Agencies in neighboring Bushwick, Brownsville, and Fort Greene—stepped up to provide space, equipment, and paraprofessionals. Enrollment tripled to almost 500 students in the fall of 1967.[42]

The Neighborhood College had no degree-granting capacity and no permanent funding source. No matter—according to its director, Rudy Bryant, the college of the streets challenged the "white established order" and its standard policy of "turning a deaf ear to the cries of oppressed people." Bryant lobbied degree-granting CUNY institutions to lower entrance requirements for students who had taken courses at the Neighborhood College, and in some cases he succeeded. But Bryant aspired to a higher purpose: to provide a model of how minority groups could "effect meaningful and ongoing changes in a decrepit situation." Clearly, such changes would require more than a non-accredited, underfunded archipelago of night classes.[43]

That's where the Restoration Corporation came in. Kennedy supported the idea of a college in Bedford-Stuyvesant, and he recruited the former provost of Long Island University, William Birenbaum, to lead the campaign. Birenbaum lived in Brooklyn Heights and had been among the volunteer professors at the Neighborhood College. A self-styled visionary, he assembled a study group dubbed the Educational Affiliate, which included Vann and James Farmer, the former national director of CORE. The group proposed a brand-new model of urban education that would integrate "an educational concept of what a college in Bedford-Stuyvesant should be and a physical interpretation of that concept." This meant, first

287

of all, eschewing plans for a unitary campus that might require large-scale demolition. A new college must belong to the "urban mix," and its facilities must mesh seamlessly with ongoing efforts to rehabilitate residential streets. As for the students, they should experience "no separation between knowledge and action"—meaning that liberal-arts education, professional skills, and internships would be fused. The college would do all it could to open its doors. Admissions standards would be lowered to accommodate most students who had graduated high school or passed a series of equivalency tests. Classes would run twelve months a year, day and night.[44]

Most important, perhaps, was that the Educational Affiliate advocated community control. The proposal insisted that the new college must evoke a "clear sense of local responsibility and control," both in its physical plant and in its curriculum, and that students and community organizations should help govern the institution. The Educational Affiliate also rejected CBCC's strategy of soliciting a two-year community college in Bed-Stuy. That solution, it was argued, would only perpetuate mediocre outcomes for black Brooklynites. Instead, Birenbaum called for a comprehensive four-year college capable of enrolling up to 8,000 students. Since that was a nonstarter for CUNY, the Kennedy group hoped to woo enough corporate donations and foundation grants to launch a free, private college in Brooklyn. But no significant private-sector funds were forthcoming.[45]

In November 1967, the Board of Higher Education announced plans to place a junior college in a yet-to-be-determined "poverty area" of Brooklyn. Everyone assumed this meant Bedford-Stuyvesant, and word circulated that Kennedy had exerted backroom pressure on CUNY's chancellor, Albert Bowker. Indeed, several aspects of the CUNY proposal resembled ideas the Restoration Corporation's Educational Affiliate had been exploring. Community College #7, as it was temporarily known, would open in the fall of 1969. The new college would have flexible admissions standards and provisions for community input in planning its curriculum. Though only a two-year institution, it would give students the option of transferring into a four-year program after only one semester of study in a "comprehensive" curriculum. On February 1, 1968, Bowker announced that the college would open in Bedford-Stuyvesant, backed by $32 million in city funds. It would initially enroll 500 students and eventually take 5,000. Kennedy applauded CUNY's "far-reaching commitment to the educational needs of the area," and Lindsay declared that the college might become "a model for the whole nation."[46]

Community leaders in Bedford-Stuyvesant were less impressed. Members of Youth in Action and CBCC, in particular, felt that Kennedy had made an end run around them by negotiating directly with CUNY. Even close Kennedy allies such as Restoration's chairman, Thomas Jones, expressed disappointment that College #7 had been conceived and announced without direct input from black Brooklyn. According to Watkins, Kennedy was widely seen as having tried to co-opt the broader movement for community control, which was at that very moment hurtling toward a confrontation with the teachers union in Ocean Hill–Brownsville. Few in black Brooklyn were prepared to accept Kennedy's argument that he had negotiated the best possible deal for Bedford-Stuyvesant on behalf of its people. Local activists expressed their disapproval with Kennedy's maneuvers by launching a grassroots campaign to force CUNY back to the negotiating table and reopen discussions about community control in the new college.

On February 10, 1968, Youth in Action hosted an "emergency mass meeting" about the college. Some 500 people attended—but Lindsay, Kennedy, and Bowker, who had been invited to address the meeting, stayed away. Tensions soon mounted, and the usual succession of incendiary speakers took the stage. But an impassioned speech by Jones changed the mood. To general surprise, the judge put himself and Restoration's board squarely on the side of the dissidents. For the first time, it seemed, all factions of the community's activist leadership were coming together. Wrote Watkins, who attended the meeting, "a variety of persons and groups, some regarded as 'Uncle Toms' and political conservatives, others regarded as the most 'radical militants,' persons who had not worked together in the past, indeed had been public opponents, were now speaking with one accord." On the spot, an alliance of twenty-five groups came together: Restoration and CBCC each signed up, along with CORE, the Urban League, several Puerto Rican groups, a variety of PTAs, the Central Brooklyn Neighborhood College, and representatives of Youth in Action's board and staff.[47]

The Bedford-Stuyvesant Coalition on Educational Needs and Services, as the alliance called itself, functioned much as CBCC had in the early 1960s. An organization of organizations, it routinely staged public meetings and was run by a steering committee of between twenty-five and thirty people, each representing one club, association, or agency. Soon two broad factions materialized, each pushing for a different kind of college. One

A poster produced by Bedford-Stuyvesant Youth in Action in February 1968 after the city's Board of Higher Education announced that it would sponsor a community college to be placed in Central Brooklyn.

group, led by Jones, wanted a local counterpart to traditional baccalaureate colleges like City College or Brooklyn College. The other group rallied behind Sonny Carson, who floated proposals for a more experimental, Afrocentric curriculum. Vann positioned himself somewhere between the two camps. What the coalition's leaders could agree on was that they wanted a four-year college with full degree-granting authority. Their main worry was that a two-year college would be focused primarily on vocational training "to provide industrial workers for newly proposed industries slated to enter the Bedford-Stuyvesant area." At best, this would be an unnecessary duplication of what the War on Poverty agencies were already doing; at worst, it would be yet another signifier of colonialism. "We reject a two-year college as inherently inferior," one coalition document stated, "and any offer which ends only in that, as grossly insulting."[48]

The coalition insisted that community representatives, rather than people named by the Board of Higher Education, should design the college's curriculum, determine its site, and choose its staff. Such demands fell far outside established CUNY policy, and it was a testament to the ferment of 1968 that CUNY was even willing to negotiate on such terms. In April, following a flurry of street protests and meetings with representatives from Bed-Stuy, CUNY announced a set of remarkable concessions. First, the Board of Higher Education would expand its presidential search committee to include five members of the community coalition in addition to the five members of the board already in place. Second, the board agreed to give the search committee considerable leeway in recommending a site for the college. Third, and perhaps most significantly, the citizens of Brooklyn would be given a say in curriculum design.

At a public meeting held on May 2, 1968, the Bed-Stuy coalition elected a seven-person negotiating team to begin discussions with the Board of Higher Education appointees. (Two of the seven were named as "alternates.") Jones and Vann headlined the team, representing the twin poles of reform politics in black Brooklyn. Joining them were Carson; Herman Patterson, a professor with ties both to CUNY and the Central Brooklyn Neighborhood College; Jack Pannigan, head of a club called Brothers and Sisters for Afro-American Unity; Ella Sease, a veteran PTA activist; and Isaura Santiago, a youth worker in the Puerto Rican community. "A more representative group of Black people would be hard to find anywhere in the world," Vann wrote the following year. It was clear that this would be a hard-nosed group: Carson, Vann, and Pannigan were all regarded as

"non-establishment militants," in Watkins's words. Yet the Restoration Corporation was also well-represented. Like Jones, Carson sat on Restoration's
board; Vann had worked closely with the Educational Affiliate and would
soon join Restoration's board as well. Less audible were the voices of the
women who had headlined CBCC's work in past years.[49]

Vann proved the key player. A teacher and assistant principal at Junior
High School 271 in Ocean Hill–Brownsville, he was quickly emerging as
one of the most eloquent advocates of community control in Brooklyn.
Tall, bearded, and grave looking, Vann had a fondness for dashikis and a
politician's ease with words. Like his former basketball teammate Franklin
Thomas, he belonged to a new generation of leaders, born during the Depression, who stood between the old-guard CBCC activists and the radical youth. He tended to sympathize with the kids, but he also knew how
to work a committee meeting. Later, in the 1970s, he would help organize
a cohort of young black reformers who shook up Brooklyn politics and
helped elect two additional black Congressmen; Vann himself would serve
almost four decades in the State Assembly and the City Council. In the
1960s, though, his base was in the public schools, where admirers called
him *Mwalimu*, the Swahili word for "Great Teacher."

Vann, along with Les Campbell, had organized AATA in 1964. At first,
they looked to Galamison as a mentor and an ally. By 1966, however, they
had broken with the older activist by repudiating the goal of integration
and articulating a Black Power critique of both the teachers union and the
public-school system. "Our philosophy is based on three concepts: self-
control, self-determination, and self-defense," Vann said in 1967. AATA
denounced the dominance of whites among the mainstream union leadership and highlighted various forms of racial bias in the school system. A
particular sore point in 1967 was a union demand that teachers be given
more leeway to remove "disruptive children" from classrooms; AATA
charged that such disciplinary measures would disproportionately affect
black and Puerto Rican students. AATA members were among the key
players in the Ocean Hill–Brownsville experiment, allying with black parents and openly clashing with the predominantly white United Federation
of Teachers. In so doing, Vann and Campbell mirrored what Youth in
Action radicals were doing: using their positions as public employees to
open up an activist space within the state apparatus.[50]

Even as tempers flared in Ocean Hill–Brownsville, the parties to the
community-college debate sat down at the bargaining table. Structured

negotiations between the community coalition and the Board of Higher Education began in June 1968. At first, compromise seemed possible. The community agreed to accept a two-year college for a trial period, and the Board of Higher Education promised to "explore the possibility" of funding four-year baccalaureate programs in the future. Meanwhile, the sides agreed on a nebulous plan by which a community board would oversee the budget, curriculum, and personnel of the college but would only exert as much autonomy "as is possible under the University system." The sides also agreed that the college would relax admissions standards for black and Puerto Rican high-school graduates. CUNY even agreed to supply the community coalition with office equipment and a planning budget to help develop a curriculum in African-American and Puerto Rican Studies. Vann lauded the Board of Higher Education for being "sincere and honest," and he optimistically trumpeted the progress being made. "A revolution in higher education is under way—a community controlled junior college rising in the heart of an educationally-economically deprived ghetto," he wrote in September.[51]

But the relationship soon soured. In the fall of 1968, the citywide teacher strikes touched off by the Ocean Hill–Brownsville dispute resulted in a torrent of bitter recriminations and racial invective. Liberal elites withdrew their support of community control; African American communities felt betrayed. Against that backdrop, it became almost impossible for the two sides in the college negotiations to resolve their differences. Even minor slights loomed as mortal sins. Vann suddenly lost faith in the CUNY board after finding out about several planning decisions that had been made without consulting the community coalition. These were small matters— for instance, the board had neglected to inform Vann of a grant application being submitted to the Ford Foundation to help plan the college—but to Vann they represented a breach of trust. The Bed-Stuy group pushed harder on the issue of community control, especially when it came time to select a principal. The community coalition preferred Rhody McCoy, who had overseen the Ocean Hill–Brownsville school district, but he was too controversial a figure for CUNY's tastes. Vann, Campbell, and Carson dug in. With charges of racism and anti-Semitism filling the air—largely as a result of the Ocean Hill–Brownsville dispute—negotiations broke down entirely.[52]

On January 2, 1969, Jones quit the negotiating team, effectively ending the grand coalition in Bedford-Stuyvesant. Slamming the door behind him, the judge heaped scorn on both sides. On the one hand, he argued, some members of the Board of Higher Education seemed hell-bent on "planning for our community without consultation with our representatives." A year into negotiations with the people of Bedford-Stuyvesant, those officials remained unable (or unwilling) to grasp "what community control and participation must be to overcome the ravages of educational deprivation suffered by the youth of Bedford-Stuyvesant." On the other hand, Jones also attacked unnamed members of his own community for failing to acknowledge the positive impact a new college might make in their community, regardless of how it was structured. "The proposed College No. 7 involves a 34 million dollar investment of public funds," he wrote, "and that . . . educational center will shape the lives and future of our ablest young men and women."[53]

By the summer of 1969, with no agreement in sight and the deadline for the school's opening long since passed, CUNY began threatening to allocate its funds elsewhere. In Bedford-Stuyvesant, meetings were getting ugly. The coalition split after Vann said he would rather have no college at all than one that wasn't community controlled. Some moderate groups, including the NAACP and the various War on Poverty agencies (CBCC, Youth in Action, Restoration), united to condemn the "inflexible position" of the radicals. Claiming to represent "the silent majority in Bedford-Stuyvesant," the moderates now called on Chancellor Bowker to find new negotiating partners.[54] The Board of Higher Education declared a final impasse with Vann's group in September 1969, and four of Brooklyn's black elected officials—Congresswoman Shirley Chisholm, State Senator William Thompson, and Assemblymen Sam Wright and Waldaba Stewart—swooped in to resolve the issue. To lose the college altogether was unacceptable, especially when so much progress had already been made.[55]

From that point forward, it was the politicians who spoke for the people of Central Brooklyn in negotiations with the Board of Higher Education. They proceeded to hammer out a compromise solution. The college, it turned out, would be built not in Bedford-Stuyvesant—where no large plots of empty land existed—but in neighboring Crown Heights, near the former site of the Dodgers' Ebbets Field. It would combine two- and four-year programs, offer innovative courses for paraprofessionals, and include some provisions for community input—though not community *control* by any stretch. Even the name was a compromise: initial plans called for the school to be named Martin Luther King College, but King's widow balked and it was another slain civil-rights leader, Medgar Evers, who received the honor. (Carson later related that he had advocated calling it Malcolm X College but that CUNY had unilaterally rejected that option.) In March 1970, Richard Trent of Brooklyn College was named president of Medgar Evers. The Brooklyn branch of the NAACP hailed Trent's appointment as a victory over "these forces in our community who would enslave the rest of us." Vann, meanwhile, denounced Chisholm and the rest of the politicians as "niggers waiting in the wings to 'do their thing'" and found little good to say about Trent. "Unfortunately for Black people it was real easy to divide and conquer," wrote Vann, who would soon enter the political arena himself and attempt to translate his experiences in grassroots organizing into legislative power.[56]

Medgar Evers College was hardly the radical experiment in Afrocentric learning imagined by Campbell and Carson. Nor did it satisfy the ambitions of the reformers affiliated with the Restoration Corporation, who dreamed of reinventing urban education. But if Medgar Evers was not the perfect college, it was *a* college, and it was a college in Central Brooklyn that would be run by and for black people. For that, it was widely celebrated as the crowning culmination of a long and difficult struggle. Medgar Evers College would turn into a valuable educational resource for Brooklyn's African American students and educators, and it served as an anchor institution for a community desperately seeking to control its fate. In the years after it opened its doors in 1971, it quickly developed an identity "as a place where struggling black women and single mothers strove," in the words of historian Russell Rickford. More than 90 percent of the school's students were black, and 75 percent were women—among whom a strong majority were mothers going back to school in their twenties. The faculty, similarly, was composed largely of black women, including, most famously, Betty Shabazz (the widow of Malcolm X), who joined the school in 1976.[57]

Through political pressure, coalition building, and policy entrepreneurship, Central Brooklyn activists had managed to dramatize an issue, offer policy solutions, and extract resources from the state. Yet it took the intercession of elected officials to close the deal. Only a few short years earlier, CBCC had negotiated directly with mayors and senators. Now, with Chisholm and five other black Brooklynites holding legislative posts, CBCC's political functions were mostly obsolete. As for Restoration, its role in the college struggle was to have articulated grand ideas before eventually pushing for a compromise solution so as to avoid losing what few concessions were on the table. With private funding for its college idea in short supply and political capital dwindling after Kennedy's death in 1968, Restoration ultimately cooperated in unprecedented ways with Youth in Action, CBCC, and the community's radical voices. That kind of improvisation and ideological flexibility would serve Restoration well in future years. But Restoration—and the neighborhood it served—remained dangerously vulnerable to the caprices of government funders and macroeconomic forces. As long as powerful patrons were about, the corporation could function. But that dependence left it ill-equipped for the future.

Soldiering On

The assassination of Robert Kennedy on June 5, 1968, traumatized a generation of young liberals who had counted on a second Kennedy administration to end the war in Vietnam, win the War on Poverty, and heal gaping wounds in the American soul. Kennedy's death prompted a slew of journalistic considerations of his antipoverty work in Brooklyn. The *Times* ran long pieces, and CBS aired a multipart investigation of urban turmoil, with a special focus on Bedford-Stuyvesant. The thrust of the coverage rankled some local activists. Youth in Action staff, in particular, loudly complained that the CBS broadcast had neglected even to mention their agency, giving the impression that Restoration was the only thing standing between order and chaos in Central Brooklyn. (Having watched the show, one YIA official savaged Restoration staffers as "pompous, pretentious traitors who never miss an opportunity to represent themselves to the white establishment as leaders of the black community.") But while many eulogies proclaimed Kennedy's work in Brooklyn to be his greatest legacy, his loss decreased the likelihood that Restoration might secure the kind of large-scale investment and job growth needed to bring about Bed-Stuy's long-term economic transformation. That would eventually force a reconsideration of what Restoration could accomplish.[58]

In the months surrounding Kennedy's death, Restoration launched several new initiatives that reflected the clout of the senator's connections: a mortgage pool to support local home ownership, an IBM plant in Bed-Stuy, and designs for a major shopping complex and community center on Fulton Street. The successive announcements of these new programs in the first half of 1968 got good press and amounted to political gold for

Kennedy in the midst of a presidential campaign. Each was a statement of noble aspirations and promised to combine outside investment in Bed-Stuy with earnest, community-based initiative. Here was Kennedy not as a ruthless partisan but as a practical-minded coalition builder.[59]

The mortgage pool was the most significant contribution to come out of the businessmen's group. Thomas officially announced the pool's creation on April 2, 1968, just as Kennedy was beginning to campaign in Indiana ahead of that state's presidential primary, but the program had been taking shape for six months beforehand. George Moore, chairman of First National City Bank, had taken the lead in raising the funds, assembling a coalition of potential contributors in the fall of 1967. A walking tour of Bed-Stuy's tidiest blocks introduced bankers to "happy children and well-scrubbed store fronts," helping to dispel the potential lenders' fears about the area. Some eighty commercial lenders and insurers—including First National, Chase Manhattan, Dime, Equitable, Prudential, and Metropolitan Life—pledged support. Total contributions surpassed $75 million.[60]

Thomas heralded the program as one that would "help restore health and vitality to the Bedford-Stuyvesant housing market." The mortgage pool would offer loans for three purposes. First and most obviously, it would help new buyers purchase homes. Second, it would help underwrite renovations—a key service in a neighborhood of aging buildings where credit was tight. Third, the pool would help those owners holding multiple mortgages on onerous terms—a common situation in Bed-Stuy—consolidate their debts. "We have absolutely no doubt," Thomas and John Doar, the executive director of D&S, wrote in April 1968, "that mortgage loan money in any volume at moderate cost will not be available in Bedford-Stuyvesant without a program of this sort. . . . We cannot overemphasize the critical nature of this program and the urgency of getting it started." Loans would be insured by the Federal Housing Administration and be available at the going rate of a 10 percent down payment and a twenty-five-year term—far more generous than anything available to most Bed-Stuy homeowners. Thomas explained that before the existence of the pool, the typical buyer of a $17,000 home would have had to take out a first mortgage for $10,000 and a second mortgage for $5,000, each of which would entail high upfront costs and also hold a relatively high interest rate. In order to make up the cash deficit, most such families put off needed renovations and converted one or more floors of their newly bought homes into rental units or rooming houses. These practices, per Thomas, typically contributed to the "ruining of sound housing."[61]

The mortgage pool provided the beginnings of a response to redlining. Its existence promised to transform the credit market in Bed-Stuy and contribute to the area's long-term beautification. In its effects, the mortgage pool dovetailed with the Civil Rights Act of 1968, also known as the Fair Housing Act, which banned housing discrimination. It also mimicked highly valued Bed-Stuy community institutions such as the Paragon Progressive Credit Union, and served as yet another indicator of Restoration's commitment to protecting Bed-Stuy's middle class. The area already boasted an owner-occupancy rate of between 15 percent and 20 percent, and Restoration's founders believed that encouraging homeownership would foster stability in the midst of crisis. But change came slowly. Within the first year, Restoration closed just 152 loans, at a total value of $2.5 million. Of those loans, only thirty-four facilitated a purchase, and the rest went to refinancing. Restoration staffers assigned to the mortgage program also helped eighty-eight underwater homeowners obtain discounts on second mortgages they had previously taken out. Only $235,000 of the refinancing money contributed to rehabilitation, though homeowners, with their heads now above water, might also be more likely to carry out renovations in the future. Either way, it was clear that the program tended to benefit existing homeowners—the very people who already possessed equity, however small. Restoration faced a conundrum: any efforts to improve housing in the area would run up against the reality that most local residents had modest incomes and dim hopes of accumulating wealth. However generous the mortgage terms made available, few among Bed-Stuy's poor could dream of buying property.[62]

If the green garbage cans emblazoned with the Restoration logo symbolized its work in the late 1960s, the corporation's new headquarters and shopping center on Fulton Street became the emblem for Restoration's work a decade later. At first, Thomas and his staff worked out of the Granada Hotel in downtown Brooklyn; there was simply no office space available in Bedford-Stuyvesant. What became known as Restoration Plaza sat in a repurposed milk factory on Fulton Street, where Thomas Jones and the Unity Democrats had once picketed for more black jobs. The factory had been abandoned in the mid-1960s, and the dilapidated block had become "a symbol of the problems of the community," in the words of one former Restoration staffer. The redesign was conceived by the Washington,

DC, firm of Arthur Cotton Moore but built by the Restoration Development Corporation, a for-profit subsidiary that, like CHIP, employed a workforce made up almost exclusively of African Americans from Central Brooklyn. The Ford Foundation put up an 85 percent guarantee on the loan that launched the project.[63]

The first phase, which housed Restoration's staff as well as office space for electric utility Con Edison and several commercial tenants, opened in 1972 and earned rave reviews. (The *Times* described it as "a stunning skylit, brick-lobbied office building flowing with lush green plants and decorated with paintings, photographs and sculpture by local artists.") The second phase, which opened in 1975, incorporated adjacent buildings; its innovative design drew comparisons to Ghirardelli Square in San Francisco. In addition to 115,000 square feet of retail space and 60,000 square feet of office space, the completed project also included a 30,000-square-foot open plaza, an ice-skating rink, an art gallery and youth arts academy, and a job-placement agency. Opposite the back end of the plaza, on Herkimer Street, was a low-income housing development Restoration itself had built. Most famously, Restoration Plaza was home to the Billie Holiday theater, where, for decades to come, Brooklynites of all ages would go to attend Afro-Caribbean dance, theater, and music performances.[64]

If the corporation's efforts to promote block associations and brownstone living echoed the ideas of Jane Jacobs and the new generation of neighborhood activists, the effort to centralize a variety of community activities in a single area was very much in keeping with the classic vision of urban renewal. Viewed from the sidewalks surrounding it, Restoration Plaza loomed as a new-age fortress—a reflection of local anxieties about rising crime and drug addiction. Its storefronts faced inward, providing small business owners and customers alike with protection from the dangers of the street. The idea was to give the community a focal point, an anchor, which over time would help revitalize a depressed stretch of Central Brooklyn's main commercial artery. But Restoration Plaza was also meant to be a place where local residents could come together and experience cultural uplift. All told, it offered a hulking, concrete incarnation of the "comprehensive" vision at the heart of Restoration.[65]

Restoration Plaza provided Bed-Stuy with a magnet for attracting new retail outlets, restaurants, and services. Meanwhile, the corporation was attempting to develop local, black-owned businesses. In the years following Kennedy's death, Restoration tackled the issue in as comprehensive a

SCATTERED SITES

Brownstones for sale, courtesy of the Bedford-Stuyvesant Restoration Corporation, 1978. These were among dozens of run-down or abandoned structures that Restoration purchased, gut-renovated, and brought to market as part of its "Brownstone Renaissance" program.

manner as could be expected from a neighborhood-based agency. Marshaling federal monies, bank loans, and equity investments, Restoration threw $20 million at 128 local businesses through the late 1970s. These ranged from mom-and-pop stores (a Laundromat and a grocery) to a recording studio called The Platinum Factory, financed jointly by Restoration and CBS. Through its various building and home-improvement projects, Restoration helped to fund thirty-two construction-related firms. It also financed twenty manufacturing firms and a similar number of retail outlets. In addition, it helped to create black-owned franchises of national chains such as Baskin-Robbins and Nathan's Famous, as well as car dealerships. Finally, the corporation spun off several subsidiaries, which assumed economic risks the private sector was unwilling to take on. For instance, after a long and frustrating effort to attract a supermarket for the newly built Restoration Plaza, the corporation created a subsidiary, the Restoration Supermarket Company, to share risk with whatever supermarket chain would be willing to take the plunge. Only at that point did the Supermarkets General Corporation agree, despite strong misgivings, to place a Pathmark store in Restoration Plaza. The supermarket, set in the middle of what later generations would dub a "food desert," served a vital need and employed 150 community residents. It would endure into the twenty-first century. Yet despite isolated successes, Restoration's efforts to alter the local business climate produced few lasting gains. Many of the small-business ventures quickly failed; those that managed to turn a profit were only so many drops in the bucket.[66]

The trends underlying such circumstances lay largely beyond Restoration's control, but the corporation also came under fire for things it *could* control—namely the impression it gave of being a program designed by and for the middle class. The mortgage pool, for instance, directed more than 60 percent of its loans to refinancing efforts, leaving the agency vulnerable to charges that it was, in the final analysis, mostly aimed at protecting and preserving the investments made by the homeowners who had pushed for its establishment in the first place. The same could be said for street renovations and exterior-rehabilitation programs, most of which were undertaken on already elegant streets whose block associations lobbied hardest for further improvements. Restoration did build hundreds of units of rental housing, but the homes it put up for sale, while cheap by Brooklyn standards, still sat far outside the reach of families living close to the poverty line. Skeptics alleged that Restoration's leadership model was similarly designed to empower a new class of black managers who proceeded to make decisions on behalf of the community.[67]

One of those critics was Jitu Weusi (formerly Les Campbell), who along with Vann had founded the African-American Teachers Association in the mid-1960s. In the aftermath of Ocean Hill–Brownsville, Weusi launched The East, a nationalist cultural organization focused on offering Afrocentric education and activating the energies of Central Brooklyn's working class. Though his erstwhile allies Carson and Vann chose to cooperate with Restoration, Weusi remained opposed to the politics practiced by what he called "the black nouveaux riches." In a 1982 article, Weusi acknowledged that Restoration filled a desperate need in the community, but he charged that the corporation had accomplished little beyond building housing and retail space that was too expensive for Bed-Stuy's working class to afford. Further, Restoration had alienated its constituents with its insularity and "disregard for community input and involvement in decision making." Thomas, per Weusi, had succeeded early on in constructing "a façade of peace and progress"—but Restoration remained an "agency built on paternalism."[68]

Another notable assessment of Restoration's activity came from Haskell Ward, the commissioner of community development under Mayor Koch, and one of the few highly placed African Americans in city government during Koch's first term. Ward wrote in 1980 that it was "valid to assume that the Bedford-Stuyvesant community would look more like the South Bronx today if it had not been for the funding received by the Restoration Corporation." Yet Bed-Stuy remained ensnared in a "classic bind," according to Ward: "With very few exceptions, manufacturers are unwilling to risk plant development in poor urban areas; taxes are high, land is limited and expensive, the labor pool is unskilled and unpredictable, and the community is not attractive to high-salaried managerial and technical staff. On the other hand, the opportunities for retail businesses are limited by the surrounding poverty. . . . The result is that Restoration has had to make equity investments from its own resources to attract business to the area and ensure that they are managed properly."[69]

Macroeconomics mystified. The small-business program suffered from a lack of affluent consumers. Renting out space in the new commercial center was a challenge. The only major corporation that stepped up to invest in the area was Watson's IBM, which opened a computer-cable manufacturing plant in 1968. By the mid-1970s, the plant employed 420 workers, and it would expand still further in 1979. On the other hand, an estimated 6,000 jobs were lost in Bedford-Stuyvesant between 1969 and 1974. Other than the IBM plant, the effort to attract large-scale industry to Central Brooklyn proved an almost total failure. Kennedy had no trouble inducing individual businessmen to sit on Restoration's board, but he could not alter capital flows. C. Douglas Dillon, who chaired the D&S board between 1967 and 1969, made entreaties asking fellow financiers to donate personal or corporate monies to the Bed-Stuy effort. "We think we can count on wide support from the business community because we believe that the private business sector of our economy has and feels a responsibility to save our cities," Dillon wrote in a 1968 letter aimed at drumming up support for Restoration. He was wrong. The Bedford-Stuyvesant effort would remain almost entirely dependent on federal funds and, to a lesser extent, support from the Ford Foundation. The lack of private investment in the community vindicated the warning one CEO had issued when Kennedy visited him, hat in hand, back in 1967: "Senator, the afternoon I walk into my board of directors and tell them that Bobby Kennedy was here today, and he thinks we should put a plant in Bedford-Stuyvesant, that is the afternoon they'll have me committed."[70]

For all that, Restoration did score tangible successes. By 1977, a decade into the corporation's work, Restoration had funded the exterior renovation of 3,682 homes on ninety-six blocks and trained more than 3,835 local residents in masonry, carpentry, and other construction trades. Through the "scattered rehabilitation" program, Restoration had bought up 342 abandoned townhouses, fixed them up, and then marketed them as a "Bedford-Stuyvesant Brownstone Renaissance." After years of struggles, the Restoration Development Corporation was turning a profit on the commercial center. The mortgage pool still functioned below capacity, but the corporation had made 1,080 loans, totaling more than $22 million. Meanwhile, Restoration claimed in the late 1970s to be the second-largest landowner in Brooklyn (after the city of New York itself), and the corporation had built 500 new units of housing, with 261 more said to be in the works. It had performed 10,792 screenings for lead poisoning and offered housing advice and assistance to 35,335 local residents. Through its efforts, 8,037 people had been placed in jobs and 512 recruits had been hired for on-the-job vocational training.[71]

Beyond that, the corporation had carried out street renovations, built parks, and led cleanup drives in empty lots. In 1973, Restoration purchased the four homes still standing from nineteenth-century Weeksville, which had been rediscovered five years earlier by James Hurley and his students at the Central Brooklyn Neighborhood College and later turned into an archaeological dig and historic-preservation effort under Youth in Action auspices. Though the task of restoring the homes was eventually spun off to a separate group, the Weeksville Society, Restoration was the only community entity in the mid-1970s that possessed the capital needed to step in and protect the homes from disappearing altogether. Preserved and protected over ensuing decades, the Weeksville Heritage Center would stand as one of Brooklyn's great historical treasures, a living reminder to future generations of Bed-Stuy's black past.[72]

Epilogue

Gloom and Boom

It's the brownstones that have kept Bedford-Stuyvesant together—they've been the stabilizing force here despite the large pockets of poverty.

—LUCILLE ROSE, 1985

On October 13, 1977, the Brooklyn bureau of the *Amsterdam News* hosted a brainstorming session. At the paper's behest, two-dozen influential Brooklynites came together to "speak very candidly about apathy among the Black masses and about the community's seeming inability to find solutions to the nagging social problems." It was a dark time. New Yorkers of all stripes seemed to be losing faith in their fellows; angry tribalism tore at the city's social fabric. Arson and abandonment were transforming neighborhoods into landscapes of doom. Looting during that summer's blackout had seemed to affirm a nihilist streak in the collective unconscious. A fiscal crisis had brought New York to its knees; the postcrisis regime tightened the screws. The plagues visited on New York City seemed endless: garbage piled up, junkies roamed the streets, firehouses were shuttered. Every year tens of thousands of citizens and hundreds of businesses were quitting the city. Hushed talk of planned shrinkage was heard. Local and national elites, it seemed, were going to let the city destroy itself in order to save it.[1]

The mood in the *Amsterdam News* conference room was suitably gloomy. Elsie Richardson was there, along with former CBCC chairman Lionel Payne, Al Vann (founder of the African-American Teachers Association and now a state assemblyman), Reverend William Jones (former chairman of Youth in Action), and William Thompson (a founding

305

Madison Street in Bedford-Stuyvesant, 2015. The sign was put up in the early 1960s by the Madison-Lewis-Sumner block association, according to the current owner of the home, whose parents moved to Bed-Stuy in the 1940s and were the second black family to purchase a house on the block. *Author photo*

member of the Restoration board and a state senator). In the 1960s, all had taken up the campaign to capture state resources and wield them in a program of neighborhood-based revitalization. Their methods had differed, as had their definitions of community. Yet they had embraced a common form of place-based politics that defined power at the intersection of race and urban space. All had bought into the community-planning and decentralization initiatives launched by the Wagner and Lindsay administrations; each in their own way, they'd taken up the refrains of the Great Society and sung them with gusto.[2]

To what end? What had come of it all? Thirty years earlier, in 1947, the Brooklyn Council for Social Planning had spawned its first gang-outreach program; a decade later, the Central Brooklyn Coordinating Council had come together; another ten years after that, the Restoration Corporation had been founded; and now, in 1977, the future of Bedford-Stuyvesant looked grim. Three decades after Brooklyn's Jackie Robinson broke baseball's color line, two decades after New York City's first-in-the-nation law banning housing discrimination, and a decade after the first community-controlled school boards had been launched, many African Americans felt increasingly marginalized within the city's body politic.

As Richardson, Jones, and the rest met that day in October 1977, Edward I. Koch was poised to become the city's next mayor. On the campaign trail, he had promised to take on "poverty pimps" and to dismantle once and for all the city's Community Action Agencies. Koch, whose power base lay among the city's white working class, charged that in places like Bedford-Stuyvesant, Crown Heights, the Lower East Side, and Harlem— the seedbeds of the War on Poverty—the city was wasting taxpayer money on antipoverty programs. The new mayor accused community corporations of having become old-style patronage mills dedicated to defending "ethnic" (by which he meant *black*) turf and political privilege. Exhibit A was Youth in Action, which had proven low-hanging fruit for politicos like City Councilman Sam Wright and State Senator Vander Beatty, along with the petty criminals in their orbits. Asked how he might respond to pressure from African American politicians eager to maintain the poverty program, Koch replied, "I don't give a damn."[3]

Koch was not the only person taking aim at Brooklyn's black leaders. Those leaders were turning on one another. Elsie Richardson expressed dismay at the lack of clout wielded by Brooklyn's growing cohort of African American officeholders. "We have more black elected officials than we've

307

ever had and yet we're less effective than we've ever been," Richardson told her fellow brainstormers at the *Amsterdam News* summit. Not everyone agreed: Sylvester Leaks, Youth in Action's executive director, blamed the old-guard community organizers—people like Richardson—for buying into the Great Society in the first place. "I think the worst thing to happen to black people in my lifetime is this concept of integration," he said. "It has done more to confuse us and to mislead us than any other single item." Reverend William Jones of Bethany Baptist Church, who had done as much as anyone in the 1960s to mobilize enthusiasm for the War on Poverty, now cast a pox on all houses. "Most of the people in this room are plantation managers," he thundered. As for the executive director of CBCC, Charles Joshua, his was the voice of despondency. "We've practically given up," he said. "In the 1950s and '60s we fought the establishment; we were successful. We had initiative; we had drive. I don't know what happened."[4]

Joshua was right to wonder what had happened. Only a few years earlier, an optimist might have turned up signs of progress in Bedford-Stuyvesant. Between 1960 and 1970, the median number of school years completed by local residents had jumped from 7.9 to 10.3. Graduation rates, though still weak, were almost 30 percent higher in 1970 than they had been a decade earlier, and the opening of Medgar Evers College promised to put more of those graduates through college than ever before. The 1960s had seen a 50 percent reduction in the number of Bed-Stuy women employed as domestics; meanwhile, War on Poverty initiatives like the Women's Talent Corps had helped bring about a corresponding increase in the number of black women working in professional or paraprofessional positions. Thanks in part to Great Society programs, the portion of black New Yorkers employed by governments had doubled, reaching 20 percent in the 1970s—and that figure would continue to rise, especially among women, in the decades to come. Given the collapse of New York's manufacturing sector during that same period, government work would prove a key source of upward mobility for the city's African Americans.[5]

While the median family income of $6,300 in Bedford-Stuyvesant in 1970 was only 7 percent higher in real terms than it had been in 1960 and still just 70 percent of the city average, even this modest growth was notable given the continuing in-migration of poor people and the dramatic increase in the numbers of children and single mothers living in the community. (The median age in Bed-Stuy dropped from twenty-eight to twenty-three between 1960 and 1970, and 43 percent of area residents were under age twenty by the start of the 1970s.) The percentage of Bed-Stuy families with incomes above the city median had increased by 80 percent in a decade, a stunning figure that reflected the efforts made by CBCC and the Restoration Corporation to consolidate the area's middle class. In 1964, Bed-Stuy residents made up 3.5 percent of New York City's total population but pulled in only 0.9 percent of the city's total income; despite a slight drop in the area's population, Bed-Stuy's relative aggregate income increased by a third in 1970 to 1.2 percent. Bed-Stuy's official unemployment rate in 1970 stood at a mere 6 percent. In 1973, the Restoration Corporation estimated that close to 60 percent of the 450,000 people living in its project area could qualify as "middle class." For those in need, the various new forms of noncash income that Great Society programs had offered poor families—Food Stamps, Medicare, Medicaid, Head Start—made daily life more tolerable.[6]

As the 1970s dawned, then, the War on Poverty, broadly defined, appeared to be working. Seemingly against all odds, Bed-Stuy's population was better educated, more affluent, healthier, and better served than it had been a decade earlier. Poverty was nowhere near licked, clearly, but the War on Poverty was providing vital services in one of America's poorest communities. Nationally, Great Society programs had, according to one study, "more than tripled real federal expenditures on health, education, and welfare." The official poverty rate had dipped sharply, reaching lows of 11.1 percent in 1973 and 11.4 percent in 1978—less than half what the figure had been when John F. Kennedy took office. Official poverty rates among African Americans remained much higher than for whites, but they too had plummeted, from 55 percent in 1960 to 30 percent in 1974. Between 1960 and 1970, the portion of black managers and administrators working for federal, state, or local governments increased from 21 percent to 35 percent—twice the rate of growth for whites. An expanding and politically savvy black middle class testified, in part, to the new policy networks linking African American leaders to the state.[7]

But that was hardly the whole story. National poverty rates had declined, but concentrated poverty was spreading. In 1977, most Bed-Stuy residents would have scoffed at the idea that things were getting better. Despite the substantial gains of the 1960s, there were profound weaknesses in the local economic structure. Brooklyn was hemorrhaging jobs. A study carried out by the Restoration Corporation in 1973 found that a third of local residents of working age had "a serious labor market problem." Local "subemployment"—a category that included people who had dropped out of the workforce, those in extremely low-wage jobs, and those working part-time—was so high as to render meaningless the official unemployment rate in Bed-Stuy. Restoration's efforts to deliver sustained job growth and commercial development in the area were too little to reverse macroeconomic trends. According to one analysis of census-tract data, Bed-Stuy's official poverty rate would rise from 27.5 percent to 34 percent between 1970 and 1990. While the neighborhood mostly escaped the death spiral of arson and abandonment that afflicted nearby Brownsville and Bushwick, Bed-Stuy's rejuvenation would be a long time coming.[8]

In assessing the afterlife of the long War on Poverty, it's tempting to conclude that the fate of places like Bedford-Stuyvesant was ultimately decided by forces so overwhelming—deindustrialization, the fiscal crisis, the lingering geography of racism—that there was nothing much any community organization could do to alter conditions on the ground. Indeed, the very basis on which power had been constituted during the 1960s, namely the neighborhood, proved a remarkably weak fortress from which to fight against the economic and political restructuring of New York and the United States. In that sense, the War on Poverty had disempowered the poor rather than empowering them. It had codified the institutions and processes through which low-income communities could gain concessions from local and federal governments, while at the same time ensuring that those institutions and processes were maddeningly bureaucratic. The fact that those institutions had originally been designed to control the behavior of young, mostly black, men made it all too easy to blame precisely that behavior—and the communities that produced it—when the institutions failed.

Maybe that had been the point of the War on Poverty all along. Maybe the poverty programs had been designed to empower an expanding black middle class with the intellectual, political, and economic clout it needed to serve as "plantation managers," to use William Jones's term. After all, Robert Wagner, Lyndon Johnson, and Robert Kennedy had said time and again that the poverty program must serve as a buffer against rioting and disorder.[9] CBCC, Youth in Action, Restoration—each had been conceived to defuse unrest, to absorb the energy of the civil-rights movement, and to incorporate African American leaders into the political structures of the Democratic Party. It was foolish, then, to expect such agencies to counterbalance macroeconomic trends, let alone eradicate poverty itself.

On the other hand, social policy does not spring from the minds of Wagners and Kennedys alone. Viewed from the local level, the War on Poverty reflected a series of clearly articulated demands issued in the late 1950s and early 1960s by grassroots activists and community leaders. They, too, wanted to preclude future riots, channel the energy of the civil-rights movement (they *were* the civil-rights movement), and integrate the Democratic Party—but they wanted to do all those things as ways of protecting, structuring, and preserving the environments in which they lived. In Bedford-Stuyvesant, they aspired both to black political power and to an ideal of community stability defined by safe streets, home ownership, business development, intellectual achievement, and civic pride.

For a time, as Charles Joshua pointed out, they had been successful. They had transformed CBCC from a government-sponsored antigang program into a social movement. They had acted as policy entrepreneurs in the areas of urban renewal, family planning, employment, higher education, and housing preservation. They had rebuilt Tompkins Park and saved Fulton Park. They had sent a generation of toddlers to preschool and shepherded a generation of teen mothers through high school. They had trained local citizens for new careers and turned government agencies into valuable sources of jobs. They had fought for a community college, they had fixed up brownstones, and they had amassed a mortgage pool to promote home ownership. Meanwhile, federal investment in the War on Poverty had provided "a huge opportunity for African American professionals to build organizations and to run them," as the Restoration Corporation's current president, Colvin Grannum, described it. By the 1970s, members of the black political class, including Shirley Chisholm, had consolidated access to government structures and begun laying down their own version of what Ira Katznelson has called "city trenches." From that perspective, things looked somewhat less bleak in the *annus horribilis* of 1977.[10]

"Don't Move, Improve"

That year also saw the end of an era for the Restoration Corporation. After ten years on the job, Franklin Thomas was calling it quits and resuming his private law practice. Unlike the half-dozen executive directors who had walked away from Youth in Action during that time, Thomas departed a hero in 1977. Under his guidance, Restoration had proven that not all War on Poverty programs were failures. After a rocky start, Restoration had managed to insulate its programs from political strife, bickering, and corruption. "While the Bedford-Stuyvesant Youth-in-Action program has been plagued with multiple probes of alleged fiscal improprieties, firing and jailing of top personnel, etc., the corporation has run like a well-oiled machine," the *Amsterdam News* commented upon Thomas's departure. That reputation spread far beyond Brooklyn. By 1977, Thomas had joined the boards of CBS, Citibank, New York Life Insurance, and Lincoln Center for the Performing Arts. He'd even received an offer—which he declined—from incoming president Jimmy Carter to be the new secretary of Housing and Urban Development.[11]

Restoration's tenth anniversary inspired a flurry of press reports heralding Bed-Stuy's minor miracle. With a Democrat occupying the White House for the first time since Lyndon Johnson's departure in 1969, many asked whether Carter—whose 1977 tour through the rubble of the South Bronx signaled the federal government's intent to reengage with urban problems—should look to Central Brooklyn for a model to follow. Michael Harrington, for one, thought so. Restoration, wrote the man whose 1962 book had sparked the federal "rediscovery" of poverty, "is a living remnant of the social imagination and innovation of the sixties—a dream, it would seem, that works." The *Times* agreed, arguing that Restoration offered an object lesson in the virtues of Great Society liberalism because it "had managed to tap the last great resources for urban revitalization: the energy, the ingenuity, the talents, and the aspirations of the local residents." The *Washington Post* heralded "the success of Bed-Stuy," calling attention to the "impressive" impact of Restoration Plaza and the façade improvement programs. Even *People* magazine got in on the act, printing a fawning profile of Thomas.[12]

By the close of the 1970s, Restoration had spent some $83 million, most of it from federal funds, to improve Bedford-Stuyvesant. To many local activists, the corporation's work loomed as evidence that they had not been tilting at windmills all along—though even the most upbeat recognized that, in Thomas's words, "there is a tremendous amount of work still to be done." The Restoration model also resonated outside Bed-Stuy's borders. With its emphasis on home ownership, job creation, physical rehabilitation, business development, and neighborhood pride, Restoration offered a template for the CDCs that were popping up in some of the country's poorest places in the 1970s. It also provided an example of how to marry the Black Power movement to what Richard Nixon dubbed "black capitalism."[13]

At the heart of Restoration's work was a simple, characteristically American insight: that black people in America, in order to thrive, must own property. The War on Poverty had enshrined in federal policy the idea that the best measure of a family's poverty was its income—and, ergo, that fighting poverty meant increasing incomes. Restoration, on the other hand, targeted *wealth*. By the 1970s, three decades into the most democratic wealth-building experiment America had ever known—the postwar housing boom—blacks remained on the outside looking in, victims of what Ta-Nehisi Coates has dubbed "plunder—quiet, systemic, submerged."[14] Deprived of investment capital because of redlining, they had watched powerlessly as their homes and communities deteriorated. Restoration hoped to nurture black asset-building and build a community where those assets retained their value long enough to be passed down.[15]

Restoration's founders astutely pinpointed the central flaw of the federal War on Poverty: that it urged community groups to pursue transformative change in partnership with political elites who, despite their rhetoric, favored incremental reform. Community action, per Restoration, was a form of political theater—one that directed grassroots energies in fratricidal directions. Thomas dispensed with politics altogether, spoke little of systemic inequities, and aspired to businesslike efficiency. Echoing Booker T. Washington, Restoration would turn inward and create new bases of black power through community economic development. It was a stark assessment of the narrow bounds within which African American neighborhoods could pursue their own empowerment, but it dovetailed nicely with the neoliberal consensus that was emerging in the aftermath of the Great Society.[16]

Skeptics argued that Restoration could not, and ought not, serve as a blueprint for other CDCs. Restoration had been born in exceptional circumstances, and Bedford-Stuyvesant's large corps of owner-occupants—upon whose presence the Restoration model was based—distinguished it from most other urban black neighborhoods. Even admirers of the corporation's work worried that its "comprehensive" model (housing rehabilitation, plus social services, plus arts and culture, plus business development, plus property leasing, and so on) made it almost impossible to replicate, absent funding on a scale that even Restoration itself never saw. A more hard-hitting critique held that Restoration, with its corporate patrons and apolitical outlook, was little more than an "administrative gatekeeper" that embodied "past dependency," as scholar Ernest Quimby put it in 1977. According to teacher turned activist Jitu Weusi, "many community residents raised the broader question of who Restoration was really restoring (preparing) the community for. Many wondered aloud whether this new form of benevolence was really a disguise for regentrification."[17]

During the 1980s, the Reagan administration slashed away at the remnants of federal support for poor urban neighborhoods. At a time when both drugs and the War on Drugs were ravaging neighborhoods like Bedford-Stuyvesant, CDCs were among the few bulwarks left guarding against further collapse. In that context, Franklin Thomas's vision looked less like a sellout to the white power structure than a pragmatic effort to spark local pride and initiative in a racist society. The thinking behind the Community Home Improvement Program, in particular, emerged as "the closest thing the far-flung community-development industry has to revealed scripture," in the words of scholar William P. Ryan. But Restoration itself was crippled by severe budget cutbacks. In part because it was trying to do too many things at once, the corporation was forced to sell off most of its physical assets, shutter its community centers, relinquish its subsidiaries, and curtail all but a small number of programs. By 1992, Restoration had cut its staff from 300 to 36. The next generation of CDCs—including several in Brooklyn—would be leaner and more single-minded in their dedication to housing.[18]

By then, the grand promises of the Great Society had receded into history. In an era of government retrenchment, community-based efforts to combat economic inequality were "swimming against the tide," as historian Alice O'Connor puts it. Yet CDCs could still achieve successes. At a basic level, such institutions "sustained many communities through long, despairing decades," in the words of one recent assessment. A Ford Foundation report from 1987 argued that the CDCs had helped create "new economic bases in troubled communities [and] become a major component of corrective capitalism; in this free-enterprise nation they are finding ways to open doors to classes and individuals otherwise excluded from the American dream."[19]

It was no surprise that the Ford Foundation would be lauding the CDC movement. The foundation had funded Restoration from the get-go, and in 1979 Ford made the ultimate gesture of support for the Bed-Stuy model when it hired Franklin Thomas as its president. After taking over, Thomas helped codify the foundation's approach to CDCs and turn community development into a nationwide movement. To run the effort, he turned to Mitchell Sviridoff, another old poverty warrior. Sviridoff later recalled a conversation with Thomas in the mid-1970s when they discussed what they would do if they were given $25 million to spend however they wished on community development. Thomas's idea was to give a half-million bucks to each of fifty community groups and ask them to launch an experimental program with the money—the idea being that out of those fifty initiatives, at least one brilliant idea would be born. It was a classic 1960s insight and, under Thomas and Sviridoff, the Ford Foundation applied it to helping CDCs navigate the age of Reagan.[20]

To that end, Ford spawned the Local Initiatives Support Corporation (LISC) and brought together a national network of funders to help underwrite CDCs, many of which, like Restoration, lost federal support after the early 1980s. In a way, LISC acted like a latter-day Office of Economic Opportunity, propping up beleaguered community organizations around the country and stoking the energies of new ones. Within a decade, LISC would be providing funds and expertise to almost 800 CDCs nationwide. By 2010, according to scholar Alexander von Hoffman, LISC had invested $11.1 billion in "the development of 277,000 affordable homes, millions of square feet of retail and community space, not to mention schools, child care facilities, and children's playing fields." Other funding networks were at work too—and CDCs, by some counts, numbered 4,000 in all. But their efficacy remained a matter of debate.[21]

Critics alleged that CDCs, like CAAs before them, reinforced the boundaries of poor neighborhoods and internalized structural inequities. What gains they did achieve were often dwarfed by the magnitude of need. According to urbanist Tom Angotti, CDCs in New York became stuck between "revolution and devolution" after becoming close allies with the city government in the 1980s. "CDCs grew out of a convergence of two trends—grassroots efforts to take control of neighborhoods and City Hall's interest in washing its hands of responsibility for neighborhood renewal," Angotti writes. Though some CDCs continued to contest government policies and promote community control of poor neighborhoods, they more often turned into "local development packagers," who ultimately benefited private real-estate interests by reviving depressed housing markets.[22]

Of course, revival was precisely the point of CDCs. In most neighborhoods where CDCs were founded, activists desperately yearned for an infusion of capital into the local landscape, and they took whatever help they could get, be it from churches, foundations, corporations, or governments. And, in that area, success stories abounded. In New York, across the United States, and in other countries, CDCs helped spur local economic growth and community revitalization simply by creating housing and jobs in places ravaged by private and public disinvestment. The CDC movement, according to journalist and preservationist Roberta Brandes Gratz, "ignited a momentum for change that persuaded conventional developers—and their institutional lenders—to follow their lead with new investment in the very neighborhoods they had previously redlined and declared hopeless."[23]

The best-known tale comes from the South Bronx, where CDCs such as Banana Kelly Community Improvement Association and the People's Development Corporation emerged from the rubble in the late 1970s and early 1980s. "Don't Move, Improve!" was Banana Kelly's motto; another Bronx CDC called itself Nos Quedamos—meaning "We Stay." The groups gained funding from LISC and planning advice from Pratt's Ron Shiffman, who brought with him lessons learned during his time working with Elsie Richardson and CBCC in Bed-Stuy. Then, in the late 1980s and early 1990s, the Bronx CDCs partnered with the city government under mayors Koch and David Dinkins to carry out the largest program of public housing undertaken anywhere in the country since the 1960s. A once-devastated area began to revive. The Bronx model would prove attractive in the 1990s, as had the Bed-Stuy model in the 1970s. As the policy journal *City Limits* recently argued, "In New York since Moses's fall and Jacobs's departure, and especially since the nadir of the fiscal crisis, the greatest engine of resurgence has been small-scale community efforts to improve a lot here, a block there, all adding up to major movements."[24]

It's a legacy of which Elsie Richardson was proud. For decades, she spoke bitterly of being shunted aside while Kennedy and the Restoration Corporation appropriated her ideas. But she slowly buried the hatchet and eventually embraced the CDC she had done so much to spawn. In her old age, Richardson became an informal advisor to Restoration, which she called a "guiding light to the community"; each year, without fanfare, she would mail Restoration's current president, Colvin Grannum, an envelope containing a donation of $250. Meanwhile, Richardson increasingly gained credit for her contributions to the black freedom struggle and the long War on Poverty. At her funeral in 2012, Grannum delivered a eulogy in which he spoke at length about her contributions to Restoration and to the national CDC movement. The postservice reception was held at Restoration Plaza, where, in the building's entrance hall, there hangs a portrait of Richardson and Shirley Chisholm, deep in conversation in the winter of 1966.[25]

"Come on Home to Bed-Stuy"

Fifty years ago, Richardson and Chisholm could scarcely have imagined that Bed-Stuy would one day become New York's hottest housing market. But some local activists had inklings of the future. In 1970, *Black News*, a monthly edited by Jitu Weusi, published a series of articles on "the great land grab" occurring in Brooklyn. "There is currently a frantic run on brownstone houses by white people in the housing market," Weusi wrote. "In the quaint jargon of the white man, brownstones are 'In.' . . . Presently white people are buying brownstone houses in Bed Stuy for outrageously low prices and the trend will accelerate."[26]

Weusi was half right: brownstones were "in," as evidenced by the new homebuyers flocking to Brooklyn neighborhoods like Park Slope and Boerum Hill at the time. But a "frantic run" on Bed-Stuy itself was decades away. In the 1960s and 1970s, the frantic run of capital *out* of the community posed a much bigger threat to its survival. Bed-Stuy's middle-class activists treated brownstones as valuable resources in the battle to halt capital flight, knit community bonds, and build black assets. To that end, some linked up with the "white people" who had settled in nearby neighborhoods. In the late 1960s, CBCC organizers helped Park Slope's Everett Ortner, founder of the citywide Brownstone Revival Coalition, run tours of "the former Bedford and Stuyvesant neighborhoods" for the Brooklyn chapter of the Victorian Society of America. Reported the CBCC newsletter in 1969: "The conviction of this group that Bedford-Stuyvesant has some of the finest architecture in the city is backed up by the reactions of the people who took the tour last November. Most were surprised, if not amazed in view of the horrible image of the community painted by the media."[27]

While CBCC was promoting Bed-Stuy's architectural heritage as a way of repairing the community's reputation, Restoration was seeking to nurture a new generation of black homeowners. In 1978, two Restoration vice presidents, Bernard MacDonald and George Glee, joined several friends in founding a civic organization named Brownstoners of Bedford-Stuyvesant. The group aimed to harness the flagging energies of local block associations and strengthen Bed-Stuy's middle class. Members met in each other's backyards to share knowledge about home renovations, refinancing, and community happenings; they also compared notes with Ortner and a growing network of preservationists from around the city. But the main event on the Brownstoners' calendar was their annual house tour, when they flung open the doors of their beautifully redone houses, alongside ones in the midst of renovations, and invited potential buyers to imagine the possibilities of life in Bed-Stuy.[28]

One of the tour organizers was Brenda Fryson, a career counselor for the Department of Education who had grown up in Fort Greene. Fryson lived with her daughter and husband, a social worker with the city's welfare department, in a 1901 brownstone on Chauncey Street, overlooking Fulton Park. They'd bought their home for $25,000 in 1974 and spent several years restoring it and decorating it with African art. Friends at the Restoration Corporation had helped secure financing for the mortgage and renovations, which had cost another $20,000.[29]

Fryson, who was thirty-seven in 1978, saw herself walking in the footsteps of Richardson and Chisholm. Her father was a bus driver, her mother a seamstress. In the 1960s, she'd joined boycotts and rent strikes; she'd also been inspired by the campaign to block slum clearance around Fulton Park, which would have demolished the house she later bought. Promoting brownstone living, she believed, was about more than just bricks and mortar; the key was to build community. "We didn't just buy a structure," Fryson later explained. "We bought the neighbors; we bought the block." She and fellow Brownstoners sat on PTAs and police–community councils, they organized block associations, and they ran voter-registration drives. They also donated the proceeds from their housing tours—which were ticketed events—to scholarships for graduating seniors at Boys and Girls High School on Fulton Street.[30]

Most members of the Brownstoners, like the Frysons, worked for nonprofits or in government jobs—the sectors that large numbers of African Americans had penetrated during the Great Society years. The group's original motto—"Come on home to Bed-Stuy"—was directed at the prodigal sons and daughters of Brooklyn's first generation of black homeowners. But the house tours also attracted African American professionals from across the country. Many bought into the Brownstoners' vision of Bed-Stuy as a place where, in Fryson's words, "black people could not only grow their families but also grow and preserve our culture and our history and our legacy." By 1985, the *Times* was reporting that prices for houses within "historically important" areas of Bedford-Stuyvesant had appreciated by 25 percent over the previous year and were fetching between $90,000 and $125,000. "In the last five years, it's like a Back to Bed-Stuy movement," observed veteran activist Lucille Rose in 1985. That same year, crack hit town; its impact, Fryson recalled, was "like an atom bomb."[31]

The Brownstoners of Bed-Stuy kept at their work through hard times. Then, in the new millennium, the landscape changed dramatically. Between 2000 and 2010, the white population increased 633 percent in the old "Bedford" section of Bed-Stuy, to the west of Throop Avenue—the largest increase of any demographic group anywhere in the city in that decade. The enclave's black population, meanwhile, dipped below 50 percent for the first time in a half-century. Suddenly, Jitu Weusi's prophesy was coming true.[32]

By 2015, the neighborhood formerly known as America's largest ghetto was awash in wealth. Though rates of concentrated poverty and incarceration in Bedford-Stuyvesant ranked among the highest in the city, brownstones were selling for $2 million and three-bedroom rentals in Stuyvesant Heights listed for $4,500 a month. Longtime homeowners regularly got early-morning phone calls asking if they were ready to sell. Some cashed in; others defaulted on mortgages or were defrauded of their homes. Private investment firms scooped up properties by the bushel; thousands of low-income tenants were priced out or turfed out by landlords eager to charge "market rates."[33] Once upon a time, speculators lined their pockets by making the ghetto; now, they would reap windfalls from its destruction.

Local leaders, meanwhile, prepared to wage another round in the battle for Bed-Stuy. "We need to protect this community," said state assemblymember Annette Robinson, who bought her first Brooklyn brownstone in the 1970s. "The indigenous people who have been here their whole lives, they're getting pushed out." Few disagreed. But identifying enemies, let alone devising strategies to combat them, was hard. And opinions differed as to how, exactly, the community could and should be protected—how to balance the interests of tenants and homeowners, how to harness local wealth without hurting local people, how (or if) to welcome newcomers while preserving what Brenda Fryson called "our culture and our history and our legacy."[34]

Had Bed-Stuy been victimized by what Jane Jacobs dubbed "oversuccess"? In their laudable efforts to create a livable, nurturing community, did the neighborhood's activists inadvertently make it *too* attractive? Perhaps. But just as community groups were mostly powerless to stem the tides of deindustrialization in the 1970s, they almost certainly did not cause the real-estate tsunami that engulfed Brooklyn—and countless other urban spaces across the globe—in the twenty-first century. What has "come on home to Bed-Stuy" is global capital.

Notes

Note on sources: Don Watkins and Sydney J. Moshette Jr. gave the author access to their private papers, which contained archival materials about Brooklyn community organizations from the 1950s, 1960s, and 1970s. The materials have since been donated to the Brooklyn Public Library's Brooklyn Collection, but they were in the author's possession and had yet to be processed when research for this book was conducted.

Abbreviations

AWP	Adam Walinsky Papers
BE	*Brooklyn Eagle*
BHS	Brooklyn Historical Society
BMP	Burke Marshall Papers
BPL	Brooklyn Public Library, Brooklyn Collection
BSRC	Bedford-Stuyvesant Restoration Corporation
BSRCOH	Bedford-Stuyvesant Restoration Corporation Oral History Project
CDCOH	Community Development Corporation Oral History Project
DWP	Don Watkins Private Papers
JFKL	John F. Kennedy Presidential Library
LBJL	Lyndon Baines Johnson Library and Museum
LGW	La Guardia and Wagner Archives
NYAN	*New York Amsterdam News*
NYCMA	New York City Municipal Archives
NYCYB	New York City Youth Board
NYPL-Sch	New York Public Library, Schomburg Center for Research in Black Culture
NYT	*New York Times*
RFKOH	Robert F. Kennedy Oral History Program
RFW	Robert F. Wagner Jr. Papers
SJMP	Sydney J. Moshette Jr. Private Papers
TMCJP	Thomas M. C. Johnston Papers

Introduction

Epigraph: Central Brooklyn Coordinating Council, "Program for Total
Rehabilitation and Renewal of Bedford-Stuyvesant and Central Brooklyn
Area," November 1964, in Ronald Shiffman, "Strategy for a Coordinated
Social and Physical Renewal Program: Bedford-Stuyvesant" (New York: Pratt
Center for Community Improvement, 1966).

1. Elsie Richardson, interview with the author, June 5, 2011.
2. Thomas R. Jones, prepared statement and testimony, Hearings of the Subcommittee on Employment, Manpower, and Poverty of the Committee on Labor
and Public Welfare, U.S. Senate, May 8, 1967, 1855–1856 (Washington,
DC: U.S. Government Printing Office, 1967).
3. Elsie Richardson, interview with the author, June 5, 2011; "Fire Death Toll
Now Five," *New York Amsterdam News (NYAN)*, September 7, 1932.
4. Elsie Richardson, interview with the author, June 5, 2011; Elsie Richardson,
Obituary (self-authored), distributed March 20, 2012; Elsie Richardson, in
Fighting for Justice: New York Voices of the Civil Rights Movement, executive
producer Patricia L. Gatling (Film series sponsored by the New York City
Commission on Human Rights and NYC Media, 2009).
5. On postwar Bedford-Stuyvesant, see Harold X. Connolly, *A Ghetto Grows in
Brooklyn* (New York: New York University Press, 1977); Jeffrey Nathan Gerson,
"Building the Brooklyn Machine: Irish, Jewish and Black Political Succession
in Central Brooklyn, 1919–1964" (PhD thesis, City University of New York,
1990); Craig Steven Wilder, *A Covenant with Color: Race and Social Power in
Brooklyn* (New York: Columbia University Press, 2000); Wilhelmena Rhodes
Kelly, *Images of America: Bedford-Stuyvesant* (Charleston, SC: Arcadia
Publishing, 2007); Brian Purnell, *Fighting Jim Crow in the County of Kings:
The Congress of Racial Equality in Brooklyn* (Lexington: University Press of
Kentucky, 2013); and the collection of oral history interviews carried out in
2008 under the joint auspices of the Brooklyn Historical Society and the
Bedford-Stuyvesant Restoration Corporation.
6. Elsie Richardson, interview with the author, June 5, 2011; Elsie Richardson,
interview with James Briggs Murray, February 2, 1990, Community Develop-
ment Corporations Oral History Project, New York Public Library, Schomburg
Center for Research in Black Culture.
7. The many published accounts of Kennedy's involvement in Bedford-
Stuyvesant include Jack Newfield, *Robert Kennedy: A Memoir* (New York:
Dutton, 1969); Evan Thomas, *Robert Kennedy: His Life* (New York: Simon and
Schuster, 2000); Edward R. Schmitt, *President of the Other America: Robert
Kennedy and the Politics of Poverty* (Amherst: University of Massachusetts
Press, 2010); Mitchell Sviridoff, ed., *Inventing Community Renewal: The Trials*

and Errors That Shaped the Modern Community Development Corporation
(New York: New School University, 2004); Kimberley Johnson, "Community
Development Corporations, Participation, and Accountability: The Harlem
Urban Development Corporation and the Bedford-Stuyvesant Restoration
Corporation," *Annals of the American Academy of Political and Social
Science* 594 (July 2004), 109–124; Tom Adam Davies, "Black Power in Action:
The Bedford-Stuyvesant Restoration Corporation, Robert F. Kennedy, and the
Politics of the Urban Crisis," *Journal of American History* 100:3 (December 2013),
736–760; Brian Purnell, "'What We Need Is Brick and Mortar': Race, Gender,
and Early Leadership of the Bedford-Stuyvesant Restoration Corporation," in
Laura Warren Hill and Julia Rabig, eds., *The Business of Black Power: Commu-
nity Development, Capitalism, and Corporate Responsibility in Postwar
America* (Rochester, NY: University of Rochester Press, 2012), 217–244; Arthur
M. Schlesinger, *Robert Kennedy and His Times* (Boston: Houghton Mifflin,
1978), Chap. 35; and Karen Ferguson, *Top Down: The Ford Foundation, Black
Power, and the Reinvention of Racial Liberalism* (Philadelphia: University of
Pennsylvania Press, 2013), Chap. 6. Also useful is a Ford Foundation report
from 1969: R. B. Goldmann, "Performance in Black and White: An Appraisal
of the Development and Record of the Bedford-Stuyvesant Restoration and
Development and Services Corporations" (February 1969), Papers of the Ford
Foundation, Box 1, John F. Kennedy Presidential Library (JFKL).

8. Ronald Shiffman, interview with Sady Sullivan, February 4, 2008, Bedford-
Stuyvesant Restoration Corporation Oral History Project, Brooklyn Historical
Society; "Brooklyn Negroes Harass Kennedy," *New York Times (NYT)*,
February 5, 1966; Elsie Richardson, interview with the author, June 5, 2011.

9. Other accounts of the confrontation contain slightly different versions of who
said what. The quotes used here and in ensuing paragraphs are taken largely
from "Brooklyn Negroes Harass Kennedy," *NYT*, February 5, 1966; "Boro Cry
to RJK, JVL: 'We're Tired of Waiting,'" NYAN, February 12, 1966; and
"Kennedy Tours Bed-Stuy," *New York Recorder*, February 12, 1966.

10. Thomas, *Robert Kennedy*, 319.

11. James L. Sundquist, "Introduction," in James L. Sundquist, ed., *On Fighting
Poverty: Perspectives from Experience* (New York: Basic Books, 1969), 3; Lyndon
Baines Johnson to cabinet members, November 11, 1966, "LG 10/1/66–12/31/66,"
Box 2, White House Central Files, Lyndon B. Johnson Presidential Library
(LBJL); President's Annual Message to the Congress on the State of the Union,
January 8, 1964, LBJL online.

12. Doris Kearns Goodwin, *Lyndon Johnson and the American Dream* (New York:
St. Martin's Griffin, 1991), 286. See also Joseph A. Califano Jr., *The Triumph &
Tragedy of Lyndon Johnson: The White House Years* (New York: Simon and
Schuster, 1991).

13. Annelise Orleck, "The War on Poverty and American Politics since the 1960s," in Annelise Orleck and Lisa Gayle Hazirikian, eds., *The War on Poverty: A New Grassroots History, 1964–1980* (Athens: University of Georgia Press, 2011), 438. Useful overviews of the War on Poverty include Sar A. Levitan, *The Great Society's Poor Law: A New Approach to Poverty* (Baltimore: Johns Hopkins University Press, 1969); Michael L. Gillette, *Launching the War on Poverty: An Oral History* (New York: Twayne Books, 1996); Robert F. Clark, *The War on Poverty: History, Selected Programs, and Ongoing Impact* (Lanham, MD: University Press of America, 2002); Carl M. Brauer, "Kennedy, Johnson, and the War on Poverty," *Journal of American History* 69:1 (June 1982), 98–119; and Martha J. Bailey and Sheldon Danzinger, "Legacies of the War on Poverty," in Bailey and Danzinger, eds., *Legacies of the War on Poverty* (New York: Russell Sage Foundation, 2013), 1–36.

14. On the connections between civil rights, black political power, and the War on Poverty, see Thomas J. Sugrue, *Sweet Land of Liberty: The Forgotten Struggle for Civil Rights in the North* (New York: Random House, 2008); Robert O. Self, *American Babylon: Race and the Struggle for Postwar Oakland* (Princeton, NJ: Princeton University Press, 2003); Susan Ashmore, *Carry It On: The War on Poverty and the Civil Rights Movement in Alabama* (Athens: University of Georgia Press, 2008); William S. Clayson, *Freedom Is Not Enough: The War on Poverty and the Civil Rights Movement in Texas* (Austin: University of Texas Press, 2010); Leonard N. Moore, *Carl B. Stokes and the Rise of Black Political Power* (Urbana: University of Illinois Press, 2002); and the essays in Hill and Julia Rabig, eds., *The Business of Black Power*.

15. For instance, Stephen Tuck, in his otherwise masterful synthesis of the black freedom struggle, writes that the War on Poverty "did not address discrimination or deindustrialization." See Stephen Tuck, *We Ain't What We Ought to Be: The Black Freedom Struggle from Emancipation to Obama* (Cambridge, MA: Harvard University Press, 2010), 335–336.

16. The classic conservative critique of the Great Society is Charles Murray, *Losing Ground* (New York: Basic Books, 1984). For a recent assessment of the War on Poverty from the right, see Scott Winship, "Actually, We Won the War on Poverty," in *Politico Magazine* online, January 24, 2014. See also Fred Siegel, *The Future Once Happened Here: New York, D.C., L.A., and the Fate of America's Big Cities* (New York: Free Press, 1997).

17. See Peter Marris and Martin Rein, *Dilemmas of Social Reform: Poverty and Community Action in the United States* (Chicago: University of Chicago Press, 1967, reprinted 1982); Daniel P. Moynihan, *Maximum Feasible Misunderstanding: Community Action in the War on Poverty* (New York: Free Press, 1969); Alice O'Connor, *Poverty Knowledge: Social Science, Social Policy, and the Poor in Twentieth-Century U.S. History* (Princeton, NJ: Princeton Univer-

sity Press, 2001); Allen J. Matusow, *The Unraveling of America: A History of Liberalism in the 1960s* (New York: Harper and Row, 1984); Judith Russell, *Economics, Bureaucracy, and Race: How Keynesians Misguided the War on Poverty* (New York: Columbia University Press, 2004); David Zarefsky, *President Johnson's War on Poverty: Rhetoric and History* (Tuscaloosa: University of Alabama Press, 1986); Sidney M. Milkis, "Lyndon Johnson, the Great Society, and the 'Twilight' of the Modern Presidency," in Sidney M. Milkis and Jerome M. Mileur, eds., *The Great Society and the High Tide of Liberalism* (Amherst: University of Massachusetts Press, 2005); Irwin Unger, *The Best of Intentions: The Triumphs and Failures of the Great Society under Kennedy, Johnson, and Nixon* (New York: Doubleday, 1996); Nicholas Lemann, *The Promised Land: The Great Black Migration and How It Changed America* (New York: Alfred A. Knopf, 1991); Jill Quadagno, *The Color of Welfare: How Racism Undermined the War on Poverty* (New York: Oxford University Press, 1994).

18. See, for instance, the essays in Bailey and Danzinger, eds., *Legacies of the War on Poverty*; and Peter Edelman, "The War on Poverty and Subsequent Federal Programs: What Worked, What Didn't Work, and Why? Lessons for Future Programs," *Journal of Poverty Law and Policy* (May–June 2006), 7–18. For an interesting perspective on the left-liberal defense of the Great Society, see Michael Katz, "Was Government the Solution or the Problem? The Role of the State in the History of American Social Policy," *Theory & Society* 39:3/4 (May 2010), 487–502.

19. A recent attempt to devise a more accurate measure of poverty, based on after-tax incomes, found that the poverty rate was 32 percent in 1963 and 14.4 percent in 1973. See Bruce D. Meyer and James X. Sullivan, "Winning the War: Poverty from the Great Society to the Great Recession," *Brookings Papers on Economic Activity* (Fall 2012), 133–200.

20. Christopher Jencks, "The War on Poverty: Was It Lost?" *New York Review of Books*, April 2, 2015; Christopher Jencks, "Did We Lose the War on Poverty?" *New York Review of Books*, April 23, 2015; Council of Economic Advisors, "The War on Poverty Fifty Years Later: A Progress Report" (January 2014), 45. See also Christopher Wimer et al., "Trends in Poverty with an Anchored Supplemental Poverty Measure," Columbia University Population Research Center, Working Paper No. 13–01 (2013); Thomas Edsall, "How Poor Are the Poor?" *NYT*, March 25, 2015; and John E. Schwartz, *America's Hidden Success: A Reassessment of Twenty Years of Public Policy* (New York: Norton, 1983).

21. On persistent inequality and concentrated poverty, see Douglas S. Massey and Nancy Denton, *American Apartheid: Segregation and the Making of the Underclass* (Cambridge, MA: Harvard University Press, 1998); Patrick Sharkey, "Neighborhoods and the Black-White Mobility Gap" (Washington, DC: The Economic Mobility Project: An Initiative of The Pew Charitable Trusts, 2009);

and William Julius Wilson, *When Work Disappears: The World of the New Urban Poor* (New York: Vintage Books, 1996).

22. Herbert J. Gans, *The War against the Poor: The Underclass and Antipoverty Policy* (New York: Basic Books, 1995). See Richard Cloward and Frances Fox Piven, *Poor People's Movements: Why They Succeed, How They Fail* (New York: Vintage Books, 1977); Cloward and Piven, "The Politics of the Great Society," in Milkis and Mileur, eds., *The Great Society and the High Tide of Liberalism*, 253–267; Ira Katznelson, *City Trenches: Urban Politics and the Patterning of Class in the United States* (New York: Pantheon Books, 1981); and J. David Greenstone and Paul E. Peterson, *Race and Authority in Urban Politics: Community Participation and the War on Poverty* (New York: Russell Sage Foundation, 1973). On the War on Poverty and crime, see Elizabeth Hinton, "A War within Our Own Boundaries: Lyndon Johnson's Great Society and the Rise of the Carceral State," *Journal of American History* 102:1 (June 2015), 100–112.

23. See the essays in Orleck and Hazirikian, eds., *The War on Poverty: A New Grassroots History*; Kent B. Germany, *New Orleans after the Promises: Poverty, Citizenship, and the Search for the Great Society* (Athens: University of Georgia Press, 2007); Wesley G. Phelps, *A People's War on Poverty: Urban Politics and Grassroots Activists in Houston* (Athens: University of Georgia Press, 2014); Mark Edward Braun, *Social Change and the Empowerment of the Poor: Poverty Representation in Milwaukee's Community Action Programs, 1964–1972* (Lanham, MD: Lexington Books, 2001); Noel Cazenave, *Impossible Democracy: The Unlikely Success of the War on Poverty Community Action Programs* (Albany: State University of New York Press, 2007); Nicole P. Marwell, *Bargaining for Brooklyn: Community Organizations in the Entrepreneurial City* (Chicago: University of Chicago Press, 2007); Nancy Naples, *Grassroots Warriors: Activist Mothering in the War on Poverty* (New York: Routledge, 1998); Felicia Kornbluh, *The Battle for Welfare Rights: Politics and Poverty in Modern America* (Philadelphia: University of Pennsylvania Press, 2007); and William Clayson, "The Barrios and the Ghettos Have Organized!: Community Action, Political Acrimony, and the War on Poverty in San Antonio," *Journal of Urban History* 28:2 (2002), 158–183.

24. "Protestants Held Stingy in Slum Aid," NYT, May 25, 1968; Barry Stein, *Rebuilding Bedford-Stuyvesant: Community Economic Development in the Ghetto* (Cambridge: Center for Community Economic Development, 1975), 1. In the 1960s, Bedford-Stuyvesant was also sometimes dubbed the "second largest ghetto" in the country (after the South Side of Chicago). See, for instance, Ford Foundation/Goldmann, "Performance in Black and White," 9, JFKL; John J. Goldman, "Good News From Bed-Stuy," *New York* 3:36 (September 7, 1970), 6.

328

1. A Suitcase Full of Knives

Epigraph: Robert F. Wagner Jr., remarks at the fifteenth anniversary dinner of the New York City Youth Board, November 15, 1962, Box 060005W, Folder 21, Robert F. Wagner Jr. Papers (RFW), La Guardia & Wagner Archives (LGW) online.

1. Eric C. Schneider, *Vampires, Dragons, and Egyptian Kings: Youth Gangs in Postwar New York* (Princeton, NJ: Princeton University Press, 1999); "17 Boys Arrested in Fatal Gang Riot," *New York Times (NYT)*, July 21, 1945.

2. William Bernard, *Jailbait: The Story of Juvenile Delinquency* (New York: Greenberg, 1948), 4–5.

3. Schneider, *Vampires, Dragons, and Egyptian Kings*, 65–67; "Youth Gang Wars Kill 10 in a Year," *NYT*, May 8, 1950; "17 Boys Arrested in Fatal Gang Riot," *NYT*, July 21, 1945. On responses to postwar gang violence in Harlem, see Michael Javen Fortner, *Black Silent Majority: The Rockefeller Drug Laws and the Politics of Punishment* (Cambridge, MA: Harvard University Press, 2015), Chap. 1.

4. Quoted in Schneider, *Vampires, Dragons, and Egyptian Kings*, 51.

5. "Brooklynites Meet to Fight Juvenile Problem in Section," *New York Amsterdam News (NYAN)*, August 4, 1945.

6. "State Conference Disapproves Tough Approach to Delinquency," *NYT*, October 6, 1955; Juvenile Delinquency Evaluation Project of the City of New York, dir. Robert M. MacIver, "Delinquency in the Great City" (July 1961).

7. "Youth Gang Wars Kill 10 in a Year," *NYT*, May 8, 1950; Brooklyn Council for Social Planning (BCSP), "Report of the Tompkins Park Leadership Project" (1950), Folder 9.1.023, Box 66, BCSP Papers, Brooklyn Public Library Brooklyn Collection (BPL).

8. Mwlina Imiri Abubadika (aka Sonny Carson), *The Education of Sonny Carson* (New York: Norton, 1972), 37.

9. Abubadika, *The Education*, 37. See also Jon Mitchell, "Jim Stark's 'Barbaric Yawp': Rebel without a Cause and the Cold War Crisis in Masculinity," in J. David Slocum, ed., *Rebel without a Cause: Approaches to a Maverick Masterwork* (Albany: State University of New York Press, 2005), 131–147.

10. BCSP, "Outlined Proposed Leadership Project with Gang Groups" (December 1946), "Neighborhood Organization," Box 22, BCSP Papers, BPL; BCSP, "Report of the Tompkins Park Youth Leadership Project," BPL.

11. BCSP, "Welcome to Brooklyn: Handbook for New Workers" (1954), Box 66, BCSP Papers, BPL; "Community Council's Aid Urged to Save Borough Welfare Units," *NYT*, January 1, 1957; BCSP, Summary of Conference on Our Expanding Negro Population, April 6, 1940, Folder 9.1.026, Box 66, BCSP Papers, BPL.

12. "Wide Program of Social Welfare Urged to Ease Crime in Brooklyn," *NYT*, November 27, 1943; "Social Plans Offered for 'Little Harlem,'" *NYT*, December 13, 1943; "Mayor Denounced by Jury for Crime in Brooklyn Area," *NYT*, November 16, 1943; "Race Tension Seen in Brooklyn Area," *NYT*, April 21, 1946; BCSP, Worker's Report on Unattached Boys' Groups, September 9, 1947, "Williamsburg-Tompkins Park Youth Leadership Project: Reports," Box 22, BCSP Papers, BPL.

13. Alice O'Connor, *Poverty Knowledge: Social Science, Social Policy, and the Poor in Twentieth-Century U.S. History* (Princeton, NJ: Princeton University Press, 2001), Chap. 1; Noel A. Cazenave, "Chicago Influences on the War on Poverty," in Martin V. Melosi, ed., *Urban Public Policy: Historical Modes and Methods* (University Park: Pennsylvania State University, 1993), 52–68; Irving A. Spergel, *Reducing Youth Gang Violence: The Little Village Gang Project in Chicago* (Lanham, MD: AltaMira Press, 2007), 5–6. On the flaws of "social disorganization theory," see Irving A. Spergel, *The Youth Gang Problem: A Community Approach* (New York: Oxford University Press, 1995), 153–154.

14. "Boro Boy Gangs Turn Mail Order Toy Guns into Lethal Weapons," *Brooklyn Eagle (BE)*, April 29, 1948; New York City Youth Board (NYCYB), Council of Social and Athletic Clubs Annual Review, 1951–1952, Folder 6.1.044, Box 37, BCSP Papers, BPL; Ralph W. Whelan, "Philosophy and Development of the Youth Board Program," in NYCYB, *Reaching the Unreached: Fundamental Aspects of the Program of the New York City Youth Board* (New York: NYCYB, 1952). On the Harlem initiative, see James R. Dumpson, "An Approach to Antisocial Street Gangs," *Federal Probation* 13 (1949), 22–29.

15. "How One Man Joined a Boy Gang, Helped It Save Itself," *BE*, April 11, 1949; BCSP, Worker's Report on Unattached Boys' Groups, BPL.

16. BCSP, Worker's Report on Unattached Boys' Groups, BPL; "Boy Gangs of Boro," *BE*, April 28, 1948.

17. BCSP, "Report of the Tompkins Park Youth Leadership Project," BPL. For more on how gangs in postwar New York defined ethnic turf, see Schneider, *Vampires, Dragons, and Egyptian Kings*.

18. BCSP, Worker's Report on Unattached Boys' Groups, BPL; BCSP, "Report of the Tompkins Park Youth Leadership Project," BPL; "Big Fight Planned by Teen-Age Gangs," *NYT*, May 11, 1950; Abubadika, *The Education*, 21–22. On gang structures and practices, see Schneider, *Vampires, Dragons, and Egyptian Kings*; and Spergel, *The Youth Gang Problem*, 75–76.

19. BCSP, "Report of the Tompkins Park Youth Leadership Project," BPL; "Reformed Boy Gang Fixed Own Quarters, Now Aids Other Lads," *BE*, April 12, 1949; "The Brewery Rats Now Good Citizens," *NYT*, January 21, 1950;

"Gang Battlefield Now a Quiet Play Area," *BE*, January 20, 1950; "Phoenix on Pulaski Street," *Christian Science Monitor*, March 4, 1950.

20. BCSP, "Report of the Tompkins Park Youth Leadership Project," BPL; "How One Man Joined a Boy Gang, Helped It Save Itself," *BE*, April 11, 1949.

21. BCSP, memo to the *BE*, August 26, 1948, "Youth Services: Youth Councils Project—Correspondence and Reports, 1948–56," Box 23, BCSP Papers, BPL; "B'klyn Welfare Groups Set Up Youth Projects," *NYAN*, June 12, 1948; "Social Planning Committee Cites Ways of Meeting Gang Menace," *BE*, June 4, 1950.

22. Urban League of Greater New York, "Tentative Project to Help Meet the Needs of Young People in an Unserviced Neighborhood of Brooklyn" (1947), Folder 7.4.001, Box 40, BCSP Papers, BPL; Urban League, "Program Plans: Group Work Department, 1948–1949," Folder 7.4.001, Box 40, BCSP Papers, BPL; "League Youth Project Holds Celebrity Party at Center," *NYAN*, September 11, 1948.

23. "Juvenile Aid Plan Is Ready for City," *NYT*, May 12, 1949; "Mayor Enlarges City Youth Board," *NYT*, June 20, 1954; "Youth Board Puts Stress on Gangs," *NYT*, June 29, 1950.

24. "Teen-Age Fighting Rises in Brooklyn," *NYT*, October 11, 1950; "Big Fight Planned by Teen-Age Gangs," *NYT*, May 11, 1950; "Eight Begin Jail Terms in Teen Zip-Gun Fight," *BE*, June 23, 1950; "Youth Gang Wars Kill 10 in a Year," *NYT*, May 8, 1950.

25. Minutes of the Conference with Judge Kaplan re: "Gang Project for Brooklyn," July 6, 1950, Folder 6.1.039, Box 36, BCSP Papers, BPL; Minutes of the Conference on Youth Board Gang Project for Brooklyn, July 10, 1950, Folder 6.1.039, Box 36, BCSP Papers, BPL; "Youth Board's Help Assures Boro of Practical Move against Gangs," *BE*, July 3, 1950; NYCYB, Council of Social and Athletic Clubs Annual Review, 1951–1952, BPL.

26. Whelan, "Philosophy and Development of the Youth Board Program"; James E. McCarthy and Joseph S. Barbaro, "Re-Directing Teen-Age Gangs," in NYCYB, *Reaching the Unreached*; "Social Workers Assigned to Brooklyn Youth Gangs," *NYT*, July 2, 1950; "$50,000 Earmarked by Youth Board to Fight Bedford-Stuyvesant Gang Menace," *NYAN*, March 24, 1951.

27. Schneider, *Vampires, Dragons, and Egyptian Kings*, 193; "Gang Wars Curbed by City Mediators," *NYT*, November 21, 1953; NYCYB, Council of Social and Athletic Clubs Annual Review, 1951–1952, BPL; Materials relating to the Advisory Committee for the Brooklyn Detached Worker Project, 1950–1951, Folder 6.1.043, BCSP Papers, BPL.

28. "Dr. Kenneth Marshall, Official of Antipoverty Programs, Dies," *NYT*, October 19, 1971.

29. "New Approach Set to Aid 'Waywards,'" *NYT*, April 24, 1949; "Citizens' Drive on Delinquency," *NYT*, May 30, 1948; "Juvenile Aid Plan Is Ready for City," *NYT*, May 12, 1949.

30. NYCYB, "Teenage Gangs" (1957), Folder 6.1.039, Box 36, BCSP Papers, BPL; "$50,000 Earmarked by Youth Board to Fight Bedford-Stuyvesant Gang Menace," *NYAN*, March 24, 1951; "Juvenile Delinquency and a Cure!" *NYAN*, October 30, 1954; and Schneider, *Vampires, Dragons, and Egyptian Kings*.

31. Judith Greene and Kevin Pranis, "Gang Wars: The Failure of Enforcement Tactics and the Need for Effective Public Safety Strategies," Justice Policy Institute (July 2007), 15–16. See also Malcolm W. Klein, "Juvenile Gangs, Police, and Detached Workers: Controversies about Intervention," *Social Service Review* 39:2 (June 1965), 183–190.

32. "52.7% Rise Reported in Youth Crime," *New York Herald-Tribune*, February 14, 1955.

33. Elizabeth A. Wells, *West Side Story: Cultural Perspectives on an American Musical* (Lanham, MD: Scarecrow Press, 2010), 194; "Delinquency Probe Brings Flood of Public Reaction," *St. Petersburg Times*, November 29, 1953.

34. "Delinquency Plan of U.S. Supported," *NYT*, November 17, 1955; "Pino, McMullen Start Legislative Drive on Juvenile Delinquency," *BE*, January 20, 1955; "Grand Jury to Urge Age Cards for Teens," *World Telegram and Sun*, October 14, 1955. On federal policy responses to juvenile delinquency in the 1950s, see Jason Barnosky, "The Violent Years: Responses to Juvenile Crime in the 1950s," *Polity* 38:3 (July 2006), 314–344. On New York gangs in the mid-1950s, see Harrison Salisbury, *The Shook-Up Generation* (New York: Harper and Row, 1958).

35. Frances Fox Piven, "Dilemmas in Social Planning: A Case Inquiry," *Social Service Review* 42:2 (June 1968), 203.

36. On the New Deal in New York, see Mason B. Williams, *City of Ambition: FDR, La Guardia, and the Making of Modern New York* (New York: Norton, 2013). On Wagner and African Americans, see Clarence Taylor, "Robert Wagner, Milton Galamison, and the Challenge to New York City Liberalism," *Afro-Americans in New York Life and History* 31:2 (July 2007); and Chris McNickle, *To Be Mayor of New York: Ethnic Politics in the City* (New York: Columbia University Press, 1993). The major work on Wagner is Richard M. Flanagan, *Robert Wagner and the Rise of New York's Plebiscitary Mayoralty: The Tamer of the Tamanny Tiger* (New York: Palgrave MacMillan, 2015).

37. Chris McNickle, "Wagner, Robert F. (ii)," in Kenneth T. Jackson, ed., *The Encyclopedia of New York City* (New Haven, CT: Yale University Press, 2010), 1371; Text of Robert F. Wagner's address to the State C.I.O. Convention, printed in *NYT*, September 27, 1953; "Mayor Wagner's Gift," *NYT*, February 13, 1991; and "Mourners Recall Wagner as Man of Subtle Grace," *NYT*, February 17,

1991. On Wagner's contributions to New York's fiscal imbalance, see Fred Siegel, *The Future Once Happened Here: New York, D.C., L.A., and the Fate of America's Big Cities* (New York: Free Press, 1997), 31–35.

38. "Our Changing City," NYT, June 20, 1955; Flanagan, *Robert Wagner*, 36; Robert F. Wagner Jr., speech to the Tammany Society Dinner, July 1, 1954, Folder 20, Box 060071W, RFW, LGW online. For contrasting views on New York's postwar welfare state, see Joshua Freeman, *Working Class New York: Life and Labor since World War II* (New York: The New Press, 2000) and Vincent J. Cannato, *The Ungovernable City: John Lindsay and His Struggle to Save New York* (New York: Basic Books, 2001).

39. E. W. Kenworthy, "The Emergence of Mayor Wagner," NYT *Magazine*, August 14, 1955; Gay Talese, "Political Walkathons and Talkathons," NYT *Magazine*, October 29, 1961.

40. Ira Katznelson, *City Trenches: Urban Politics and the Patterning of Class in the United States* (New York: Pantheon Books, 1981), 142; "Thelma Boozer Named Civil Defense Aide in N.Y.," *Jet*, January 28, 1954, 4; Office of the President of the Borough of Manhattan, press release, August 2, 1950, Robert F. Wagner Documents Collection, Speeches Series, Folder 116, Box 060039W, RFW, LGW online; "Harlem District Planning Council Formed," NYAN, July 7, 1951; "Planning Board Praised for Winning Improvements," NYAN, January 31, 1953; Seth Forman, "Community Boards," *Gotham Gazette*, September 20, 2000. On community-based planning, see Marci Reaven, "Citizen Participation in City Planning: New York City, 1945–1975" (PhD thesis, New York University, 2005), esp. Chap. 3.

41. On Moses and urban renewal, see Robert A. Caro, *The Power Broker: Robert Moses and the Fall of New York* (New York: Alfred A. Knopf, 1974); Joel Schwartz, *The New York Approach: Robert Moses, Urban Liberals, and Redevelopment of the Inner City* (Columbus: Ohio State University Press, 1993); Samuel Zipp, *Manhattan Projects: The Rise and Fall of Urban Renewal in Cold War New York* (New York: Oxford University Press, 2010); and Kenneth T. Jackson and Hilary Ballon, eds., *Robert Moses and the Modern City: The Transformation of New York* (New York: Norton, 2007).

42. "Vacancies Scarce in Housing Here," NYT, November 5, 1955; "Rate of Vacancy Low in Tenements," NYT, November 13, 1955.

43. See Taylor, "Robert Wagner, Milton Galamison, and the Challenge."

44. Robert F. Wagner to A. Phillip Randolph, September 5, 1961, Folder 9, Box 060296, RFW, LGW online; Robert F. Wagner Jr., speech to the National Committee Against Discrimination in Housing, May 20, 1954, Folder 40, Box 060039W; Robert F. Wagner, speech to the National Urban League and the Urban League of Greater New York, March 16, 1954, Folder 9, Box 060070W, RFW, LGW online.

45. Among the men and women who joined what was something of a municipal black cabinet during Wagner's second and third terms were Robert C. Weaver, who headed the city's rent-control board before moving to the federal Home Finance Administration; John King, superintendent of schools; Robert Magnum, deputy commissioner of the city's hospitals; James Dumpson, welfare commissioner; Harry C. Harris, who oversaw the Housing and Rehabilitation Board; Arthur C. Logan, chairman of the Council Against Poverty; Anne Roberts, staff director of the Economic Opportunity Committee; and Reverend Gardner C. Taylor, who acted as one of three Democratic co-leaders in Brooklyn after Wagner's 1961 split with the Kings County Democratic machine.

46. "Where We Stand," NYAN, September 2, 1961; Wagner campaign materials, 1961, Folder 9, Box 060296, RFW Papers, LGW online; Taylor, "Robert Wagner, Milton Galamison, and the Challenge," 124; "Jack Weighs Suit against Detractors," NYT, February 28, 1956; Elsie Richardson, interview with the author, June 5, 2011.

47. Fox Piven, "Dilemmas in Social Planning," 203; " 'Number 1' Project for the City," NYT, June 29, 1958.

48. "Mayor Enlarges City Youth Board," NYT, June 20, 1954; Greene and Pranis, "Gang Wars," 15; Robert F. Wagner, speech at meeting of the Advisory Council of President's Committee on Juvenile Delinquency and Youth Crime, January 3, 1963, Folder 44, Box 060014W, RFW, LGW online; Robert F. Wagner Jr., speech before the Senate Sub-committee on Juvenile Delinquency, March 9, 1961, Folder 22, Box 060046W, RFW, LGW online; Robert F. Wagner, speech at public forum on juvenile delinquency, September 24, 1957, Folder 3, Box 060043W, RFW, LGW online.

49. "City Is Expanding its Street Clubs," NYT, September 23, 1957; "Mayor Mobilizes Full City Attack on Teen Violence," NYT, September 7, 1957; "Youth Board Sifts Work Camp Plans," NYT, August 28, 1957; "Wagner Orders Teen Crime Fight," NYT, August 27, 1957; Gertrude Samuels, "One Answer to Delinquency: Work Camps," NYT Magazine, September 8, 1957.

50. Robert F. Wagner, speech at the conference on the Church's responsibility in the present juvenile delinquency crisis, October 30, 1959, Folder 35, Box 060083W, RFW, LGW online; and Robert F. Wagner, speech before the Senate Sub-committee on Juvenile Delinquency, March 9, 1961, Folder 22, Box 060046W, RFW, LGW online; City of New York, "Perspectives on Delinquency Prevention," 13, 38, Folder 8.1.080, Box 59, BCSP Papers, BPL.

51. NYCYB, "Teenage Gangs" (1957), BPL. On discourses surrounding black criminality in the early twentieth century, see Khalil Gibran Muhammad, *The Condemnation of Blackness: Race, Crime, and the Making of Modern Urban America* (Cambridge, MA: Harvard University Press, 2010).

52. Robert F. Wagner Jr., remarks at the Fifteenth Anniversary Dinner of the New York City Youth Board, November 15, 1962, Box 060005W, Folder 21, RFW, LGW online.

53. "Another Boy Shot as Teen War Flares," NYAN, November 9, 1957; "Wagner Praises City Youth Board," NYT, October 31, 1957; "New York," NYT, September 6, 1959; Mark A. McCloskey, "State and Municipal Youth Authorities (Or Commissions) and Their Role in Juvenile Delinquency Prevention," *Journal of Negro Education* 28:3 (Summer 1959), 341; NYCYB, "Teenage Gangs" (1957), BPL.

54. City of New York, "Perspectives on Delinquency Prevention," BPL; Robert F. Wagner Jr., press release, April 13, 1948, Folder 36, Box 060039W, RFW, LGW online.

55. "Mayor Mobilizes Full City Attack on Teen Violence," NYT, September 7, 1957; "Joint Action by Agencies Urged in Teen-Crime Report to Mayor," NYT, October 15, 1957; "Map Full-Scale Drive on Teenage Hoodlums," NYAN, February 1, 1958.

56. The New York Welfare Council would later become the Welfare and Health Council of New York City and subsequently the Community Council of Greater New York. In 1957, when the Greater New York Fund stipulated that its monies no longer be used by the Community Council to fund borough agencies, the Brooklyn Council was forced to cease operations (as were its sister organizations in Queens, the Bronx, and Staten Island). "Community Council's Aid Urged to Save Borough Welfare Units," NYT, January 1, 1957.

57. See Andrew Morris, "The Voluntary Sector's War on Poverty," *Journal of Policy History* 16:4 (2004), 275–305; and Eleanor L. Brilliant, "Community Planning and Community Problem Solving: Past, Present, and Future," *Social Service Review* 60:4 (June 1986), 568–589.

2. Mobilizing the Forces

Epigraph: J. Archie Hargraves, "Recommendation for a People's Program to Combat Juvenile Delinquency," [1956], Folder 5.3.003, Box 28, Papers of the Brooklyn Council for Social Planning (BCSP), Brooklyn Public Library Brooklyn Collection (BPL).

1. "Map Full-Scale Drive on Teenage Hoodlums," *New York Amsterdam News (NYAN)*, February 1, 1958; "$50,000 Earmarked by Youth Board to Fight Bedford-Stuyvesant Gang Menace," NYAN, March 24, 1951. See also Eric C. Schneider, *Vampires, Dragons, and Egyptian Kings: Youth Gangs in Postwar New York* (Princeton, NJ: Princeton University Press, 1999); and Harrison Salisbury, *The Shook-Up Generation* (New York: Harper and Row, 1958).

2. "Coincidence Seen in Youth Violence," *New York Times (NYT)*, January 30, 1958; "Map Full-Scale Drive on Teenage Hoodlums," NYAN, February 1, 1958.

3. Brooklyn Council for Social Planning, "Welcome to Brooklyn: Handbook for New Workers" (1955 edition), 7, Folder 9.1.032, Box 66, BCSP, BPL.

4. Suleiman Osman, *The Invention of Brownstone Brooklyn: Gentrification and the Search for Authenticity in Postwar New York* (New York: Oxford University Press, 2011), 23. See also Craig Steven Wilder, *A Covenant with Color: Race and Social Power in Brooklyn* (New York: Columbia University Press, 2000).

5. "Mayor Denounced by Jury for Crime in Brooklyn Area," *NYT*, November 16, 1943; "Our Negro Neighbors," *Brooklyn Eagle (BE)*, June 29, 1938. On the naming of Bedford-Stuyvesant, see Harold X. Connolly, "Bedford-Stuyvesant," in Charlene Claye Van Derzee, ed., *An Introduction to the Black Contribution to the Development of Brooklyn* (Brooklyn: New Muse Community Museum of Brooklyn, 1977), 91–97; and Harold X. Connolly, *A Ghetto Grows in Brooklyn* (New York: New York University Press, 1977).

6. "Negroes Getting Bigger Political Plums as Party Leaders Realize Their Power," *BE*, August 6, 1955; Bedford-Stuyvesant Youth in Action (BSYIA), "The Bedford-Stuyvesant Proposal," August 20, 1964, Don Watkins Papers (DWP); BSYIA, "Planned Intervention to Halt and Reverse the Vicious Cycle," March 11, 1965, DWP; Proceedings of CBCC Conference, December 10, 1966, Bedford-Stuyvesant Restoration Corporation Oral History Project (BSRCOH), Brooklyn Historical Society (BHS); Center for Urban Education, "Community Attitudes in Bedford-Stuyvesant: An Area Study" (Summer 1967), 4, DWP.

7. Connolly, *A Ghetto Grows in Brooklyn*, 5; Joan Bacchus Maynard and Craig Steven Wilder, "Weeksville," in Kenneth T. Jackson, ed., *The Encyclopedia of New York City* (New Haven, CT: Yale University Press, 2010), 1392; Joan Maynard, "Weeksville Revisited," in Van Derzee, *Black Contribution to the Development of Brooklyn*, 85–89. On Weeksville, see Judith Wellman, *Brooklyn's Promised Land: The Free Black Community of Weeksville, New York* (New York: New York University Press, 2014).

8. Osman, *The Invention of Brownstone Brooklyn*, 28; Edwin G. Burrows and Mike Wallace, *Gotham: A History of New York City to 1898* (New York: Oxford University Press, 1999), 972–973. On urban growth in the nineteenth century, see Kenneth T. Jackson, *Crabgrass Frontier: The Suburbanization of the United States* (New York: Oxford University Press, 1985), Chap. 2.

9. "Wealthy Negro Citizens," *NYT*, July 14, 1895; Connolly, "Bedford-Stuyvesant." See Wilder, *A Covenant with Color*, Chaps. 6–7.

10. BCSP, Summary of Conference on Our Expanding Negro Population, April 6, 1940, 1, Folder 9.1.026, Box 66, BCSP Papers, BPL; Anna Arnold Hedgeman, *The Trumpet Sounds: A Memoir of Negro Leadership* (New York: Holt, Rinehart

and Winston, 1964), 74–75, 125–126. On the Great Migration, see Isabel
Wilkerson, *The Warmth of Other Suns: The Epic Story of America's Great Migration* (New York: Vintage, 2010).

11. Connolly, *A Ghetto Grows in Brooklyn*, Chap. 2; Osman, *The Invention of Brownstone Brooklyn*, Chap. 1.

12. "200 Brooklyn Citizens Plan Housing Fight," NYAN, August 13, 1938; "Brooklyn Federation Ready to Demand Immediate Clearance of Local Slums," NYAN, September 3, 1938; BCSP, Summary of Conference on Our Expanding Negro Population, 3, BPL.

13. BCSP, "Growing Up in Brooklyn: Report of Brooklyn's Little White House Conference on Children and Youth" (1951), Folder 3.2.016, Box 16, BCSP Papers, BPL. See also Wilder, *A Covenant with Color*.

14. BCSP, "Welcome to Brooklyn: Handbook for New Workers" (1954 edition), 8–9, Folder 9.1.031, Box 66, BCSP Papers, BPL; Kenneth T. Jackson, "The Arsenal of Democracy," essay accompanying *WWII & NYC* (New York Historical Society exhibition, 2012).

15. BCSP, "Welcome to Brooklyn" (1954), 8–9, BPL.

16. Martha Biondi, *To Stand and Fight: The Struggle for Civil Rights in Postwar New York City* (Cambridge, MA: Harvard University Press, 2003), 21–22.

17. The number of Puerto Ricans living in New York City rose from 61,000 in 1940 to 817,712, or 10 percent of the city's total population, three decades later. See Carmen T. Whalen, "Colonialism, Citizenship, and the Making of the Puerto Rican Diaspora: An Introduction," in Carmen T. Whalen and Víctor Vázquez-Hernández, eds., *The Puerto Rican Diaspora: Historical Perspectives* (Philadelphia: Temple University Press, 2008), 3. On workplace discrimination in postwar Brooklyn, see Wilder, *A Covenant with Color*, Chap. 7.

18. It is worth noting that census figures in this era generally classified Puerto Ricans as "white."

19. Wilder, *A Covenant with Color*, 212; Hamill, "Brooklyn: The Sane Alternative," *New York*, July 14, 1969.

20. Wilder, *A Covenant with Color*, 185–205; Ta-Nehisi Coates, "The Case for Reparations," *The Atlantic* (June 2014). On redlining, see Jackson, *Crabgrass Frontier*, Chap. 11. On white flight and resistance to black neighbors, see Arnold R. Hirsch, *Making the Second Ghetto: Race and Housing in Chicago, 1940–1960* (New York: Cambridge University Press, 1983); Thomas J. Sugrue, *The Origins of the Urban Crisis: Race and Inequality in Postwar Detroit* (Princeton, NJ: Princeton University Press, 1996); Becky M. Nicolaides, *My Blue Heaven: Life and Politics in the Working-Class Suburbs of Los Angeles, 1920–1965* (Chicago: University of Chicago Press, 2002); and Jonathan Rieder, *Canarsie: The Jews and Italians of Brooklyn Against Liberalism* (Cambridge: Harvard University Press, 1985).

21. Hospital Council of Greater New York, "Hospital Needs of the Bedford-Stuyvesant Area in Brooklyn" (December 1953), Folder 5.3.008, Box 28, BCSP Papers, BPL. On poverty statistics, see Gordon M. Fisher, "An Overview of (Unofficial) Poverty Lines in the United States from 1904 to 1965" (revised version, 1997), posted on www.census.gov.

22. "Big Season Flourishes with Elegant Events," NYAN, January 12, 1957; "Navy Ball Opens Social Season," NYAN, October 15, 1960; " 'Deep Are the Roots' in Brooklyn Society," NYAN, March 28, 1959; "2,000 at 40th Annual Dance of Comus Club," NYAN, January 11, 1964; "How the Comus Club Became Brooklyn's Snootiest," NYAN, January 12, 1963. See also Connolly, *A Ghetto Grows in Brooklyn.*

23. Gardner C. Taylor, Oral History interview, undated, National Visionary Leadership Project, www.visionaryproject.org/taylorgardner; Wilhelmena Rhodes Kelly, *Images of America: Bedford-Stuyvesant* (Charleston, SC: Arcadia, 2007), 100, 108; "Brooklyn Banker Defends Bedford Stuyvesant Area," NYAN, December 9, 1961.

24. Robin D. G. Kelley, "House Negroes on the Loose: Malcolm X and the Black Bourgeoisie," *Callaloo* 21:2 (Spring 1998), 421. On traditions of "racial uplift" among African Americans, see Karen Ferguson, *Black Politics in New Deal Atlanta* (Chapel Hill: University of North Carolina Press, 2002); Evelyn Brooks Higginbotham, *Righteous Discontent: The Women's Movement in the Black Baptist Church, 1880–1920* (Cambridge, MA: Harvard University Press, 1993); and Kevin K. Gaines, *Uplifting the Race: Black Leadership, Politics, and Culture in the Twentieth Century* (Chapel Hill: University of North Carolina Press, 1996). See also E. Franklin Frazier, *Black Bourgeoisie: The Rise of a New Middle Class in the United States* (Collier Books, 1962).

25. Paule Marshall, "Rising Islanders of Bed-Stuy," NYT *Magazine*, November 3, 1985; Paule Marshall, "Black Immigrant Women in Brown Girl Brownstones," in Constance R. Sutton and Elsa M. Chaney, eds., *Caribbean Life in New York City: Sociocultural Dimension* (New York: Center for Migration Studies, 1987), 89; Reuel R. Rogers, *Afro-Caribbean Immigrants, African Americans, and the Politics of Incorporation* (Cambridge: Cambridge University Press, 2006), 57–58; F. Donnie Forde, *Caribbean Americans in New York City, 1895–1975* (Charleston, SC: Arcadia, 2002), 79; Mary H. Manoni, *Bedford-Stuyvesant: The Anatomy of a Central City Community* (New York: Quadrangle, 1973), 16.

26. Shirley Chisholm, *Unbought and Unbossed* (Boston: Houghton Mifflin, 1970), 14–15.

27. Chisholm, *Unbought and Unbossed*, 4–5, 18; Constance R. Sutton and Susan R. Makiesky-Barrow, "Migration and West Indian Racial and Ethnic Consciousness," in Constance R. Sutton and Elsa M. Chaney, eds., *Caribbean Life in New York City: Sociocultural Dimension* (New York: Center for

Migration Studies, 1987), 94–95, 104–105; Forde, *Caribbean Americans in New York City*, 33. See also Yndia S. Lorick-Wilmot, *Creating Black Caribbean Ethnic Identity* (El Paso, TX: LFP Scholarly Publishing, 2010).

28. Calvin B. Holder, "The Rise of the West Indian Politician in New York City, 1900–1952," *Afro-Americans in New York Life and History* 4:1 (January 1980), 45. For more on interethnic political conflicts within black Brooklyn, see Evrick Brown, "Fried Chicken or Ox Tail: An Examination of Afro-Caribbean and African-American Conflict in New York City" (PhD thesis, SUNY-Albany, 2005). See also Jim Sleeper, *The Closest of Strangers: Liberalism and the Politics of Race in New York* (New York: Norton, 1990), 57–60.

29. By the mid-1970s, Paragon had around 9,000 members and close to $7 million in assets. Yet these numbers masked its decline, a process accelerated by the growing clout of the Bedford-Stuyvesant Restoration Corporation and federal legislation like the Civil Rights Act of 1968 and the Community Reinvestment Act of 1977, which provided African Americans with increasing access to lines of credit. In 1981, Paragon closed its doors in ignominious fashion, with a team of federal examiners packing its records into cardboard boxes and shipping them to Boston for examination by officers of the National Credit Union Administration. Thanks to the credit-union deposit-insurance program passed in 1970, Paragon's 6,000 shareholders saw their investments up to $100,000 refunded. See Beverly Jensen, "Credit Unions: The Story of Do-It-Yourself Banking," *Black Enterprise* (October 1976), 47–53, 87–91; Stephen Gayle, "Paragon Hits Bottom," *Black Enterprise* (March 1981), 19; C. Gerald Fraser, "The 'Union' Immigrants Built," *Black Enterprise* (April 1980), 31; "Paragon Credit Union Honors 12 Founders at Achievement Dinner," *NYAN*, April 26, 1952; "Eyes on Brooklyn," *New York Age*, June 21, 1958; "Paragon Marks 25th Yr.," *NYAN*, July 25, 1964; and Clyde Atwell, *A Passion to Survive: A Credit Union Grows in Brooklyn* (New York: Pageant-Poseidon Press, 1976).

30. Bedford-Stuyvesant Development and Services Corporation (D&S), Minutes of the Board of Directors, January 12, 1967, "Planning 1966–1967, Vol. 1," Box 44, Burke Marshall Papers, John F. Kennedy Library (JFKL); Adelaide Sanford, interview with Laurie Cumbo, January 24, 2008, BSRCOH, BHS. The exploitative real-estate transactions that accompanied Bedford-Stuyvesant's transformation into a majority-black neighborhood are described in Wilder, *A Covenant with Color*, Chap. 9.

31. Marshall, "Rising Islanders of Bed-Stuy"; Raymond & May Associates, "Vest Pocket Housing in Bedford-Stuyvesant: A Summary Report to the Community and City on Some of the First Steps in New York's Model Cities Program" (1968), Avery Architectural & Fine Arts Library, Columbia University; Pratt Institute Planning Department, "Stuyvesant Heights: A Good Neighborhood in Need of Help" (1965), Pratt Center for Community Development online.

32. Ronald Shiffman, "Strategy for a Coordinated Social and Physical Renewal Program: Bedford-Stuyvesant" (unpublished draft, 1966), courtesy of New York State Library; "Restoration's Mortgage Pool Totals 100 Million Dollars," *Restoration* Newsletter, October 1969, Papers of the Bedford-Stuyvesant Restoration Corporation (BSRC), Folder 4, BPL; Michael Harrington, "The South Bronx Shall Rise Again," *New York*, April 3, 1978.

33. Ford Foundation (R. B. Goldmann, author), "Performance in Black and White: An Appraisal of the Development and Record of the Bedford-Stuyvesant Restoration and Development and Services Corporations" (February 1969), Box 1, Ford Foundation Papers, JFKL.

34. "'Terrorism' Is Laid to Brooklyn Group," *NYT*, December 17, 1937; "Candidate for Assembly Reveals Odd Information," *NYAN*, September 17, 1938. According to Thomas R. Jones, his father organized a block association on Hancock Street in 1935 or 1936. See Thomas R. Jones, interview with James Briggs Murray, February 10, 1990, Community Development Corporation Oral History Project, New York Public Library, Schomburg Center for Research in Black Culture.

35. "Brooklyn's Block Program Progresses," *NYAN*, October 2, 1948; "Stuyvesant's 'Clean-Up' Drive," *NYAN*, February 19, 1949; "'Beautify Your Block' Is Aim of Boro Associations," *NYAN*, September 25, 1948; "Banker Defends Bedford Stuyvesant Area," *NYAN*, December 9, 1961.

36. "Merger of Groups in Bedford Area Planned," *NYAN*, May 20, 1939; "Bedford-Stuyvesant Council Backbone of the Community," *NYAN*, July 16, 1960; "Council Plans for Annual Cleanup Drive," *NYAN*, August 20, 1955; "Salute Stuyford Council," *NYAN*, November 26, 1955; Thomas R. Jones, interview with Jeffrey Gerson, June 10, 1993, courtesy of LGW; "Banker Defends Bedford Stuyvesant Area," *NYAN*, December 9, 1961.

37. Steven Gregory, "The Changing Significance of Race and Class in an African-American Community," *American Ethnologist* 19:2 (May 1992), 260; N. D. B. Connolly, *A World More Concrete: Real Estate and the Remaking of Jim Crow South Florida* (Chicago: University of Chicago Press, 2014), 7.

38. On the "long" civil rights movement in the North, see Jeanne F. Theoharis and Komozi Woodward, eds., *Freedom North: Black Freedom Struggles Outside the South, 1940–1980* (New York: Palgrave Macmillan, 2003), 145–173; Thomas J. Sugrue, "Affirmative Action from Below: Civil Rights, the Building Trades, and the Politics of Racial Equality in the Urban North, 1945–1969," *Journal of American History* 91:1 (June 2004); Thomas J. Sugrue, *Sweet Land of Liberty: The Forgotten Struggle for Civil Rights in the North* (New York: Random House, 2008); and Jacquelyn Dowd Hall, "The Long Civil Rights Movement and the Political Uses of the Past," *Journal of American History* 91:4 (March 2004), 1233–1263.

39. "Signed on the Last Day," *New York Tribune*, June 16, 1895; "To Influence Colored Voters," *NYT*, January 13, 1896. See also Evan Friss, "Blacks, Jews, and Civil Rights Law in New York, 1895–1913," *Journal of American Ethnic History* 24:4 (Summer 2005), 70–99.

40. "Discrimination," *NYAN*, December 30, 1931; "Gains Ruling Over Municipal Judge's Race Ban Decision," *NYAN*, June 4, 1930; "A Just Decision," *NYAN*, June 11, 1930; "Negro Congress Fights Coney Island Jim Crow," *NYAN*, August 16, 1941; "School-Zoning Protest Confab Stirs Parents in Uptown Area," *NYAN*, August 30, 1941; "School Conditions Assailed," *NYAN*, February 3, 1945; "First Lady Visits Boro," *NYAN*, December 18, 1943; "Accuse School Board of Bias," *NYAN*, October 20, 1945. On civil-rights struggles in 1930s and 1940s New York City, see Connolly, *A Ghetto Grows in Brooklyn*; and Martha Biondi, *To Stand and Fight: The Struggle for Civil Rights in Postwar New York City* (Cambridge, MA: Harvard University Press, 2003).

41. "Brutality Inquiry by Council Asked," *NYT*, February 25, 1953; "Rally to Stop Brutality Is Held by NAACP," *NYAN*, April 9, 1949; "Stuyford Group Protests Police Brutality Here," *NYAN*, September 11, 1948.

42. Bed-Stuy's rate of fifty-two infant deaths per one thousand in the late 1950s compares to the rates in countries like Sudan and Swaziland in 2015. See Central Intelligence Agency, *The World Factbook 2015*, accessed online at www .cia.gov/library/publications/the-world-factbook/index.html.

43. "City Budget Held to Neglect Young," *NYT*, April 12, 1955; Rev. B. J. Lowry, memo, October 6, 1955, Folder 5.3.006, Box 28, BCSP Papers, BPL.

44. "A New Leader," *NYAN*, March 24, 1956; "Trade with Pride," *NYAN*, May 5, 1956.

45. "Rights Group Tells of Bias Battles," *NYAN*, April 25, 1959. On the peculiarities of black protest in postwar New York City, see Martha Biondi, "How New York Changes the Story of the Civil Rights Movement," *Afro-Americans in New York Life and History* 31:2 (July 2007), 15–31.

46. Ford Foundation/Goldmann, "Performance in Black and White," 6, JFKL.

47. On interethnic relations within the Brooklyn Democratic Party, see Jeffrey Nathan Gerson, "Building the Brooklyn Machine: Irish, Jewish and Black Political Succession in Central Brooklyn, 1919–1964" (PhD thesis, City University of New York, 1990).

48. Chisholm, *Unbought and Unbossed*, 30.

49. Biondi, *To Stand and Fight*, 208; Wallace S. Sayre and Herbert Kaufman, *Governing New York City: Politics in the Metropolis* (New York: Norton, 1965; first edition 1960); J. Phillip Thompson, *Double Trouble: Black Mayors, Black Communities, and the Call for a Deep Democracy* (Cary, NC: Oxford University Press, 2005), 177.

50. Julie A. Gallagher, *Black Women and Politics in New York City* (Urbana: University of Illinois Press, 2012), 78–80; "New Stuyford Councilman Has Boro

Respect," NYAN, December 14, 1957. The concept of the "sub-machine" is borrowed from John Louis Flateau, "Black Brooklyn: The Politics of Ethnicity, Class, and Gender" (PhD thesis, City University of New York, 2005). See also Gerson, "Building the Brooklyn Machine"; and Jeffrey Gerson, "Bertram L. Baker, the United Action Democratic Association, and the First Black Democratic Succession in Brooklyn, 1933–1954," *Afro-Americans in New York Life and History* 16:2 (July 1992), 17–46.

51. "Dean of Black Brooklyn Politics a Power at 85," NYT, October 10, 1982; "Negroes Gaining in Political Power," BE, August 6, 1954; Gallagher, *Black Women and Politics*, 92–93. See also Connolly, *A Ghetto Grows in Brooklyn*; Chris McNickle, *To Be Mayor of New York: Ethnic Politics in the City* (New York: Columbia University Press, 1993); Flateau, "Black Brooklyn"; and Gerson, "Building the Brooklyn Machine."

52. "New Nazarene Minister Installed Last Sunday," *New York Age*, June 23, 1956; William W. Ellis, *White Ethics and Black Power: The Emergence of the West Side Organization* (Chicago: Aldine, 1969), 94–96; J. Archie Hargraves, *Stop Pussyfooting through a Revolution: Some Churches That Did* (New York: Stewardship Council of the United Church of Christ, 1963); "Do Christians Oppose the Way of Violence?" *New York Age*, June 20, 1959. In later years, Hargraves would gain national prominence as a founder of the Urban Training Center in Chicago and as president of Shaw University.

53. Hargraves, *Stop Pussyfooting through a Revolution*; "Church Begins New Slum Plan on N.Y.'s Sidewalks," *Chicago Defender*, May 2, 1959.

54. Bedford-Stuyvesant Area Project, docket for meeting on pilot project, February 25, 1957, Sydney J. Moshette Jr. Papers (SJMP); "Church Begins New Slum Plan on N.Y.'s Sidewalks," *Chicago Defender*, May 2, 1959.

55. J. Archie Hargraves, "Recommendation for a People's Program to Combat Juvenile Delinquency," [1956]; [J. Archie Hargraves], "We Have Heard the Discussion," [1956]; J. Archie Hargraves, memo, November 9, 1956, all in Folder 5.3.003, Box 28, BCSP Papers, BPL.

56. "Stuyford Leaders Blast Papers, Jury Foreman, for 'Vicious' Stories," NYAN, February 8, 1958.

57. Hargraves, "Recommendation for a People's Program," BPL.

58. On Pinkston and the connections between the Youth Board and CBCC, see Ernest Quimby, "Black Political Development in Bedford-Stuyvesant as Represented in the Origin and Role of the Bedford-Stuyvesant Restoration Corporation" (PhD thesis, City University of New York, 1977), 122–134. Quimby argues that because CBCC emerged from the Youth Board, it was not a grassroots organization and symbolized the community's "dependency" on outside power structures.

59. Elsie Richardson, interview with the author, June 5, 2011; "New School Aims at Art for All," NYAN, May 30, 1959; "It's Greek to Me!" NYAN, August 3, 1957; "Pinkston Named to Head YIA," NYAN, December 10, 1966.

60. "Rheingold Salutes a Good Neighbor" advertisement in *Ebony* (June 1961), 11; "Charles A. Ward New League Head," *Chicago Defender*, March 24, 1956.

61. "Rheingold Salutes a Good Neighbor" advertisement.

62. "Map Full-Scale Drive on Teenage Hoodlums," NYAN, February 1, 1958; "Steering Unit Takes Name," NYAN, March 22, 1958; CBCC, Organizational Profile [1962], SJMP; CBCC, roster of attendance at the board meeting of November 1, 1962, SJMP; Elsie Richardson, interview with the author, June 5, 2011.

63. James E. McCarthy, for instance, was a Youth Board official who in 1950 worked alongside the Brooklyn Council for Social Planning to design the blueprints for the original Brooklyn detached-worker program. He would go on to lead the Lower East Side's Mobilization for Youth experiment during its formative years. Robert Cooper, a one-time director of street-club workers for the Youth Board, in 1965 became executive director of Harlem's Associated Community Teams group. See NYCYB, Council of Social and Athletic Clubs Annual Review, 1951–1952, Folder 6.1.044, Box 37, BCSP Papers, BPL; Materials relating to the Advisory Committee for the Brooklyn Detached Worker Project, 1950–1951, Folder 6.1.043, BCSP Papers, BPL; "City Widens Drive on Street Gangs," NYT, November 10, 1950.

64. "Stuyford Leaders Blast Papers, Jury Foreman, for 'Vicious' Stories," NYAN, February 8, 1958.

65. For a different perspective on the black middle class and crime, see Michael Javen Fortner, *Black Silent Majority: The Rockefeller Drug Laws and the Politics of Punishment* (Cambridge, MA: Harvard University Press, 2015).

66. "They Buried Maude B. in Her Beloved Boro," NYAN, June 5, 1976; "Maude Richardson, 82, Dead," NYT, May 31, 1976; "Maude B. Richardson Praised for 30 Years of Civic Work," NYAN, April 28, 1945; "Brooklyn and Queens Personalities," NYAN, April 13, 1940; "Precinct Council Will Open Center," NYAN, March 25, 1944; Julie Gallagher, "Building a More Just Society, One Struggle at a Time: Grassroots Activists in New York City, 1940–1960," prepared for delivery at the 2009 Congress of the Latin American Studies Association, Rio de Janeiro, Brazil, June 11–14, 2009.

67. Julie A. Gallagher, "Women of Action, in Action: The New Politics of Black Women in New York City, 1944–1972" (Doctoral dissertation, University of Massachusetts at Amherst, 2003), 7, 17; Ford Foundation/Goldmann, "Performance in Black and White," 6, JFKL.

68. "Volunteer Youth Aides Begin Training Program," NYAN, February 15, 1958; "Achievement Awards Earmarked for 31," NYAN, April 12, 1958; "Project Will Aid Youths in Brooklyn," *New York Age*, July 26, 1958; "New Youth Program," *New York Recorder*, August 9, 1958; "Brainy Teenagers Open 3-year Civic Program," NYAN, July 12, 1958.

69. "Operation Teens Rapidly Nearing Goal for Summer," NYAN, July 26, 1958; "A Good Project," NYAN, February 28, 1959; "Teens-In-Industry Is a Successful Project," NYAN, October 24, 1959; "Rheingold 'Good Neighbor' Aids Bklyn Teens-In-Industry," NYAN, July 29, 1961; "Rheingold Salutes a Good Neighbor" advertisement; "Teen Project Gets More $$," NYAN, May 14, 1960; "Seek 100 Jobs for Teenage Students," NYAN, June 11, 1960; Central Brooklyn Coordinating Council, Organizational Profile [1962–1963], SJMP.

70. "Contact Us," NYAN, August 6, 1960; "Teenagers to Get Summer Jobs through Council," *New York Age*, July 19, 1958; "What's Next? By Dr. Robert Palmer," *New York Recorder*, June 9, 1962.

71. "City Director Will Discuss Curbing Slums," NYAN, November 14, 1959.

3. From the Clubhouse to the White House

Epigraph: "Incumbents Allowing Area 'to Deteriorate': Jones," *New York Amsterdam News*, June 16, 1962.

1. Robert F. Wagner Jr., speech before the Advisory Council of the President's Committee on Juvenile Delinquency (PCJD), January 3, 1963, Folder 44, Box 060014W, Robert F. Wagner Jr. Papers (RFW), La Guardia Wagner Archives (LGW) online. The "dual city" concept is borrowed from John Mollenkopf and Manuel Castells, eds., *Dual City: Restructuring New York* (New York: Russell Sage Foundation, 1991).

2. Hugh Heclo has identified a peculiar "sixties civics," which he argues was defined by a seeming paradox: "Americans were taught that so far as the governing system is concerned, one should both expect more and trust less than ever before." See Hugh Heclo, "Sixties Civics," in Sidney M. Milkis and Jerome M. Mileur, eds., *The Great Society and the High Tide of Liberalism* (Amherst: University of Massachusetts Press, 2005), 54.

3. On this dichotomy, see Ira Katznelson, *City Trenches: Urban Politics and the Patterning of Class in the United States* (New York: Pantheon Books, 1981); Marci Reaven, "Citizen Participation in City Planning: New York City, 1945–1975" (PhD thesis, New York University, 2005); and Noel Cazenave, *Impossible Democracy: The Unlikely Success of the War on Poverty Community Action Programs* (Albany: State University of New York Press, 2007).

4. Thomas R. Jones, interview with James Briggs Murray, February 10, 1990, Community Development Corporation Oral History Project (CDCOH), New

York Public Library, Schomburg Center for Research in Black Culture
(NYPL-Sch); Bedford-Stuyvesant Youth in Action (YIA), "The Bedford-
Stuyvesant Proposal," August 20, 1964, Don Watkins Papers (DWP).

5. "Crocuses and City Bloom on 70 Day," *New York Times (NYT)*, March 6, 1961;
   "Weather Reports Throughout the Nation," *NYT*, March 6, 1961.
6. "Youth Gangs, Attorney General Talk," *The Sun*, March 9, 1961; David
   Hackett, quoted in Edward R. Schmitt, *President of the Other America: Robert
   Kennedy and the Politics of Poverty* (Amherst: University of Massachusetts
   Press, 2010), 69.
7. Delinquency was linked to a generalized rise in crime: arrests of adults for
   "major crimes" in New York doubled during the 1950s. See Juvenile Delin-
   quency Evaluation Project of the City of New York, dir. Robert M. MacIver,
   "Delinquency in the Great City" (July 1961).
8. Robert F. Wagner Jr., speech before the Senate Subcommittee on Juvenile
   Delinquency, March 9, 1961, Folder 22, Box 06046W, RFW, LGW online;
   "City's Gang Wars Ascribed to Girls," *NYT*, March 10, 1961.
9. Robert F. Wagner, speech at Brandeis University, November 16, 1965, Folder 7,
   Box 060249, RFW, LGW online.
10. John F. Kennedy, Executive Order 10940, establishing the President's
    Committee on Juvenile Delinquency and Youth Crime, May 11, 1961, John F.
    Kennedy Presidential Library (JFKL) online; Allen J. Matusow, *The Unrav-
    eling of America: A History of Liberalism in the 1960s* (New York: Harper and
    Row, 1984), 107–108.
11. On the delinquency program and its antecedents, see, among others, Alice
    O'Connor, *Poverty Knowledge: Social Science, Social Policy, and the Poor in
    Twentieth-Century U.S. History* (Princeton, NJ: Princeton University Press,
    2001); Noel A. Cazenave, "Chicago Influences on the War on Poverty," in
    Martin V. Melosi, ed., *Urban Public Policy: Historical Modes and Methods*
    (University Park, PA: Pennsylvania State University, 1993), 52–68; and Joseph
    H. Helfgot, *Professional Reforming: Mobilization for Youth and the Failure of
    Social Science* (Lexington, MA: Lexington Books, 1981). For an insider's look at
    how the Ford Foundation's work came to influence Great Society programs,
    see Mitchell Sviridoff, ed., *Inventing Community Renewal: The Trials and
    Errors that Shaped the Modern Community Development Corporation* (New
    York: Community Development Research Center, 2004), especially the
    transcripts of Sviridoff's reminiscences.
12. PCJD, Criteria for Evaluating Applications for Grants to Conduct Demonstra-
    tion Action Projects (draft), May 1, 1963, "Key Documents, 1961–1965," Box 4,
    Daniel Knapp Papers, JFKL. On the Gray Areas program, see Alice O'Connor,
    "Community Action, Urban Reform, and the Fight against Poverty: The Ford
    Foundation's Gray Areas Program," *Journal of Urban History* 22:5 (July 1996),

586–625; and Robert Halpern, *Rebuilding the Inner City: A History of Neighborhood Initiatives to Address Poverty in the United States* (New York: Columbia University Press, 1995), Chap. 3. On Ford's efforts throughout the 1960s, see Karen Ferguson, *Top Down: The Ford Foundation, Black Power, and the Reinvention of Racial Liberalism* (Philadelphia: University of Pennsylvania Press, 2013).

13. Michael L. Gillette, *Launching the War on Poverty: An Oral History* (New York: Twayne Books, 1996), 85; Matusow, *The Unraveling of America*, 107–108; Schmitt, *President of the Other America*, 71–72.

14. Robert F. Kennedy, remarks to the Citizens Advisory Council of the PCJD, September 21, 1962, "President's Committee File, Undated," Box 4, Richardson White Papers, JFKL.

15. Grants Awarded Under P. L. 87–274, December 31, 1963, "10/63–12/63 and undated," Box 5, Daniel Knapp Papers, JFKL; Juvenile Delinquency Evaluation Project, "The Planning of Delinquency Prevention and Control" (February 1961), Folder 9, Box 060300, RFW, LGW online; Wagner, speech before the Advisory Council of the PCJD, January 3, 1963, LGW online.

16. Judith Greene and Kevin Pranis, "Gang Wars: The Failure of Enforcement Tactics and the Need for Effective Public Safety Strategies," Justice Policy Institute (July 2007), 16. On Mobilization for Youth, see Marris and Rein, *Dilemmas of Social Reform*; Cazenave, *Impossible Democracy*, esp. Chap 1; and Sonia Lee and Andre Diaz, "'I Was the One Percenter': Manny Diaz and the Beginnings of a Black–Puerto Rican Coalition," *Journal of American Ethnic History* 26:3 (2007), 52–80.

17. Cloward quoted in Cazenave, *Impossible Democracy*, 26.

18. O'Connor, *Poverty Knowledge*, 126–127; Lillian B. Rubin, "Maximum Feasible Participation: The Origins, Implications, and Present Status," *Annals of the American Academy of Political and Social Science* 385 (September 1969), 8–9. See also Cazenave, *Impossible Democracy*, Chap. 2.

19. Richard A. Cloward and Lloyd E. Ohlin, *Delinquency and Opportunity: A Theory of Delinquent Gangs* (Glencoe, IL: Free Press, 1960), 78; Mobilization for Youth, "A Proposal for the Prevention and Control of Delinquency by Expanding Opportunities," second edition (August 1962), 45.

20. "War on Youth Crime to Start Downtown," *NYT*, February 2, 1959; Juvenile Delinquency Evaluation Project, "The Planning of Delinquency Prevention and Control" (February 1961), LGW online.

21. "Mobilization for Youth," *NYT*, December 16, 1959; "U.S. to Aid Plan for Youths Here," *NYT*, December 16, 1959; "Agency to Conduct Youth Project," *NYT*, June 28, 1961; "U.S. and City Open 12.6-Million War on Delinquency," *NYT*, June 1, 1962; Greene and Pranis, "Gang Wars," 16. See also Mobilization for Youth, "A Proposal for the Prevention and Control," 1962.

22. Robert F. Kennedy, remarks to the Citizens Advisory Council of the PCJD, September 21, 1962, JFKL; Minutes of the Citizens Advisory Council of the PCJD, January 3–4, 1963, Folder 1, Box 1, Eleanor Charwat Personal Papers, JFKL; Leonard W. Stern to Richardson White, May 21, 1969, "Comments on Chapters," Box 1, Richardson White Papers, JFKL.

23. Gerald Markowitz and David Rosner argue that Clark's work with the Northside clinic during the 1950s in fact anticipated the opportunity theory put forth by Cloward and Ohlin. Gerald Markowitz and David Rosner, *Children, Race, and Power: Kenneth and Mamie Clark's Northside Center* (Charlottesville: The University Press of Virginia, 1996), 187–188. See Chapter 4 of the current volume for more about Clark's work in Harlem.

24. Address by Lloyd Ohlin, April 20, 1966, "Office of Juvenile Delinquency, 4/68," Box 3, Richardson White Papers, JFKL.

25. "Gang Wars Upset Area in Brooklyn," *NYT*, May 2, 1961; Gangland Summit," *New York Amsterdam News (NYAN)*, May 27, 1961; "City Opens Drive on Youth Crime," *NYT*, July 27, 1961.

26. "Powell Supporting Levitt; Assails Policies of Mayor," *NYT*, July 28, 1961; "City Opens Drive on Youth Crime," *NYT*, July 27, 1961"; Mayor Acts to Curb Teenage Violence!" *NYAN*, July 29, 1961; "The Right Way," *NYAN*, July 29, 1961.

27. "Youth Board Probe," *NYAN*, September 8, 1962; "Ignoring an Area," *NYAN*, August 11, 1962.

28. "Say Each Looks Out for Himself Alone," *NYAN*, September 22, 1962; "Stuyvesant Leaders Score City Planning Officials," *NYAN*, September 29, 1962.

29. "Clarion Call," *NYAN*, October 13, 1962; "Say Commission Moves Is Step in Right Direction," *NYAN*, October 6, 1962.

30. Minutes of the CBCC meeting, December 5, 1962, Sydney J. Moshette Jr. Papers (SJMP); "Stuyvesant Leaders Score City Planning Officials, *NYAN*, September 29, 1962.

31. Elsie Richardson, interview with Deborah Jones, January 22, 2008, Bedford-Stuyvesant Restoration Corporation Oral History Project (BSRCOH), Brooklyn Historical Society (BHS); Ronald Shiffman, interview with Sady Sullivan, February 4, 2008, BSRCOH, BHS.

32. CBCC, Roster of Attendance for the Bedford-Stuyvesant Leadership Meeting, November 1, 1962, SJMP; CBCC, Membership mailing list [1962], SJMP.

33. CBCC, Minutes of the Bedford-Stuyvesant Leadership Meeting, November 1, 1962, SJMP; CBCC, Roster of Attendance, November 1, 1962, SJMP; "'Deep Are the Roots' in Brooklyn Society," *NYAN*, March 28, 1959; "Navy Ball Opens Social Season," *NYAN*, October 15, 1960; "2,000 at 40th Annual Dance of Comus Club," *NYAN*, January 11, 1964; "Pinkston Promoted," *NYAN*,

December 15, 1962; "Say Commission Move Is Step in Right Direction,"
NYAN, October 6, 1962; "Council Elects Officers," NYAN, November 10, 1962.

34. Susan Brownmiller, "This Is Fighting Shirley Chisholm," *NYT Magazine*,
April 13, 1969; Julie Gallagher, "Waging 'The Good Fight': The Political
Career of Shirley Chisholm, 1953–1982," *Journal of African American
History* (June 22, 2007), 394–395; "King's Diary," NYAN, December 5, 1959;
"First Brooklyn Negro Woman Running for the Assembly," NYAN, May 9,
1964; Joshua Guild, "To Make That Someday Come: Shirley Chisholm's
Radical Politics of Possibility," in Dayo F. Gore, Jeanne Theoharis, and
Komozi Woodard, eds., *Want to Start a Revolution? Radical Women in the
Black Freedom Struggle* (New York: New York University Press, 2009),
258–280.

35. Brownmiller, "This Is Fighting Shirley Chisholm"; Shirley Chisholm,
Unbought and Unbossed (Boston: Houghton Mifflin, 1970); "The Lady Is Also
a First," NYAN, November 7, 1964.

36. "Letter of the Week," NYAN, December 5, 1964; Gallagher, "Waging 'The
Good Fight,'" 395–397; "Socially Yours by Glenora Watkins," *New York
Recorder*, August 10, 1963; CBCC, Constitution and By-Laws, endorsed
December 5, 1962, SJMP.

37. CBCC, Organizational Profile [1962], SJMP.

38. CBCC, Program Committee reports, December 5, 1962 and January 24, 1963,
SJMP; Sydney J. Moshette Jr. interview with the author, June 8, 2011; CBCC,
"The Reporter: The Eyes and Ears of the Community" (December 1962),
SJMP; "Council to Act on Boro Problems," NYAN, February 2, 1963.

39. An alternate interpretation of the ferment of 1960s New York, offered by Robert
Pecorella, argues that community-based movements (which Pecorella calls
"postreform politics") emerged as a direct reaction to the kinds of "reform
politics" practiced by the city administration. Whereas the reformers emphasized "professional administration of government" on a citywide basis, the
advocates of postreform politics stressed citizen participation and took
neighborhoods as their unit of analysis. See Robert Pecorella, *Community
Power in a Postreform City: Politics in New York City* (Armonk, NY: M. E.
Sharpe, 1994), Chap. 3.

40. Herbert H. Lehman, speech, July 9, 1961, Folder 23, Box 060300, RFW, LGW
online; Robert F. Wagner Jr., speech to the Tammany Society Dinner, July 1,
1954, Folder 20, Box 060071W, RFW, LGW online; Robert F. Wagner Jr.,
interview with Don Swaim, March 7, 1973, Wired for Books online; "Robert
Wagner, 80, Pivotal New York Mayor, Dies," *NYT*, February 13, 1991. On
Wagner's split with DeSapio and the rise of the reform clubs, see Chris
McNickle, *To Be Mayor of New York: Ethnic Politics in the City* (New York:
Columbia University Press, 1993), Chap. 8; and Charles Brecher and Ray-

mond D. Horton, *Power Failure: New York City Politics and Policy since 1960* (New York: Oxford University Press), 80–83.

41. "Democrats Face Factional Fights," *NYT*, March 20, 1962; Suleiman Osman, *The Invention of Brownstone Brooklyn: Gentrification and the Search for Authenticity in Postwar New York* (New York: Oxford University Press, 2011), 134–136.

42. Thomas R. Jones, interviewed by James Briggs Murray, February 10, 1990, CDCOH, NYPL-Sch; Thomas R. Jones, interview with Jeffrey Gerson, June 10, 1993, courtesy of LGW; Jeffrey Nathan Gerson, "Building the Brooklyn Machine: Irish, Jewish and Black Political Succession in Central Brooklyn, 1919–1964" (PhD thesis, City University of New York, 1990); Gallagher, "Waging 'The Good Fight.'" On Jones, see Brian Purnell, "'What We Need Is Brick and Mortar': Race, Gender, and Early Leadership of the Bedford-Stuyvesant Restoration Corporation," in Laura Warren Hill and Julia Rabig, eds., *The Business of Black Power: Community Development, Capitalism, and Corporate Responsibility in Postwar America* (Rochester, NY: University of Rochester Press, 2012), 225–226.

43. "King's Diary," NYAN, December 5, 1959; "Parents Win Wide Support in School Boycott," NYAN, November 17, 1962; "May Picket Milk Co.," NYAN, November 11, 1961; "Incumbents Allowing Area 'to Deteriorate': Jones," NYAN, June 16, 1962; "Mrs. Roosevelt Re-states Support of Attorney Jones," NYAN, September 1, 1962.

44. Julie Gallagher, *Black Women and Politics in New York City* (Urbana: University of Illinois Press, 2012), 95; "Kings Diary," NYAN, September 22, 1962.

45. On Brooklyn's civil-rights struggles, see Clarence Taylor, *Knocking at Our Own Door: Milton Galamison and the Struggle to Integrate New York City Schools* (New York: Columbia University Press, 1997); and Brian Purnell, *Fighting Jim Crow in the County of Kings: The Congress of Racial Equality in Brooklyn* (Lexington: University Press of Kentucky, 2013). On consumer boycotts in the North, see Stacy Kinlock Sewell, "The 'Not-Buying Power' of the Black Community: Urban Boycotts and Equal Employment Opportunity, 1960–1964," *Journal of African American History* 89:2 (Spring 2004), 135–151.

46. "200 Racial Pickets Seized at Building Projects Here," *NYT*, July 23, 1963; Clarence Taylor, "'Whatever the Cost, We Will Set the Nation Straight': The Ministers' Committee and the Downstate Center Campaign," *Long Island Historical Journal* 1:2 (Spring 1989), 136–146; Clarence Taylor, *The Black Churches of Brooklyn* (New York: Columbia University Press, 1994), 139. On Brooklyn CORE, see Brian Purnell, "A Movement Grows in Brooklyn: The Brooklyn Chapter of the Congress for Racial Equality (CORE) and the Northern Civil Rights Movement during the Early 1960s" (PhD thesis, New York University, 2006). On the 1962 strike at Beth-El Hospital in Brownsville,

which also ended in a negotiated settlement with Governor Rockefeller, see Wendell E. Pritchett, *Brownsville, Brooklyn: Blacks, Jews, and the Changing Face of the Ghetto* (Chicago: University of Chicago Press, 2002), Chap. 6.

47. Thomas J. Sugrue, "Racial Romanticism," *Democracy* 13 (Summer 2009), 72; Purnell, "A Movement Grows in Brooklyn," 21, 43, 49–56.

48. "Merger of Groups in Bedford Area Planned," NYAN, May 20, 1939; "Council Plans for Annual Cleanup Drive," NYAN, August 20, 1955; "Salute Stuyford Council, NYAN, November 26, 1955; "Bedford-Stuyvesant Council Backbone of the Community," NYAN, July 16, 1960; "Housing Worsens in Brooklyn Area," NYT, November 10, 1963; "Bedford-Stuyvesant Neighborhood Council Study to Lower Prices," NYAN, January 15, 1966; Brian Purnell, "'Taxation without Sanitation Is Tyranny': Civil Rights Struggles Over Garbage Collection in Brooklyn, New York During the Fall of 1962," *Afro-Americans in New York Life and History* (July 2007), 61–88.

49. Purnell, "A Movement Grows in Brooklyn," 138.

50. On Jacobs's activism in the West Village, see Robert Fishman, "Revolt of the Urbs: Robert Moses and His Critics," in Kenneth T. Jackson and Hilary Ballon, eds., *Robert Moses and the Modern City: The Transformation of New York* (New York: Norton, 2007); and Jennifer Hock, "Jane Jacobs and the West Village: The Neighborhood against Urban Renewal," *Journal of the Society of Architectural Historians* 66:1 (March 2007), 16–19. On Thabit, see Reaven, "Citizen Participation in City Planning." See also Christopher Klemek, *The Transatlantic Collapse of Urban Renewal: Postwar Urbanism from New York to Berlin* (Chicago: University of Chicago Press, 2011); Samuel Zipp, *Manhattan Projects: The Rise and Fall of Urban Renewal in Cold War New York* (New York: Oxford University Press, 2010); and Colin Gordon, "Blighting the Way: Urban Renewal, Economic Development, and the Elusive Definition of 'Blight,'" *Fordham Urban Law Journal* 31:2 (January 2004), 305–337.

51. "Urban Renewal," NYAN, April 13, 1963.

52. See, for instance, Craig Steven Wilder, *A Covenant with Color: Race and Social Power in Brooklyn* (New York: Columbia University Press, 2000), Chap. 9.

53. Robert F. Wagner Jr., speech to the U.S. Conference of Mayors, May 25, 1964, Folder 16, Box 060019W, RFW, LGW online.

54. "Looking Ahead," NYAN, September 9, 1961.

55. Bedford-Stuyvesant Development and Services Corporation, Minutes, January 12, 1967, JFKL.

56. "Urban Renewal," NYAN, April 13, 1963; "Renewal 'Trickle' Irks Coordinating Council," NYAN, January 1, 1966; Ronald Shiffman, interview with the author, July 16, 2015.

57. "Renewal 'Trickle' Irks Coordinating Council," NYAN, January 1, 1966; Elsie Richardson, statement, August 2, 1967, in "A Report to the Community by the Bedford-Stuyvesant Better Housing Committee," DWP. Emphasis in original.

58. "Brooklyn Banker Defends Bedford Stuyvesant Area," NYAN, December 9, 1961.

59. "Urban Renewal—Yes! But Don't Change Face of Area, Residents Plea," NYAN, August 11, 1962; Ronald Shiffman, interview with the author, July 16, 2015.

60. Robert F. Wagner Jr., speech to the National Urban League and the Urban League of Greater New York, March 16, 1954, Folder 9, Box 060070W, RFW, LGW online; Harry C. Harris, "An Interim Report on Neighborhood Conservation in New York City" (June 1963), Folder 181, Box 9, RFW, LGW online; "City Says It Saved 7 Rundown Areas," NYT, July 3, 1963; "Tough Housing Idealist," NYT, April 3, 1962.

61. "5th Ward Area Plans Fight to Prevent Blight," *Chicago Daily Tribune*, May 11, 1950; "70% of Cities Enforce Housing Laws," *Washington Post*, November 29, 1953; Alexander von Hoffman, "The Quest for a New Frontier in Housing" (Joint Center for Housing Studies, Harvard University, 2010), 8–9.

62. New York City Housing and Redevelopment Board, "Neighborhood Conservation in New York City" (1966), courtesy Internet Archive and Columbia University Libraries, 11–12; "Community Fight on Slums Is Urged," NYT, February 11, 1959; "Mayor Initiates Sweeping Study of All Housing," NYT, August 21, 1959; "Lack of Money Stops Harlem Rehabilitation," NYAN, August 15, 1959; "First Case Is Won in Slum Clean-up," NYT, January 14, 1960; "Community Asked to Aid Slum Fight," NYT, May 12, 1959; Sixth Annual Report of Mayor Robert F. Wagner Jr. to the City Council and to the People of New York City, 1959.

63. Jane Jacobs, *The Death and Life of Great American Cities* (New York: Vintage Books, 1961); Osman, *The Invention of Brownstone Brooklyn*, 100.

64. "Mayor Initiates Sweeping Study of All Housing," NYT, August 21, 1959; "New Title 1 Plan Outlined for City by Housing Board," NYT, June 5, 1960; "Excerpts from Panuch Report to Wagner on Need for New Housing Board," NYT, March 10, 1960; "3-Man Authority to Guide Housing Urged on Mayor," NYT, March 10, 1960; Wendell Pritchett, *Robert Clifton Weaver and the American City: The Life and Times of an Urban Reformer* (Chicago: University of Chicago Press, 2010), 199–203; Klemek, *The Transatlantic Collapse of Urban Renewal*, 43.

65. Joel Schwartz, "Tenant Power in the Liberal City, 1943–1971," Section 3, in Ronald Lawson, ed., *The Tenant Movement in New York City, 1904–1984* (New Brunswick, NJ: Rutgers University Press, 1986), tenant.net/Community/history /histo4c.html; "Realty Men at City Hall," NYT, June 19, 1960; "New Group

Seeks Funds to Purchase and Repair Slums," *NYT*, September 19, 1961; Harry C. Harris, "An Interim Report on Neighborhood Conservation in New York City" (June 1963), Folder 181, Box 9, RFW, LGW online.

66. "No Higher Rents for Brower Pk.," *NYAN*, August 31, 1963; "Landlords Side," *NYAN*, September 14, 1963; "Urban Renewal—Yes! But Don't Change Face of Area, Residents Plea," *NYAN*, August 11, 1962.

67. "City Director Will Discuss Curbing Slums," *NYAN*, November 14, 1959; CBCC, Minutes, February 7, 1963 (handwritten notes), SJMP. On the interrelationship of public-health discourse and progressive reform, see Samuel Kelton Roberts, *Infectious Fear: Politics, Disease, and the Health Effects of Segregation* (Chapel Hill: University of North Carolina Press, 2009).

68. "Housing Program to Get New Chief," *NYT*, June 30, 1962; "City Plans Drive on Arverne Area," *NYT*, September 7, 1961; "2 More City Areas Due for Renewal," *NYT*, October 31, 1961; "Neighborhood Study Clubs in Operation," *NYAN*, November 23, 1963; New York City Housing and Redevelopment Board, "Neighborhood Conservation in New York City" (1966), 159; City of New York, Office of the Mayor, Press Releases, August 18 and August 21, 1963, Folder 7, Box 060224, RFW, LGW online.

69. In 1968, the Procopes would successfully lobby Governor Nelson Rockefeller to create the Fair Access to Insurance Requirements plan. Around that time, E. G. Bowman diversified into the realm of commercial insurance, and the Bed-Stuy Restoration Corporation became the firm's first client. Bowman eventually gained a clientele that included the New York City Housing Authority and several Fortune 500 companies. In 1979, it became one of the first black-owned firms with offices on Wall Street. See "John L. Procope, 82, Publisher of Black Newspaper in Harlem, Dies," *NYT*, July 18, 2005; "Largest Black Insurance Firm to Mark Year-Long Anniversary," *NYAN*, January 30, 1993; Nicole Marie Richardson, "Ernesta G. Procope: America's Insurance Maven," *Black Enterprise* 36:2 (September 2005), 26; and Henry Stimpson, "Ernesta Procope," *Financial History* (Winter 2000), 25–27.

70. "Council Wants Slum Housing Clearance," *NYAN*, March 16, 1963.

71. CBCC, Minutes, February 7, 1963 (handwritten notes), SJMP; New York Department of City Planning, "Summary of Alternatives for Area Services Project, Bedford Stuyvesant," February 7, 1963, SJMP.

72. "Council to Act on Boro Problems," *NYAN*, February 2, 1963; "City to Act on Bedford-Stuyvesant," *Brooklyn Eagle*, March 28, 1963; "Project Fights Blight in 22-Block Bklyn Area," *NYAN*, July 20, 1963; "Call 600 Landlords," *NYAN*, August 31, 1963.

73. "Bedford-Stuyvesant Neighborhood Council Study to Lower Prices," *NYAN*, January 15, 1966; "Clean-Up Campaign Planned," *NYAN*, June 22, 1963; CBCC, Meeting minutes, October 3, 1963 (handwritten notes), SJMP; "B-S

Hails Proposed New Tompkins Park," NYAN, September 12, 1964; "Expect
Work on Tompkins Park to Start," NYAN, November 14, 1964; "Cultural
Center Set for Tompkins Park," NYAN, February 19, 1966; "More Facilities in
Tompkins Pk.," NYAN, March 28, 1964. Tompkins Park was renamed in honor
of Von King in 1985; in 2011, the Parks Department named the band shell after
Coursey.

74. Paul R. Screvane, speech before the Central Brooklyn Coordinating Council,
August 30, 1965, Folder 10, Box 060058W, RFW, LGW online.

75. Walter C. Pinkston, CBCC Memo on Labor Office, February 16, 1963, Folder
13, Box 060295, RFW, LGW online; Cecil C. Gloster to James J. McFadden,
February 18, 1963, Folder 13, Box 060295, RFW, LGW online; "No Surveys,
Mr. Mayor," NYAN, February 16, 1963.

76. "Leaders Question Mayor on Unemployment," NYAN, February 16, 1963;
"Summary of Requests from Bedford-Stuyvesant Community, February 19,
1963, Folder 13, Box 060295, RFW, LGW online; CBCC, meeting minutes,
October 3, 1963 (including handwritten notes), SJMP; "McFadden, Leaders
Make Up," NYAN, June 22, 1963.

77. "Leaders Question Mayor on Unemployment," NYAN, February 16, 1963; "Say
They Were Bypassed in Labor Office Setup," NYAN, June 15, 1963.

78. Robert F. Wagner Jr., speech at the opening of the Bedford-Stuyvesant office of
the New York City Department of Labor, July 1, 1963, Folder 2, Box 060068W,
RFW, LGW online; Partial List of Programs of the New York City Government on Equal Opportunity, [1963], Folder 7, Box 060224, RFW, LGW online.

79. YIA, "The Bedford-Stuyvesant Proposal," DWP.

80. "Two Groups with One Idea Start Youth Service Program," NYAN, Au-
gust 10, 1963; "Robert Kennedy Drops in for a Day," NYT, August 15, 1963;
CBCC, minutes, November 21, 1963, SJMP; YIA, "The Bedford-Stuyvesant
Proposal," DWP.

81. "Council's Youth Services Project Gets in Motion." NYAN, August 24, 1963;
"Jones Plans Drive for Youth Program," NYAN, August 10, 1963.

4. War and Rumors of War

Epigraph: Sargent Shriver, address to the National Bar Association, August 3,
1966, Sargent Shriver Peace Institute online.

1. "Outlook for '64: A War on Poverty," *Washington Post,* January 1, 1964.

2. Lyndon B. Johnson, Annual Message to the Congress on the State of the
Union, January 8, 1964, Lyndon Baines Johnson Library and Museum (LBJL)
online.

3. Ted Sorensen, *Counselor: A Life at the Edge of History* (New York: Harper-
Collins, 2008), 386. The War on Poverty, Michael Gillette has written,

"seemed to embrace the entire Great Society agenda." Michael L. Gillette, *Launching the War on Poverty: An Oral History* (New York: Twayne Books, 1996), xii.

4. Johnson, Annual Message to the Congress on the State of the Union, January 8, 1964, LBJL online.

5. Bruce J. Schulman, *Lyndon B. Johnson and American Liberalism: A Brief History with Documents* (Boston: Bedford/St. Martin's, 1995), 70. On Johnson, see, among others, Joseph A. Califano Jr., *The Triumph & Tragedy of Lyndon Johnson: The White House Years* (New York: Simon and Schuster, 1991); and Randall B. Woods, *LBJ: Architect of American Ambition* (New York: Free Press, 2006).

6. Lyndon B. Johnson, remarks at the University of Michigan, May 22, 1964, LBJL online. On Johnson's emphasis on "quality" over "quantity," see Sidney M. Milkis, "Lyndon Johnson, the Great Society, and the 'Twilight' of the Modern Presidency," in Sidney M. Milkis and Jerome M. Mileur, eds., *The Great Society and the High Tide of Liberalism* (Amherst: University of Massachusetts Press, 2005), 8–9.

7. Allen J. Matusow, *The Unraveling of America: A History of Liberalism in the 1960s* (New York: Harper and Row, 1984), 217–218. On the consequences of Johnson's rhetorical choices, see David Zarefsky, *President Johnson's War on Poverty: Rhetoric and History* (Tuscaloosa: University of Alabama Press, 1986). For an insightful look at how martial rhetoric serves both to enlarge and to constrain the range of effective policies, see William Leuchtenberg, "The New Deal and the Analogue of War," in John Braeman, Robert H. Bremner, and Everett Walters, eds., *Change and Continuity in Twentieth-Century America* (Columbus: Ohio State University Press, 1964), 81–143.

8. Johnson, Annual Message to the Congress on the State of the Union, January 8, 1964, LBJL online; Economic Opportunity Act of 1964; Maurice Isserman and Michael Kazin, *America Divided: The Civil War of the 1960s* (New York: Oxford University Press, 2008), 109; Schulman, *Lyndon Johnson and American Liberalism*, 71–73, 84–85.

9. Lyndon B. Johnson to Sargent Shriver, February 12, 1964, "FG 11–15, 11/22/63–11/24/64," Box 124, White House Central Files, LBJL. On Johnson and FDR, see William E. Leuchtenberg, "Lyndon Johnson in the Shadow of Franklin Roosevelt," in Milkis and Mileur, eds., *The Great Society.*

10. Bureau of Economic Analysis, "Gross Domestic Product: Percent Change from Preceding Period, Based on Chained 2005 Dollars," www.bea.gov/national/index.htm#gdp; "The U.S. Unemployment Rate, Jan. 1948 to Aug. 2011," www.miseryindex.us; Benjamin M. Friedman, *The Moral Consequences of Economic Growth* (New York: Alfred A. Knopf, 2005), 183–184.

11. Daniel Patrick Moynihan, speech before the New Democratic Club, June 10, 1964, Folder 7, Box 060249, RFW, LGW online; Charles R. Morris, "Of Budgets, Taxes, and the Rise of a New Plutocracy," in Joseph P. Viteritti, ed., *Summer in the City: John Lindsay, New York, and the American Dream* (Baltimore: Johns Hopkins Press, 2014), 83; "Mayor Says City Can't Afford Poverty Fight," *New York Times (NYT)*, October 28, 1964; "Wagner to Press for Minimum Pay of $1.25 an Hour," *NYT*, December 17, 1959; Community Council of Greater New York, "Poverty in New York City: Facts for Planning Community Action" (New York: Community Council of Greater New York, January 1965, second printing), iv. On the decline of New York as a working-class city, see Joshua Freeman, *Working Class New York: Life and Labor since World War II* (New York: The New Press, 2000). See also John Hull Mollenkopf, "The Postindustrial Transformation of the Political Order in New York City," in John Hull Mollenkopf, ed., *Power, Culture, and Place: Essays on New York City* (New York: Russell Sage Foundation, 1988), 223–258.

12. "Mayor Says City Can't Afford Poverty Fight," *NYT*, October 28, 1964; "Only New Jobs Here in 5 Years Have Been in Construction Field," *NYT*, December 17, 1964; "Training Resources for Youth: Brooklyn, U.S.A.," Report by the YMCA of Greater New York, June 1965; Robert F. Wagner Jr., statement to the American Municipal Association, July 25, 1964, Folder 5, Box 060245, RFW, LGW online.

13. The next and last time official unemployment fell below the 4 percent barrier was in 2000. See Bureau of Economic Analysis, "Gross Domestic Product: Percent Change from Preceding Period, Based on Chained 2005 Dollars," www.bea.gov/national/index.htm#gdp; "The U.S. Unemployment Rate, Jan. 1948 to Aug. 2011," www.miseryindex.us.

14. Michael Harrington, *The Other America: Poverty in the United States* (New York: Macmillan, 1962); Administrative History of the Office of Economic Opportunity, Volume I, Box I, 4, LBJL.

15. Harrington, *The Other America*, 160. See Oscar Lewis, "The Culture of Poverty," in Daniel P. Moynihan, ed., *On Understanding Poverty: Perspectives from the Social Sciences* (New York: Basic Books, 1968), 187–200. On Harrington, see Maurice Isserman, "50 Years Later: Poverty and *The Other America*," *Dissent* (Winter 2012).

16. Alice O'Connor, *Poverty Knowledge: Social Science, Social Policy, and the Poor in Twentieth-Century U.S. History* (Princeton, NJ: Princeton University Press, 2001), 122, 151. On social science and the War on Poverty, see Daniel P. Moynihan, *Maximum Feasible Misunderstanding: Community Action in the War on Poverty* (New York: The Free Press, 1969); Peter Marris and Martin

Rein, *Dilemmas of Social Reform: Poverty and Community Action in the United States* (Chicago: University of Chicago Press, 1967, reprinted 1982); and Noel Cazenave, *Impossible Democracy: The Unlikely Success of the War on Poverty Community Action Programs* (Albany: State University of New York Press, 2007).

17. Dwight MacDonald, "Our Invisible Poor," *The New Yorker*, January 19, 1963; John F. Kennedy, speech at Sheraton Park Hotel, Washington, DC, September 20, 1960, accessed via the American Presidency Project online; Gillette, *Launching the War on Poverty*, Chap. 1. See also Edward R. Schmitt, *President of the Other America: Robert Kennedy and the Politics of Poverty* (Amherst: University of Massachusetts Press, 2010).

18. James L. Sundquist, *Politics and Policy: The Eisenhower, Kennedy and Johnson Years* (Washington, DC: Brookings Institution, 1968), 113–114.

19. Gillette, *Launching the War on Poverty*, Chap. 1; Robert Lampman quoted in Herman Phillip Miller, "Income Distribution in the United States," U.S. Dept. of Commerce, Bureau of the Census, 1960 (second printing, 1968), 31.

20. Gillette, *Launching the War on Poverty*, 83–85; David Hackett to Robert F. Kennedy, January 2, 1964, "President's Committee File, 1/64," Box 4, Richardson White Papers, John F. Kennedy Presidential Library (JFKL).

21. Gillette, *Launching the War on Poverty*, Chap. 1; Schulman, *Lyndon B. Johnson and American Liberalism*, 71. For more on the planning phases of the War on Poverty, see, among others, Nicholas Lemann, *The Promised Land: The Great Black Migration and How It Changed America* (New York: Alfred A. Knopf, 1991); and Moynihan, *Maximum Feasible Misunderstanding*.

22. As early as 1973, David Greenstone and Paul Peterson found that community action unfolded differently in each of the five cities they studied. See J. David Greenstone and Paul E. Peterson, *Race and Authority in Urban Politics: Community Participation and the War on Poverty* (New York: Russell Sage Foundation, 1973).

23. Walter Heller to Lyndon B. Johnson, December 20, 1963, LBJL.

24. "Mayor Mobilizes Full City Attack on Teen Violence," *NYT*, September 7, 1957; "Attack on Slums," *NYT*, December 10, 1958; "Text of Mayor's State-of-City Message," *NYT*, April 15, 1959; "Clean-Up of Slums in West Side Area Begun by Wagner," *NYT*, July 11, 1961; Institute of Public Administration, "The Administration of Services to Children and Youth in New York City" (1963); "Fighting Bob," *NYT*, July 12, 1961.

25. Meeting of Council on Expanded Employment Opportunity with Mayor Wagner, December 15, 1963, Folder 11, Box 060239, RFW, LGW online; Robert F. Wagner Jr., speech at Youth Week Conference sponsored by the New York City Youth Board, November 22, 1965, Folder 18, Box 060029W, RFW, LGW online.

26. "Wagner Directs Agencies to Push Minority Rights," *NYT*, June 5, 1963.

27. Notes on caucus meeting, City Hall, December 15, 1963, Folder 11, Box 060239, RFW, LGW online; Meeting of Council on Expanded Employment Opportunity with Mayor Wagner, December 15, 1963, LGW online; YMCA of Greater New York, "Training Resources for Youth: Brooklyn, U.S.A.," June 1965, accessed via eric.ed.gov; Wallace S. Sayre and Herbert Kaufman, *Governing New York City: Politics in the Metropolis* (New York: Norton, 1965; first edition, 1960), xlix. For a contemporary analysis of Wagner's contributions to the fiscal crisis, see Barry Gottehrer, ed., *New York City in Crisis: A Study in Depth of Urban Sickness* (New York: D. McKay, 1965).

28. "Wagner Backers to Open Drive for Vice-Presidency," *NYT*, December 11, 1963; "Mayor Deplores Moves to Put Him in Federal Arena," *NYT*, December 20, 1963; "Johnson Invites Mayor to Capitol," *NYT*, November 27, 1963.

29. Others were even more outraged. "His ineptitude, hypocrisy, self-serving bumbling, and sheer stupidity (if not outright corruption) have made our city bankrupt, morally, functionally, and financially," wrote two self-described Democrats, adding that they would greet a Johnson-Wagner ticket by voting for "<u>any</u> Republican offered in opposition." A protest emanating from Columbia University's Philosophy Hall was even more blunt: "I consider him a zero." See the following in "Gen PL / Wagner, Robert 11/22/63–1/13/64," Box 25, White House Central Files, LBJL: Alice Kramer to Lyndon B. Johnson, December 13, 1963; Corrine and Lily Nevelson to Lyndon B. Johnson, December 14, 1963; and Eric Bentley to Lyndon B. Johnson, August 1, 1964.

30. "The Mayor Weighs His Future," *NYT*, November 28, 1963.

31. "Wagner Meets Johnson but Bars Politics as Topic," *NYT*, December 21, 1963; "Wagner Preparing Attack on Poverty," *NYT*, January 8, 1964.

32. Robert F. Wagner Jr., address to the New York City Council, January 14, 1964, Folder 19, Box 060021W, RFW, LGW online.

33. Wagner, address to the New York City Council, January 14, 1964, LGW online; "The Mayor and the Poor," *NYT*, January 16, 1964.

34. "How City Spends to Fight Poverty," *NYT*, March 23, 1964; City Accelerates Fight on Poverty," *NYT*, July 28, 1964.

35. "Wagner Backs War on Poverty," *Christian Science Monitor*, March 24, 1964; "Mourners Recall Wagner as Man of Subtle Grace," *NYT*, February 17, 1991; Taylor, "Robert Wagner, Milton Galamison and the Challenge to New York City Liberalism," *Afro-Americans in New York Life and History* 31:2 (July 2007), 124; "148 Elementary Schools Remain Open 8 Weeks," *New York Amsterdam News* (NYAN), May 29, 1965; Robert F. Wagner Jr., address to the New York City Council, January 14, 1964, LGW online.

36. Community Council of Greater New York, "Poverty in New York City." On the U.S. poverty threshold, see Howard Glennerster, "United States Poverty

Studies and Poverty Measurement: The Past Twenty-Five Years," *Social Service Review* 76:1 (March 2002), 83–107; Rebecca M. Blank, "Presidential Address: How to Improve Poverty Measurement in the United States," *Journal of Policy Analysis and Management* 27:2 (2008), 233–254.

37. That figure did not include individuals living alone. See Community Council of Greater New York, "Poverty in New York City."

38. Bedford-Stuyvesant Youth in Action (YIA), "Let Us Face the Facts: A Portrait of Bedford-Stuyvesant, as Reflected by Bedford-Stuyvesant Youth in Action's Studies, and Seen by Its Residents," undated, Don Watkins Papers (DWP); YIA, "Supplementary Data Sheet Based on 1960 Census," [1964], DWP; YIA, "Living Conditions in Bedford-Stuyvesant," [1966], DWP; YIA, "The Bedford-Stuyvesant Proposal," August 20, 1964, DWP; "Training Resources for Youth: Brooklyn, U.S.A.," Report by the YMCA of Greater New York, June 1965; National Opinion Research Center, "Neighborhood Reactions to a Local Riot," [1964], DWP.

39. "Living Conditions in Bedford-Stuyvesant," [1966], DWP; YIA, "A Survey of Comparative Consumer Prices in Bedford-Stuyvesant and Surrounding Areas," September 8, 1966, DWP; YIA, "Fulton Street Business Survey" (1965), DWP, 4–5; Pratt Institute Planning Department, "Stuyvesant Heights: A Good Neighborhood in Need of Help," (1965), Pratt Center for Community Development online.

40. YIA, "The Bedford-Stuyvesant Proposal," DWP.

41. Ronald Shiffman, interview with the author, July 14, 2015; YIA, "The Bedford-Stuyvesant Proposal," DWP.

42. "B'klyn Council Gets $26,000 from Youth Bd," NYAN, November 9, 1963; "Community Council Dedicates H. Q.," NYAN, February 15, 1964.

43. YIA, "The Bedford-Stuyvesant Proposal," DWP; City of New York, Office of the Mayor, press release, July 25, 1964, "War on Poverty" binder, New York City Municipal Archives (NYCMA); YIA, "Profile of Board Members," [1964], DWP; "Brooklyn Antipoverty Program Is Set," NYT, July 26, 1964; "Living Conditions in Bedford-Stuyvesant," [1966], DWP.

44. City of New York, Office of the Mayor, press release, July 25, 1964, NYCMA; YIA, "Profile of Board Members," [1964], DWP.

45. Bayard Rustin, "From Protest to Politics: The Future of the Civil Rights Movement," *Commentary* 39:1 (1965), 25. See also Thomas J. Sugrue, *Sweet Land of Liberty: The Forgotten Struggle for Civil Rights in the North* (New York: Random House, 2008), Chap. 11.

46. YIA, "The Bedford-Stuyvesant Proposal," DWP; Don Watkins, conversation with the author, July 2, 2009.

47. Almira Coursey, "An Appeal for Unity," *Central Brooklyn Coordinator*, September 16, 1965, CBCC Papers, Brooklyn Historical Society.

48. "Screvane Links Reds to Rioting," *NYT*, July 22, 1964; "Wagner Meeting Unity Council on Next Move," *NYAN*, August 8, 1964; "Manhattan Rioting Crosses Bridge, Spreads to Brooklyn," *NYAN*, July 25, 1964; "Hot Summer," *NYT*, July 26, 1964; "Brooklyn Riots Continue; Police Shoot 2 as Looters," *NYT*, July 23, 1964. On the roots and responses to the Harlem riot, see Cathy Lisa Schneider, *Police Power and Race Riots: Urban Unrest in Paris and New York* (Philadelphia: University of Pennsylvania Press, 2014), Chap. 1; and Alex Elkins, "Fifty Years of Get Tough," Urban History Association blog, July 16, 2014, urbanhistorians.wordpress.com.

49. "City Begins Drive for 20,000 Jobs," *NYT*, July 30, 1964.

50. Lyndon B. Johnson: "Remarks on the City Hall Steps, Dayton, Ohio," October 16, 1964, accessed via the American Presidency Project online; YIA, "The Bedford-Stuyvesant Proposal," DWP; list of approved projects, [1965], Papers of the Lindsay Administration, Microfilm Roll 5, Folder 115, NYCMA; YIA, "Recap on Youth in Action, Inc., Funding" (May 1966), DWP; City of New York, Office of the Mayor, press release, July 25, 1964, NYCMA; City Accelerates Fight on Poverty," *NYT*, July 28, 1964. On riots and the Great Society, see Richard Cloward and Frances Fox Piven, *Regulating the Poor: The Functions of Public Welfare* (New York: Vintage Books, 1971); Gerald Horne, *Fire This Time: The Watts Uprising and the 1960s* (New York: Da Capo Press, 1995); and Kevin Mumford, *Newark: A History of Race, Rights, and Riots in America* (New York: New York University Press, 2007).

51. YIA, "The Bedford-Stuyvesant Proposal," DWP; "Cite Negro Beatings at John Jay High," *NYAN*, October 12, 1963; "Say White Gang Preys on Negro School Kids," *NYAN*, December 1, 1962; "Probe Beatings of Negroes by White Students," *NYAN*, March 23, 1963.

52. YIA, "The Bedford-Stuyvesant Proposal," 2, 13–14, DWP; statement by the Chairmen of the Projects, Council for Youth and Community Development Projects, July 24, 1964, Papers of the Wagner Administration, NYCMA.

53. YIA, "The Bedford-Stuyvesant Proposal," 1, 2, 6, DWP.

54. Joseph Bensman, "The Sociologist on the Cutting Edge," in Bernard Rosenberg and Ernest Goldstein, eds., *Creators and Disturbers: Reminiscences by Jewish Intellectuals of New York* (New York: Columbia University Press, 1982); O'Connor, *Poverty Knowledge*, 124–126; Harlem Youth Opportunities Unlimited, Inc., "Youth in the Ghetto: A Study of the Consequences of Powerlessness and a Blueprint for Change," second edition (New York: Harlem Youth Opportunities Unlimited, 1964); Kenneth B. Clark, *Dark Ghetto: Dilemmas of Social Power* (New York: Harper and Row, 1965). On the Clarks, see Gerald Markowitz and David Rosner, *Children, Race, and Power: Kenneth and Mamie Clark's Northside Center* (Charlottesville: The University Press of Virginia, 1996).

55. YIA, "Planned Intervention to Solve Problems Resulting from Segregation and Poverty in the Ghetto," first draft, January 20, 1965, 3, 8, 10, DWP; YIA, "Planned Intervention to Halt and Reverse the Vicious Cycle," March 11, 1965, 17, DWP.

56. Daniel P. Moynihan, *The Negro Family: The Case for National Action* (Washington, DC: Office of Policy Planning and Research, 1965); Michael Katz, *In the Shadow of the Poorhouse: A Social History of Welfare in America* (New York: Basic Books, 1986), 256. On the emphasis placed by "experts" on the supposedly damaged psyches of African Americans during the War on Poverty years, see Daryl Michael Scott, *Contempt and Pity: Social Policy and the Image of the Damaged Black Psyche* (Chapel Hill: University of North Carolina Press, 1997), esp. Chap. 8. On the "culture of poverty" debate, see Mario Luis Small, David J. Harding, and Michèle Lamont, "Reconsidering Culture and Poverty," *Annals of the American Academy of Political and Social Science* 629:1 (2010), 6–27.

57. YIA, "The Bedford-Stuyvesant Proposal," 55, 53, 45, DWP; William M. Chisholm to Paul Screvane, August 24, 1964, DWP. See Mobilization for Youth, "A Proposal for the Prevention and Control of Delinquency by Expanding Opportunities," second edition (August 1962).

58. YIA, untitled pamphlet [1964/1965], DWP; Katz, *In the Shadow of the Poorhouse*, 255; O'Connor, *Poverty Knowledge*, 165. Cloward and Fox Piven reject the thesis that "the stupidity or cupidity of particular political leaders or their 'idea men'" shaped the War on Poverty. See Cloward and Fox Piven, *Regulating the Poor*, 249n.

59. Don Watkins, conversation with the author, July 2, 2009.

60. YIA, "History & Development of Bedford-Stuyvesant Youth in Action, Inc.," [1967], DWP; YIA, "Supplementary Data Sheet Based on 1960 Census," undated, DWP.

61. "New Poverty Group to Study Causes," *New York World-Telegram*, December 9, 1964; City of New York, Office of the Mayor, press release, July 25, 1964, NYCMA.

62. YIA, "Programming Planned Intervention: Guidelines for Development," second draft, January 26, 1965, DWP; YIA, "Planned Intervention," March 11, 1965, 14, DWP; YIA, "Comprehensive Program Proposals," [1965], Introduction, Papers of the Wagner Administration, Microfilm Roll 5, NYCMA; "Brooklyn Agency Asks Youth Corps," *NYT*, May 8, 1965.

63. YIA, "Planned Intervention," January 20, 1965, 13, 15, DWP; YIA, "Programming Planned Intervention: Guidelines for Development," second draft, January 26, 1965, 13, DWP; YIA, "Comprehensive Program Proposals," [1965], Foreword, 5, NYCMA.

64. "RFK Sets B-S Housing Tour," *NYAN*, February 5, 1966.

65. Office of Economic Opportunity (OEO), "Dimensions of Poverty in 1964," "OEO, 6/1965–11/1965," Box 31, Adam Walinsky Papers (AWP), JFKL.

66. White House press release, March 16, 1964, "Federal Government 11–15, 11/22/63–11/24/64," Box 124, White House Central Files, LBJL; Fact Sheet: Economic Opportunity Amendments of 1965, "OEO, 6/1965–11/1965," Box 31, AWP, JFKL.

67. Task Force on Urban Areas, Preliminary Report, April 8, 1964, "President's Committee File, 4/64," Box 4, Richardson White Papers, JFKL; David L. Hackett to Sargent Shriver, February 11, 1964, "Poverty, Hackett, David: Memoranda, 1963–1964," Box 33, AWP, JFKL.

68. Mark H. Furstenberg to Jack Conway and Richard Boone, August 7, 1964; Mark H. Furstenberg to Julius Edelstein, August 15, 1964, both in "Poverty, Hackett, David: Memoranda, 1963–1964," Box 33, AWP, JFKL.

69. Taylor, "Robert Wagner, Milton Galamison, and the Challenge," 134, 124; "All Alone," *NYAN*, February 1, 1964; "148 Elementary Schools Remain Open 8 Weeks," *NYAN*, May 29, 1965; Brian Purnell, "Revolution Has Come to Brooklyn: Construction Trades Protests and the Negro Revolt of 1963," in David Goldberg and Trevor Griffey, eds., *Black Power at Work: Community Control, Affirmative Action, and the Construction Industry* (Ithaca, NY: Cornell University Press, 2010), 23–47. See also Chris McNickle, *To Be Mayor of New York: Ethnic Politics in the City* (New York: Columbia University Press, 1993), on the shifting politics of the time. On school politics, see Diane Ravitch, *The Great School Wars: A History of the New York City Public Schools* (Baltimore: Johns Hopkins University Press, 2000).

70. On the changing role of settlement houses, see Herbert J. Gans, "Redefining the Settlement's Function for the War on Poverty," *Social Work* 9:4 (October 1964), 3–12; and Andrew Morris, "The Voluntary Sector's War on Poverty," *Journal of Policy History* 16:4 (2004), 275–305.

71. Sonia Lee and Andre Diaz, "'I Was the One Percenter': Manny Diaz and the Beginnings of a Black–Puerto Rican Coalition," *Journal of American Ethnic History* 26:3 (2007), 52–80; Cazenave, *Impossible Democracy*, 118. See also Marris and Rein, *Dilemmas of Social Reform*.

72. "The Right to Fight City Hall," *NYT*, November 11, 1964; Cazenave, *Impossible Democracy*, Chap. 6. See also Mobilization for Youth correspondence from 1964 in Folder 7, Box 060236, RFW, LGW online.

73. Cazenave, *Impossible Democracy*, 105–117; Kenneth B. Clark, Oral History interviews with Ed Edwin, April 7, 1976, and May 10, 1976, Columbia University Libraries Oral History Research Office. On Powell's treatment of Clark, see Markowitz and Rosner, *Children, Race, and Power*, 198–199.

74. "Screvane to Scan Poverty Budgets," *NYT*, July 2, 1964. Peterson and Greenstone write that Wagner "opposed a participatory CAP because he, too,

perceived through the juvenile delinquency program the threat to the pluralist bargaining order posed by participation." See Greenstone and Peterson, *Race and Authority in Urban Politics*, 274.

75. Bertram M. Beck, "Organizing Community Action," *Proceedings of the Academy of Political Science* 29:4 (1969), 162–163.

76. OEO, *Community Action Agency Atlas* (January 1969), Columbia University Social Work Agency Collection; Beck, "Organizing Community Action," 162–163.

77. New York City Council Against Poverty, "New York City War on Poverty, 1965: A Report to the Citizens of New Yrok," 60, DWP; Stephen David, "Leadership of the Poor in Poverty Programs," *Proceedings of the Academy of Political Science* 29:1 (1968), 86–100.

78. Beck, "Organizing Community Action," 164; Arnold Bornfriend, "Political Parties and Pressure Groups," *Proceedings of the Academy of Political Science* 29:4 (1969), 58.

5. Maximum Feasible Bureaucratization

Epigraph: Timothy Vincent, testimony before the Senate Subcommittee on Labor and Public Welfare, June 24, 1966, "Poverty, 4/1966–6/1966," Box 32, Adam Walinsky Papers (AWP), John F. Kennedy Library (JFKL).

1. "Former Lady Professor Taking Youth Program over the Top," *New York Amsterdam News* (NYAN), December 18, 1965; "Antipoverty Director Is Named in Brooklyn," *New York Times* (NYT), March 27, 1965; Elsie Richardson, interview with the author, June 5, 2011.

2. Seymour Gray, "A View from the Top: Dorothy Orr," *Black Enterprise* 7:7 (February 1977), 60–63; "Ten Best Places to Work," *Black Enterprise* 12:7 (February 1982), 37–44; "Former Lady Professor Taking Youth Program over the Top," NYAN, December 18, 1965. In an interesting twist, the executive director of the Interracial Council for Business Opportunity during the early 1970s was Darwin W. Bolden, the man Orr replaced as executive director of Bedford-Stuyvesant Youth in Action (YIA). See "Drive on for More Negro Businesses," NYT, July 28, 1968.

3. "Directs Brooklyn Youth Project," NYAN, April 3, 1965; "Poor to Control a Poverty Plan," NYT, May 20, 1966.

4. Fact Sheet: Economic Opportunity Amendments of 1965, "Office of Economic Opportunity, 6/1965–11/1965," Box 31, AWP, JFKL.

5. "We Have Not Yet Begun to Fight," *New York World-Telegram*, March 11, 1965; Ford Foundation (R. B. Goldmann author), "Performance in Black and White: An Appraisal of the Development and Record of the Bedford-Stuyvesant

Restoration and Development and Services Corporations" (February 1969), 8, Box 1, Ford Foundation Papers, JFKL.

6. Joseph P. Viteritti, "Times a-Changin': Mayor for the Great Society," in Joseph P. Viteritti, ed., *Summer in the City: John Lindsay, New York, and the American Dream* (Baltimore: Johns Hopkins Press, 2014), 6–7; "Screvane Scores Antipoverty Unit," *NYT*, May 15, 1964; "$9,183,626 U.S. Aid Given City to Open Poverty Program," *NYT*, June 6, 1965.

7. Dorothy Orr, YIA Executive Director's Progress Report, February 17, 1966, March 17, 1966, Don Watkins Papers (DWP).

8. YIA, "Recap on Youth in Action, Inc. Funding" (May 1966); Orr, YIA Executive Director's Progress Report, February 17, 1966; YIA, Minutes of the Board of Directors, September 16, 1965, December 16, 1965, February 23, 1966, DWP; "Few Programs Use Quotas," *NYT*, August 4, 1966.

9. Quoted in "Few Programs Use Quotas," *NYT*, August 4, 1966; YIA, "Recap on Youth in Action, Inc. Funding" (May 1966), DWP.

10. Jerald E. Podair, *The Strike That Changed New York: Blacks, Whites, and the Ocean Hill–Brownsville Crisis* (New Haven, CT: Yale University Press, 2002), 36; Joseph P. Viteritti, "After the Fall," in Viteritti, ed., *Summer in the City*, 229. For more on the personality and promise of Lindsay, see the essays contained in Sam Roberts, ed. *America's Mayor: John V. Lindsay and the Reinvention of New York City* (New York: Columbia University Press, 2010). For Lindsay on Lindsay, see John V. Lindsay, *The City* (New York: Norton, 1970).

11. Vincent J. Cannato, *The Ungovernable City: John Lindsay and His Struggle to Save New York* (New York: Basic Books, 2001), 109; Podair, *The Strike That Changed New York*, 36–42. According to Podair, Lindsay's coalition shared a fundamental commitment to the idea of "community control," though that coalition was unable to withstand the strains caused by the Ocean Hill–Brownsville controversy of 1968–1969. For an argument about how Lindsay's Great Society programs doomed the city, see Fred Siegel, *The Future Once Happened Here: New York, D.C., L.A., and the Fate of America's Big Cities* (New York: Free Press, 1997). For a perspective on Lindsay's work as a coalition builder, see Chris McNickle, *To Be Mayor of New York: Ethnic Politics in the City* (New York: Columbia University Press, 1993). See also the essays in Viteritti, ed., *Summer in the City*; and Arnold Bornfriend, "Political Parties and Pressure Groups," *Proceedings of the Academy of Political Science* 29:4 (1969), 55–57.

12. Office of John Lindsay, press release, December 5, 1965, Papers of the Lindsay Administration, Microfilm Roll 5, Folder 115, New York City Municipal Archives (NYCMA); Elsie Richardson, interview with the author, June 5, 2011. On Lindsay's relationship with the city's black communities, see Clarence

Taylor, "Race, Rights, Empowerment," in Viteritti, ed., *Summer in the City*, 60–78.

13. Office of John Lindsay, press release, December 5, 1965, NYCMA.
14. "Voice of Poverty Demands Action," NYT, February 4, 1966.
15. Ibid.
16. "Haryou to Mayor: Where's the Cash?" NYT, February 19, 1966; YIA, press release, February 21, 1966, DWP; YIA, Minutes of the Board of Directors, February 23, 1966, DWP; Jacob Javits to Sargent Shriver, February 16, 1966, DWP. Journalist Tom Wolfe parodied such "mau-mau" tactics—and ridiculed the cowed responses of politicians—in a 1970 essay about San Francisco's poverty program. See Tom Wolfe, *Radical Chic & Mau-Mauing the Flak Catchers* (New York: Farrar, Straus and Giroux, 1970).
17. Dorothy Orr, YIA Executive Director's Progress Report, February 17, 1966, DWP; Dorothy Orr, Editorial, *YIA Monthly Newspaper*, June 1966, DWP.
18. "'Happenings' in Park Unsponsored Chaos," NYAN, August 19, 1967; Jack Newfield, *Robert Kennedy: A Memoir* (New York: Dutton, 1969), 103; Brian Purnell, "A Movement Grows in Brooklyn: The Brooklyn Chapter of the Congress for Racial Equality (CORE) and the Northern Civil Rights Movement during the Early 1960s" (PhD thesis, New York University, 2006), 440. See Mwlina Imiri Abubadika (Sonny Carson), *The Education of Sonny Carson* (New York: Norton, 1972).
19. Dorothy Orr, Editorial, *YIA Monthly Newspaper*, June 1966, DWP; Stephen E. Cotton, "Politics and Poverty," *The Harvard Crimson*, April 29, 1967.
20. Robert "Sonny" Carson, "Brooklyn Core," *YIA Monthly Newspaper*, August 3, 1967; YIA, Minutes of the Board of Directors, April 5, 1966; YIA, press release, April 4, 1966, all in DWP.
21. "The Rev. William A. Jones, Civil Rights Activist, Dies at 71," NYT, February 8, 2006; author's conversation with Sydney J. Moshette Jr. and Don Watkins, September 27, 2011.
22. Clarence Taylor, *The Black Churches of Brooklyn* (New York: Columbia University Press, 1994), 139.
23. "YIA Groups Threaten Own Poverty War," *New York World-Telegram and Sun*, March 24, 1966; "'Poor' Run YIA's First Open Meeting," *Williamsburg News*, April 15, 1966; YIA, press release, April 4, 1966, DWP; "War Declared on Bedford-Stuyvesant Poverty," *YIA Monthly Newspaper*, June 1966, DWP.
24. "Rally to Protest Delay in Anti-Poverty Setup," [New York] *Daily News*, June 17, 1966; Citizens Committee for the Preservation of Bedford-Stuyvesant Youth in Action, Inc., press release, June 1966, DWP; YIA, posters publicizing June 17, 1966, rally, DWP.
25. William Jones to John Lindsay, May 25, 1966, DWP.

26. "Youth Leadership Institute," YIA *Monthly Newspaper*, July 1967, DWP; Timothy Vincent, testimony before the Senate Subcommittee on Labor and Public Welfare, June 24, 1966, "Poverty, 4/1966–6/1966," Box 32, AWP, JFKL.

27. YIA, "Where the Youth in Action Dollar Goes," [1967], DWP; YIA, Minutes of the Board of Directors, July 27, 1967, DWP; YIA, budget materials and salary charts, 1966–1968, DWP.

28. YIA, Statement from the Executive Director, September 26, 1966, DWP.

29. Orr, YIA Executive Director's Progress Report, February 17, 1966, DWP.

30. "C.B.C.C. Asks: Clarify Charges"; Elsie Richardson, letter to William Chisholm; Almira Coursey, "An Appeal for Unity," all printed in the *Central Brooklyn Coordinator*, September 16, 1965, CBCC Papers, Brooklyn Historical Society; "Brawl Disrupts Poverty Session," NYT, September 4, 1965; "Chisholm Quits YIA in Clash," NYAN, April 9, 1966; "Jones Heads YIA Bd.; Galamison Also Quits," NYAN, April 16, 1966.

31. "Four in Brooklyn Quit Poverty Unit," NYT, September 24, 1966; "Brooklyn Poverty Board Names Acting Chief Despite Opposition," NYT, September 27, 1966; "Pinkston Takes Over as Director of YIA," NYAN, October 1, 1966; YIA, Minutes of the Board of Directors, August 18, 1966, DWP.

32. William Jones to George Nicolau, October 3, 1966, DWP.

33. "Kafka and Poverty," NYT, June 14, 1966; " 'We Must Move Mountains,' " NYT, June 27, 1966; "City Poverty War Defended," *New York Post*, June 30, 1966.

34. Alice O'Connor, *Poverty Knowledge: Social Science, Social Policy, and the Poor in Twentieth-Century U.S. History* (Princeton, NJ: Princeton University Press, 2001), 131, 233; William P. Ryan, interview with Mitchell Sviridoff, in Sviridoff, ed., *Inventing Community Renewal: The Trials and Errors That Shaped the Modern Community Development Corporation* (New York: New School University, 2004); "Antipoverty Expert," NYT, June 14, 1966; "Mitchell Sviridoff, 81, Dies," NYT, October 23, 2000.

35. Institute of Public Administration, "Developing New York City's Human Resources" (aka the Sviridoff Report), June 1966, DWP; "Plan to Aid Poor Widely Praised," NYT, June 28, 1966; "Giant City Agency to Reorganize Aid to Poor Is Urged," NYT, June 27, 1966. On Lindsay's attempts to rationalize the city's bureaucracies, see David Rogers, "Management Versus Bureaucracy," in Viteritti, ed., *Summer in the City*, 110–114.

36. New York City Council Against Poverty, Guidelines for the formation of Community Corporations (Approved by the Council on October 27, 1966), DWP; Institute of Public Administration, "Developing New York City's Human Resources," DWP.

37. Bertram M. Beck, "Organizing Community Action," *Proceedings of the Academy of Political Science* 29:4 (1969), 165.

38. YIA, publicity materials relating to neighborhood board elections, 1966, DWP; D.S.W., Incorporated, "Consultation and Review of the Bedford-Stuyvesant Youth in Action Program," May 22, 1967, DWP; "Poor to Control a Poverty Plan," *NYT*, May 20, 1966.

39. YIA, Minutes of the Special Committee, October 13, 1966; Don Watkins to YIA Board, October 26, 1966; YIA, Executive Director's Progress Report, January 19, 1967; YIA, press releases, November 14, 1966, December 9, 1966; Ad Hoc Planning Committee for the Bedford-Stuyvesant Community Corporation, "Plan for Conversion of Youth in Action Inc. into the Community Corporation in Bedford-Stuyvesant," [1966]; YIA, "History and Development of Bedford-Stuyvesant Youth in Action, Inc.," [1967], all in DWP.

40. Board of Directors lists, February 16, 1967 and May 10, 1967; Ray H. Williams to board members, April 25, 1967; D.S.W., Incorporated, "Consultation and Review," May 22, 1967, all in DWP.

41. YIA, Minutes of the Board of Directors, May 11, 1967, June 22, 1967, June 29, 1967, July 20, 1967, DWP. The federal directive was the result of an amendment to the Economic Opportunity Act proposed by Congresswoman Edith Green, which also stipulated that CAAs be officially established and overseen by local governments. The clause had little effect in New York City, where such a setup had long been in place, but critics within the Republican Party termed it "the bosses and boll weevil amendment." See Lillian B. Rubin, "Maximum Feasible Participation: The Origins, Implications, and Present Status," *Annals of the American Academy of Political and Social Science* 385 (September 1969), 27.

42. New York City Human Resources Administration (HRA), "An Evaluation of the Agency (Bedford-Stuyvesant Youth in Action)" (January–February 1967), 5–6, DWP.

43. D.S.W., Incorporated, "Consultation and Review: The Bedford-Stuyvesant Youth in Action Program," May 22, 1967, i, DWP.

44. D.S.W., Incorporated, "Consultation and Review," DWP.

45. Ibid., 92–93.

46. HRA, "An Evaluation of the Agency," DWP.

47. "Maximum Feasible Participation: A Hope or a Hustle?" *Mobilization for Youth News Bulletin* (Summer 1966), DWP.

48. YIA, Minutes of the Board of Directors, February 17, 1966, DWP; D.S.W., Incorporated, "Consultation and Review," i, DWP; Paul R. Screvane, speech before the Central Brooklyn Coordinating Council, August 30, 1965, Folder 10, Box 060058W, RFW, LGW online; Audit of YIA, conducted by Emsar Bradford Jr. for the period ending October 31, 1966, DWP; List of New York

City Head Start sponsors, [1968, probably May], Papers of the Lindsay
Administration, Microfilm Roll 44, Folder 1644, NYCMA. On Head Start, see
Maris A. Vinovskis, *The Birth of Head Start: Preschool Education Policies in the
Kennedy and Johnson Administrations* (Chicago: University of Chicago Press,
2005); and Richard P. Nathan, ed., "How Should We Read the Evidence
About Head Start?" *Journal of Policy Analysis and Management* 26:3 (2007),
673–689.

49. D.S.W., Incorporated, "Consultation and Review," DWP; New York City
Council Against Poverty, Annual Report, 1966–1967, Columbia University
Social Work Library Agency Collection; "Over 1,000 Jobs Available Through
MCDA," YIA *Monthly Newspaper*, October 27, 1967, DWP; James Hurley,
interview with Ashley Bowden, November 12, 2011, Weeksville Heritage
Center.

50. "Brooklyn to Get Day-Care Center," NYT, August 29, 1971; "School for Unwed
Mothers to Be Dedicated," NYAN, June 4, 1975; Andy Cooper, "One Man's
Opinion," NYAN, April 16, 1977.

51. YIA, "The Unwed Mother" (1965), DWP.

52. YIA, "Welcome to Young Mothers," [1967], DWP.

53. YIA, "Welcome to Young Mothers," [1967], DWP; "Pregnant Girls Earn
Diplomas," NYT, December 18, 1966.

54. YIA, untitled pamphlet (undated), DWP; YIA, "Welcome to Young Mothers,"
[1967], DWP; YIA, "The Unwed Mother" (1965), DWP; "Unwed Mothers
Project Support Urged," NYAN, November 18, 1967.

55. YIA, "The Unwed Mother" (1965), 7, 11, DWP; YIA, press release, April 6,
1966, DWP.

56. "Community Sponsors Fund Drive," NYAN, June 17, 1967; "Unwed Mothers
Project Support Urged By CSI," NYAN, November 18, 1967; "$1.1 Million Loan
Agreement Signed By Brooklyn Women," *Atlanta Daily World*, September 5,
1971; "Pregnant Girls Earn Diplomas," NYT, December 18, 1966.

57. Elsie Richardson, for instance, mentioned Young Mothers when asked in a
1990 interview to reflect on her proudest accomplishments with CBCC. In
conversations with the author, Don Watkins, Jitu Weusi, and Sydney Moshette
Jr. all reserved special praise for DeFreitas's work.

58. Andy Cooper, "One Man's Opinion," NYAN, April 16, 1977.

59. Audrey C. Cohen to Sargent Shriver, June 28, 1965, Folder 2, Box 060242, RFW,
LGW online; Audrey C. Cohen, "The Women's Talent Corps: Proposal"
(1965), accessed via eric.ed.gov. On Cohen's life and work, see Grace G.
Roosevelt, *Creating a College That Works: Audrey Cohen and Metropolitan
College of New York* (Albany: State University of New York Press, 2015).

60. Women's Talent Corps, Progress Report for March–April 1967, accessed via
eric.ed.gov; Nick Juravich, "'Opportunity of a Lifetime': Paraprofessionals and

the UFT in New York City, 1966–78" (2012), 6–7. The author is grateful to Nick Juravich for granting permission to use this unpublished article.

61. Barbara J. Walton, "Second Annual Report and Evaluation of the Talent Corps/College of Human Services" (April 1969), 3; Wilbur J. Cohen to Sargent Shriver, June 18, 1965, Folder 2, Box 060242, RFW, LGW online.

62. YIA, "The Women's Talent Corps," [1966], DWP.

63. "Talent Corps Graduates Sent Afield," *Christian Science Monitor*, January 20, 1967; "Summary: The Women's Talent Corps," [1966], DWP; "Self-Help in the Ghetto," *NYT*, July 2, 1967; "A Graduation from Poverty into Jobs in Community Service," *NYT*, June 17, 1967; Juravich, "'Opportunity of a Lifetime.'"

64. Women's Talent Corps, Progress Report, March–April 1967, accessed via eric .edu. See Michael Katz, "Why Don't American Cities Burn Very Often?" *Journal of Urban History* 34:185 (2008), 185–208.

65. Barbara J. Walton, "Second Annual Report and Evaluation of the Talent Corps/College of Human Services" (April 1969); Audrey C. Cohen, "College for Human Services: A Model for Innovation in Urban Higher Education" (May 1967), 1, accessed via eric.ed.gov; "Self-Made College," *Time*, July 6, 1970; Henry Weil, "A New Degree Challenges Tradition," *Change* 6:10 (Winter 1974–1975), 18–20; Metropolitan College of New York website, www.mcny.edu/about/history1.php; Juravich, "'Opportunity of a Lifetime,'" 10–11, 31.

66. For an example of this critique, see Judith Russell, *Economics, Bureaucracy, and Race: How Keynesians Misguided the War on Poverty* (New York: Columbia University Press, 2004).

67. Carl McCall to Walter Offutt, March 7, 1967, DWP.

68. YIA, Minutes of the Board of Directors, October 19, 1967, DWP. The board attempted on several occasions to fire Pinkston, and he finally left the agency in 1970. See "Pinkston Ouster Demanded by YIA Dissidents," *NYAN*, June 7, 1969; "Boro YIA Board Fires Pinkston," *NYAN*, September 13, 1969; and "YIA Discord Cause for Dismissal of Director," *NYAN*, October 25, 1969.

69. YIA, "Community Action Area I's Questions and Grievances" (June 21, 1968), DWP.

70. The archives abound with examples of planners' confusion about how funds flowed from OEO to local agencies. For instance, in 1968, the Council Against Poverty held a marathon orientation session to walk new board members through what the chairman, Edwin Greenidge, called the "Rube Goldberg" structures linking federal, state, regional, and city policymaking bodies. "Try not to be snowed by it all," was Greenidge's advice to the men and women charged with vetting the city's poverty policies. See Minutes of the New York

City Council Against Poverty, April 18, 1968, New York Public Library: Science, Industry, and Business Library.

71. "'Happenings' in Park Unsponsored Chaos," NYAN, August 19, 1967; YIA, Minutes of the Board of Directors, July 27, 1967, DWP; YIA, Minutes of public meeting with the Board of Directors, August 9, 1967, DWP.

72. Mitchell Sviridoff, "Conclusion," in Sviridoff, ed., *Inventing Community Renewal*, 242.

73. Task Force on Urban Areas, Preliminary Report, April 8, 1964, "President's Committee File, 4/64," Richardson White Papers, Box 4, JFKL. On the influence and limitations of "community development" ideals in other countries, see Daniel Immerwahr, *Thinking Small: The United States and the Lure of Community Development* (Cambridge, MA: Harvard University Press, 2015).

74. Carson, "Brooklyn Core," YIA *Monthly Newspaper*, August 3, 1967, DWP.

75. "Hard Work Helps Land $1.1 Million Construction Loan," *Jet* (September 16, 1971); "'I'm Finished Caring': DeFreitas," NYAN, April 16, 1977; "Acquit YIA Exec in Fraud," NYAN, July 22, 1978.

76. The answer, according to Carson, was CORE—"the sole group who unselfishly, untiringly and without material reward is champion of the plight of the oppressed." See Carson, "Brooklyn Core," YIA *Monthly Newspaper*, August 3, 1967, DWP.

77. Melvin B. Mogulof to David Hackett, March 11, 1964, "Community Action Programs: Poverty (2)," Richardson White Papers, Box 6, JFKL.

6. The Power to Act

Epigraph: Robert F. Kennedy, statement before the Annual Conference on Community Development in Bedford-Stuyvesant, hosted by the Central Brooklyn Coordinating Council (CBCC), December 10, 1966, Don Watkins Papers (DWP).

1. "Redevelopment Plan Set for Bedford-Stuyvesant," *New York Times (NYT)*, December 11, 1966; "Community, Government and Business Unite to Rehabilitate Bedford-Stuyvesant," *Central Brooklyn Coordinator*, January 1967, DWP.

2. Proceedings of CBCC Conference, December 10, 1966, Bedford-Stuyvesant Restoration Corporation Oral History Project (BSRCOH), Brooklyn Historical Society (BHS); "Community, Government and Business Unite to Rehabilitate Bedford-Stuyvesant," *Central Brooklyn Coordinator*, January 1967, DWP.

3. Proceedings of CBCC Conference, December 10, 1966, BSRCOH, BHS.

4. Ibid.

5. Ibid.

6. Ibid.; Robert F. Kennedy, statement, December 10, 1966, DWP. On Kennedy's reasons for getting involved in Bedford-Stuyvesant, see note 6 in the Introduction to this volume.

7. Proceedings of CBCC Conference, December 10, 1966, BSRCOH, BHS.

8. The borders of Clinton Hill are a matter of dispute. In the nineteenth century, the wealthy area known as "The Hill," centered around majestic Clinton Avenue, included much of the former town of Bedford, as well as most of what are today known as Clinton Hill and Fort Greene. Today, Clinton Hill is defined as the rectangle bordered by Vanderbilt Avenue, Bedford Avenue, Myrtle Avenue, and Atlantic Avenue. In the late 1960s, this area was usually considered a part of Bedford-Stuyvesant, especially as its white residents decamped. See Brian Merlis, *Brooklyn's Historic Clinton Hill and Wallabout* (Brooklyn, NY: Israelowitz Publishing, 2011), 22–26; and Ronald Shiffman, interview with the author, July 16, 2015.

9. The Center is known today as the Pratt Center for Community Development. See Pratt Center for Community Development, "The Pratt Center Story" (2008), www.prattcenter.net/pratt-center-story. On the Pratt Center's activist tradition, see Laura Wolf-Powers, "Expanding Planning's Public Sphere: *STREET* Magazine, Activist Planning, and Community Development in Brooklyn, New York, 1971–1975," *Journal of Planning Education and Research* 28 (2008), 180–195.

10. "New Center Aids Area Replanning," NYT, July 31, 1966; George M. Raymond and Ronald Shiffman, "The Pratt Center for Community Improvement: A University Urban Action Program," *Pratt Planning Papers* 4:4 (January 1967), 27–40. On Jacobs and the revolt against planning, see Christopher Klemek, "Dead or Alive? Reading Jane Jacobs on Her Golden Anniversary, *Dissent* (Spring 2011), 73–77; Christopher Klemek, "From Political Outsider to Power Broker in Two 'Great American Cities': Jane Jacobs and the Fall of the Urban Renewal Order in New York and Toronto," *Journal of Urban History* 34:2 (January 2008), 309–332; Roberta Brandes Gratz, *The Battle for Gotham: New York in the Shadow of Robert Moses and Jane Jacobs* (New York: Nation Books, 2010); and Steven A. Goldsmith and Lynne Elizabeth, eds., *What We See: Advancing the Observations of Jane Jacobs* (Oakland: New Village Press, 2010).

11. "Aide Says City Clears Slums but Fails to Improve Environs," NYT, December 29, 1960; George Raymond, "Successful Rehabilitation Calls for New Approach: 'Continuous Renewal,'" *Journal of Housing* 17:4 (April 1960), 135–137; George M. Raymond, "Editorial: Seward Park Extension," *Pratt Planning Papers* 1:2 (May 1962), 6; Marci Reaven, "Citizen Participation in City Planning: New York City, 1945–1975" (PhD thesis, New York University, 2005), 177, 211; George Raymond, "Needed: A Vote of Confidence," *Pratt Planning Papers* 1:1 (February 1962), 8.

12. Raymond and Shiffman, "The Pratt Center," 27–28; Jennifer Stern, "Pratt to the Rescue: Advocacy Planning Is Alive and Well in Brooklyn," *Planning* (May 1989), 26–28. On the brownstoners of Cobble Hill, see Suleiman Osman, *The Invention of Brownstone Brooklyn: Gentrification and the Search for Authenticity in Postwar New York* (New York: Oxford University Press, 2011), Chap. 6.

13. Raymond, "Needed: A Vote of Confidence," 8; George Raymond, "Pratt Institute Planning Department Recipient of a $94,000 Rockefeller Brothers Fund Grant," *Pratt Planning Papers* 1:4 (January 1963), 1.

14. Raymond, "Pratt Institute Planning Department Recipient," 1.

15. Ronald Shiffman, interview with Sady Sullivan, February 4, 2008, BRSCOH, BHS; Ronald Shiffman, "Strategy for a Coordinated Social and Physical Renewal Program: Bedford-Stuyvesant" (draft edition, 1966), courtesy New York State Public Library; Ronald Shiffman, interview with Todd W. Bressi, *Places* 12:2 (1999), 53; Stern, "Pratt to the Rescue," 27.

16. Paul Davidoff, "Advocacy and Pluralism in Planning," *Journal of the American Institute of Planners* 31:4 (1965), 546.

17. Davidoff, "Advocacy and Pluralism in Planning," 545; emphasis in original. On Davidoff's thinking and impact, see Allan David Heskin, "Crisis and Response: A Historical Perspective on Advocacy Planning," *Journal of the American Planning Association* 46:1 (1980), 50–63; and Barry Checkoway, "Paul Davidoff and Advocacy Planning in Retrospect," *Journal of the American Planning Association* 60:2 (1994), 139–143. On the limits of advocacy planning, see Robert Goodman, *After the Planners* (New York: Simon and Schuster, 1971). For a perspective that links Davidoff's views to Jane Jacobs's, see Chester Hartman, "Steps Toward a Just Metropolis," in Goldsmith and Elizabeth, eds., *What We See*, 167–175.

18. Ronald Shiffman, interview with Todd W. Bressi, 53; Ford Foundation, "Urban Extension: A Report on Experimental Programs Assisted by the Ford Foundation" (October 1966), at www.eric.ed.gov; "New Center Aids Area Replanning," *NYT*, July 31, 1966.

19. H. Carl McCall, interview with the author, September 23, 2014; "Church Unit Surveys B-S Housing Ills," *New York Amsterdam News (NYAN)*, July 25, 1964; "Churches Start $100,000 Program for Negro Youth," NYAN, August 1, 1964; "39 Area Churches Helping B-S Youths," NYAN, January 22, 1966.

20. Ronald Shiffman, interview with the author, July 16, 2015.

21. "Worst City Slums Due for Renewal in New Program," *NYT*, April 14, 1964; "Plan Urban Renewal," NYAN, April 25, 1964.

22. "Church Unit Surveys B-S Housing Ills," NYAN, July 25, 1964; "New Center Aids Area Replanning," *NYT*, July 31, 1966; Pratt Institute Planning Department, "Stuyvesant Heights: A Good Neighborhood in Need of Help" (1965),

Pratt Center for Community Development online; Ronald Shiffman, interview with Sady Sullivan, February 4, 2008, BSRCOH, BHS.

23. Ronald Shiffman, interview with the author, July 16, 2015; Raymond and Shiffman, "The Pratt Center for Community Improvement," 30–31.

24. Raymond and Shiffman, "The Pratt Center for Community Improvement," 30–31.

25. CBCC, "Program for Total Rehabilitation and Renewal of Bedford-Stuyvesant," presented at CBCC War on Poverty Conference, November 21, 1964, and published as an appendix in Shiffman, "Strategy for a Coordinated Social and Physical Renewal Program."

26. The classic argument about misapplied social science in the War an Poverty is Daniel P. Moynihan, *Maximum Feasible Misunderstanding: Community Action in the War on Poverty* (New York: The Free Press, 1969).

27. At different times, Richardson served as the representative to CBCC for either the Parkway-Stuyvesant Civic Council or the Brower Park Civic Council; both groups acted as umbrella organizations for block associations in Crown Heights. Elsie Richardson, Obituary (self-authored), distributed March 20, 2012; Elsie Richardson, interview with James Briggs Murray, February 2, 1990, Community Development Corporation Oral History Project (CDCOH), New York Public Library, Schomburg Center for Research in Black Culture (NYPL-Sch); Elsie Richardson, interview with the author, June 5, 2011.

28. Ronald Shiffman, interview with Sady Sullivan, February 4, 2008, BSRCOH, BHS; Proceedings of CBCC Conference on Community Development in Bedford-Stuyvesant, December 10, 1966, BSRCOH, BHS; Ronald Shiffman, interview with the author, July 16, 2015. Shiffman and Richardson continued to profess their mutual admiration almost a half-century after they first met. In a eulogy delivered at Richardson's funeral on March 20, 2012, Shiffman said: "I earned my degree from Pratt, but my education really began when I met Elsie."

29. Ronald Shiffman, interview with Sady Sullivan, February 4, 2008, BSRCOH, BHS; Elsie Richardson, interview with James Briggs Murray, February 2, 1990, CDCOH, NYPL-Sch.

30. CBCC, Final Report for the Eighth Annual Meeting (1965–66), "Annual Report, 1965–66," CBCC Papers, BHS; "Bedford-Stuyvesant Needs More," *Central Brooklyn Coordinator*, August 16, 1965, CBCC Papers, BHS.

31. "Poverty Fighters Back Street Plan," *NYT*, December 20, 1964; "$5 Million Poverty Plan," *New York World-Telegram*, December 17, 1964; CBCC, "Program for Total Rehabilitation and Renewal of Bedford-Stuyvesant," November 21, 1964, in Shiffman, "Strategy for a Coordinated Social and Physical Renewal Program"; CBCC, Recommendations of the Housing and Planning

Workshop, November 21, 1964, in Shiffman, "Strategy for a Coordinated Social and Physical Renewal Program."

32. CBCC, "Program for Total Rehabilitation and Renewal of Bedford-Stuyvesant," November 21, 1964, in Shiffman, "Strategy for a Coordinated Social and Physical Renewal Program."

33. "Training Resources for Youth: Brooklyn, U.S.A.," report by the YMCA of Greater New York, June 1965.

34. Osman, *The Invention of Brownstone Brooklyn*, 100; Thomas J. Sugrue writes that "in 1963, a remarkable 83 percent of blacks saw the federal government as 'helpful' to them." See Sugrue, *Sweet Land of Liberty: The Forgotten Struggle for Civil Rights in the North* (New York: Random House, 2008), 357.

35. CBCC, "Program for Total Rehabilitation and Renewal" and CBCC, Recommendations of the Housing and Planning Workshop, both in Shiffman, "Strategy for a Coordinated Social and Physical Renewal Program."

36. Ford Foundation (R. B. Goldmann, author), "Performance in Black and White: An Appraisal of the Development and Record of the Bedford-Stuyvesant Restoration and Development and Services Corporations" (February 1969), 4, 92, Box 1, Ford Foundation Papers, John F. Kennedy Presidential Library (JFKL); Shiffman, "Strategy for a Coordinated Social and Physical Renewal Program," 6–12.

37. The proposal submitted by the Citizens Housing and Planning Council encapsulated the integrated approach that Shiffman and CBCC were just beginning to contemplate in late 1963 and early 1964: "The problem of such a section—the slum problem, in a word—is, as has been said for years, a problem of the physical deterioration of buildings. Yet it is not simply the problem of buildings. It is a social problem, growing out of and contributing to the deterioration of families and individuals. Yet it is not simply a social problem. It is an economic problem, growing out of the lack of economic investment in slum areas, the lack of job opportunities, and the shortage of government funds." See Michael Coffey, "Proposal for a Demonstration Program in Total Community Development" (April 1963), 1, Folder 11, Box 060239, Robert F. Wagner Papers (RFW), La Guardia & Wagner Archives (LGW) online.

38. Karen Ferguson argues that Sullivan, a Ford Foundation protégée, offered Kennedy and foundation officials a template for the kind of leadership they desired in Bedford-Stuyvesant. See Karen Ferguson, *Top Down: The Ford Foundation, Black Power, and the Reinvention of Racial Liberalism* (Philadelphia: University of Pennsylvania Press, 2013), 214.

39. Elsie Richardson would later insist that the ideas picked up in the Model Cities program were largely a restatement of the plans hatched by CBCC and Pratt in 1964. See Elsie Richardson, interview with James Briggs Murray, February 2, 1990, CDCOH, NYPL-Sch; Elsie Richardson to Robert F.

Kennedy, March 27, 1967, "Correspondence, 1/10/67–4/4/67," Box 1, Thomas M. C. Johnston Papers (TMCJP), JFKL. On evolving federal policy in 1966, see Alexander von Hoffman, "Into the Wild Blue Yonder: The Urban Crisis, Rocket Science, and the Pursuit of Transformation" (Joint Center for Housing Studies, Harvard University, 2011).

40. New York City Council Against Poverty, Guidelines for the formation of Community Corporations (Approved on October 27, 1966), DWP; New York City Council Against Poverty, "New York City Poverty Areas (Maps and Boundary Descriptions)," 1970, New York City Municipal Archives (NYCMA).

41. Ronald Shiffman, "Beyond the Marketplace: Towards an Equitable Housing Program," lecture delivered at the New York Center for Architecture (2006), 7.

42. Paul R. Screvane, speech before the CBCC, August 30, 1965, Folder 10, Box 060058W, RFW, LGW online; "Javits, RFK to Appear in Housing Talk," NYAN, October 30, 1965; Ronald Shiffman, interview with the author, July 16, 2015; Shiffman, "Strategy for a Coordinated Social and Physical Renewal Program," 105; "Bedford-Stuyvesant Needs More," *Central Brooklyn Coordinator*, August 16, 1965, CBCC Papers, BHS; Ronald Shiffman, interview with Sady Sullivan, February 4, 2008, BSRCOH, BHS.

43. Arthur M. Schlesinger, *Robert Kennedy and His Times* (Boston: Houghton Mifflin, 1978), Chap. 35; Joseph A. Palermo, *In His Own Right: The Political Odyssey of Senator Robert F. Kennedy* (New York: Columbia University Press, 2001), 3; Edward R. Schmitt, *President of the Other America: Robert Kennedy and the Politics of Poverty* (Amherst: University of Massachusetts Press, 2010), 16. Another biographer, Jack Newfield, has referred to the "consistently moralistic and emotional root of Kennedy's politics." See Jack Newfield, *Robert Kennedy: A Memoir* (New York: Dutton, 1969), 69. For Kennedy in his own words, see Robert F. Kennedy, *To Seek a Newer World* (Garden City, NY: Doubleday, 1967).

44. Richard W. Boone, "Reflections on Citizen Participation and the Economic Opportunity Act," *Public Administration Review* 32 (September 1972), 447.

45. "How the Average Negro Is Thinking," NYAN, June 23, 1962. The extent of the Kennedys' commitment to civil rights during these critical months remains a matter of debate. John Dittmer, in his account of the Mississippi freedom struggle, writes that both Kennedys "preferred order to justice" until mid-1963, and even the civil-rights legislation proposed that year was seen by activists as weak. See John Dittmer, *Local People: The Struggle for Civil Rights in Mississippi* (Champaign: University of Illinois Press, 1995), 169. In contrast, Edward Schmitt writes that by early 1963, "most African Americans remained convinced—in spite of serious disappointments—that both the attorney general and the president were firmly on their side, and were increasingly

treating blacks as full political partners." See Schmitt, *President of the Other America*, 53. See also Palermo, *In His Own Right*, 5, 163.

46. Newfield, *Robert Kennedy*, 30–31; Evan Thomas, *Robert Kennedy: His Life* (New York: Simon and Schuster, 2000), 319–320.

47. Robert Caro, "The Transition," *The New Yorker*, April 2, 2012. Kennedy maintained in 1964 that his brother had been planning an antipoverty program of considerable magnitude. As Johnson's $1 billion program was set to begin, RFK claimed that President Kennedy had foreseen dedicating "several billions of dollars each year" to the antipoverty effort. See Schmitt, *President of the Other America*, 96–97.

48. Quoted in Schlesinger, *Robert Kennedy and His Times*, 778; quoted in Mitchell Sviridoff, ed., *Inventing Community Renewal: The Trials and Errors That Shaped the Modern Community Development Corporation* (New York: New School University, 2004), 59. See also Thomas, *Robert Kennedy*, 318.

49. Robert F. Kennedy to Lyndon B. Johnson, January 16, 1964, "Hackett, David: Memoranda, 1963–1964," Box 33, Adam Walinsky Papers (AWP), JFKL.

50. Hackett to Kennedy, December 20, 1963; Hackett to Charles L. Schultze, January 22, 1964; Hackett to Sargent Shriver, February 11, 1964, all in "Poverty, Hackett, David: Memoranda, 1963–1964," Box 33, AWP, JFKL.

51. Robert F. Kennedy, speech, June 26, 1964, "Poverty, Hackett, David: Memoranda, 1963–1964," Box 33, AWP, JFKL.

52. Kennedy to Johnson, January 16, 1964, JFKL; quoted in Stuart Gerry Brown, *The Presidency on Trial: Robert Kennedy's 1968 Campaign and Afterwards* (Honolulu: University Press of Hawaii, 1972), 21.

53. "Kennedy Urges All to Join Campaign," NYAN, September 11, 1965; Robert F. Kennedy, speech, June 26, 1964, "Poverty, Hackett, David: Memoranda, 1963–1964," Box 33, AWP, JFKL.

54. Ford Foundation/Goldmann, "Performance in Black and White," 10, JFKL; Schmitt, *President of the Other America*, 111–112; Adam Walinsky to Robert F. Kennedy, Re. Program for the fall [1966], "Bedford-Stuyvesant: Memoranda," Box 2, AWP, JFKL; Adam Walinsky to Robert F. Kennedy, Re. Activities for this year [1967], "Bedford-Stuyvesant: Memoranda," Box 2, AWP, JFKL; Peter B. Edelman, interview with Larry Hackman, January 3, 1970, Robert F. Kennedy Oral History Program (RFKOH), JFKL.

55. Adam Walinsky, "Keeping the Poor in Their Place," *New Republic* 151:1 (July 4, 1964), 15–18.

56. Adam Walinsky, Review of Daniel P. Moynihan's *Maximum Feasible Misunderstanding*, NYT, February 2, 1969.

57. On Kennedy's response to Watts, see Schmitt, *President of the Other America*, Chap. 5.

58. Robert F. Kennedy, "Reflections on the 1965 Watts Riots, Aug. 18, 1965," in Edwin O. Guthman and C. Richard Allen, eds., *RFK: Collected Speeches* (New York: Viking, 1993), 162.

59. Peter B. Edelman, interview with Larry Hackman, January 3, 1970, RFKOH, JFKL; Peter B. Edelman, interview with the author, August 29, 2014.

60. Kennedy, "Reflections on the 1965 Watts Riots."

61. David Hackett and Thomas Johnston to Robert Kennedy, August 27, 1965, "Memoranda, miscellaneous, 8/27/65–1/16/68 and undated," Box 2, TMCJP, JFKL.

62. Guthman and Allen, *RFK*, 165; Schmitt, *President of the Other America*, 124. For a sophisticated take on Kennedy's thought process, see Tom Adam Davies, "Black Power in Action: The Bedford-Stuyvesant Restoration Corporation, Robert F. Kennedy, and the Politics of the Urban Crisis," *Journal of American History* 100:3 (December 2013), 740–744.

63. Peter B. Edelman, interview with Larry Hackman, January 3, 1970, RFKOH, JFKL.

64. Robert F. Kennedy, speech at Borough President's Conference on Harlem (draft), January 21, 1966, "Speeches: Drafts: 1/21/1966–1/22/1966," Box 34, AWP, JFKL.

65. Lyndon B. Johnson, "Special Message to the Congress Recommending a Program for Cities and Metropolitan Areas, Jan. 26, 1966," accessed via the American Presidency Project online; Walter Thabit, *How East New York Became a Ghetto* (New York: New York University Press, 2003), 138. By 1967, Elsie Richardson and others in the CBCC leadership group were arguing that their ideas, as put forth in 1964, had influenced the task force that conceived of the Model Cities program. Whether or not any direct lines of influence existed, the claim is nonetheless intriguing, as it points up CBCC's self-conscious attempts to influence federal policymaking. See Elsie Richardson to Robert F. Kennedy, March 27, 1967, "Correspondence, 1/10/67–4/4/67," Box 1, TMCJP, JFKL.

66. Ford Foundation/Goldmann, "Performance in Black and White," 11, JFKL; Guthman and Allen, *RFK*, 176.

67. Geoffrey Faux, "Politics and Bureaucracy in Community-Controlled Economic Development," *Law and Contemporary Problems* 36:2 (Spring 1971), 279–280.

68. Ronald Shiffman, interview with Sady Sullivan, February 4, 2008, BSRCOH, BHS; Shiffman, "Beyond the Marketplace"; Colvin Grannum, interview with the author, August 22, 2014.

69. Graves would go on to found *Black Enterprise* magazine in 1970 and become one of the wealthiest black men in the country.

70. Carter Burden, interview with Roberta W. Greene, February 13, 1974, RFKOH, JFKL; Newfield, *Robert Kennedy*, 95.

71. Robert F. Kennedy to McGeorge Bundy [1966], "Bedford-Stuyvesant: Ford Foundation," Box 1, AWP, JFKL; Ford Foundation/Goldmann, "Performance in Black and White," 13, JFKL.

72. CBCC, "List of Priorities for Bedford-Stuyvesant, Presented to the office of Robert F. Kennedy, Feb. 22, 1966," published as an appendix in Shiffman, "Strategy for a Coordinated Social and Physical Renewal Program."

73. Peter B. Edelman, interview with the author, August 29, 2014; Ford Foundation/Goldmann, "Performance in Black and White," 25–26, JFKL.

74. Ford Foundation/Goldmann, "Performance in Black and White," 15–20, JFKL; "Bklyn Leaders Get Support from RFK," NYAN, October 22, 1966.

75. CBCC, "Bedford-Stuyvesant Renewal and Rehabilitation Corporation: A Proposal," [1966], "Bedford-Stuyvesant, 1/1968 and undated," Box 1, AWP, JFKL; H. Carl McCall, interview with the author, September 23, 2014; Schmitt, *President of the Other America*, 154–155.

76. Elsie Richardson, interview with James Briggs Murray, February 2, 1990, CDCOH, NYPL-Sch; Ford Foundation/Goldmann, "Performance in Black and White," 25–26, JFKL.

77. William P. Ryan, "Bedford-Stuyvesant and the Prototype Community Development Corporation," in Sviridoff, ed., *Inventing Community Renewal*, 70–71.

78. Lawrence F. Parachini, *A Political History of the Special Impact Program* (Cambridge, MA: Center for Community Economic Development, 1980); EBS Management Consultants, "Initial Evaluation of the Bedford-Stuyvesant Special Impact Program," prepared for the U.S. Department of Labor, June 30, 1969.

79. Office of Economic Opportunity, "Narrative Summary of the Economic Opportunity Amendments of 1966," 4–5, DWP; Ford Foundation/Goldmann, "Performance in Black and White," 14–15, JFKL; Thomas R. Jones, interview with James Briggs Murray, February 10, 1990, CDCOH, NYPL-Sch. Kennedy and Javits also proposed to create something they called the Economic Opportunity Corporation, which would in effect have been a vehicle for taking the poverty fight outside of the control of the White House and the OEO bureaucracy. Aimed at promoting the industrial and commercial revival of poor neighborhoods, it would have issued up to $1 billion in capital stock and been authorized to help fund a variety of initiatives related to the poverty program: job training, small-business loans, slum rehabilitation, and so forth. "The intent here is to establish the EOC as the one-stop service point for involving the private sector in activities aimed at improving slum and ghetto

conditions," a planning document stated. "Senator Javits's Proposal to Establish an Economic Opportunity Corporation," [January 1967], "Office of
Economic Opportunity, 1/1967–12/1967," Box 31, AWP, JFKL.

80. Planning documents, November 15, 1966, and undated, "Planning/Structure,
9/28/66–5/3/67 and undated," Box 2, TMCJP, JFKL; Newfield, *Robert Kennedy,* 95.

81. George M. Raymond and Ronald Shiffman to Thomas Johnston, September
7, 1966, "Correspondence, 7/31/66–10/14/66," Box 1, TMCJP, JFKL; "Bedford-
Stuyvesant Program," [Fall 1966], "Bedford-Stuyvesant: Memoranda," Box 2,
AWP, JFKL.

82. Walinsky to Kennedy, Re. Program for the fall [1966], JFKL.

83. Kennedy, statement before the CBCC, DWP; "Community, Government, and
Business Unite in Bedford-Stuyvesant," *Central Brooklyn Coordinator,* January
1967, DWP; "Redevelopment Plan Set for Bedford-Stuyvesant," NYT, De-
cember 11, 1966; "RFK Announces Big N.Y. Anti-Slum Program," *Washington
Post,* December 11, 1966; "Remaking Brooklyn's Slums," NYT, December 12,
1966; "A Giant Step in Right Direction," NYAN, December 24, 1966; "New
Look Coming to Bedford-Stuy," NYAN, December 17, 1966; Proceedings of
CBCC Conference, December 10, 1966, BSRCOH, BHS.

7. Whose Community, What Action?

Epigraph: Elsie Richardson, "Ring around the Rosy," *Central Brooklyn
Coordinator,* January 1967, Don Watkins Papers (DWP).

1. Bedford-Stuyvesant Development and Services Corporation (D&S), Minutes
of the Board of Directors, January 12, 1967, "Planning 1966–1967, Vol. 1,"
Box 44, Burke Marshall Papers (BMP), John F. Kennedy Library (JFKL).

2. James F. Oates, the chairman of Equitable Life insurance, would join the
board in mid-1967.

3. Robert F. Kennedy, statement before the Central Brooklyn Coordinating
Council Conference on Community Development, December 10, 1966, DWP;
Cary Reich, *Financier: The Biography of André Meyer* (New York: William
Morrow and Company, 1983); "The Greatest Capitalist in History," *Fortune,*
August 31, 1987; D&S, Minutes, January 12, 1967, JFKL. On the motives of the
businessmen for joining the Kennedy project, see Jack Newfield, *Robert
Kennedy: A Memoir* (New York: Dutton, 1969), 98–102.

4. Jeff Shesol, *Mutual Contempt: Lyndon Johnson, Robert Kennedy, and the Feud
that Defined a Decade* (New York: W.W. Norton, 1997), 249; "Redevelopment
Plan Set for Bedford-Stuyvesant," *New York Times (NYT),* December 11, 1966.

5. Robert F. Kennedy, statement, December 10, 1966, DWP; D&S, Minutes,
January 12, 1967, JFKL.

6. Franklin A. Thomas, interview with Roberta W. Greene, March 23, 1972, Robert F. Kennedy Oral History Program (RFKOH), JFKL.

7. Benno C. Schmidt, interview with Roberta W. Greene, July 17, 1969, RFKOH, JFKL; "Bedford-Stuyvesant: A Ghetto Action Prototype," *Pratt Planning Papers* 4:4 (January 1967), 3.

8. William P. Ryan, "Bedford-Stuyvesant and the Prototype Community Development Corporation," in Mitchell Sviridoff, ed., *Inventing Community Renewal: The Trials and Errors That Shaped the Modern Community Development Corporation* (New York: New School University, 2004), 73; Ford Foundation (R. B. Goldmann, author), "Performance in Black and White: An Appraisal of the Development and Record of the Bedford-Stuyvesant Restoration and Development and Services Corporations" (February 1969), 22–23, Box 1, Ford Foundation Papers, JFKL; Reich, *Financier*; "Master of Mergers," *NYT*, October 16, 1983; "Bklyn Leaders Get Support From RFK," *New York Amsterdam News (NYAN)*, October 22, 1966.

9. Benno C. Schmidt, interview with Roberta W. Greene, July 17, 1969, RFKOH, JFKL.

10. Thomas, *Robert Kennedy*, 325; Benno C. Schmidt, interview with Roberta W. Greene, July 17, 1969, RFKOH, JFKL; Ford Foundation/Goldmann, "Performance in Black and White," 24, JFKL.

11. Adam Walinsky to Robert F. Kennedy, Re. Program for the fall [1966], "Bedford-Stuyvesant: Memoranda," Box 2, Adam Walinsky Papers (AWP), JFKL.

12. Ibid.; Adam Walinsky to Robert F. Kennedy, Re. Activities for this year [1967], "Bedford-Stuyvesant: Memoranda," Box 2, AWP, JFKL.

13. "Air Thick with Plans for Ghetto," *Washington Post*, September 29, 1966; Ford Foundation/Goldmann, "Performance in Black and White," 28, JFKL; Arthur M. Schlesinger, *Robert Kennedy and His Times* (Boston: Houghton Mifflin, 1978), 234, 742.

14. Karen Ferguson, *Top Down: The Ford Foundation, Black Power, and the Reinvention of Racial Liberalism* (Philadelphia: University of Pennsylvania Press, 2013), 214; Benno C. Schmidt, interview with Roberta W. Greene, July 17, 1969, RFKOH, JFKL.

15. Leonard N. Moore, *Carl B. Stokes and the Rise of Black Political Power* (Urbana: University of Illinois Press, 2002), 68.

16. Robert F. Kennedy, statement, December 10, 1966, DWP; Ford Foundation/Goldmann, "Performance in Black and White," 41, JFKL. See also Ryan, "Bedford-Stuyvesant and the Prototype Community Development Corporation," 82–83.

17. Raymond & May Associates, David A. Crane, I. M. Pei and Partners, and William R. McGrath, "A Proposal for Planning and Design Services: Preliminary

Physical Development Plan," submitted to Edward J. Logue, February 9, 1967, "Bedford-Stuyvesant: Memoranda," Box 2, AWP, JFKL; Edward Logue to Donald Elliott, Frank Thomas, and Eli Jacobs, July 10, 1967, "Planning, 1966–1967, Volume 1," Box 45, BMP, JFKL.

18. D&S, Minutes, January 12, 1967, JFKL.

19. Ford Foundation/Goldmann, "Performance in Black and White," 40, JFKL.

20. D&S, Minutes, January 12, 1967, JFKL; "Bedford-Stuyvesant Given Grant to Plan a Network of Parks," *NYT*, March 26, 1967.

21. D&S, Minutes, January 12, 1967, JFKL.

22. D&S, Minutes of the Board of Directors, March 8, 1967, "Board of Directors: Rehabilitation Committee Meeting, 3/8/67," Box 1, Thomas M. C. Johnston Papers (TMCJP), JFKL; D&S, Minutes, January 12, 1967, JFKL; "A Proposal for Planning and Design Services: Preliminary Physical Development Plan," April 11, 1967, "Planning, 1966–1967, Volume 1," Box 45, BMP, JFKL; George Raymond to Eli Jacobs, October 3, 1967, "Planning, 1966–1967, Volume 1," Box 45, BMP, JFKL.

23. Franklin A. Thomas, interview with Roberta W. Greene, March 23, 1972, JFKL; Thomas R. Jones to Thomas Johnston, March 10, 1967, and March 19, 1967, "Memoranda, miscellaneous, 8/27/65–1/16/68 and undated," Box 2, TMCJP, JFKL.

24. Jones quoted in Ford Foundation/Goldmann, "Performance in Black and White," 40, JFKL; Eli Jacobs, interview with Roberta Greene, October 27, 1976, RFKOH, JFKL. Logue remained affiliated with the project through the summer of 1967, but his role was cut down significantly. Though he periodically protested the marginalization of his plans, by that point he was running for mayor of Boston and had little time to devote to Bedford-Stuyvesant. See Edward J. Logue, memo, August 7, 1967, "Planning, Volume 1, 1966–1967 (6)," Box 45, BMP, JFKL.

25. Bryant George, Purpose and Structure: Bedford-Stuyvesant Renewal and Rehabilitation Corporation, February 14, 1967, "Bedford-Stuyvesant: Memoranda," Box 2, AWP, JFKL; memo, [1966, possibly Edward Logue], "Bedford-Stuyvesant: Memoranda," Box 2, AWP, JFKL.

26. Memo re. Tasks immediately ahead in Bedford-Stuyvesant, [December 1966, likely Adam Walinsky or Thomas Johnston], "Bedford-Stuyvesant: Memoranda," Box 2, AWP, JFKL.

27. Elsie Richardson, "Ring around the Rosy," *Central Brooklyn Coordinator*, January 1967, DWP.

28. Tavis Smiley, *Death of a King: The Real Story of Dr. Martin Luther King Jr.'s Final Year* (New York: Little Brown, 2014).

29. Ford Foundation/Goldmann, "Performance in Black and White," 31–32, JFKL.

30. Bedford-Stuyvesant Renewal and Rehabilitation Corporation, Insert for Minutes of Meeting of Board of Directors, March 31, 1967, "Board of Directors: Renewal and Rehabilitation Corporation," Box 1, TMCJP, JFKL; Ronald Shiffman, interview with Sady Sullivan, February 4, 2008, Bedford-Stuyvesant Restoration Corporation Oral History Project (BSRCOH), Brooklyn Historical Society (BHS); Ronald Shiffman, interview with the author, July 16, 2015; "McQueen Heads Coordinating Unit," NYAN, April 30, 1966.

31. Central Brooklyn Coordinating Council (CBCC), Final Report for the Eighth Annual Meeting (1965–66), "Annual Report, 1965–66," Papers of the CBCC, BHS.

32. Ford Foundation/Goldmann, "Performance in Black and White," 7, JFKL; Brian Purnell, "'What We Need Is Brick and Mortar:' Race, Gender, and Early Leadership of the Bedford-Stuyvesant Restoration Corporation," in Laura Warren Hill and Julia Rabig, eds., *The Business of Black Power: Community Development, Capitalism, and Corporate Responsibility in Postwar America* (Rochester, NY: University of Rochester Press, 2012), 221.

33. "Lucille Rose Captures NAACP Title," NYAN, January 13, 1945; "Lucille Rose Dead at 68," NYAN, August 22, 1987; "Lucille Mason Rose, First Woman Named as a Deputy Mayor," NYT, August 18, 1987; Ruth Edmonds Hill, "Lucille Mason Rose," *Notable Black American Women, Book II* (Detroit: Gale Research, 1996), 573–574; "Introducing Mrs. Lucille Rose," NYAN, October 21, 1961; "NAACP Credited," NYAN, March 16, 1963; "Woman Director Sworn In," NYAN, October 3, 1964.

34. "New Life for the Brownstones of Bedford-Stuyvesant," NYT, October 10, 1985; "Lucille Rose Dead at 68," NYAN, August 22, 1987.

35. For instance, in February 1963, when Mayor Wagner hosted a "united front" of ten Stuyford leaders at City Hall, Chisholm was the only woman among them. Similarly, a key 1963 meeting between CBCC and city housing officials was a mostly male affair. See "Leaders Question Mayor on Unemployment," NYAN, February 16, 1963; and CBCC, Minutes, February 7, 1963, Sydney J. Moshette Jr. Papers.

36. Proceedings of CBCC Conference on Community Development, December 10, 1966, BSRCOH, BHS.

37. Thomas R. Jones, interview with Roberta W. Greene, November 26, 1971, RFKOH, JFKL; Franklin A. Thomas, interview with Roberta W. Greene, March 23, 1972, RFKOH, JFKL; Carter Burden, interview with Roberta W. Greene, February 13, 1974, RFKOH, JFKL; Ronald Shiffman, interview with Sady Sullivan, February 4, 2008, BSRCOH, BHS.

38. Elsie Richardson, interview with Deborah Jones, January 22, 2008, BSRCOH, BHS; Carter Burden, interview with Roberta W. Greene, February 13, 1974, RFKOH, JFKL; Ronald Shiffman, interview with the author, July 16, 2015. For

an astute analysis of the gendered dynamics of Restoration's founding, see Purnell, "'What We Need Is Brick and Mortar,'" 226–233.

39. Ford Foundation/Goldmann, "Performance in Black and White," 7, 31, JFKL. Karen Ferguson writes that "the CBCC group was vilified by received wisdom that unquestioningly elevated both men and youth as the true representatives of black America." See Ferguson, *Top Down*, 226.

40. Thomas R. Jones, interview with Jeffrey Gerson, June 10, 1993, La Guardia & Wagner (LGW) Archives. See also John Louis Flateau, "Black Brooklyn: The Politics of Ethnicity, Class, and Gender" (PhD thesis, City University of New York, 2005).

41. Franklin A. Thomas, interview with Roberta W. Greene, March 23, 1972, JFKL; Ford Foundation/Goldmann, "Performance in Black and White, 13, JFKL.

42. Ferguson, *Top Down*, 224–226; Ford Foundation/Goldmann, "Performance in Black and White," 8, JFKL.

43. "Call Celler Traitor to Afro-Americans," NYAN, May 20, 1967; "Bed-Stuy Launches Afro-Congress Drive," NYAN, June 3, 1967. On the *Cooper v. Power* case, which forced the redistricting of Bedford-Stuyvesant, see Wayne Dawkins, *City Son: Andrew W. Cooper's Impact on Modern-Day Brooklyn* (Jackson: University Press of Mississippi, 2012), Chap. 5. On Chisholm's career, see Julie Gallagher, "Waging 'The Good Fight': The Political Career of Shirley Chisholm, 1953–1982," *Journal of African American History* (June 22, 2007), 392–416.

44. The Ford Foundation study authored by R. B. Goldmann in 1969 claims that "Jones had ardently aspired" to the Congressional seat and that "it was well known that Jones and Mrs. Chisholm were bitter political enemies." Ford Foundation/Goldmann, "Performance in Black and White," 26, JFKL.

45. "Afro-American Congressman Search Brings Many Choices," NYAN, December 2, 1967; "CNC Picks Shirley Chisholm for Congress Race," NYAN, December 30, 1967; Susan Brownmiller, "This Is Fighting Shirley Chisholm," NYT *Magazine*, April 13, 1969.

46. Franklin A. Thomas interview with Roberta W. Greene, March 23, 1972, JFKL; Franklin A. Thomas, interview with James Briggs Murray, January 26, 1990, CDCOH, NYPL-Sch; Ronald Shiffman, interview with Sady Sullivan, February 4, 2008, BSRCOH, BHS.

47. Earl Graves to Eli Jacobs and Thomas Johnston, [March 1967], "Community, Undated," Box 1, TMCJP, JFKL; Elsie Richardson to Robert F. Kennedy, March 27, 1967, "Correspondence, 1/10/67–4/4/67," Box 1, TMCJP, JFKL.

48. Bryant George to Thomas Johnston, March 28, 1967, "Correspondence, 1/10/67–4/4/67," Box 1, TMCJP, JFKL; R&R, Minutes, March 31, 1967, JFKL;

Thomas R. Jones, interview with James Briggs Murray, February 10, 1990, CDCOH, Sch-NYPL.

49. Thomas R. Jones, interview with Roberta W. Greene, November 26, 1971, RFKOH, JFKL; Ford Foundation/Goldmann, "Performance in Black and White," 5–9, 26–35, JFKL. The extent to which Jones's actions had been greenlighted by Kennedy or his staff is unclear. Karen Ferguson, for instance, argues that the entire scheme had been "cooked up" in advance and that the telegrams were prearranged. See Ferguson, *Top Down*, 225.

50. Quoted in Ryan, "Bedford-Stuyvesant and the Prototype Community Development Corporation," 79; Lionel Payne, telegrams to Robert F. Kennedy, April 2, 1967, "Bedford-Stuyvesant, 4/1967," Box 1, AWP, JFKL.

51. "Brooklyn Groups Charge Meddling," NYT, April 6, 1967.

52. "Bitter Charges Hurled by Warring Blight Groups," NYAN, April 15, 1967.

53. "800 Demand Vote on Renewal Unit," NYT, April 7, 1967; "Bitter Charges Hurled by Warring Blight Groups," NYAN, April 15, 1967; Ford Foundation/Goldmann, "Performance in Black and White," 34, JFKL; Newfield, *Robert Kennedy*, 103.

54. "Bitter Charges Hurled by Warring Blight Groups," NYAN, April 15, 1967; Ford Foundation/Goldmann, "Performance in Black and White," JFKL; Franklin Thomas, interview with James Briggs Murray, January 26, 1990, CDCOH, NYPL-Sch; Earl Graves to Eli Jacobs and Thomas Johnston, [March 1967], JFKL.

55. Walter C. Pinkston, Confidential memorandum to Youth in Action board members, December 14, 1966, DWP; Walter Pinkston, "Position Statement," *YIA Monthly Newspaper*, August 1967, DWP.

56. "Jane Bolin, the Country's First Black Woman to Become a Judge, Is Dead at 98," NYT, January 10, 2007; "Rev. Walter Offutt, Jr. Dead at 63," NYAN, October 12, 1974; "NAACP Church Head Appeals for Inter-Faith Civil Rights Support," *Atlanta Daily World*, December 2, 1947; "Meet to Hear Account of Recent Florida Shootings," NYAN, December 1, 1951; "New Harlem Hospital Demanded at Rally," NYAN, September 27, 1958; "Store Front Drive Helped Registration," NYAN, October 22, 1960; "38 Harlem Groups Plan United Program," NYAN, June 18, 1960.

57. Walter P. Offutt Jr., "Poverty Lives Next Door to All of Us," *YIA Monthly Newspaper*, March 1967.

58. Reverend Walter P. Offutt, testimony, Hearings of the Subcommittee on Employment, Manpower, and Poverty of the Committee on Labor and Public Welfare, U.S. Senate, Part 6, May 9, 1967 (Washington, DC: U.S. Government Printing Office, 1967), 1936–1940.

59. Ibid.

60. Ibid.

61. Thomas R. Jones, prepared statement and testimony, Hearings of the Subcommittee on Employment, Manpower, and Poverty, May 8, 1967, 1855–1857, 1882–1883; Offutt, testimony, Hearings of the Subcommittee on Employment, Manpower, and Poverty, May 9, 1967, 1939.

62. Walter Pinkston, "Position Statement," *YIA Monthly Newspaper*, August 1967, DWP; Walter C. Pinkston to Youth in Action board members, December 14, 1966, DWP.

63. Thomas M. C. Johnston to Lionel Payne, April 4, 1967, "Correspondence, 1/10/67–4/4/67," Box 1, TMCJP, JFKL.

8. From the Ground Up

Epigraph: Franklin A. Thomas, interview with Sady Sullivan, February 1, 2008, Bedford-Stuyvesant Restoration Corporation Oral History Project (BSRCOH), Brooklyn Historical Society (BHS).

1. "Bedford-Stuyvesant Development Project Overview," April 4, 1967; "Preliminary Two-Year Action Program Outline: Bedford-Stuyvesant Development Program," April 6, 1967; "Industrial Development: Job Creation Program," April 1967; Paul F. O'Rourke to Peter Edelman, April 21, 1967, all in "Bedford-Stuyvesant, 4/1967," Box 1, Adam Walinsky Papers (AWP), John F. Kennedy Presidential Library (JFKL). See also Ford Foundation (R. B. Goldmann, author), "Performance in Black and White: An Appraisal of the Development and Record of the Bedford-Stuyvesant Restoration and Development and Services Corporations" (February 1969), 41–43, Box 1, Ford Foundation Papers, JFKL.

2. William P. Ryan, "Bedford-Stuyvesant and the Prototype Community Development Corporation," in Mitchell Sviridoff, ed., *Inventing Community Renewal: The Trials and Errors That Shaped the Modern Community Development Corporation* (New York: New School University, 2004), 82–83.

3. Karen Ferguson argues that Thomas's managerial style mirrored the desires of Kennedy and his establishment supporters on Wall Street and at the Ford Foundation, whose disillusionment with the Community Action Program spurred them to embrace more conservative forms of neighborhood governance in black urban communities. See Karen Ferguson, *Top Down: The Ford Foundation, Black Power, and the Reinvention of Racial Liberalism* (Philadelphia: University of Pennsylvania Press, 2013), Chap. 6.

4. "A Man Who Keeps Faith in Bed-Stuy," *New York Times* (NYT), May 14, 1972; John J. Goldman, "Born in a Brooklyn Slum, Frank Thomas Discovers You Can Go Home Again—and Fix it Up," *People*, May 16, 1977; Erica Hurtt, "A Private Man in Public Life," courtesy of www.ivyleaguesports.com; Franklin A. Thomas, interview with Sady Sullivan, February 1, 2008, BSRCOH, BHS.

5. John C. Hancock to Franklin Thomas [1967], "Community, 2/23/67–5/24/67 and undated," Box 1, Thomas M. C. Johnston Papers (TMCJP), JFKL; D&S, Minutes, JFKL. According to Kennedy aide Carter Burden, there was a lengthy debate between Thomas and the D&S board over whether Thomas should get an Oldsmobile or a Cadillac. Carter Burden, interview with Roberta Greene, February 13, 1974, Robert F. Kennedy Oral History Program (RFKOH), JFKL.

6. Tom Adam Davies, "Black Power in Action: The Bedford-Stuyvesant Restoration Corporation, Robert F. Kennedy, and the Politics of the Urban Crisis," *Journal of American History* 100:3 (December 2013), 738; Eli Jacobs, interview with Roberta Greene, October 27, 1976, RFKOH, JFKL; Franklin A. Thomas, interview with James Briggs Murray, January 26, 1990, Community Development Corporation Oral History Project (CDCOH), New York Public Library, Schomburg Center for Research in Black Culture (NYPL-Sch); Ford Foundation/ Goldmann, "Performance in Black and White," 123, JFKL.

7. Franklin A. Thomas, interview with James Briggs Murray, January 26, 1990, CDCOH, NYPL-Sch; Claude Collin, *Mon Amérique à moi: Voyage dans l'Amérique noire* (Paris: L'Harmattan, 2002), 52.

8. "New Poverty Aide Asks Unity in Bedford-Stuyvesant Program," *NYT*, May 11, 1967; Mitchell Sviridoff to Samuel Jackson, September 12, 1967, "Planning, 1966–1967, Volume 2," Box 45, Burke Marshall Papers (BMP), JFKL; Franklin A. Thomas, interview with Roberta W. Greene, March 23, 1972, JFKL; Earl Graves to Thomas Johnston, May 22, 1967, "Memoranda, miscellaneous, 8/27/65–1/16/68 and undated," Box 2, TMCJP, JFKL. See also Ryan, "Bedford-Stuyvesant and the Prototype Community Development Corporation," 78–79.

9. Elsie Richardson, "Letter to Concerned Members of Bedford-Stuyvesant," July 12, 1967, "Press Releases, 1967–68," BHS; Franklin Thomas, interview with William P. Ryan and Mitchell Sviridoff, October 24, 1966, in Sviridoff, ed., *Inventing Community Renewal*, 221.

10. Jack Newfield, *Robert Kennedy: A Memoir* (New York: Dutton, 1969), 75–76.

11. Kimberley Johnson, "Community Development Corporations, Participation, and Accountability: The Harlem Urban Development Corporation and the Bedford-Stuyvesant Restoration Corporation," *Annals of the American Academy of Political and Social Science* 594 (July 2004), 109–124.

12. Tamar Jacoby, "Sonny Carson and the Politics of Protest," *City Journal* (Summer 1991); Rhonda Y. Williams, "The Pursuit of Audacious Power: Rebel Reformers and Neighborhood Politics in Baltimore, 1966–1968," in Peniel E. Joseph, ed., *Neighborhood Rebels: Black Power at the Local Level* (New York: Palgrave Macmillan, 2010), 232.

13. Franklin A. Thomas, interview with Roberta W. Greene, March 23, 1972, JFKL; Eli Jacobs, interview with Roberta Greene, October 27, 1976, RFKOH, JFKL. Kennedy aide Carter Burden later recalled that "There was a basic

reluctance to put all the marbles in the Jones-Thomas corporation. There's no question about that." Carter Burden, interview with Roberta W. Greene, February 13, 1974, RFKOH, JFKL.

14. Thomas J. Watson Jr., interview with Roberta W. Greene, January 6, 1970, RFKOH, JFKL.

15. Franklin Thomas, interview with William P. Ryan and Mitchell Sviridoff, October 24, 1966, in Sviridoff, ed., *Inventing Community Renewal*, 226–227.

16. Geoffrey Faux, "Background Paper," in *CDCs: New Hope for the Inner City* (New York: Twentieth Century Fund, 1971), 71; "Worries Mar Restoration Group's Birthday," *NYT*, May 7, 1973; Edward K. Carpenter, "Good News from Bed-Stuy," *Design and Environment* (January 1976); Barron Tenny, interview with the author, January 18, 2012; Franklin A. Thomas, interview with Roberta W. Greene, March 23, 1972, JFKL.

17. New York City Community Development Agency, Program Directories for Years G, H, and I (November 1971, January 1973, and January 1973), NYPL-SIBL.

18. "Brooklyn Antipoverty Agency Is under Federal Investigation," *NYT*, May 14, 1974; "Former YIA Chairman Given Suspended Sentence," *New York Amsterdam News (NYAN)*, August 12, 1978; "4 Seized in Hijacking of Truck Cargoes," *NYT*, September 29, 1974; "Antipoverty Fraud Is Charged to Four," *NYT*, April 2, 1977; "Chessa Is Arrested, Bailed, Suspended," *NYAN*, May 18, 1974; "Maurice Chessa Indicted," *NYAN*, November 22, 1980; Jim Sleeper, "The Battle for Black Brooklyn," *Village Voice*, August 31, 1982; "Wright, YIA Indictments Stagger Black Community," *NYAN*, April 9, 1977; "Ex-State Senator Beatty Slain in Storefront Office in Brooklyn," *NYT*, August 31, 1990. See also Jack Newfield and Paul Du Brul, *The Abuse of Power: The Permanent Government and the Fall of New York* (New York: Penguin, 1978); and Jim Sleeper, *The Closest of Strangers: Liberalism and the Politics of Race in New York* (New York: Norton, 1990).

19. Barron Tenny, interview with the author, January 18, 2012; quoted in Barry Stein, *Rebuilding Bedford-Stuyvesant: Community Economic Development in the Ghetto* (Cambridge, MA: Center for Community Economic Development, 1975), 5–6.

20. On the lessons gleaned by CDCs from community action, see Lawrence F. Parachini, *A Political History of the Special Impact Program* (Cambridge, MA: Center for Community Economic Development, 1980), 22–24.

21. Devorah Heitner, "The Good Side of the Ghetto: Visualizing Black Brooklyn, 1968–1971," *The Velvet Light Trap* 62 (Fall 2008), 48–61; Benjamin Glascoe, interview with Sady Sullivan, August 31, 2007, BSRCOH, BHS; EBS Management Consultants, "Initial Evaluation of the Bedford-

Stuyvesant Special Impact Program," prepared for the U.S. Department of Labor, June 30, 1969.

22. Ford Foundation/Goldmann, "Performance in Black and White," 111, JFKL; Bedford-Stuyvesant Restoration Corporation (BSRC), Final Report of the Home Improvement Program, March 31, 1968, "Housing: Exterior Renovation Program," Box 42, BMP, JFKL.

23. This resonated with other efforts carried out in late 1960s New York City to determine what those who lived in what the city dubbed "poverty areas" wanted government to do for them. The highest priority for people surveyed in one study after another was housing. Be it in poor, majority-black areas or in "transition neighborhoods," where low-income blacks and Puerto Ricans coexisted with white middle-class residents, people insisted that they needed better housing conditions and help from government in attaining them. "It is evident that the public wants a real thrust behind the construction of low and middle income housing," one survey noted. "Solid majorities of the public also want the city to help builders and landlords on renovation." See Louis Harris and Associates, Inc., "Transition Neighborhoods in New York City: The People's View of Their Housing Environment" (December 1969), Folder 40, Box 060279, RFW, LGW online.

24. BSRC, Final Report of the Home Improvement Program, March 31, 1968, JFKL; EBS Management Consultants, "Initial Evaluation"; Barron Tenny, interview with the author, January 18, 2012. On the linkages between CHIP and past neighborhood-improvement efforts, see Brian Purnell, " 'What We Need Is Brick and Mortar': Race, Gender, and Early Leadership of the Bedford-Stuyvesant Restoration Corporation," in Laura Warren Hill and Julia Rabig, eds., *The Business of Black Power: Community Development, Capitalism, and Corporate Responsibility in Postwar America* (Rochester, NY: University of Rochester Press, 2012), 237.

25. EBS Management Consultants, "Initial Evaluation."

26. BSRC, Final Report of the Home Improvement Program, March 31, 1968, JFKL.

27. Ibid.; Ryan, "Bedford-Stuyvesant and the Prototype Community Development Corporation," 84–86.

28. Goldman, "Born in a Brooklyn Slum"; Barron Tenny, interview with the author, January 18, 2012.

29. Dozens of letters are reprinted as appendices to BSRC, Final Report of the Home Improvement Program, March 31, 1968, JFKL.

30. BSRC, Final Report of the Home Improvement Program, March 31, 1968, JFKL.

31. Ibid.

32. "Rebuilding Effort Helps Street in Slums to Become Untypical," *NYT*, December 25, 1967; Franklin Thomas, interview with William P. Ryan and Mitchell Sviridoff, October 24, 1966, in Sviridoff, ed., *Inventing Community Renewal*, 222–225; New York City Landmarks Preservation Commission, "Stuyvesant Heights Historic District: Designation Report" (September 14, 1971).

33. Don Watkins, "Education and Urban Poverty: A Research Essay on Education in Bedford-Stuyvesant" (unpublished, 1965), Don Watkins Papers (DWP).

34. Watkins, "Education and Urban Poverty," DWP; Bedford-Stuyvesant Youth in Action (YIA), "Why Do Bedford-Stuyvesant Youths Drop Out of School? A Study of the Bedford-Stuyvesant Community by the Neighborhood Youth Corps Research Aides" (September 8, 1966), DWP.

35. At the time, only 8 percent of the city's teachers, and barely 3 percent of all administrators, were black, despite the fact that blacks and Puerto Ricans made up more than 50 percent of all students enrolled. See Jerald E. Podair, "The Ocean Hill–Brownsville Crisis: New York's *Antigone*," paper presented at the Conference on New York City History, October 6, 2001.

36. The most complete retelling of the Ocean Hill–Brownsville crisis is Jerald E. Podair, *The Strike That Changed New York: Blacks, Whites, and the Ocean Hill–Brownsville Crisis* (New Haven, CT: Yale University Press, 2002). See also Wendell Pritchett, *Brownsville, Brooklyn: Blacks, Jews, and the Changing Face of the Ghetto* (Chicago: University of Chicago Press, 2002); Clarence Taylor, *Knocking at Our Own Door: Milton Galamison and the Struggle to Integrate New York City Schools* (New York: Columbia University Press, 1997); Michael Usdan, "Citizen Participation: Learning From New York City's Mistakes" *Urban Review* (September 1969), 9–12; and Thomas J. Sugrue, "Shanker Blows Up the World," *The Nation*, October 25, 2007.

37. Don Watkins, conversation with the author, July 2, 2009.

38. Major Owens to Community Corporation chairmen and directors, December 11, 1968, DWP; Jonathan Kozol, *Death at an Early Age: The Destruction of the Hearts and Minds of Negro Children in the Boston Public Schools* (Boston: Houghton Mifflin, 1967).

39. Memo, John L. Procope to CBCC members, ca. 1964; Memo, Cecil C. Gloster to CBCC members, March 2, 1964, both in Sydney J. Moshette Jr. Papers.

40. "Forces Fight Dawn–Dusk Battle for New College," *NYAN*, March 7, 1964; "Pastor Assails Officials," *NYAN*, March 7, 1964; "Tempers Flare on College Sit," *NYT*, February 28, 1964.

41. Don Watkins, "A Community College: Conceived without Consultation" (Chap. 1 of unpublished study, 1970), I-1, DWP.

42. "Central College Triples Students," *NYAN*, October 21, 1967; "Volunteers Give Slum Students a Second Chance," *NYT*, December 10, 1967; James Hurley, interview with Ashley Bowden, November 12, 2011, Weeksville Heritage Center; "Proposed Central Brooklyn College Opportunities Program" [1967, probable author Pratt Institute for Community Improvement], DWP.

43. "College Director Defends Boro Neighborhood College," *NYAN*, October 12, 1968.

44. Educational Affiliate of the Bedford-Stuyvesant Restoration Corporation, "A College in the City: An Alternative" (1968), DWP.

45. Ibid.

46. Watkins, "A Community College," DWP; "City U. Will Build in Brooklyn Slum," *NYT*, February 2, 1968; Board of Higher Education of the City of New York, "Fact Sheet on the City University Community College to Be Established in Brooklyn's Bedford-Stuyvesant Area" (February 1, 1968), DWP.

47. YIA, press release, February 6, 1968; Coalition on Educational Needs and Services, list of current representatives to the Steering Committee [1968]; Don Watkins, "The Community Responds" (Chap. 2 of unpublished study, 1970), II-3; YIA, publicity poster, February 1968, all in DWP.

48. Undated document, DWP; draft of statement to be distributed to Coalition members, June 1968, DWP; Don Watkins, conversation with the author, July 2, 2009.

49. Don Watkins, "Initial Negotiations" (Chap. 4 of unpublished study, 1970), DWP; Al Vann, "Is, or Was There, a Community College in Bedford-Stuyvesant?" *Black News* 1:8 (January 1970), Brooklyn Public Library Brooklyn Collection (BPL).

50. Ron Howell, "Al Vann and the Revolution. Unplugged," *City Limits* (November 1, 1997); Jitu Weusi, interview with the author, January 13, 2012; Joe Klein, "The Power Next Time: Albert Vann Is the City's Hottest Black Politician," *New York* (October 10, 1983), 38–45; "Workshop Is Held in Brooklyn to Teach Parents How to Teach," *NYT*, September 9, 1967; "Negro Teachers Define Their Stand," *NYT*, September 21, 1967.

51. Draft of statement to be distributed to Coalition members, June 1968; Watkins, "Initial Negotiations"; Bedford-Stuyvesant Coalition on Educational Needs and Services (Negotiating Team), memo, June 11, 1968; Albert Vann, letter to candidates, September 5, 1968, all in DWP. For a look at how the Bedford-Stuyvesant college negotiations compared with similar episodes elsewhere in the country, see William Ellison Chalmers, *Racial Negotiations: Potentials and Limitations* (Ann Arbor: Institute of Labor and Industrial Relations, University of Michigan–Wayne State University, 1974). A portion of the study produced by Don Watkins about the Bedford-Stuyvesant college dispute was later incorporated into Chalmers's publication.

52. Don Watkins, "From Issues to Impasse" (Chap. 5 of unpublished study, 1970), DWP; Albert Vann, Progress Summary to the Community, circulated by Elsie Richardson, July 1969, DWP.
53. Thomas R. Jones to Albert Vann, January 2, 1969, DWP.
54. Don Watkins, in a 2010 conversation with the author, said that the militant faction led by Carson was "most likely not representative of the community." According to Watkins, most people at the time sided with the old-guard community organizations and the elected officials, not necessarily because they disagreed with Vann's point about community control but because they were ultimately more worried about where their children would be educated.
55. Members of the Bedford-Stuyvesant Coalition for Community College # 7 to Albert Bowker, June 10, 1969; Concerned Members of the Negotiating Team to Albert Vann, July 17, 1969; Julius C. C. Edelstein to Albert Vann, September 17, 1969; "News from NAACP" (March 16, 1970); Watkins, "From Issues to Impasse," all in DWP.
56. "News from NAACP" (March 16, 1970), DWP; Russell J. Rickford, *Betty Shabazz, Surviving Malcolm X: A Journey of Strength from Wife to Widow to Heroine* (Napierville, IL: Sourcebooks, 2005), 367; Vann, "Is, or Was There, a Community College in Bedford-Stuyvesant?" BPL.
57. Rickford, *Betty Shabazz*, 367–368.
58. "Kennedy's Plans Gain in Brooklyn," *NYT*, June 28, 1968; "Two Ex-Employees Now Businessmen," *NYT*, July 10, 1968; Community Development Institute, "Position on C.B.S. Program 'The Cities' Part II" [1968], DWP; James Miller to Walter Pinkston, Memorandum re. CBS broadcast (July 3, 1968), DWP; YIA to CBS, memorandum [1968], DWP; Newfield, *Robert Kennedy*, 108.
59. "IBM Plans 300-Worker Plant in Slums of Bedford-Stuyvesant," *NYT*, April 18, 1968; "Promise More Bed-Stuy Jobs with IBM Plant," *NYAN*, April 20, 1968; "Mortgage Funds Pledged to Slum," *NYT*, April 2, 1968.
60. Ford Foundation/Goldmann, "Performance in Black and White," 93, 97, JFKL; Arnold Spellun to Eli Jacobs, November 7, 1967, "Mortgage Pool (Folder 1)," Box 42, BMP, JFKL; "Mortgage Funds Pledged to Slum," *NYT*, April 2, 1968; Carpenter, "Good News from Bed-Stuy."
61. Proposed Goals, Structure and Staff for Mortgage Program in Bedford-Stuyvesant, January 31, 1968, "Mortgage Pool (Folder 1)," Box 42, BMP, JFKL; Franklin A. Thomas and John Doar to Donald P. Turner, April 18, 1968, "Mortgage Pool (Folder 2)," Box 42, BMP, JFKL; "Senators, in Bedford-Stuyvesant, Hear Praise for Development Unit," *NYT*, June 12, 1971.
62. "Mortgage Funds Pledged to Slum," *NYT*, April 2, 1968; Marshall Kaplan to Eli Jacobs and Franklin Thomas, June 27, 1967, "Bedford-Stuyvesant, 5/1967-6/1967," Box 1, AWP, JFKL; Marshall Kaplan, Proposed Housing Program for

Bedford-Stuyvesant, June 27, 1967, "Bedford-Stuyvesant, 5/1967-6/1967," Box 1, AWP, JFKL; BSRC Mortgage Pool, Monthly Report, May 1969, "Mortgage Pool (Folder 7)," Box 42, BMP, JFKL; BSRC Mortgage Pool, Progress Report, January 1, 1968 to June 30, 1969, "Mortgage Pool (Folder 6)," Box 42, BMP, JFKL.

63. Barron Tenny, interview with the author, January 18, 2012; "Bedford-Stuyvesant Group to Build $6-Million Center," *NYT*, June 29, 1972; Franklin Thomas, interview with William P. Ryan and Mitchell Sviridoff, October 24, 1966, in Sviridoff, ed., *Inventing Community Renewal*, 230–231.

64. Carpenter, "Good News from Bed-Stuy"; "Worries Mar Restoration Group's Birthday," *NYT*, May 7, 1973.

65. Michael Harrington, "The South Bronx Shall Rise Again," *New York* (April 3, 1978), 36. On crime fears among Bed-Stuy merchants, see Michael Javen Fortner, *Black Silent Majority: The Rockefeller Drug Laws and the Politics of Punishment* (Cambridge, MA: Harvard University Press, 2015), 140–141.

66. BSRC, "The Restoration Story" (January 1980, unpublished), DWP; BSRC, Restoration Boxscore Through September 1979, DWP; Barron Tenny, interview with the author, January 18, 2012.

67. For an example of this perspective, see Ernest Quimby, "Black Political Development in Bedford-Stuyvesant as Represented in the Origin and Role of the Bedford-Stuyvesant Restoration Corporation" (PhD thesis, City University of New York, 1977).

68. Jitu Weusi, "The Demise of the Black Nouveaux Riches," *NYAN*, December 24, 1977; Jitu Weusi, "Which Way for Bed-Stuy Restoration?" *NYAN*, June 19, 1982.

69. Haskell Ward, "Bedford-Stuyvesant: An Assessment," *Journal of the Institute for Socioeconomic Studies* 5:4 (Winter 1980), 51–52.

70. C. Douglas Dillon, open letter [1968], "Bedford-Stuyvesant, 1/1968 and undated," Box 1, AWP, JFKL; Ferguson, *Top Down*, 249; Ward, "Bedford-Stuyvesant," 51; "The Success of Bed-Stuy," *Washington Post*, April 22, 1978; Ron Shiffman, interview with author, July 16, 2015; Newfield, *Robert Kennedy*, 98.

71. BSRC, *Restoration* newsletter, September 1977; Ward, "Bedford-Stuyvesant," 45–54; Harrington, "The South Bronx Shall Rise Again."

72. Judith Wellman, *Brooklyn's Promised Land: The Free Black Community of Weeksville, New York* (New York: New York University Press, 2014), 229–233.

Epilogue

Epigraph: "New Life for the Brownstones of Bedford-Stuyvesant," *NYT*, October 10, 1985.

1. "*Amsterdam News* Hosts Community Leaders Confab," *New York Amsterdam News (NYAN)*, October 22, 1977. On New York in 1977, see Jonathan Mahler,

Ladies and Gentlemen, the Bronx Is Burning: 1977, Baseball, Politics, and the Battle for the Soul of a City (New York: Picador, 2006); and Jack Newfield and Paul Du Brul, *The Abuse of Power: The Permanent Government and the Fall of New York* (New York: Penguin, 1978). On the fiscal crisis, see Kim Moody, *From Welfare State to Real Estate: Regime Change in New York City, 1974 to the Present* (New York: The New Press, 2007).

2. "*Amsterdam News* Hosts Community Leaders Confab," NYAN, October 22, 1977.

3. "Democratic Mayoral Rivals Hold Debate Filled with Recriminations," *New York Times (NYT)*, September 2, 1977; "Owens Blasts Koch," NYAN, September 17, 1977; "Koch Warns Blacks," NYAN, December 31, 1977. On Koch, see Michael Goodwin, ed., *New York Comes Back: The Mayoralty of Edward I. Koch* (New York: Powerhouse Books, 2005).

4. "*Amsterdam News* Hosts Community Leaders Confab," NYAN, October 22, 1977.

5. Mary H. Manoni, *Bedford-Stuyvesant: The Anatomy of a Central City Community* (New York: Quadrangle, 1973). See also Michael Katz, "Narratives of Failure? Historical Interpretations of Federal Urban Policy," *City & Community* 9:1 (March 2010), 13–22.

6. Manoni, *Bedford-Stuyvesant*, 28; "The State of the Community," *Restoration* Newsletter (January/February 1974), "Bedford Stuyvesant Restoration Corp. I," Brooklyn Public Library Brooklyn Collection (BPL); John E. Schwartz, *America's Hidden Success: A Reassessment of Twenty Years of Public Policy* (New York: Norton, 1983), 26–27.

7. Martha J. Bailey and Nicolas J. Duquette, "How Johnson Fought the War on Poverty: The Economics and Politics of Funding at the Office of Economic Opportunity" (online publication, December 2013); Edward Berkowitz, "Losing Ground? The Great Society in Historical Persepctive," in David Farber and Beth Bailey, eds., *The Columbia Guide to America in the 1960s* (New York: Columbia University Press, 2001), 98; Sharon M. Collins, "The Making of the Black Middle Class," *Social Problems* 30:4 (April 1983), 373.

8. "The State of the Community," *Restoration* Newsletter (January/February 1974), "Bedford Stuyvesant Restoration Corp I," BPL; David Rusk, *Inside Game/Outside Game: Winning Strategies for Saving Urban America* (Washington, DC: Brookings Institution Press, 2001), 33–34. On the changing dimensions of inequality, see Michael B. Katz, Mark J. Stern, and Jamie J. Fader, "The New African American Inequality," *The Journal of American History* 92:1 (2005), 75–108.

9. See Elizabeth Hinton, " 'A War within Our Own Boundaries': Lyndon Johnson's Great Society and the Rise of the Carceral State," *Journal of American History* 102:1 (June 2015), 100–112.

10. Colvin Grannum, interview with the author, August 22, 2014; Ira Katznelson, *City Trenches: Urban Politics and the Patterning of Class in the United States* (New York: Pantheon Books, 1981).

11. "Who Will Be Restoration's New President?" NYAN, January 1, 1977; John J. Goldman, "Born in a Brooklyn Slum, Frank Thomas Discovers You Can Go Home Again—And Fix It Up," *People*, May 16, 1977.

12. Michael Harrington, "The South Bronx Shall Rise Again," *New York*, April 3, 1978; "Throwing Money in the Proper Fashion," NYT, January 11, 1977; Goldman, "Born in a Brooklyn Slum."

13. Goldman, "Born in a Brooklyn Slum"; Ronald Shiffman, "Beyond the Marketplace: Towards an Equitable Housing Program," lecture delivered at the New York Center for Architecture (2006). On the Restoration Corporation and Black Power, see Tom Adam Davies, "Black Power in Action: The Bedford-Stuyvesant Restoration Corporation, Robert F. Kennedy, and the Politics of the Urban Crisis," *Journal of American History* 100:3 (December 2013), 736–760. See also the essays in Laura Warren Hill and Julia Rabig, eds., *The Business of Black Power: Community Development, Capitalism, and Corporate Responsibility in Postwar America* (Rochester, NY: University of Rochester Press, 2012).

14. Ta-Nehisi Coates, "The Case for Reparations," *The Atlantic* (June 2014).

15. Despite such efforts, the wealth gap between black and white Americans has widened dramatically since the 1980s. See Institute on Assets and Social Policy, Brandeis University, "The Racial Wealth Gap Increases Fourfold" (Research and Policy Brief, May 2010).

16. On the dilemmas faced by CDCs, see Joyce Mandell, "CDCs and the Myth of the Organizing-Development Dialectic," *Comm-Org Papers, The On-Line Conference on Community Organizing* 15 (2009).

17. Ernest Quimby, "Black Political Development in Bedford-Stuyvesant as Represented in the Origin and Role of the Bedford-Stuyvesant Restoration Corporation" (PhD thesis, City University of New York, 1977), 1; Jitu Weusi, "Which Way for Bed-Stuy Restoration?" NYAN, June 19, 1982. See also Geoffrey Faux, "Background Paper," in *CDCs: New Hope for the Inner City* (New York: Twentieth Century Fund, 1971).

18. William P. Ryan, "Bedford-Stuyvesant and the Prototype Community Development Corporation," in Mitchell Sviridoff, ed., *Inventing Community Renewal: The Trials and Errors That Shaped the Modern Community Development Corporation* (New York: New School University, 2004), 85; "The Hope Business," NYT, May 26, 1992; Colvin Grannum, interview with the author, August 22, 2014; Barron Tenny, interview with the author, January 18, 2012. On Restoration's influence, see Lawrence F. Parachini, *A Political History of the Special Impact Program* (Cambridge, MA: Center for Community Economic

Development, 1980); Stewart E. Perry, "Federal Support for CDCs: Some of the History and Issues of Community Control," *Review of Black Political Economy* 3:3 (Spring 1973), 17–42; and Kimberley Johnson, "Community Development Corporations, Participation, and Accountability: The Harlem Urban Development Corporation and the Bedford-Stuyvesant Restoration Corporation," *Annals of the American Academy of Political and Social Science* 594 (July 2004), 109–124.

19. Alice O'Connor, "Swimming against the Tide: A Brief History of Federal Policy in Poor Communities," in Ronald F. Ferguson, ed., *Urban Problems and Community Development* (Washington, DC: Brookings Institution Press, 1999); Julia Rabig, "'A Fight and a Question': Community Development Corporations, Machine Politics, and Corporate Philanthropy in the Long Urban Crisis," in Hill and Rabig, eds., *The Business of Black Power*, 265; Neal R. Peirce and Carol F. Steinbach, *Corrective Capitalism: The Rise of America's Community Development Corporations* (New York: Ford Foundation, 1987), 9.

20. "Activist Making Switch to Academia," NYT, December 29, 1985; Alexander von Hoffman, "The Past, Present, and Future of Community Development in the United States," in Nancy O. Andrews and David J. Erickson, eds., *Investing in What Works for America's Communities* (Federal Reserve Bank of San Francisco, 2012), 27, 49.

21. Hoffman, "The Past, Present, and Future of Community Development in the United States," in Andrews and Erickson, eds., *Investing in What Works*, 49. On the legacies of the CDC movement, see The Urban Institute, *The Impact of Community Development Corporations on Urban Neighborhoods* (Washington, DC: Urban Institute, 2005); and Paul S. Grogan and Tony Proscio, *Comeback Cities: A Blueprint for Urban Neighborhood Revival* (Boulder, CO: Westview Press, 2000).

22. Tom Angotti, *New York for Sale: Community Planning Confronts Global Real Estate* (Cambridge, MA: MIT Press, 2008), 102–103. On the limitations of CDCs, see Robert Halpern, *Rebuilding the Inner City: A History of Neighborhood Initiatives to Address Poverty in the United States* (New York: Columbia University Press, 1995), Chap. 4; and Karen Ferguson, *Top Down: The Ford Foundation, Black Power, and the Reinvention of Racial Liberalism* (Philadelphia: University of Pennsylvania Press, 2013).

23. William M. Rohe, Rachel G. Bratt, and Protip Biswas, "Evolving Challenges for Community Development Corporations: The Causes and Impacts of Failures, Downsizings and Mergers" (Center for Urban and Regional Studies, University of North Carolina at Chapel Hill, 2003), 1–2; Roberta Brandes Gratz, *The Battle for Gotham: New York in the Shadow of Robert Moses and Jane Jacobs* (New York: Nation Books, 2010), 32. See also Avis C. Vidal,

Rebuilding Communities: A National Study of Urban Community Development Corporations (New York: Community Development Research Center, New School for Social Research, 1993).

24. Jill Jonnes, *We're Still Here: The Rise, Fall, and Resurrection of the South Bronx* (New York: Fordham University Press, 2002); and Jarrett Murphy, "Moses, Jacobs, and You: The Battle for Gotham," citylimits.org (December 22, 2010). On Koch's housing programs, see Michael Gecan and Johnny Ray Young-blood, "A Housing Legacy," in Goodwin, ed., *New York Comes Back.*

25. Elsie Richardson, interview with the author, June 5, 2011; Elsie Richardson, interview with James Briggs Murray, February 2, 1990, Community Development Corporations Oral History Project, New York Public Library, Schomburg Center for Research in Black Culture; Elsie Richardson, interview with Deborah Jones, January 22, 2008, Bedford-Stuyvesant Restoration Corporation Oral History Project, Brooklyn Historical Society.

26. "The Great Land Grab Continues," *Black News* 1:7 (January 10, 1970), BPL; "The Priceless Land Value of Bed. Stuy.," *Black News* 1:8 (January 25, 1970), BPL.

27. Suleiman Osman, *The Invention of Brownstone Brooklyn: Gentrification and the Search for Authenticity in Postwar New York* (New York: Oxford University Press, 2011); "Second Brownstone Tour of Bed-Stuy Sold Out," Central Brooklyn Coordinating Council News Briefs, May 17, 1969, CBCC Papers, BPL.

28. Brenda Fryson, interview with the author, July 16, 2015; Brownstoners of Bedford-Stuyvesant, Inc., informational pamphlet, 2015.

29. Robert Curvin and Bruce Porter, *Blackout Looting! New York City, July 13, 1977* (Gardner Press, 1979), 164–168; Brenda Fryson, interview with the author, July 16, 2015.

30. Brenda Fryson, interview with the author, July 16, 2015; "Mayor of Stoops," *NYT,* November 18, 2013.

31. "New Life for the Brownstones of Bedford-Stuyvesant," *NYT,* October 10, 1985; Jeff Coplon, "The Tipping of Jefferson Avenue," *New York* 38:14 (April 25, 2005), 46.

32. "Striking Change in Bedford-Stuyvesant as White Population Soars," *NYT,* August 4, 2011.

33. On real-estate scams in and around Bedford-Stuyvesant, see "Real Estate Shell Companies Scheme to Defraud Owners Out of Their Homes," *NYT,* November 7, 2015; "How a Homeowner's Foreclosure Deal Turned into a Scam Horror Story," *New York Post,* October 24, 2015; and "Family Says its $1.5 Million Brownstone Was Stolen in Deed-Theft Scam," *DNA Info,* May 12, 2015. See also "The Boy From Oz: Alan Dixon Buys Bed-Stuy Brownstones for Australian Fund," *Brooklyn Eagle,* August 6, 2014; "Investors Are Behind 73%

of Bed-Stuy's Cheaper Home Sales," *The Real Deal*, October 1, 2013; and Citizens Committee for Children, "Concentrated Poverty in New York City: An Analysis of the Changing Geographic Patterns of Poverty," April 2012, available at cccnewyork.org.

34. Annette Robinson, Remarks at the Brownstoners of Bedford-Stuyvesant 37th Annual Housing Tour, October 17, 2015. For contrasting perspectives on recent trends in Central Brooklyn, see DW Gibson, *The Edge Becomes Center: An Oral History of Gentrification in the Twenty-First Century* (New York: The Overlook Press, 2015); Lance Freeman, *There Goes the Hood: Views of Gentrification from the Ground Up* (Philadelphia: Temple University Press, 2006); Justin Davidson, "Is Gentrification All Bad?" *New York*, February 2, 2014; Rachel D. Godsill, "Transforming Gentrification into Integration," Furman Center, May 20, 2014, furmancenter.org/research/iri/godsil; "In Bed-Stuy Housing Market, Profit and Preservation Battle," *NYT*, June 19, 2015; and Joe Coscarelli, "Spike Lee's Amazing Rant Against Gentrification," *New York*, February 24, 2014.

Acknowledgments

Finishing a book is hard, and this one would've been abandoned long ago were it not for the support network that sustained me. I'm lucky to have spent six years at Columbia University, where my advisor, Kenneth Jackson, taught me more than I thought I could ever learn about writing, about history, and about New York. Ken's enthusiasm for his craft, even after five decades on the job, remains infectious, and his knowledge is encyclopedic—literally. Another beacon was Elizabeth Blackmar, whose generosity is matched only by her brilliance. This book could not have been written were it not for her awesome ability to anticipate her students' thoughts, make sense of them, and nudge them several steps further. Ira Katznelson, Dorian Warren, and David Rosner each provided unique insights into my work and pushed me to think harder about the implications of my research. I'm also thankful for the support and guidance of Eric Foner, Anders Stephanson, Alan Brinkley, and Samuel K. Roberts.

This book originated in a seminar led by Sarah Phillips, who served up great portions of her time while helping me untangle my ideas. My clever comrades at Columbia—Jessica Adler, Melissa Borja, Thai Jones, Megan French-Marcelin, Tamara Mann, Trent MacNamara, Yuki Oda, Nick Osborne, Victoria Phillips, Matt Spooner—inspired me to work harder whenever I traveled uptown. Nick Juravich shared findings from his own research, and Mason Williams generously read the manuscript in its entirety. Suleiman Osman, Barbara Winslow, and Michael Blum also offered valuable scholarly input at different stages of this project. My editor at Harvard University Press, Brian Distelberg, offered razor-sharp insight and kindly put up with me through several missed deadlines and bouts of indecision. Joyce Seltzer, Kathi Drummy, and Kim Giambattisto deserve praise for their patience, vision, and hard work.

No work of history could be written without librarians and archivists. Joy Holland and Ivy Marvel at the Brooklyn Public Library let me spend weeks in a lovely research room on the edge of Prospect Park. I'm also grateful to Sady Sullivan of the Brooklyn Historical Society; Alix Ross and Michael Ryan, formerly of Columbia's Rare Books and Manuscript Library; Allen Fisher at the LBJ Library; and the staffs at the JFK Library, the Schomburg Center, and the New York Municipal Archives. The Anti-Discrimination Center, the Lehman Center for American History, and the Bancroft Awards Committee at Columbia University offered precious grant monies.

For the past four years, I've had the privilege of teaching at Bard High School Early College in Queens, where my students fill me with hope for the future of this city. I thank Val Thomson and Pat Sharpe for their support and flexibility. I don't know where I'd be without Jenna Alden's warm friendship, fierce intellect, and constant cheerleading. I'm also grateful to my wonderful colleagues in the Social Studies department, who sacrificed their time to help move the project along. In moments of writerly angst, I couldn't have asked for better buddies than Kris Porter and Kolby Yarnell, who made me laugh and helped with logistics. Misha Franta and Steve Slater made me see the big picture. My loving in-laws, Kathy and Bill Farley, read portions of the work, asked tough questions, and urged me on. Finally, I owe a deep debt of gratitude to friends and family members too numerous to mention, who expressed interest and held my hand at key moments.

My own parents—all four of them—have showered me with love and stimulation all my life. Lindsay Crysler, who long ago inspired me to become a writer, spills red ink all over my copy whenever I ask him to, like the wise old pro he is. Lana Seabrooke, forever a tender and adoring fan, has continued to cheer me on in recent years, despite trying times. Pat Woodsworth, who loves nothing more than a good debate over a good beer, has been exhorting me to stake intellectual claims and defend them since I was about three years old. Thanks to him, I stand on the shoulders of a giant. My biggest booster, Judy Woodsworth, closely read every single word and punctuation mark of this work, endnotes included—even as she raced toward publication deadlines of her own. She is and always has been an inspiration.

No person contributed more to this effort than my senior editor, Amy Farley. Living in cramped Brooklyn apartments with two children underfoot, Amy smilingly endured the infinite clutter of a disorganized historian. Her emotional, intellectual, and financial support never wavered; I'll never figure out what I did to deserve a companion so smart and funny and wise. About those kids: Will has filled our lives with hilarity and wonder, and though he wishes his dad had pursued paleontology instead of urban history, he earnestly sat down more than once to peruse the book-in-progress. Eleanor, meanwhile, has radiated joy, curiosity, and beauty every day of her short life. She knows no limits.

I owe this work to my grandfather, David Woodsworth. A social worker, scholar, and activist, he held his beliefs passionately. The policy questions I've investigated in my research were first introduced to me in his living room, when I was a teenager and we'd spend hours each week deep in conversation. Before he died in 2010, he gave me pointers on an early version of this work. I'd like to believe that both he and my grandmother, Sheila Woodsworth, would find a lot to discuss, and critique, in the finished version. My other grandparents, Zsuzsanna and Zoltán Weisz, didn't live long enough to know I would become a historian, but I carry within me their personal histories of persecution, displacement, and overcoming.

One of the great joys of this project was getting to know some of the men and women who participated in the events chronicled here. Don Watkins offered up a rich trove of archival materials, rigorous edits, and sharp-edged recollections of events fifty years past, told over multiple coffee dates and phone conversations. Sydney Moshette Jr. provided lively conversation, invitations to community events, and fascinating documents. I was also lucky enough to spend time with Alma Carroll and Jitu Weusi before they died; both generously shared their stories, wisdom, and passion. Peter Edelman, Brenda Fryson, Colvin Grannum, H. Carl McCall, Ron Shiffman, and Barron Tenny all sat down for long chats that deepened my understanding of Bedford-Stuyvesant and the War on Poverty. Elsie Richardson, though ailing, graciously allowed me to visit her home for an interview, on the condition that I keep it short; two and a half hours later, she was still telling stories. Her life, and the broader activism she embodied, leave me humbled: humbled by what was accomplished, and humbled by the work that remains.

Index

Jacobs, Jane: ideas and influence of, 62, 113, 204, 244, 299, 320; activism, 107, 205; departure from New York, 316

Javits, Jacob K., 104, 170; involvement in Bed-Stuy, 200, 201, 231, 234, 239, 240–242, 256; policy proposals of, 232–233, 377n79

jazz musicians, 56

Jews: and Brooklyn Council for Social Planning, 21–22; and youth gangs, 21, 23; charitable organizations, 22, 27, 225; in Central Brooklyn, 51, 146; in Democratic Party, 69, 101, 156, 284; in American Labor Party, 71; in Boerum Hill, 102; and CORE, 105; and CBCC, 119, 206

Jim Crow. *See* segregation

Job Corps, 8, 145, 154, 165

job creation and placement: as CBCC goal, 4, 5, 10, 82, 119, 311; as antigang tactic, 24, 28, 31, 87, 90; during World War II, 53; within Area Services program, 115; and planning for War on Poverty, 134–135; in response to 1964 riots, 145; as HARYOU goal, 148; as YIA goal, 151–152, 164, 182–183, 184, 185, 197; and Job Corps, 154; and WTC, 191–194; as source of community tensions, 195; as RFK goal, 202, 222, 224, 226, 229, 240; and SIP, 232–233; and BSRC programs, 277–279, 281–282; and IBM plant, 302–303; and CDCs, 316; in government, 318

Job Orientation in Neighborhoods (JOIN), 134, 137, 141

Johnson, Bernice, 98

Johnson, Lyndon B. (LBJ): declaration of War on Poverty, 2, 4, 14, 122–126, 166; vision of Great Society, 7–8, 34, 270; vision of War on Poverty, 10, 154, 163, 189, 196; and riots, 11–12, 145–146, 310; appointees of, 113, 126; and economic growth, 128; and creative federalism, 133, 163; and Wagner, 135–138, 156, 158, 357n29; and Congress, 164, 173; backlash against, 169, 234; rhetoric of, 198; urban policies of, 216, 226; and civil rights, 219; rivalry with RFK, 220–221, 227, 242; departure from office, 312

Johnston, Thomas, 246, 270; critique of the War on Poverty, 224–225; work in Bedford-Stuyvesant, 229, 240, 247, 263–264, 273

Jones, J. Raymond, 59, 68, 70

Jones, Thomas R., Jr., 7; West Indian heritage of, 58, 60, 102; as activist and reformer, 71, 82, 85, 99, 102–104, 119–121, 143, 153, 298; as chairman of R&R, 200, 201, 231–233, 238–239, 245–246, 248–249, 252–259, 383n49; and RFK, 228, 234, 238, 249, 251–255, 289; rivalries with CBCC activists, 232, 248–249, 251–259, 262, 263, 266, 270, 382n44; gendered discourse of, 251–252; and black nationalists, 259, 271–272, 291; as chairman of BSRC, 269, 272, 289, 292; and block associations, 280, 340n34; and community-college campaign, 284, 286, 289, 291–294

Jones, Thomas R., Sr., 102, 280, 340n34

Jones, William A., 57, 106, 248, 260, 305, 307; and YIA, 142, 143, 172, 173, 177; critique of community leadership, 308, 310

Joshua, Charles, 308, 311

juvenile delinquency. *See* crime; President's Committee on Juvenile Delinquency and Youth Crime; youth gangs

Juvenile Delinquency and Youth Offenses Control Act, 88

Juvenile Delinquency Evaluation Project, 37, 90

Kaplan, Nathaniel, 28, 43

Kellar, Charles, 60, 67

Kennedy, John F., 5, 124, 240, 309; assassination of, 7, 93, 122, 135, 220; and PCJD, 14, 88, 92, 93, 130; administration of, 84, 126; and RFK, 86, 218–219, 221, 311; and civil rights, 120, 219, 374n45; and poverty, 127, 130–132, 221, 375n47

Kennedy, Robert F. (RFK), 6, 8, 14, 15, 201; tour of Bed-Stuy, 1–2, 4–7, 228; as sponsor of community action, 85, 88, 92–93; tour of East Harlem, 86; early ideas about juvenile delinquency, 86–87; oversight of PCJD, 88–90, 92–93, 121, 130, 218–219; pledging support for PCJD program in Bed-Stuy, 121; encounters with poverty, 130, 228; announcement of Bed-Stuy initiatives, 200–203, 212; vision of community development, 202–203, 226–235; and Sullivan initiatives, 216; personal transformation, 218–220; and civil rights, 219; critique of War on Poverty, 220–222; response to Watts, 223–225;